To Norman & An

MABREY BASS'S TARB(

FROM 1950 TO 1990

Mabrey Bass's Tarboro

From 1950 to 1990

Including Twenty-Two Articles
of Historical Interest by Dr. Spencer P. Bass

RTP
Research Triangle Publishing, Inc.

Published by
Research Triangle Publishing, Inc.
PO Box 1130
Fuquay-Varina, NC 27526

Library of Congress Catalog Card Number: 97-76539
ISBN 1-884570-77-1

Cover Design by Kathy Holbrook
Edited by Roland Taylor

Photo credits: M. S. Brown collection
Parts of the present work originally appeared in *The Southerner*

Printed in the United States of America
10 9 8 7 6 5 4 3 2 1

PREFACE

Mabrey Bass's Tarboro was the inspiration of Mabrey's younger brother William M. Bass, still remembered by everyone as "Bill." A Tarboro native, Bill also grew up under the cool oak and elm trees that lined Main Street and is now a resident of Dallas, Texas. The purpose of the book is simply to commemorate Mabrey's life-time love affair with his home town as reflected in his *Daily Southerner* column, "Ramblin' Round." Bill Bass financed the project and Roland Taylor, another Tarboro native and newspaperman, volunteered to edit approximately 10,000 items in the 2,000 columns that reflected Mabrey's deep devotion to Tarboro and all its people.

The logistics were monstrous. They began at the Edgecombe Public Library's microfilm records. Mrs. Jennifer Bobbitt and her daughter, Melissa, patiently looked up each issue of the newspaper from June of 1950 until Mabrey's death in 1990. They searched for and printed out every column. Many of those early newspapers were so smudged or blurred that they were sometimes impossible to read. Sometimes the type on the copies w so small it required a magnifying glass to decipher.

Mrs. Bobbitt passed the copies on to this editor who those items to be published, trying to avoid duplicati the way.

Every good newspaperman enjoys re-telling goo Mabrey was no exception. He loved the accoun Confederate monument in the Common was sho of his metal pants. And there was the tale about rect a scorched brunswick stew. And the night exploded at Simmons Furniture Store and the tir Hargrove delivered Goodfellow Christmas pre ιunately, there was room for only one version of each of those stories.

After the initial selection process, this editor passed the items on to Bill Bass in Dallas before the final selection was made. The most arduous task of all was proofreading each item and there were several reasons for that. Mabrey was not a gifted speller and the newspaper could not afford someone to read and edit his columns. Knowing that a writer is his own worst editor, Mabrey sent his stuff to the printers to be set into type because he had no other choice.

There, further damage was done for another variety of reasons. Sometimes a Linotype machine malfunctioned. One temporarily lost all the "e's" in its magazine. A sentence that should have read, "They were never there and needed a sentence to keep them in jail," came out, "Thy wr nvr thr and ndd a sntnc to kp thm in jail." There were also legendary tales about how much liquor a printer could consume on a single shift.

After the final selections were made, the microfilm copies were turned over to the skillful fingers of Vivian Johnson in Carrboro and she keyboarded the items onto floppy computer disks. Ms. Johnson was close to perfection but the process still opened the door for other possible errors. Those things, along with poor copies some original newspapers that barely had enough ink to read, made proof reading in 1997 a risky business.

It took a team of readers to finish the project with Bill Bass, 'arl Rosenbaum and his wife Betty carrying most of the load. yet another Tarboro native and lifelong friend of Mabrey, best of the lot, finding errors in names and places that else had missed. The team did its best, understands may be errors and hopes they are neither offensive rassing.

ımn items are presented in chronological order, be- year in January and concluding with December. vas made to preserve Mabrey's style of writing as ersonal rhythms and punctuations. Editor's notes lly sparse and used only to help guide the readers mes and the issues being considered.

The 22 stories by Dr. Spencer P. Bass in the addendum came from Dr. Bass's personal scrap book and are printed here as they appeared, with no editing. All the stories except one, an incredible account of his grandfather's wound at Petersburg during the Civil War, were published in local newspapers in Tarboro and Rocky Mount. All the articles have much historical value.

A note about the photographs: There were few photographs of Mabrey during his working years because he was more often taking pictures than posing for them. The two pictures of him in this volume are from the family collection. All the others came from the personal archives of M. S. Brown. The sponsor of *Mabrey Bass's Tarboro* will forever be grateful to M. S. (Sonny) Brown Jr. for allowing unlimited access to his father's collection of pictures in and around Tarboro. A skilled amateur photographer, Mr. Brown, known to everyone as "Coca Cola" Brown, took pictures of anything and everything from the 1930's through the 1950's. Beloved and generous, he often stepped in to take Tarboro High School yearbook photographs—at no charge—if the students could not find a professional. Mr. Brown practically adopted the high school band and was at every parade and municipal function that mattered. The pictures selected for this volume represent the times, people and places that were important in the formulative years of Mabrey Bass's life. The photographs are priceless; the Brown family's generosity is immeasurable.

This editor began the project with some trepidation, not sure "Ramblin'" was as good as he remembered or that it would hold up in the ultimate test of time. In reality, "Ramblin'" was much better. It not only held up over time, it remained consistent and readable with logic that never faltered and a love for Tarboro that never wavered. There is a softness about this text that is warm and comfortable. And there is not a single mean-spirited comment in all the 39 years the column was published. Instead, it is clear that "Ramblin" was the glue that held Tarboro together during five decades.

There was another intangible quality about Mabrey that is easily sensed but difficult to describe. This editor's 90-year old mother probably expressed it best in her uncomplicated diagnosis: "If you didn't like Mabrey Bass, there was something wrong with you."

This editor was also blessed by being able to read ALL the columns but to reproduce all of them here would be impossible. We picked what we thought was best, those which represented Mabrey best and ask your forgiveness if your personal favorite item is not included here.

Roland. L. Taylor
Durham, NC
August, 1997

Going Home

The Town Common makes Tarboro different. The four-block tree-filled park at the edge of the downtown business district was laid out in 1760 and always gave Tarboro a sense of grace and dignity not enjoyed by larger cities in the eastern North Carolina coastal plains. At mid-century—1950—the Common and countless oaks and magnolias lining city streets absorbed the blazing, suffocating summer heat and returned gentle, inviting breezes of comfort and friendship, hospitality and home.

On such a summer day in 1950 before air conditioning and closed windows, you could walk around your block and smell what every neighbor was having for supper. After supper, as darkness fell, they sat in outside rocking chairs or in the front porch swing waiting for the house to cool down enough for sleeping. The town had just begun a DDT mosquito-killing campaign but in some neighborhoods where the porches were small and the trees were few, residents put their chairs in the yard and burned little piles of rags to repel insects.

Tarboro was also home to Baker Mabrey Bass Jr. who was born, reared and educated there, who landed with the Marines at Iwo Jima and survived to get his journalism degree from the university at Chapel Hill. Pinned down in a deep volcanic ash foxhole on Iwo, he promised himself that if he ever got out of the hole, he would return to Tarboro and never leave again.

And there were other reasons.

There was a predictability about the place. Many of the farmers had recently converted to oil burners for their flue-cured bright leaf tobacco that grew in the heavily fertilized sandy loam soil. But some of the hard heads—or those who simply did not have the capital to make improvements—continued to cut wood all winter and sit up summer nights tending the fire in the barns. When those fires got out of hand through carelessness or drunkenness the burning barn could be seen for five miles.

The fuel for curing might change but the tobacco would always be there. In late summer, large tobacco warehouses were filled with the sweet, lethal aroma of golden leaves and the fascinating mumbbla-mumbbla auctioneers' chants that sometimes ended with "Sold American." It was a good time of the year because everyone, even the desperate sharecroppers, had money. It would always be that way despite a growing, uncomfortable realization that there was something wrong with an economic system that left farmers more in debt at the end of each year. They never seemed to get ahead but they would still be there. They would always be there. It was the only way to grow tobacco. That's just the way it was.

There were also cotton and soybeans and corn and everyone feasted on fresh boiled peanuts after the vines were pulled up and stacked in the fields. Like watermelons, fresh peanuts were fair game for those brave enough to stop at a field and pile heavily laden vines over car fenders before roaring away into the darkness. Peanuts, like cotton, meant extra money. Youngsters could pick enough cotton or stack enough peanuts to buy things— a sweater, a new pair of tennis shoes or maybe even a bicycle if they worked very, very hard. They did that every fall. They always would. It was as predictable as the rise and fall of the river that almost circled the town on its slow relentless flow towards Little Washington.

In town, Hart Mill made cotton cloth and the workers who ran the looms lived in those easily recognized, monotonous company-owned houses. From time to time the mill shut down and that was hard on everybody. Sometimes it shut down because of over production or falling sales and once the workers even went on strike and that was hard on everybody too. But that's just the way it was.

On the other side of town Fountain Mill had not turned out a bolt of cloth since the Great Depression. A tall, black water tank stood endless guard over the boarded-up red brick building with the blue tinted windows. Around the mill the old company houses continued to decay. To live in a Fountain Mill house was an admission of social and economic defeat because even the dreams that it might operate again had died.

A quarter mile down Fountain Street, Runnymede Mill knitted cotton crew socks and everybody there had a vegetable garden, produced the best baseball players in the county and lived in the ugliest company houses in the free world. Runnymede would always be there too and the houses would always be the color of fresh cow manure. It was also as predictable as the river.

As decrepit as Fountain Mill was, the houses were still better than those on the black side of Tarboro and all-black Princeville across the river. Princeville was one of only two towns in America with an all-black population and a black governing body. With no industry and very little business it had a dirt-poor tax base and struggled to survive, losing ground to flood waters each time the river jumped its banks. And Princeville would always be that way too.

Although they made up 50 per cent of Edgecombe County, the black folks were almost invisible during the week but appeared in large numbers on the south end of Main Street every Saturday evening. White folks were under the impression that everybody got along just fine.

All of those things made Tarboro comfortably constant. There was the slightest hint of a change at Carolina Telephone and Telegraph Company because that Tarboro- based company offered opportunity for a much-needed middle class. But in 1950 the highly structured caste system of old-family-well-to-do-landowners, doctors and lawyers looked down at the merchants, clerks, mill workers and tenant farmers. All of those looked down on the blacks in East Tarboro and Princeville.

Tarboro had the same entertainment facilities as any other small down in the South— two segregated movie theaters. The Colonial near the Town Commons showed first-run films during the week but Saturday was still cowboy day, with a serial, a cartoon or a Three Stooges comedy. The Majestic Theater (later the Tar)at the other end of Main Street featured B pictures and reruns along with a heavy stench from the urinal that was located behind the screen. Whites sat downstairs in both theaters; blacks sat in the balcony.

In summer, the whites had a swimming pool that featured refrigerated water. Black kids swam in Tar River. They all watched organized baseball at Bryan Park where the Class D Tarboro Tars played a full season. The grandstand was available for white fans who could afford it. Black fans sat in bleachers down the right field line. White bleachers were down the left field line.

The local newspaper, *The Daily Southerner*—"Second Oldest Daily In North Carolina"—ignored the poor quality of life as well as most local news that normally holds a community together. It was owned jointly by local attorney Henry C. Bourne and Victor Herman Creech, a Tarboro florist. Bourne acquired the newspaper about 1915 and Creech operated it. Bourne's family said he never took any money out of the newspaper because there was none to take.

The Creech florist shop was on W. St. James Street and also served as the newspaper office. His greenhouse was behind his home on St. Andrews Street in Tarboro's best residential neighborhood. To an outsider, it was an unusual marriage that mixed roses, dahlias and chrysanthemums with grunting, grinding heavy machinery, messy printer's ink and molten lead.

Before World War II, the press and Linotype machine were already worn out. Soon after the war started, the old eight-page flat bed press broke down for lack of spare parts. It sat in the back corner of the flower shop gathering dust and rust while the newspaper was printed on an antique backup, a 50-year old job press that was limited to only four pages per issue. Just getting those four pages printed was mind-numbing monotony that took the better part of the day. The operator hand-fed the press one sheet of paper at a time for a daily run of 2,000 copies.

Carrier boys took their own papers off the press and folded the single sheet so that pages 1, 2, 3, and 4 were in sequence. It was then folded in half with only the top of the front page visible, just as if it had come off a press that way. Most carriers had over 100 customers and the folding usually took half an hour. The subscription rate was ten cents a week. The carrier got three cents of that.

When Creech's son, Herman Jr., got out of the Army in 1945, he tried to sell the paper but the best offer was only $2,500. Shocked, he turned it down and continued to publish. He eventually got spare parts for the old flat bed but the Linotype machine continued to clank along, spitting out lines of type, held together with coat hangers and black tape.

Type for wedding announcements, business cards and "Posted" signs to keep hunters out of pastures and fields were set by hand, one letter at a time from a type case, just as Benjamin Franklin had done it.

Mechanical inadequacies were only half the problem. There was no editorial staff. There was no sports writer, much less a sports editor; no news editor or reporter, no feature writers, no police beat reporter, no city hall reporter, no one to ponder the problems of the world and no editorials to show the way to peace and happiness for all mankind. One person did all those things and was called the Editor. Sometimes the lady who answered the telephone in the flower shop would take an obituary or a wedding notice for the society page if the caller were a recognized member of Tarboro society but the Editor did everything else.

In 1950, the paper had been without an editor for some time, apparently because of salary limitations. Even the drunks and has-beens who were once so numerous in the business had disappeared. The cool shade of the Town Common could not make car payments; the oaks and magnolias could not put a child through school nor buy necessities from the local liquor store. One editor gave it a good try but he lived in Rocky Mount 16 miles away, could not afford a car and had to hitchhike to work. After he left, Herman tried to fill the void himself but often complained that news took time away from selling advertising. With no one to call on them, merchants often left their ad copy out front on a flower shop desk.

Surely Herman was pleased at the possibility of landing a local World War II veteran with a journalism degree. Salary considerations were being worked out but there were few guidelines available. The sports editor of the Rocky Mount Evening Telegram was making $50 a week but that paper was very profitable. Starting wages for a clerk in a Tarboro men's store was $27.50. This would suggest that the new editor might make as much as $40 or even $45 a week.

The printer, Bill Evans Sr., did not need directions from an editor. He merely tore stories off the teletype himself and used what he needed to fill up a page. If he got to the end of a column and needed four inches of type, he found a four-inch story, set it, and then wrote the headline as large as he needed to fill the hole. News content was immaterial and Evans relied heavily on the weak little feature service that provided pictures, charts, maps and columns about Hollywood.

The Southerner's feature service made no pretense about being timely. There were one-column mug shots of men charged with rape in New York or maybe Texas, beauty contest winners from Montana or the Prime Minister of Patagonia. If Evans had a five-inch deep hole and the beauty queen fit, he ran her picture even though the contest had been held three months earlier.

It took some attention and common sense to know which pictures to use, but in an emergency, when time was against them, printers often filled up a hole with whatever fit and was available. Tarboro readers were accustomed to seeing baseball pictures in November or Washington officials waving as they were either getting on or getting off an airplane going to or coming from an unknown destination.

So it was in June of 1950. Armed with a diploma from the University of North Carolina Department of Journalism and a bride named Pat, Mabrey Bass took the job as Editor of *The Daily Southerner*. There was no fire in his belly to right the wrongs around him. He did not come to crusade or take up causes or to disturb or change things. He had no hidden agenda, no axe to grind, no snake oil to sell.

He had simply come home. That's all he ever wanted to do. The town and its people that he loved so much would all be the better for it but it was not a good start. For some unaccountable reason, no one was in the front office when he reported to work. He didn't even know where the bathroom was or where to hang his hat and quickly realized there was nothing in the curriculum at Chapel Hill to prepare him for what he encountered. It remained etched on his brain until his death and he always began the story with, "I'll never forget that first day."

Almost in shock, he practically stumbled his way to the back shop and nervously introduced himself to the gray-whiskered Evans. He knew how to get news, he said, and write it, but beyond that, he was lost.

Evans told him, "Don't you worry a damn bit about it. Just go out there and get some local stuff. We'll work out the rest when you get back." "We" consisted of only two people, Evans and printer-pressman Joe Payjac.

Mabrey obeyed, hit Main Street and came back with three stories. Sam McDuffie, the state ABC agent, told him about a raid on a still on Saturday night. E. D. Johnson tipped him off about plans for school building additions and Tarboro Police Chief Robert Worsley gave him a bonus of three separate items. City police had arrested a purse snatcher over the weekend and investigated an automobile accident. The third incident involved what Worsley called a "Saturday night carving party" in East Tarboro, something more or less expected on that side of town.

Bass returned to his office, found the typewriter and pounded out the stories. Evans offered his basic letters-per-column measurements for *The Southerner's* limited headline type. Mabrey edited all the stories, ripped some AP stories off the wire and wrote headlines for what he had produced and sent everything back to the printers, a bonus for them because they normally had to write the headlines.

It was something of a miracle but they went to press on time, or at least within the parameters established by his predecessors, which was before dark. The new editor breathed a sigh of relief before realizing it was just another normal day for the back shop. They would have to start all over the next morning. Although no record was kept about what happened at the end of that day, chances are they all had a couple of big drinks to celebrate with Mabrey providing the refreshments.

He knew it was not going to be easy. Large newspapers had huge news staffs and advertising salesmen and circulation managers too. It was not in Mabrey's genetic code to wish for those things. He had been anxious to get the job covering the news in his beloved home town and was delighted when it was offered. He would simply tough it out and do the best he could.

Six months later, practically exhausted and his back was to the wall, he realized it would take 10 reporters to properly cover Tarboro and Edgecombe County. A court case might take four or five days of constant attention. A city or county commission meeting could drone on for hours—often at night. In desperation he contrived a partial and temporary solution. He would gather up all the little news items and report them in an occasional column for his readers. It was also a plea for his readers to help him by calling in the news. He named the column "Ramblin' Round" and promised it would not be a regular feature of the newspaper.

His temporary solution lasted 39 years.

The first column, reproduced here in its entirety, was published Saturday afternoon January 20, 1951:

❧

This column will definitely not become a regular feature of *The Southerner*, so don't worry too much about it. 'Twil be concerned with small items which may possibly be of interest to some of the folks who read the paper.

Understand Porter McNair has a new novelty . . . has something to do with a dog.

New Colonial Store rapidly nearing completion, and when completed it will really be a beauty. No doubt Mr. David Pender would have been quite proud of it.

Wonder why the habitual drunkards are continually sent to the county jail? Why not send them to the roads where they can work the alcohol out of their system. One of the drunks gets out of jail on Friday morning, but is again locked up Friday afternoon—the charge . . . public drunkenness.

Much work is being done on Romaine Howard's office building on St. James Street.

Let's find a way to encourage more industry for Edgecombe County. We need it.

Harry Hull has done an excellent job as president of the Merchants Association during the past year, and there is no doubt but what Carroll Barnhart will continue the tradition.

NEEDED: Names in *The Southerner* other than those appearing on the court docket. We appreciate all news, including society. After Monday dial 3106.

Regardless of personal feelings the Municipal Milk Plant is selling milk for less than all surrounding towns. Greenville and Rocky Mount have recently announced prices increases, and yet one dairyman told a reporter from the Evening Telegram that he (the dairyman) sold his milk to the Tarboro plant because Tarboro paid the producer more than Rocky Mount.

Letters to the editor are few and far between, as a matter of fact we haven't been called a dirty name since last July.

Many folks are expressing favorable comment on H. G. (Gilly) Nicholson's fine sermon at Calvary Church last Sunday.

That's attractive shrubbery outside the Municipal Milk Plant—it should be—rates are high enough for them to plant orchids.

Several folks are talking about forming an Edgecombe County Historical Society.

Hope to have more news in the paper next week . . .

Had an opportunity to meet one of the applicants for the Merchant's Association job. Seems he would be an excellent choice but he wants to work for a Chamber of Commerce that lives up to its name. He would do a world of good for Tarboro provided he could get cooperation but we suppose that is a big order.

Yes, folks we really realize that there is more to getting industry for Tarboro than talking about it, but we understand that a delegation went to Raleigh this week to look into the situation.

Want to hear an excellent radio commentator? Take a listen to Robert Montgomery on Thursday right at 9:45. He broadcasts over ABC, and you can probably get them at about 700 on your dial.

We understand that one of the first fire engines purchased by the town is still in Tarboro. If we could get it, the device would look fine at parades such as Hospitality Day.

NEEDED: More news from the folks on Office Street, Maryland Avenue, Carolina Avenue, Hall Street, Howard Avenue, St. Patrick Street. Having a party? Tell us about it. It has been proven that more folks read the society column than read the front page.

We apologize to Mr. Baldwin for his story getting in the paper late. *(There was no hint about who Mr. Baldwin was but Ramblin's often sprinkled personal messages in his new column.)*

Why all this talk about drafting 18-year-olds? How about the reserves? They expressed a willingness to serve when they sign their papers.

Mistakes—a good excuse for a second column a week later.

Last week we promised that this column would definitely not become a regular feature, but due to a mistake in last week's Ramblin' Round we are running the column again to correct the error.

If you remember, last week we commented that the shrubs around the milk plant were among the prettiest in town, but rates were high enough for the town to have planted orchids. As many of our readers guessed we were talking about the light plant shrubs instead of those at the milk plant in correcting the error we add milk prices are reasonable and there is nothing pretty about the shrubbery at the milk plant.

With the school bond election now a thing of the past, (it passed) the attention of local voters will soon turn to a $40,000 bond issue for the proposed memorial library. Unless something is done to contradict rumors that the building will be placed on the west end of the Town Common, the bond issue is going to run into a whole passel of opposition.

And the third week— still more corrections.

Again we start by straightening out a comment made the preceding week. Regarding the comment on the location of the Memorial Library: The final decision rests with the town commissioners, and not with the Edgecombe Public Library Board, we are informed. Perhaps a statement from the group will be made public before the 40 thousand dollar bond issue. We hope so. If the group would state positively that the new library would not be on the Common it greatly ups the chances of the issue meeting the approval of the voters.

First entry of a spring ritual: When are the shad coming?

The Spring-like weather this past week brought out the Japonicas, jonquils, camellias and the crowd which annually builds up callouses sitting on the cement curbs in front of the courthouse.

Several reports have been received from local fishermen saying that shad have been caught in the river here during the past week. However, the names of the fishermen making the catches are not known. Better wait for a more definite report before straining Tar River water with your nets.

Mamas and Papas in Tarboro would do well to get a piece of smoked glass or exposed film for themselves and the youngsters for the eclipse which will be visible here next Wednesday afternoon. At 5:45 the moon is scheduled to have covered 31 per cent of the sun's apparent diameter.

The clock on the front of the Security Bank was taken down this week, and although it was often incorrect, the folks on the hotel block say they miss it.

March 10—Rock coming upstream.

In spite of the cold weather last Sunday at least three local fishermen had luck while trolling for rock in a stream near the coast. Pete Clark, Buck Clark and Carl Rosenbaum brought home nine stripers to make up for their shivers.

The old clock, recently removed from the front of the Security Bank, is sorely missed. Folks walking up the west side of Main Street in the business section now have to cross the street to get a look at the town clock. Often folks catch themselves glancing up at the spot formerly occupied by the old clock, just to get a vague idea of the time-of-day.

April.

The warm breezes which have prevailed here for the past several days have caused many of the beautiful flowers and shrubs to blossom forth. One of the most beautiful of Tarboro's many flowering shrubs is located behind Dr. Curtis Norfleet's home on Howard Circle, just across the street from Rob Howard's home. The shrub, or tree, is visible from the street and it is worth a Sunday afternoon drive just to view it.

Police Chief Robert Worsley resigns—no explanation.

The surprise of the week as far as the general public was concerned was the resignation of Bob Worsley as chief of police, and the appointment of Otley Leary as his successor. In Tarboro as in other towns in the state there are now and always will be a pro-chief and anti-chief factions regardless of who is in office. A man cannot be a chief of police without making someone mad.

The resignation is causing some raised eyebrows in town especially since election is just around the corner. (*There was an ironic twist to this item. Worsley replaced former Chief Berry Lewis who also resigned without explanation 15 years earlier.)*

~

(Tarboro native Harvie Ward became one of America's top amateur golfers, winning both the U. S. and British amateur titles. In the days before multi-million dollar tournament purses, Harvie did not join the PGA tour but was employed by an insurance company, using his golf talents to assist the company's business. This gentle jab only shows Bass's fondness for his friend.)

It's mighty hard to get use to those press releases telling of the exploits of Harvie Ward on the golf courses throughout the nation . . . especially since all accounts of Harvie now list his address as "Southern Pines." For a long time Harvie was known as Tarboro's best publicity agent, but since Harvie "took up with them insurance people" we've lost him. However, the change of address hasn't hurt his golfing ability . . . he's still tops.

~

Up at Shiloh this week J. R.. Satterthwalte caught two giant cat fish. One of the fish tipped the scales slightly more than 18 pounds. The other weighed in at approximately 16 pounds.

~

For folks who don't get their fill of baseball in this paper, here's an item that was passed on to us by Alva Clark. Clark's hobby is operating an amateur radio station and last week he contacted another "ham" from the Panama Canal Zone.

Clark inquired about Roy Kennedy and Eddie Neville, who played ball here several years back, but who live in the Canal Zone during the winter months. Clark was told that Kennedy has given up baseball and is in school in the States this summer. Neville, the "ham" said had injured his leg while playing ball this past winter, and will probably be out of action this summer. *(Neville also became part of an international baseball legend as a star pitcher for the Durham Bulls. His battery mate, catcher Ralph Caldwell, joined him there. Caldwell raised his family in Tarboro and his son, Mike, was a major league pitcher.)*

That new traveling band stand which Mr. M. S. Brown had constructed for the use of the high school band is certainly an outstanding attraction. It will be a great asset when the band begins its regular summer concerts at the swimming pool.

Back to Main Street.

Window of the Week: Rosenbaum's gets the title of window of the week from this column. The window display gives detail the story of nylon from the time it is mixed as a chemical to the time you buy it in Rosenbaum's in the form of a bathing suit, a shirt, trousers, underwear or a dress. The display is cleverly arranged and well deserves the title "Window of the Week."

From what we have seen of Tarboro's gardens, one of the prettiest is Charlie Clayton's. His iris, peonies and roses are lovely.

Of time and the river.

The river is lower now than many of the local folks can remember. Even the piling of the old Bell's Bridge are sticking several inches out of the water. Both creek and river fishing are reported to be excellent.

And lots of folks still kept chickens.

June weather often produced unexpected sanitary problems—especially for the chickens.

Sprite Barbee's suggestion that chicken raising be outlawed within the town limits seems to have met with approval of quite a few local folks, including some who raise chickens. All who approached us this week complain that after recent rains, the chicken lots produce a smell that rivals the Plymouth pulp mill. As Barbee pointed out, it is practically impossible to control rats and insects around the coops, and such places can be a health hazard. We sympathize with the folks who have chicken yards, but let's not forget that those yards are usually located as far as possible from the owners house and usually against the neighbors back fence. So its the neighbor, and not the owner who has to contend with the smell, the rats, and the insects.

Hot weather.

As we understand it, last Sunday's crowd at the swimming pool was the largest in recent years, with the gate receipts totaling $115.

Although A.D. Anderson of the Old Sparta section brought in the first cotton blossom of the year, two other Edgecombe farmers brought us blossoms on the same day. They were Claude Braddy of the Wiggins Farm and Ed Andrews of Mildred. However, the most "complete" blossom was brought to *The Southerner* office by Brink Howell. Brink's blossom had a boll weevil in it.

Most people didn't even have an attic fan.

Thursday night was the hottest of the week with the mercury sitting on 77 degrees. Last night the temperature dropped to a cool 70 degrees from yesterday's high of 96. The .42 inches of rain is credited with the relief.

❧

The newest addition to the local police department is Patrolman Bo Carpenter who began walking the night beat on Main Street last week. Bo was a first class football star back in the early 40's for both Tarboro and Rocky Mount High schools. He was also formerly employed by the Edgecombe Motor Company.

And for those without air conditioning...

Here's a nice refreshing—but untimely thought for these hot July days: To keep snow from sticking to the shovel, rub the shovel with a candle stump or a piece of paraffin . .

❧

This week someone asked us why we didn't write st[illegible] about tobacco barn that catch fire and burn in Edgecombe C[illegible] Our reply was that it is might difficult—sometimes pr[illegible] impossible—to get the details. So our friend suggeste[illegible] write the story with only the details available. Here'[illegible] would sound like.

"A tobacco barn burned down sometime last night[illegible] in the county somewhere. It was either near Speed or B[illegible]

The owner of the barn, who lives on a farm, said that the barn and the tobacco were valued at "right much money."

The owner said he thought he had insurance but he wasn't sure just how much or when he paid the premium. He described the blaze as "right bad."

Now is the season for one of Edgecombe's greatest gastronomic pleasures—the scuppernong grape. They tell us that there was time when almost every farm in the county had a well-kept grapevine, but now the vines—at least—the well-kept variety are a rarity. There's one bad thing about the scuppernong, however, they're a lot like boiled peanuts—you eat so many you end up with a stomach ache.

Summer is gone.

Tomorrow marks the first day of Fall and already the maple and the sycamore trees are changing color. The nights are cooler and the temptation to sleep a bit later in the morning is greater. The fish, even in Tar River, are biting. No longer are the July flies heard about sundown, and somehow the air smells a bit different. Fluffs of white cotton mark the fields of Edgecombe County, and farmers are beginning to "hog down" cornfields. The dull roar of shotguns can be heard in the late afternoon as hunters blast away at doves, and on many fields, bird dogs lope along the ditch banks limbering up for the November quail season. The swimming pool is empty and the splashing and yelling will be missed until next May. Summer has ended.

There's more water in a wet sponge that there is in Tar River [illegible] present, but local fishermen aren't complaining. Last week[illegible] a number of carp weighing over 10 pounds were pulled [illegible] the water after battles ranging from five to fifteen minutes. [illegible]balls were used for bait.

[illegible]ome back to the old clock at the Security Bank Build[illegible] pleasant to hear those chimes every 15 minutes, and to [illegible]t the office window to tell the time of day. That old [illegible] become something of a local institution.

❧

To us one of the most interesting places in town is Dr. J.P. Keech's office window. The local historian keeps an ever-changing display of interesting articles in the window and almost everyone passing the building stops to give the articles—particulary the papers—a once-over.

Ramblin' ended the year as he began—explaining mistakes.

Missing from last week's Christmas edition was the Fabric Shop ad wishing a happy holiday to all. It seems the ad wasn't picked up in time for publication, but Mrs. Mewborn wants the folks hereabouts to know she was thinking about them.

Two new carrier boys have started routes for *The Southerner* since the holidays, and we have high hopes that they will be much better than the boys they replaced. However, if you don't get a paper call us here at the office. The number is 3106.

1952

The long hard path through 1951 evidently proved too much for our old friend the Security National Bank clock. At this writing it's four and a half hours slow.

Skirting around the word "toilet."

According to Bill Stell and S.J. Brewer in the Town Clerk's office, Fireman George Cherry is something of an unofficial hero. Stell explains that last week George was credited with rescuing a local lady who became temporarily locked in one of the smaller rooms in the Town Hall. Stell says George is the man who managed to open the door.

Politics.

The announcement this week that Hubert Olive would enter the race for Kerr Scott's job brings long expected opposition for Bill Umstead who announced his intention last September. However, the field still isn't full . . . we haven't heard from Ollie Ray Boyd, the Pinetown pig man. One thing we like about Mr. Boyd is that we've never heard him claim to be a veteran, a Sunday school teacher, or a school teacher. He's just what he claims to be—a farmer.

❧

Those new trees that were set out in the Common this week were a welcome addition. They'll be greatly enjoyed by future generations, provided there is a Common fifty years from now.

End of professional baseball?

The big question in Tarboro at present seems to be "is we is or is we ain't?" because the baseball picture here has changed from rosy red to the deepest shade of black. But if we don't get baseball, at least we've learned one thing—don't publicize baseball activities in the State papers until you get a contract signed. Many local folks seem to think that the publicity resulted in a better offer being made the Petersburg directors, but then that's something we didn't know about at the time.

(The following advertisement appeared on the same page with Ramblin' and offered a glimmer of hope that the old Farrar Hotel on Main Street might be salvaged.)

ANNOUNCEMENT. . .
HOTEL COFFEE SHOP
NOW OPEN
Under New Management
Hours: 6:00 a.m. 'til 9 p.m.
OPEN SUNDAYS
Your Patronage Will Be Greatly
Appreciated
C.H. Whitaker, Manager

Always pushing for improvements.

The boys on the police force are working harder than ever these days. More than one local merchant has received a night phone call informing him that he forgot to lock the door of his store. All that walking and inspection wears out plenty of shoe leather, yet the town police remain the lowest paid of any law enforcement men in Edgecombe. The cost of living hasn't fallen any in past months either.

We understand the Edgecombe Wildlife Club has been offered the site for a 15-acre pond. Most of the site already has been cleared, but the Club will have to build a dam.

Sex ed.

The Southerner is reserving editorial comment until further details of the course are made public. However, one point is crystal-clear: The school is being asked to shoulder a responsibility which is rightly that of the parents.

We note with interest the announcement that a sex education program has been approved and personally, we believe any parent who becomes embarrassed while attempting to explain the so-called "facts of life" to a child, has no business being a parent in the first place. Enough said.

The pond project of the Edgecombe Wildlife Club is moving ahead slowly but surely. At present Bip Carstarphen is ironing out legal details, and trying to have the pond site surveyed. When he completes the ground work, members will be called to help clear logs and brush from the basin.

The rat killing campaign conducted by Martin Sasser and Lory Bullock was masterful. Scene of the attack was the alley next to the Church Street Apartments where several local establishments dumped their garbage. Using carbon monoxide and Chloraden, the two health department workers killed an uncounted number of rats, some of them the size of small dogs. Many died in their burrows, but Sasser and Bullock killed 16 with sticks as the furry creatures crawled from their holes to escape the gas.

The vandals are at it again. During the past week we have received several reports of flowers being cut from graves in Greenwood. We would like to remind those responsible that they are breaking laws by such doings.

No less than six folks called this week to comment on our editorial concerning the local airport, and all expressed the same opinion—continued operation under the present financial setup should be stopped.

The first rockfish caught here-about was landed in the Tar last Sunday (in early April) by Josh Satterthwaite so we are informed.

Local politics are almost too quiet. There's no word on any contests in the municipal elections, and the county elections are equally as dormant. On the district level, L.H. Fountain is making the rounds in all eight counties, but the Kerr activity is expected to start when the Judge comes home for the Easter Holiday.

Our congratulations this week to Capt. Stamps Howard, Jr., a retired naval officer who is giving freely of both his time and money to promote tennis among the young folks of Tarboro. It was Capt. Howard who formed the high school tennis team and initiated matches with surrounding towns. The program has been successful since the beginning thanks to the efforts of one man to make his town a better place for the young folks.

The new gymnasium at Pattillo High will be dedicated Monday and it is a structure of which all Tarboro citizens may well be proud. The new building is comparable to any in the State and will afford the Pattillo students and faculty many hours of enjoyment.

This Little League baseball proposition seems excellent to us, and if local citizens cooperate, then it should be a major attraction here this summer.

Spring.

There can be no doubt that spring is definitely here. We have reliable information that Deputy Sheriff Charlie Pridgen took off his long drawers last Saturday.

Speaking of spring, we hear that several county farmers have started setting out tobacco plants.

When you are out for a Sunday drive don't forget to take a look at the Federal housing project which is going up at the end of West Hope Lodge Street. That contractor is certainly doing some fast work.

The Tarboro Jaybirds are playing Middlesex at Runnymeade this afternoon and it promises to be a fast game. The local boys are doing an excellent job of providing their own recreation and they have a good team...haven't lost but one game.

❧

The movie, "Carbine Williams," which showed here last Monday and Tuesday had more local interest than most folks know about. Luke Sheffield tells us that the Capt. Peoples portrayed in the film is the uncle of Mrs. Wiley Newsome of 900 St. James Street.

❧

Those tobacco stems spread over the town common were placed there to make the grass greener and thicker. The entire carload of stems was given the town by a tobacco company in Rocky Mount.

June.

This Harvie Ward Day promises to be the biggest thing that ever happened to Tarboro, and present indications are that it will dwarf Hospitality Days' of the past. Bill Babcock and his committees are doing an excellent job in handling all arrangements. Incidentally, Buster Walker, who is in charge of part of the parade, today asked that all persons having convertibles that they are willing to have used in the parade call him at either his store on Main Street or his home after 6 p.m.

After a long bout with illness Dr. Spencer Bass is back at his office. He comes down each afternoon to see patients, and his appearance marks the first time since Christmas that he has been able to get out.

❧

Blossom, blossom, who's got a blossom? From scattered sections of eastern Carolina have come reports of cotton blossoms, but as yet we have heard nothing from Edgecombe. The owner of the first blossom brought into *The Southerner*'s office will receive a one-year subscription to the paper free of charge.

❧

There are those who claim that hunting is a past time for those who have nothing better to do. These scoffers claim little is accomplished by those of the hunting fraternity, but there is a story making the rounds in Tarboro this week which proves otherwise. According to what we heard, Dr. J.G. Raby has suffered from back trouble for the past year. It has caused quite a bit of pain and resulted in at least one trip to Duke Hospital for treatment and a hoped-for cure. However, the pain persisted, that is until the good doctor went hunting this week. While crossing a field he tripped, and for a minute it looked as though he would be in bed with injuries more serious than a painful back. But, no, when Dr. Raby straightened up he found that for the first time in months the pain has disappeared.

The doctors look after us, but apparently the good Lord is keeping a close eye on the doctors.

Miss Mattie.

Miss Mattie Shackleford tells us that children with slingshots and air rifles have been killing birds at an alarming rate in the old cemetery. These youngsters evidently find good hunting there, for Miss Mattie has a large number of bird baths set up for her feathered friends. Miss Mattie says it is against the law to kill birds in Tarboro and she promises full prosecution if the bird killers are caught.

Lt. George Earnhart has completed 100 missions as a jet pilot in Korea and is on his way home. Incidentally, George is getting married in August. He has finished one dangerous tour of duty and is ready to begin another.

The courthouse seemed to be a favorite spot for lightning to strike during the storm this week. The zig-zag danced off the building several times, and once knocked Bill Babcock from his seat in the clerk of court's office.

The boys at Fountain Bonded Warehouse this week called to say they were frying eggs on a steel gang plank. According to reports, the eggs were done in three minutes. That was a mighty hot sun.

Edgecombe's two convention delegates were on television last night. The state delegation finally decided to request a poll and home folks got a brief glimpse of Cap Eagles and Henry Bourne, each casting a vote for Senator Russell.

~

Well, Brother Bill got married last Saturday in Texas. It's a funny thing about those Bass boys; both of us had to go miles from home before we could find anyone who would marry us.

Civic pride.

Did you know that Tarboro has two firemen who have a combined total of 96 years of fire-fighting experience with the local fire department? Billy Bryan and Ed Morris have probably helped extinguish more blazes than any other two individuals in eastern Carolina. As volunteers they haven't been paid for their efforts through the years and there is no way of knowing just how much the fire fighting has cost them. Suits have been ruined. Shoes water-soaked and worn. Shirts burned, and hundreds of dollars paid out to the cleaners. That's true public service for you.

~

The chief topic of discussion on Main Street this week came with the announcement that the price of haircuts had advanced to 85 cents. We can't help but remember that old ditty, "Shave and a haircut—two bits," so cut it slowly; Jim, I want to get my money's worth.

~

Lt. Ashley Spier, Jr. son of Mr. and Mrs. A.C. Spier is now attending an Associate Officers Battery Course at Fort Bliss, Texas. He'll spend 15 weeks studying anti-aircraft gunnery and tactics, communications and guided missiles.

September.

The big news this week came at Monday's meeting of the town board as Chief Leary admitted that police could do nothing to stop illegal traffic in whiskey by local taxi drivers. The situation is more serious than most people believe because those ordering whiskey from cab drivers are folks who shouldn't have liquor under any condition, they aren't even allowed to buy whiskey at the local ABC store.

The police are faced with a major problem, for even if they nab one of the drivers making a delivery, the driver can contend that he only purchased the whiskey for the individual to whose home he is making the delivery. It is a bad situation and one which required immediate action by the commissioners. The people of Tarboro should tolerate no situation which makes the police the subject of abuse and scorn by any group.

At the last meeting of our town commissioners we heard talk of the possibility of installing parking meters in Tarboro. The board members said they would discuss the matter with the merchants, but from what we learn there has been no meeting of the Merchants Association. Is it that they don't care or is it that they haven't been notified? We confess that we don't know the answer to that one, but we firmly believe that this town of ours isn't so large that mechanical nickle-snatchers are needed either for the purpose of regulating parking or for extra revenue.

Carp fishing is now at its best in the Tar River, so we're told. During the past two weeks we have received reports of local folks who caught fish weighing 12, 16 and 20 pounds. We'll have to see them to believe that such large ones have been landed.

A letter from Duck Lewis now working as a "wheel" in the Burlington Chamber of Commerce bears out our statements concerning parking meters. Graham, N.C. can tell about parking meters. They hurt business after they are installed. Duck concludes his letter, "Happy Headache" . . .

Tuesday night will be a special night at *The Southerner* office. All amateur photographers are invited to come into the office and watch the new Fairchild engraver in action, and they are invited to bring their favorite photos with them. We'll show how the machine works and what is required of pictures for publication. Time of the demonstration is 8 o'clock. *(The Fairchild engraver was one of the first capital improvements made after Ramblin' became editor.)*

Scolding the health department.

Despite the health department's threat of prosecution we continue to see a large number of condemned garbage cans around Tarboro. That's hard to take for those who bought the new legal can to do their part to keep garbage from rats. Let's either enforce the law or get it off the books.

❧

George Earnhart's plan to move to Florida comes as a shock to most of us. Although it will probably benefit his health, it certainly is not for the good of Tarboro. For many years genial George has served as toastmaster for the majority of local banquets. His sense of humor is second to none and for years he served as clown prince of Edgecombe County.

❧

Tuesday we said that last night's game marked the first Pattillo High School team competed for a double-A championship. That's not so, we are told by Dave Hilliard who recalls that Pattillo had a championship team in 1935.

According to Dave the team in that year met the Henderson Training School for the title and went down to defeat by a score of 30-0.

❧

The Southerner's election was won by Capt. Stamps Howard. We have only recently completed tabulating the entries, and see that he came closest to predicting the number of votes Ike and Adlai polled in the general election. He missed the correct figure by less than one thousand votes, and predicted Ike's county total by less than 200 votes.

❧

Mrs. Ivy Priest, who was recently appointed to a high government post by President-elect Eisenhower, is no stranger to many people of Tarboro. Mrs. Priest, so we are told, is the first wife of the late Harry Hicks of Tarboro. She has many friends in Tarboro among whom are Misses Lucy and Emma Parker. Always interested in politics, it was not too many years ago that the present Mrs. Priest addressed the local Rotary Club.

Another policeman has resigned from the local department. Cecil Varnell's resignation, which becomes effective December 30, brings to three the number of patrolmen who have quit the department this year. Bo Carpenter and Gus Andrews are the two who resigned earlier.

The airport is still a problem. We still wonder why the town commissioners do not cancel the lease on the local airport and close it completely. It is certainly no asset to this town of ours.

Whiskey sales are off all over the county, according to a report from the ABC office. But that's nothing to worry about. Dave Lee tells us that the town is selling less water this month than any December in the past three years. We wonder how ginger ale sales are holding up.

1953

Although the health department didn't list any recommended treatment for children who might eat some of the rat poison distributed this week, we assume that the old treatment still goes: Stick your finger down the throat and call the doctor.

❧

Municipal elections are not until May but Main Street this week was buzzing this week with all kinds of political rumors. It seems that Mayor Johnson means it when he says that he will not seek reelection. For a while Clarence Wickham was reported to have wanted the town's top post, but now comes a different story. As we hear it, the post was offered to Don (Dinksie) Gilliam Jr. Most of the folks we talked with think "Gilly" Nicholson would also be a good choice, but if "Dinksie" decides he wants the job and announces first, it is unlikely that "Gilly" would oppose him since the men are first cousins. Rumors, rumors . . . but one thing is certain, with Slim Johnson out of the race there is going to be a first class fight for the job.

As of now, the future of Coastal Plain baseball has not been decided, but local fans are making an all-out effort to raise the necessary money. The female fans are planning a supper next week, and although the date hasn't been announced, it promises to be a lu lu—plenty of fine food at low prices. We'll announce the date as soon as it is set.

❧

We certainly hated to see Levy's Store close this week after so many years in business here. We hope Lou and Jenny Novey will be around town for a long while.

The closing of Levy's leaves three vacant stores in that block on Main Street. Two blocks further down are two stores which were destroyed by fire and have never been rebuilt. Across the street is still another vacancy (the store formerly occupied by Tarboro Furniture Co.) At this rate Tarboro won't be long in having a Main Street like that of Conetoe. That's something to think about!

Ramblin'—a natural environmentalist.

Before we begin criticizing Rocky Mount too much for sending Tarboro a supply of oil to taint the local water supply, let's consider what we are doing to Greenville by pouring raw sewage into the river. A river clean up is a project which should be undertaken by the county wildlife club immediately. Let's clean our own house before we start picking on our neighbors up the river.

Town politics heated up.

It is no secret that many citizens are hoping that "Gilly" Nicholson will seek the job (of mayor). While others say that the favorite of local politicians is 'Dinksie" Gilliam. Still others guess that "Slim" Johnson will run gain despite the fact he constantly denies he's running.

March 14.

Yesterday was Friday 13th, the second in as many months. But we can never understand how this day is considered unlucky. Of course, 13 itself is supposed to be bad medicine but Friday the 13th is supposed to have a double-whammy. The United States started out with 13 states and look what that grew into.

Separate but equal.

We understand that within the next several months Tarboro's commissioners will receive a petition calling for construction of a Negro swimming pool.

After the election.

Mayor-elect Nicholson has indicated that he will not make any committee changes in the immediate future. However, M.S. Brown's decision not to seek re-election coupled with the resignation of Commissioner Fred Fowler presents the new mayor with appointment problems of major importance. At present the town is without a water plant and cemetery commissioner, and when Brown leaves the board Monday night Tarboro will be without a milk plant commissioner and a swimming pool commissioner.

Each time we look over the police court list of persons charged with public drunkenness we remember the saying that drinking is like falling out of a window. Stopping is harder than starting.

From Old Sparta comes word that the herring are running in the Tar. We are told that a colored man caught several in a dip net he was using at the site of the old bridge this week.

Springtime.

Flowers, flowers and more flowers! Spring has brought to Tarboro its usual wreath of blossoms, and they were never more beautiful. All shades of azaleas flame forth from local gardens. Among the prettiest is the garden of Misses Annie and Virginia Sledge. Of course, we haven't seen all the local gardens, however, we've seen some beautiful tulips at Mrs. Carlisle Moore's and Mrs. Ed Patterson's.

How times change—We hadn't given the matter too much thought, but one local mother was telling us a story the other day which will make any 20-year-old feel even older. It seems this lady needed a loaf of bread so she turned to her 10-year-old son and said, "Son, go down to the D.P. Store and get me some bread." The youngster looked a bit puzzled and asked, "Where is the D.P. Store?" We wonder just like many folks in Tarboro can't remember or else don't know that the Colonial Store was formerly a part of the D.P. chain. As far as we are concerned the words "Colonial" and "D.P." are still interchangeable.

Yesterday we received a letter from Lt. George Earnhart, Jr. who is now stationed in Nevada. Buck saw one of the recent atomic tests on the Nevada desert and said, "I'm not worried too much about Russia anymore."

Prodding, prodding, prodding, to improve Tarboro.

Next week Tarboro High School and Pattillo High will award diplomas to nearly one hundred young men and women. A speaker will use flowery phrases to tell the graduates of their responsibilities to the nation and to themselves, but chances are he will not answer the question foremost in the minds of his listeners, "Where do we go from here?"

For the minority that question is easily answered. They will spend the next four years in college. But what of the others?

Where will they find employment? What kind of future can Tarboro offer?

Very little, we're afraid. And as a result we are forcing our human resources to go to other towns and states in search of jobs.

By the way, Washington was selected as the site of a woolen industry this week. The new plant will employ an estimated 600 persons.

❧

More good news reaches us this week in the form of a Raleigh announcement that the old Bell's Bridge will soon be replaced. The bridge has long been a traffic hazard and has accounted for more than one serious accident during the years it has spanned the river between Tarboro and Leggett.

Swimming pool valuable attraction for business.

The lack of an active Chamber of Commerce here has definitely taken a toll of local business, and with surrounding towns promoting heavily.

However, at this time of year Tarboro is fortunate in having a ready-made trade booster which functions for the benefit of the entire town. We are, of course, speaking of the municipal swimming pool and anyone who doubts its ability to attract segments of Edgecombe's rural population should have seen activity at the pool almost any morning this week.

With a little push the pool would become an even bigger crowd attraction . Most of us realize that parents go where their kids go. So would it not be a good idea for the management of local stores to purchase strips of pool admission tickets and give these tickets, one or two of them at a time, to county youngsters whose parents are trading in local stores. Any youngster with a ticket is going to make sure that his parents bring him back to Tarboro for a dip. Papa and Mama will probably stop in at the same store for shopping before returning home. Just thought we'd pass the idea along.

June and the big oaks pay their dividend.

Those hot days earlier this week sent local folks scurrying to their favorite store to purchase electric fans. Others bought air conditioning units and still others resorted to huge quantifies of ice water. However, the coolest individual was a gentleman stretched out on a bench under the large oaks in the Town Common. His tie was loosened, his shoes were untied , he was beating the heat and enjoying life to the fullest.

We note that the construction company which is to build a structure to replace Bells Bridge has been hampered by high water. This week a heavy bulldozer was clearing trees and undergrowth for the new road but now the water covers most of the job.

Tomato day.

Here's an item which should have gone in last week's column. Mark Ruffin pulled the first ripe tomato from his garden Wednesday, June 24. This marks the third year that Mark produced the first tomatoes in Tarboro.

July and the airport—again.

The controversy about the local airport still rages between town officials and George Hatch, the operator. We have a good idea how it will turnout. The municipal property is now used only as a parking place for local lovers. Congratulations to the new town commissioners and Mayor Nicholson for finally deciding to take a long-needed action.

A number of high school boys are looking for summer jobs. They're willing to give a good day's work for a fair wage, but several of the offers we've heard about during the past week sound as though they were set back in the Depression. How anyone can expect a youngster to accept a job for 30 or 40 cents an hour is more than we can understand. However, if you have a decent job to offer a high school boy who's willing to work just drop us a card here at *The Southerner* office.

This week goes down in our book as Cotton Blossom Week. Since Tuesday we've been constantly besieged with white and purple blossoms. They were brought from Whitakers, Pinetops Old Sparta, Penny Hill and a variety of places in between. The blossom-toters said the same, "Here's the first blossom from Edgecombe." All were crestfallen to learn that Arthur Edmondson brought the "first" into the office early Tuesday morning. He called Monday to say that he had found one. Incidentally, newspapers in Pitt, Edgecombe and Nash reported first blossom on the same day.

Good news despite the complaints about a weak Chamber.

Building boom on Main Street! The Constantine brothers are hard at work enlarging their building to include a show room and used car lot. Charlie Dandelake is completing an addition to house the new air conditioning unit at the Colonial Theatre. Carpenters are renovating the space formerly occupied by Patty's. At W.S. Clark and Sons a remodeling program is underway. In the old Levy Store fixtures have been ripped out to make way for a new business. Further down the street Joels is planning to open an enlarged store in the building formerly occupied by Tarboro Furniture Co.

(In later years, news reporters distanced themselves from every small favor or gratuity. Ramblin' was more practical and used the old standards: If you can wear it, drink it or eat it, take it.)

Thanks to the person unknown who left the watermelon on our porch this week. We sure like those gifts, but would appreciate it much more if we could identify the giver. How about leaving a note next time?

Bill Long made news for the Associated Press and the majority of the State's newspapers this week with the introduction of his tobacco harvester. But the Long Manufacturing Company attracted national attention when "Esso Oilways" a trade journal, carried a story on Long's tobacco curer. The story, aptly enough was titled, "The Long way for Quick Cures."

GOD IS GOOD to Edgecombe County! If you doubt it, just visit some of the surrounding counties and see what the prolonged drought has done to their crops. Stop in at any of the tobacco warehouses and look at the leaf being offered for sale. Then come home and look at Edgecombe crops and the tobacco on the local warehouse floor. We have indeed been fortunate in having rain at the right time, and that was particularly true of the tobacco crop. As one farmer put it, "God didn't want to hurt the Edgecombe farmers, but He held back the rain long enough to scare us half to death."

Tarboro trees were protected and preserved as long as possible.

If you see a dab of yellow paint at the base of your favorite tree you'll know the tree is earmarked for cutting. We were talking with Mayor Nicholson yesterday however, and he assured us that before any tree cutting program gets underway here there will be a public meeting to determine public sentiment. As we understand it, if the town wants to cut a tree on your property, but you object, it will not be cut PROVIDED you sign a waiver releasing the town from any responsibility should the tree fall. The mayor told us that a young tree would be planted for each old one cut. We like that plan, but we would like it even more if the plan called for two replacements. That would assure a good future growth for Tarboro.

Late October.

Christmas toys have made their appearance in local stores and a number of merchants tell us that customers have already started buying on the lay away plans. Christmas parade plans are progressing rapidly and all indications are that we will welcome old Santa in style this year.

The Town Common has been seeded for the winter, and at present it looks terrible. But just think how beautiful it will be in about a month when all that grass begins coming up. Many thanks to the town for doing the job.

We ain't very big and we ain't very important, but we keep turning up in the darndest places. The latest is a prominent mention a recent copy of "Quick," the weekly news magazine. Yep "Tarboro" is compared rather unfavorably with Cuba in an article by sports writer Red Smith. Smith writes about the big league ball players who spend the winter knocking the apple around in Cuban ball parks, and in his opening paragraph sums up the general observations of a player watching the moon rise over historic Moro Castle. The imaginary player then comments, "Tarboro, North Carolina, was never like this."

Does anyone know how Mr. Smith happened to pick Tarboro for the comparison? Could it be that Tony Napoles or some other former Tarboro ball player was overheard by Mr. Smith? To tell the truth we just don't know and it's worrying the heck out of us.

All indications point to an outstanding Christmas parade here next Friday afternoon. We are told the floats will be the most attractive ever to roll down local streets.

Another bouquet to Pattillo High for winning the Eastern Championship Thursday night. The State AA championship will be determined Wednesday night when the Trojans meet a western team here.

The fire in Princeville yesterday makes us wonder why the citizens there don't demand fire protection. We understand they pay taxes on their property, yet every time a building catches on fire the local fire department is called, but the town of Tarboro receives nothing to offset the risk of its men and equipment.

We love food whether it be collards or hog killings and when we receive gifts of food we always like to thank the giver. For that reason we express our heartfelt appreciation to the unknown person who left a sack of oysters on our side porch last week. They were delicious.

Window displays of local stores are worthy of a walk down Main Street any night. No doubt about it, the displays are some of the best seen in several years.

December 17.

It's a good thing the local Rotary and Kiwanis clubs booked Barbara and Andy Griffith when they did for the price of their entertainment will probably skyrocket now that Andy's record "What It Was Was Football" seems well on the way to national popularity. Capitol Records has purchased the copyright with an advance royalty of $5,000 and that company is lining up night club engagements for the couple. That will certainly place the price of their entertainment far beyond the reach of local civic organizations.

1954

A very positive note to start the New Year.

The robins have arrived in Edgecombe on their way northward. Quite a few have been seen around town during the past ten days, and farmers report large flocks of the birds in their fields.

❧

Fires in Tarboro this week stressed the need for two important improvements—both could well be done immediately.

The first improvement we suggest is that all fire hydrants be given an immediate inspection by members of the water department. The fire at the Cox home revealed that the hydrant at the corner of St. Andrew and Johnson Streets would not work. We have an idea that this isn't the only hydrant in Tarboro which isn't in operating condition.

❧

The town has planted a large number of young trees in the Town Common, thus assuring a new growth of oaks for future generations.

The new Tarboro High gymnasium is nearly completed, and the lockers for the dressing rooms appear to be the only obstacle preventing a formal opening of the long needed building. Mr. W.A. Mahler has expressed hope that the lockers will arrive here next week.

Always a boy at heart, Ramblin' understood boys.

As this is being written the boys who carry *The Southerner* are gathered in the alley outside our window. Two of the youngsters are chasing another up the hotel fire escape, while two others shout and beat one another with their newspaper bags. Another is hiding his friend's bicycle in the alley behind the

Security Bank. While all this is happening several other boys are watching quietly.

Sounds like a gang of juvenile delinquents, doesn't it?

But the odd thing about it is that the boys who are raising all the devilment are the best carriers. They keep their accounts in order and it's seldom their customers complain. The youngsters who are watching quietly are the ones, generally speaking, whose customers are constantly calling the office with complaints.

February 23.

The crocus poked its lovely golden head through many local lawns this week, and the elms lining Main Street are beginning to bud. Jonquils, japonica and camellias are showing off their finery. That's sign enough of Spring, regardless of what kind of weather is to follow.

A patriotism that never diminished.

Whenever a speaker mentions "this wonderful country of ours" in glowing terms he is accused of "flag waiving". Frankly, we've never liked to hear the term used in that respect. Our dislike became even greater nine years ago this week when a group of men from the 28th Marine Regiment fought its way to the top of a volcano on a God-for-saken piece of Pacific real estate called two Jima. Once atop the shell-battered peak they used a long piece of pipe to raise the Stars and Stripes. Every pair of field glasses on the Island were focused on the distant waving flag. Behind the glasses was many a wet eye. It was an inspiring sight one we'll never forget.

An environmentalist's love for Tar River and everything green.

In discussing a program of municipal improvements for Tarboro, the town commissioners have paid little attention to the acute need for a sewage disposal plant. We are told that the plant would cost at least $500,000 and, of course, that would require a bond issue. One argument used against construction of a disposal plant at this time is that the State Stream Sanitation Committee is surveying pollution conditions of all Tar Heel streams and will eventually get to the Tar. The surveys will lead to reports and recommendations for cleaning up the rivers. And it is argued here that it would be foolish to build a plant now and in a few years have the committee tell the town that the plant did not meet the requirements. Such a situation, however, cannot exist and such an attitude is not justified, for any municipality can submit to the sanitation committee plans for any proposed treatment plant. If the plan is approved a certificate is issued, giving the holder binding assurance that (if the terms of the certificate are compiled with) he will not be required to take further action relating to the control of pollution.

Such certificates have been issued to Durham, Charlotte, Liberty, Salisbury and Washington.

In our opinion Tarboro needs a sewage disposal plant more than it needs additional curbing and several other items included in the long-range planning report.

The recent warm weather brought out flowers and leaves and it also brought the crack of baseball bats and the smell of well-oiled fielder's gloves to the local school grounds. That serves as a reminder that we'll have two excellent varieties of baseball in Tarboro this summer, and it won't be too long before the Little League and Pony League practice begins.

The announcement that Miss Siddie Mallette will seek election to the Tarboro Board of Commissioners is a healthy sign. We have long believed that this town would be a better place if more women took an active part in political affairs. For quite some time now Miss Siddie has kept a watchful eye on the doings of the commissioners, and at times she has been an outspoken critic. We seriously doubt if the race will see any active politicking, such as handshaking and door knocking, but its going to be interesting to see Miss Siddie opposing Dr. Ed Roberson for election as representative of the Fourth Ward.

Snake plant.

Mr. J.R. Satterthwaite called this week to remind us to look at the snake plant in Dr. Jack Riley's office. The plant was the seen in bloom, and some local folks who raise snake plants tell us that it is most unusual. In fact, some of them didn't know the plants ever bloomed.

Election

Monday is election day in Tarboro and voters in four wards will name the commissioner who will represent them for the next two years. Although there is opposition in three wards, we haven't seen signs of much interest from the voters. *(Miss Siddie did not make it.)*

Mid-May.

Cold weather this week has certainly nipped Edgecombe crops.

The frost Tuesday night killed cotton and beans in low-lying fields, and the increased activity of the wireworms and cutworms has taken its toll of the county tobacco crop. It's hard to decide which is worse on the farmer—the weather or the Republicans.

A few weeks later.

This hot weather of the past week has certainly helped business at the swimming pool, the ice plant, the stores which sell fans, and the soda fountains. Come to think of it, we haven't heard anyone complain of coffee prices lately.

❧

Well, the first ripe tomato of the year for Tarboro was reported yesterday by Mark Ruffin. This makes the fourth consecutive year that Mr. Ruffin has placed first in the unofficial contest.

❧

Last week the first ripe tomato of the year was reported. This week it was the first cotton blossom and the first tobacco curing. That just about shoots the works on the firsts for this time of year.

A report on the taxpayers' money—a bit of economic history.

A item-by-item check of the town budget for the next year reveals the following facts which we believe are interesting enough to pass along to you readers:

The Long Manufacturing Company will receive from the town a tax refund amounting to $4,750.20. It seems someone placed a valuation of about $370,000 on a building which should have been valued on the tax books at $37,000.

The power plant expects to spend $100,000 for fuel all next year. It will purchase from VEPCO $40,000 worth of power during the year.

Lighting the major streets of Tarboro will cost an estimated $14,000 during 1954-55. It's also interesting to note that the Christmas lights used last year cost the town $1,428.74.

A new item in the budget this year provide the police chief $300 allowance for the use of his car. The police department also is allotted $500 for travel and investigation expense.

The superintendent of public works is provided with a car allowance of $400.

Maintenance of the airport property dropped from $273.66 in 1953 to $50 in 1954.

July 4.

More pleasant thoughts of the Fourth recall to us the not too-distant days past when autos were used for short trips, and the most pleasant way to enjoy the holiday was to get yourself an invitation to Mr. Ed Winslow's annual barbecue at the Cromwell Place.

We only remember one or two of those delightful events, but they made a lasting impression. That unforgettable aroma of pork cooking over a bed of hot coals—the sight of hundreds of squeezed lemons floating among crystal blocks of ice in big cypress tubs—while the ladies and young'uns dipped up cups of ice cold lemonade, the men ambled off to the barn for more fortifying drinks.

Such nice things to think about.

The old Farrar Hotel continued its struggle to stay alive.

Clarence Garrison, hotel manager, had his share of troubles and more this week. The morning after the heavy rain, Clarence found the hotel basement full of water. But the rain didn't do it.

Seems a large pipe in the walls of the old building gave way and the resulting flow of water poured into the basement.

Mid August and a sign of the times.

At least twice each week for the past couple of weeks we've called the fire station to inquire of any possible activity on the fire-fighting front. Jesse Broome usually answered the phone and before we could ask about tobacco barn fires, Jesse would shout, "No we haven't had any, and don't you even say that word." The words of course, were "tobacco barn fire," and to that time the firemen hadn't been called to the scene of a country blaze during the current curing season.

Early this week we called and without thinking innocently asked if any tobacco barns had burned. Jesse, worried as usual, shouted, "Now you've done it! We're sure to have a fire now that you've gone and talked about one."

Sure enough, that night at 11:30 the alarm came in and the firemen sped to the Floyd Lovelace farm where a tobacco barn was blazing.

Since that time Jesse has had much to say about newspaper editors who should keep their mouths shut.

Town workmen are determined that the new trees planted in the Common will not die during the drought. We have seen them watering the saplings several times, in recent weeks.

The following late summer column needs no explanation.

TO THE MAN WHO KILLED MY DOG—I don't know who you are and I hope I never do. I suppose you couldn't help hitting the big brown and white pointer shortly after 2 o'clock yesterday afternoon. After all, he was in the street, although he paid no gasoline tax and had no driver's license. At this writing, I hate you because you didn't have the common decency to stop and see how badly the dog was hurt. You didn't see if perhaps you could take him to a veterinarian. I guess you just didn't care whether the dog was dead or alive. I sincerely hope that the sound of your car hitting my dog haunts you for many a night, but I doubt that it will for the man who refuses to aid an animal he has hurt would not worry about such things.

The pointer's name was Lyn. He was only about four years old but he was one of the best dogs a man ever owned. It's odd that he should be killed today for in this morning's mail I received a clip sheet which carried an article written by William Faulkner after a hit-and-run driver killed his pointer, Pete. Here's a portion of it which I hope is read by the man who killed Lyn:

"He was just a dog. He expected little of the world into which he came and nothing of immortality either—Food (he didn't care what nor how little just so it was given with affection—a touch of the hand, a voice he knew even if he could not understand and answer the words it spoke); the earth, to run on; air to breathe; sun and rain in their season and the covied quail which were his heritage long before he knew the earth and felt he sun, whose scent he knew already from his staunch and faithful ancestry before he himself ever winded it. That was all he wanted. But that would have been enough to fill eight or ten years of his natural life because 12 years are not very many and it doesn't take much to fill them."

I called Lyn my dog, but he really belonged to my father who raised the pointer from a playsome pup, taught him to retrieve, and the two of them enjoyed many hours hunting together through the broomstraw and bean fields of the county. Lyn wasn't a street dog. He had a chain which was attached to a wire, and he roamed the backyard on the contraption. But you can't keep a bird dog leashed all day, and it was customary for him to be released at noon and at night for a jaunt down to the corner.

Lyn probably wouldn't be mad at the driver who didn't have time to stop, for Lyn had nothing but kindness for humans. He was of Carolina Farnk stock and their was no meanness in his breeding. He would have been willing to give his life for the driver who was in too big a hurry to stop.

❧

Work on the memorial library is progressing nicely, and before the building is completed, workmen will have started construction of the armory. Elrod and Gurkins have already moved their construction shack to the armory site.

Southern food—one delicacy after another.

This has certainly been a busy week for the editor. It has been a week of eating out. Monday night it was barbecue and brunswick stew with the wildlife club. Tuesday, we spent at home. Wednesday we had brunswick stew with the Elks in Rocky Mount. Thursday it was fried chicken as guest of the Long Manufacturing Company, and last night it was barbecue and brunswick stew at the Christian Church supper in Macclesfield.

After the hurricane.

Miss Hazel is now history, but tales of her visit to our county will be passed along to many generations.

Take, for instance, what happened out at Harper's Store at Leggett.

The first strong winds peeled the roof from the store, rolling up the tin as neatly as any tinsmith could do the job. However, when the wind changed into the west the tin was lifted from where it hung over the roof, uncurled and laid neatly back in its proper place. All the store owner had to do was climb to the roof and nail the tin back into place.

Time's relentless erosion of good things continues.

The Atlantic Coastline ended 64 years of passenger train service to Tarboro Tuesday night, and although there was no local "ceremony" to mark its end, the people of Ahoskie turned out in numbers to bed the train goodbye. The last train was greeted by a crowd of 300, and as it pulled from the station trumpeters of the Ahoskie band sounded taps.

(The Korean War was over but the year ended on an ominous sign reflecting the still very hot Cold War. It was a classified ad that ran next to Ramblin and speaks for itself: "FOR SALE: Ford 2-door sedan, one owner, low milage, very clean, bargain. Reason selling: son leaving for Korea. See A. C. Spier at Marrow-Pitt Hardware Co." The son, Lt. Ashley Spier, was a graduate of the U. S. Military Academy, finished his tour of duty in Korea and made the Army his career.)

1955

Local politics was always a favorite topic in early January.

Rumor has it that all the members of the present board of town commissioners will seek re-election this Spring. That included Mayor Nicholson. Even the mayor's political enemies admit that he has done an exceptional job as the town's chief executive. He has led the fight for a bond issue to bring the neglected town up to date. Despite pressure, he has not interfered with municipal department heads who are carrying out their job properly. Personal friendships have not interfered with his sense of responsibility toward the people of Tarboro. This town of ours could well stand another two years of Nicholson administration.

New homes are going up fast in Tarboro. The Cromwell Heights section is mushrooming, and there's plenty of construction in Forest Acres. When the weather breaks, another building boom should begin, and that is good news both for the contractors and the tax collectors!

From Raleigh comes word that the state is pushing small local industries and is encouraging areas to package goods they are familiar with.

Think how great it would be if we had a plant which produced quick frozen barbecue of the quality offered by Cap Wooten and Harry Gibbs, peanut brittle comparable in quality to that made by Mrs. Slim Johnson, kosher pickles equal to those made by Mrs. Aldene Creech or Mrs. Slim Johnson, watermelon rind pickle and brunswick stew like that made by Mrs. Mabrey Bass, Sr. Oh! there are countless other items of excellent local cookery which—if mass produced—would bring fame to Tarboro.

Although the new library appears to be completed, much work remains on the interior. Fixtures must be installed, and there is quite a bit of other inside work. However, the exterior work is about complete. Knox Porter has finished the job of landscaping the grounds, and incidentally the nursery man also contributed well over a hundred dollars to the building fund. The library is tentatively scheduled to open in May.

❧

The lights around the Confederate statue in the Town Common are in bad shape and need repairs. Several residents have told us that the Common is too dark to walk through at night.

❧

We'd like to call someone's attention to the fact that the historic old cotton press in the Town Common is in need of repair.

The foundation of the old press is beginning to rot away, and it seems a shame to allow such a fine relic of the days when cotton was king to rot away.

❧

Work on the memorial library is progressing nicely. Yesterday workmen were busy planting shrubs around the structure. Grass has already been planted and soon all will be ready for the formal dedication.

Writing about the library reminds us of a letter which we received this week. It was unsigned and we usually do not print anonymous letters, but it contained some fine bits of local history and for this reason it is reprinted below:

"Your paper has on several occasions carried articles on the obsolescence of the city hall and intimated that it is a monstrosity. Do you realize that 65 years ago this building was the latest style in architecture and the envy of our neighboring town?

In pre-City Hall days the opera house was in the second story of the building now occupied by Marrow-Pitt. If you will look closely you will see a bricked up doorway on the courthouse side of the building. The entrance was by outside steps. The citizens decided that the building was totally inadequate for theatrical purposes and so built the city hall with the opera house on the second floor.

The interior of this theatre was decorated and the scenery and drop curtains painted by Mr. Zoeller, grandfather of Harvie Ward. He was quite an artist as one can readily see in the scenic remains of today.

Road companies came to Tarboro because its opera house was the most pretentious east of Raleigh, and visitors came from miles around to view the plays.

Just prior to the period when the movies were becoming popular across the country, the road companies did not come to Tarboro as often as in the past and to make things more attractive the opera house was renovated and the huge box-like structure was planned on top of the building to house scenery.

The road companies still did not come, but the movies did.

Soon the opera house was a movie theatre, but the patrons had to climb a flight of steps, with the result that attendance was poor. Tarboro had too many fat people for stairs.

It was soon abandoned in favor of a ground-level building.

Now, as I already said, the City Hall was once held in high esteem. Some old timers now have plates and dishes with the picture of the City Hall in color, burned into them, and underneath is the inscription, "Made in Dresden, Germany for W.H. McNair."

Mr. McNair was a druggist who sold china as well as drugs. Some good merchant today might make money by having made new Edgecombe Library china. None of us thinks the City Hall is a thing of beauty, but remember that when built it was the last word in modern architecture."

No spring was complete without a rock fish report.

The area between the boat landing and Shiloh has been producing more rock per fisherman than any other single stretch of river.

Rumor has it that Gilly Nicholson will seek re-election as Tarboro's mayor if the city manager form of government is approved by voters Tuesday. Will he have opposition if he runs in May? According to at least one person on the inside politically, those who oppose Nicholson's policies are attempting to interest a well-known and respected citizen into running against the incumbent. The name was mentioned, but we can't conceive of that particular person entering Tarboro's political picture. However, strange things have happened.

Last week something happened here which to us is a disgrace to the court system of Edgecombe County. However, in all fairness it must be said that Edgecombe isn't alone—other county courts are the same.

We refer to the incident where a former resident of Tarboro sped down a local street at speeds alleged to be more than 50 miles per hour, sped through a school yard and crashed into a tangle of undergrowth. We understand he was charged with speeding, drunken driving and driving after his license had been revoked. The last charge did not come, however, until a check of the record revealed that this person had his license revoked in another county for two major traffic violations.

Our complaint is that this same person was indicted here last fall for drunken driving, yet time and time again his case has been continued in Superior Court.

In some cases, of course, there is justification for continuing cases, but we have noticed that in this particular case, the man has come to town several weeks before court was in session. Yet, some excuse was always found to have the case continued.

What happened last week could easily have resulted in the death of children who might have attempted to cross the street in front of the speeding car.

We also recalled several years ago that a youth was killed while speeding in a car after a very serious traffic charge against him had been continued several times.

Long Manufacturing Company is hard at work turning out equipment which will be used throughout the United States and several foreign countries. Harvester production has been in full swing for several weeks, and daily shipments by both truck and train are leaving Tarboro. The tobacco curers are in production again to meet the early demand from Georgia, and the haybalers plant is running full blast. The local company has a contract for balers to fill for the Ford Motor Company.

❧

One of the nicest things for young boys in Tarboro this year will be the farm teams for the kids who can't quite make the grade to the Little League. The boys have uniforms and play each Friday. Win or lose, doesn't seem to make too much difference, for they have those uniforms. One father was telling us that it was almost a fight at his house to make his son discard his uniform for pajamas.

❧

The first Tarboro tomato from this year's crop has been reported to *The Southerner* by Mr. Mark Ruffin. This makes the third consecutive year that Mark has brought us his first.

City Manager William Howard who takes over on July 1, was in town this week, and town employees tell us he is a man who believes in economy. They wouldn't elaborate.

July and a momentous change in city government.

Capt. William Baker Howard officially took the oath of office as town manager yesterday from Mrs. Ruth Mason, the county's lovely assistant court clerk. On hand for the brief ceremony was only one member of the town council, A.B. "Pug" Bass, who has been a local representative for more than 30 years.

The fact that Tarboro's new town manager is a retired Navy man has opened a gold mine of material for the comedians among us.

For example, there are those who insist that town employees will soon be told to report to work at 0 nine hundred rather than at the land-lubbery time of nine o'clock. They will work until seventeen hundred instead of five o'clock.

The jokers say the manager will issue an order proclaiming that municipal sweepers will man their brooms for a clean sweep down fore and aft. Municipal decks (streets) will be holystoned at each striking of the ship's bell in the town hall.

There are countless other stories being told, all, of course, in fun.

At the end of the month.

Monday night the town council will probably hear Manager W. B. Howard report on his first month of supervising municipal affairs. While we haven't discussed the matter with the manager, we imagine the first month has been a tough one, for it was the unofficial town policy to postpone almost all decisions for a period of several months before the captain arrived. That meant that much of his time had to be given over to minor details.

Historic milk plant gets a reprieve.

The eight councilmen who represent you, the people of Tarboro, decided to maintain the municipal milk plant because you indicated your desire to keep it. They are making a sincere effort to place the plant on a paying basis—a basis which will make you proud that it is a municipal plant.

However, the goals set for the plant cannot be reached without the active cooperation of every person who believes that the town should continue in the milk business. That means that each of the citizens who believes in the town-operated plant should do all that is possible to support the plant.

Without that support the plant cannot continue. The acting manager, Mr. Virgil Truitt, our excellent water plant manager, is stressing the fact that the plant is "YOUR" municipal milk plant.

Selling out of the movie business seems to be the popular thing to do this year. First, Charlie Dandelake disposed of the Colonial and Tar and now we learn that Charlie Holliday of Pinetops has sold his Pines Theatre there and has leased the drive-in at Cobbs Crossroad to Roy Champion, owner of Rocky Mount and Wilson movie houses.

Prod, push and plead for street repairs.

That water pipe leak on North Main has been fixed by the town, and several holes in Main have been repaired. The next time the town heats any asphalt we wish they would fix that deep hole in the pavement at the intersection of Albemarle and Howard Avenue. The hole is on the west side of Howard and it is almost impossible to miss it when turning west into Howard from Albemarle.

Bill Long has recently made a large addition to his tobacco harvester section. Rumor has it that the hay baler will soon get into operation again.

One of the more important things in life.

We realize that this isn't much of a column, but the doves are flying and the season for banging away at them with the old 12-guage is here again. We promise better fare next week.

Inflation rolls onward and upward.

Local barbers have upped the tariff on haircuts to an even dollar and even now the hair is growing down the back of the neck. The wife permitting, we are going to let this head of hair grow until the barber who cuts it really earns his dollar.

The price of municipal milk increased this week, but the hike wasn't made to make anyone rich. To the contrary, if Tarboro is to stay in the milk business, then vast improvements must be made tin the local plant. That extra penny will greatly aid in offsetting such costs, both now and in the future.

New attempt to salvage the old hotel on Main Street and Ramblin' promoted it heavily.

Two of the nicest people in town are the Westbrooks who operate the Hotel Tarboro dining room. We had occasion to eat there twice during the past week and both times we found the food to be excellent and there was plenty of it at very, very reasonable prices. The only thing wrong, as far as we could tell, was there simply were not many people in the dining room as there should have been, considering the excellent quality and the generous portion. Mr. Westbrook handles the kitchen while Mrs. Westbrook works in the dining room where she sees that coffee cups are kept filled and generally manages the business end of the operation.

In short, it's a pleasant place to enjoy a meal.

Judging from the stacks of brick around the Sunday School building, it appears, unofficially, that the Pentecostal Holiness Church is about to embark on another building program.

We thought the homecoming parade staged by students of Pattillo High yesterday was excellent. The floats showed a great deal of originality and were a credit to the school.

Our congratulations to Charlie Clayton who surprised all of us and took himself a bride last Saturday.

The two-liter plastic bottle was decades away.

There was considerable concern in *The Southerner* office this week about a "king-size Coke"—the 10 ounce version of Coca-Cola which is being marketed experimentally in larger cities. Most of the folks who glimpsed the bottle on the front desk were silent for a few moments, when asked, "Are my eyes playing tricks or is that bigger than a regular Coke bottle?"

October, skeeters and World Series.

The fogging machine being used in the fight against mosquitoes is doing a good job in some areas. Weather conditions are a big factor in the success of the fogging. Damp still nights are the big time for fogging.

The new television station in Washington made thousands of friends over Eastern Carolina this week when they provided viewers with the World Series, despite the fact that no programs—not even video station breaks—could originate from the studio. The successful effort to bring the series to ball fans will not soon be forgotten.

(The following account of a 1900 wedding attracted little attention in 1955 but in the late 1980's the public screamed for more of flowery accounts of Tarboro social events at the turn of the century.)

To many of the readers it is always interesting to look back to the bygone days and recall events which were much talked of at the time.

For that reason we are reprinting here a clipping from the June 19, 1900, *Southerner*, entitled, "A Very Pretty Marriage." The story tells of the wedding of Mr. Harvey Lewis and Miss Mattie Howard. We hope it recalls the names of folks some of you may have forgotten over the years.

Here goes:

"One of the prettiest marriages ever witnessed in this town took place last evening in Calvary Church, with Rev. E.W. Gamble officiating.

"The contracting parties, both natives of this place and widely popular, were Miss Mattie Howard, daughter of Wm. Howard and E. Harvey Lewis, son of T.E. Lewis.

"The ushers were Misses Kate Nash, Anna Baker, Barbara Staton and Susie Grey Baker.

"Just before these came in twos, marching up the central isle, a quartet, sang the wedding hymn. After which came in twos the little tots, Catherine Pender, Penelope Weddell, Elizabeth Howard and Alice Thurston Pender.

"Then came the bridesmaids and grooms, alternating with two maids and two grooms. In leaving the church these came out in the reverse order given:

"Miss Annie Baker of Battleboro with Manley Baker, Miss Annie Leggett of Palmyra with George Pennington, Miss Mary Howard with Wm. Grimes Clark, Miss Mary Bynum with Robert Nash of Wilmington, Miss Mamie Simmons with Robert Brown, Miss Anna Powell with W. Stamps Howard, Miss Lizzie Nash with Spencer Bass, Miss Lizzie Cotton with W.B. Howard. Miss Hester Lewis was maid of honor and T.W. Jacocks was best man.

"White and green constituted the decorations at both the church and the residence of the bride, where a reception was given them after the ceremony.

The table in the dining room was in the shape of a clover leaf. The refreshments were dainty and delicious.

"They were the recipients of many presents, with as large a proportion of valuable and useful ones as falls to the lot of Hymen's votaries(sic). and Mrs. Lewis will continue to reside here and *The Southerner* sincerely hopes they will do this long and happily.

Year's end: Not a bad year for a one-man staff.

Staring at us from the desk is the memo book which we used throughout the year to schedule our local news stories. It is turned to the final page for 1955—the page dated Dec. 31.

In looking back over the past 12 months, we find we have brought you somewhere between 2,600 and 3,000 local news stories. We have written about 8,500 headlines, and more than 200 editorials, which is not bad at all for a one-man news staff.

In addition, our tally sheet in the back of the book informs us that we've been cussed out—face-to-face—16 times, mostly by folks who objected to our cutting the "news" releases they gave us. The other side of the ledger sheet recalls that 36 folks were nice enough to tell us they liked what we had written, or that they thought we had done a good job in publicizing some project such as the recreation program or the Easter Seals drive.

All in all, it was a good year for news, but for our money the biggest story was the announcement last January 10 that General Plywood would rebuild here. Others included the capture and conviction of The Prowler, Eddie Lee Leonard, and the jail break of Lillian McCall.

1956

Keeping town officials on their toes.

The work of diverting the flow of polluter water from a point it enters the river above the municipal water intake to a point below the boat landing came to a sudden stop Wednesday afternoon when town officials discovered they had failed to get the necessary right-of-way from Mr. George Howard Fountain, owner of the 50 by 300-foot strip of property. The town offered Mr. Fountain $50 for the privilege of crossing the land with the ditch, but he wanted more. While bargaining was going on Wednesday afternoon and for a couple of hours Thursday morning the idle dragline was costing the town 15 bucks per hour.

An agreement was reached Thursday, but it now appears the issue will bring on quite a bit of discussion at the next meeting of the town council.

While searching through the personal papers of his wife's late father, Joe Bunn found some of the oldest paper money we've ever seen. It bears the inscription "Carolina Curren" and was issued at Halifax on April 2, 1776.

WENT UP TO Jack Mobley's last week to see how his remodeling sale was coming along and as I stood in the center of the new store I couldn't help but recall the days I worked there about 16 or 17 years ago. If I do say so myself, I was a first-class soda-jerker because I learned under Benny Sorey who could do almost anything around a drug store or fountain. As we remember it, Bennie also cut his cigars in half, puffing on one half during the afternoon and the other half at night. He took great pride in his work and had the reputation of making the best ice cream sodas in town. He was proud of the fact that he could put a "head" on a soda which would stay there for the life of the drink. To him, making a soda or a good Coke was an art; something not to be taken lightly.

However, during my days at Jack's, Lyn Williamson was Bennie's assistant and I worked under Lyn. Bennie worked on both of us. In those days Lyn was courting Gal Bardin, and had the reputation of blushing a deeper shade red than anyone else in town. Bennie never overlooked an opportunity to make him blush whenever Gal came into the store.

Don't know whether you readers think much of this bit of reminiscence, but perhaps you also will recall some of the pleasant happenings of times past.

Mr. Billy Bryan called me yesterday to advise that his Pink Perfection Camellia was blooming. I drove around to see the lovely shrub and learned the flowers had been damaged slightly by Thursday night's freeze. Still, the Camellia was a thing of beauty, and Mr. Billy was just as proud of it as he was 30 years ago when he planted it.

There's an air of sadness about the gaunt skeleton of the passenger shed at the ACL depot, in fact it may be entirely dismantled by the time this appears in print.

The removal of the shed and the conversion of the waiting room to a freight station removes from the ACL property the last vestige of passenger service on the Rocky Mount-Norfolk line.

While watching workmen tear down the shed we couldn't help but remember back about 25 years when the annual summer excursion to Ocean View via the Coast Line's special train was just about the biggest thing in my life. I don't remember how many cars the train pulled, but at the time it seemed to be the longest train in the entire world. The passengers would climb aboard early in the morning, mothers struggling under the load of a big box lunch, a small suitcase packed with bathing suits, and the noisy kids.

Yep, there's something sad about the change at the depot.

May 4 and—It's A Boy.

The three most wonderful words in this old world are not "I love you," "I'll marry you," or "Here's a raise."

To the contrary, the three most wonderful words are those spoken by a doctor in a green surgical gown when he declares: "It's a boy!"

John, who was born yesterday morning, is certainly his father's child. He came into the world squalling at the top of his lungs, and his mouth, like his father's, is the size of that a Tar River catfish.

Tobacco revolution begins quietly.

Bill Long is putting up a prefabricated tobacco barn on the front section of the Hope Lodge Farm. We understand it will be used to demonstrate how efficiently tobacco can put transferred directly from one of Long's harvesters into the barn thereby eliminating another hand-handling process in the curing of tobacco.

The legend of what happened to the monument in the Common.

The wreath at the foot of the Confederate monument in the Town Common looked rather lonely Thursday afternoon as the sun began dropping behind the big oaks.

I stopped the car on Wilson Street, got out, and walked over to the granite shaft, topped by the solemn old soldier. And as I recalled all the old gentleman stands for in the history of the South, I also remembered the humorous story of an indignity he suffered when the monument was dedicated.

The whole town turned out for the ceremony. The old veterans were there, at attention, with an honor guard with rifles loaded, supposedly with blanks, to fire a salute.

The speeches were long as the orators of that day recalled the glories of the days past, and when time for the salute came, the riflemen pointed upward and fired away.

The crowd drifted homeward and that night the old veterans rocked away on the front porches, remembering the battles, the long marches, and the cold winters of the war years.

But the next day a wave of horror swept the town. The ladies, especially, were in an uproar, for some uncouth member of the honor guard—probably a Yankee spy—had committed the unpardonable sin of loading his rifle with a "real bullet," taking careful aim and shooting at the stature on the monument. The bullet veered neither to the right nor left. It struck the soldier smack dab in the middle of the seat of his pants.

The wound was just too embarrassing, for, after all, North Carolina's soldiers were first at Bethel and last at Appamattox.

Quickly, and at considerable expense, the wound was repaired. But from that day to this the Confederate soldier in the Town Common has been unable to sit down.

The river has been too high and muddy for rock fishing this week so billboard artist Jack Griffin has devoted himself to painting a new Roller Champion Flour sign on the side of Mr. Browning's grocery store. Look's good, too.

Construction of the bath house for the East Tarboro pool has started, and work on the pool itself is scheduled as soon as the contracts are received from the pool makers. The contracts calls for completion in 35 working days.

June—On writing a column.

This week marks the beginning of this column's seventh year in *The Southerner*, and all in all, they have been good years. The column has been used as a sounding board for ideas regarding various improvements that could be made. We've made it as a slingshot to hurl a few brickbats, but we've tossed out an equal number of orchids. There are some of you who have told us you look forward to it each week; there are others who merely scan it, but we don't believe there are many of you who do not read at least part of it one week or another.

Some folks have asked why we didn't make "Ramblin' a daily feature of *The Southerne*r. Our answer was that we had rather attempt to write a good column once weekly than a poor one six days a week. Most of the daily columns that have appeared in this sheet from time to time carried a number of items which could be developed into full news articles. And we believe folks had rather see a headline over an account of their doings than to have it tucked away in a column under another's by-line.

Most folks don't realize it, but writing a column is a mighty time-consuming job - although there are times when it certainly doesn't appear so. We usually try to jot down items during the week to pass along to you on Saturday, but sometimes we forget and the result is usually a poor job of writing.

Folks in the register of deeds office and the clerk of court's office no longer have to dread working in the oppressive heat. Air conditioners were installed in both offices this week.

Prod, push, pull.

We certainly wish the town would do something to repair or move the Wyatt fountain in the Town Common. This monument to an Edgecombe hero has gradually fallen apart. One of the posts is down, and no longer does water spout from the top of the fountain. In short, we have permitted the memorial to become something of an eyesore.

If the fountain cannot be repaired, then steps should be taken to replace it with another monument.

When you read this I'll be in Pennsylvania to drive my family home from their much-deserved two-week's vacation from me. It's going to be a fast trip. Train up to Philadelphia Thursday night and a return trip by car tomorrow, but I've been planning for two years to take Betsy to the zoo. That will be about the extent of my activities in Yankeeland.

Fountain getting fixed.

Town Manager Howard tells us that a new spout and drain have been ordered for the Wyatt fountain in the Town Common and the memorial will be repaired just as soon as the replacements arrive.

The job of getting local warehouses ready for the opening of the tobacco market continues in full swing. This week workmen were busy replacing flooring in a couple of the houses, and the roof of at least one was being checked for leaks.

⁂

Work on the East Tarboro swimming pool is progressing nicely, according to the town manager who is still hoping for a September 12 completion date.

Incidentally, there are two other pools under construction in town. Jap Fulford has about completed the pool in his side yard, and the tile has been laid around the rim of the pool at the Hilma Country Club.

Late Summer and a little trip to one of Ramblin's favorite places.

The family had a grand time down at Salter Path this week just relaxing in the sun, enjoying the cool southwest wind, and eating some of the best seafood in the world.

There's a fish house at Salter Path which sells soft shell crabs six for a dollar, so we bought a half-dozen and a couple of fresh mullets and a quart of clams. That was really eating!

Rode down to Emerald Isle one day and suggest they change the name of the place to Sahara Sands. There are a number of beautiful homes there, but that is just about the most desolate place we've ever seen.

⁂

I came across another old *Southerner* clipping this week, one published in 1901 which recorded the death of 19-year-old Mark Cosby, brother of Howard (Deep Sea) and Bob Cosby.

In writing of Mark's death, Editor Frank Powell stated, "He was a compositor on *The Southerner* force, by whom he was esteemed, and who, in his untimely taking of, keenly feel a personal bereavement.

"He was a good son and brother and had no bad habits. He was an active member of the Hook and Ladder Company and of the Edgecombe Guards.

"No one ever worked on this paper who was more reliable or who more sincerely studied its interests.

"Three words describe him and his qualities; capable, faithful and true. He was all these in the broadest, fullest, and best sense."

Those are mighty comforting words to come from an employer.

Amazing is perhaps the best word to use in describing the speedy construction of the big water tank on St. Andrews Street, and fantastic is about the best word I can think of to describe the position taken by the steelworkers on their lofty perch.

In defense of music—any kind of music.

Just about every time I pick up the state papers I find someone has written a letter or an article condemning the latest fad in music—rock and roll. Most of the letters echo the line that the music is sending our teen-agers straight down the road to hell, so I decided to listen to a stack of rock and roll platters and form my own opinion about the stuff.

Ted Taylor up at the Variety Music Shop provided the loan of the records and I sat down to a full hour of everything from Fats Domino to Elvis Presley, with The Cadets and Shirley and Lee thrown in for good luck.

I don't see where anyone has anything to worry about.

If folks are worried about the dancing that goes with the rock and roll beat; well, there's nothing to worry about there either. In years past the older folks worried about the shimmy, the black bottom and the Charleston. Some even said the fox trot was strictly the work of the devil.

In my generation my first experience with anything but the fox trot was the so-called Big Apple, complete with truckin'. I got along all right there, but I got lost when the Big Apple developed into jitterbuggin'. And so far as dancing to fast tunes are concerned I've been lost ever since. Anything faster than "Moonlight Bay" sends me to the sidelines where I have to be satisfied with foot patting.

As for the rock and roll singers, the folks also raised cane about Rudy Vallee, Russ Columbo and Gene Austin. Later they said nothing good could come of the squeals which accompanied the moanings of Frankie Sinatra and Perry Como.

But, 15 years ago about the nearest thing to rock and roll was provided by Louis Jordan and Cab Calloway. Today it's Elvis.

Rest easy, Ma. Neither Elvis nor any other of the rock and roll idols are going to corrupt Junior. He's going to wear out a couple of pair of shoes dancing and he's going to borrow ahead on his allowance in order to buy records, and he's going to have a good time doing it. And the kids will be just as good as if they had spent their teen-age years singing "Down by the Old Mill Stream."

~

The Wyatt fountain in the Town Common is due to begin spouting water again this weekend. According to the town manager's office the parts for the fountain have been made and installed. In addition, the drainage lines have been cleaned, and the entire thing has been painted.

And lo, Ford created the Edsel.......

The Ford Motor Company is coming out with a new line of cars known as the Edsel, in honor of the late Edsel Ford. However the new contender in the medium-price field will be sold entirely separate from dealers now selling Ford, Mercury, Lincoln and Continental.

Good football season.

The Tarboro Tigers deserve a record breaking crowd at the game to determine the State AAC championship here next Friday night. The boys started the season slow but when they won the Warrenton game they seemed to discover the joy of playing hard football. As a result they played exception ball for the remainder of the season despite the fact that the crowds were far below expectation.

~

The municipal milk plant lost $2,300 during the last quarter, but James Harrell, the new manager is hard at work seeking new customers to bring production up to a profitable level. Cost of producing a quart of milk during the quarter was reported by the auditor to be 27 cents. And you know what it sells for!

The holiday season arrives.

Tarboro's Christmas lights went on for the annual parade yesterday and highlighting the attraction was the town's traditional display in the Common. Charlie Cooper and his crew got the display in place this week.

The cold weather that has come (and gone) reminds us that the big backyard hog killings of winters a decade or so back are apparently a thing of the past.

It has been a number of years since anyone has stopped by with a gift of the best of all meats—tenderloin.

Real old-timey hog killings have for the most part been replaced by freezer locker which make it possible to kill hogs safely in any kind of weather, winter or summer.

In just a few short days 1956 will become history leaving us only memories of a year which we will recall with mixed emotions. It will go down in history as a year which pushed the U.S. even nearer the brink of war. Just how near is something only history will tell. However, a Christmas card from one of our friends in Germany told of how frantic the families of our servicemen were only a short month ago when it appeared that war would come at any second. Those people were terrified, while most of us here at home didn't realize the danger.

The 1957 hurricane season does not begin until June 15, but the weather bureau believes in being prepared. It has announced a long list of names for possible Atlantic tropical storms—names such as Bertha, Esther, Gracie, Hannah and Kathie—will be used, plus some unusual ones like Inga, Odelle, Quinta, Undine and Zita. Let's hope that most hurricanes, at worst, go only as far as Bertha.

1957

Someone asked me yesterday why I keep up my editorial yapping about the need for new industry and new sources of farm income. "It won't mean a cent to you if Tarboro gets more income," he said. That is undoubtedly true. But it will mean a great deal to Tarboro and Edgecombe County. It will mean more money for the merchants and it will mean additional methods of making a living for our people. We have little or nothing to offer our high school graduates; nothing to hold them in their native community.

I suppose I'm just old-fashioned enough to have a deep love for my town and county. I want to see it prosper and grow, not only for those of us who live here today but for the future generations.

Stopped in at the Coca-Cola plant Tuesday for a chat with Mr. M.S. Brown. He was looking over some changes he was having made in his darkroom and told me that in the course of removing some old cabinets he had come across a stack of what was Tarboro's most widely distributed newspapers—the Homefront News.

That paper, published during World War II endeared itself to thousands of Edgecombe boys. It was eagerly awaited in Europe, and the Pacific, and because of it more than one Yankee came to know and love Tarboro and its people. There were a number of issues which featured bathing beauty pictures as were some of Tarboro's landmarks. In addition to "photos by Brown" there was some fine art work by Alice Evans, and plenty of spicy stories by George Earnhart and Bill Babcock. Rotarians handled the mailing chores.

Just looking over those papers brought back a lot of memories.

The Town Common is a popular place for tourists to stop and take a few pictures. For example, on two occasions this week I saw cars from West Virginia and Ohio stop on the east side of the Common. The families piled out a few minutes of leg stretching and shutter snapping. Mama and the kids posed in front of the fountain and the monument while Pa did the picture taking.

Still trying to keep the old downtown hotel alive.

The Hotel Dining Room continues to pack in the customers we have learned of the dining room's growing reputation for serving good food and plenty of it.

❧

Mayor Gilly Nicholson threw the political door wide open when he announced he will not seek re-election. There's a tremendous amount of speculation about a successor. Just about everybody in town has been named today as a possible candidate but at this stage only one thing seems certain—no member of the present council seems interested in the post.

Oops

The job of repairing the new water tank on Wagner Street wasn't as difficult as it at first seemed. Inspection by the contractors revealed that the tank hadn't sprung a leak. One of the workmen had failed to completely shut off a valve and that made it appear the tank was leaking. That particular valve has now been closed and capped.

Hotel continues to fight back.

It's getting to be kinda dangerous to walk the sidewalk under any Hotel Tarboro window.

For example, a couple of weeks ago a Coke bottle toppled from a second floor window and smashed to bits on the Main Street sidewalk. The flying glass narrowly missed several people passing on the street.

As if that weren't bad enough a similar thing happened Wednesday afternoon when half of a large pane of glass fell from a third window on St. James Street. It narrowly missed a local lady. A few minutes later the other half of the pane splintered to bits on the pavement.

Perhaps screens would help protect passer-bys.

Congratulations to Tarboro's new college trustees. It isn't often that a town is so honored twice in a single week. But that's what happened. Cam Weeks was named to the board of the University of North Carolina and Luke Hill was elected chairman of the board of N.C. Wesleyan at Rocky Mount. Mr. Hill has been a trustee since the college was organized.

Separate but equal pool opens.

The East Tarboro swimming pool got off to a good start Thursday, considering the weather. Charlie England said about 250 braved the chilly wind to take a charter dip. He also said that Jerry Johnson is planning to conduct swimming classes in a couple of weeks.

Seven years ago this week I walked into this office, fresh out of college, newly married and with something of a chip on my shoulder for having knocked around the Pacific for three years with a bunch of Marines.

During those years the chip has disappeared and the marriage has been cemented into something of seemingly eternal value.

Tomorrow is Fathers Day, an occasion for which we publish this bit of verse which found its way to the writer's desk earlier this week:

On Fathers Day we honor Dad
To give his heart a lift;
'Tis just like Mother's Day,
Except he gets a cheaper gift.

Heavy rains this week showed up quite a few leaks in the courthouse roof. Commissioners plan to make some roof repairs this summer, but a new roof is out of the question, at least for this year. Replacement cost is estimated at $15,000.

And old friend is back in the news again, ailing.

A local landmark, the Security Bank clock, has been on the blink for several days this week. For at least two days the south face showed the time to be 7 o'clock.

Those old cars which came through Tarboro this week provoked a tremendous amount of comment. As I've wondered before, how many of the present models will be around 30 or 40 years from now?

A number of those cars have features which have again come into style. Still others have features which are above what is being offered in today's models. For example, the old Franklins in the procession have aluminum bodies. No rust problem there. There weren't the many "extras" to rattle either. And I doubt if there's a car on the road which offers the comfort of that '24 Rolls.

The Southerner's classified ads this week aided in locating "Pablo" the parakeet owned by the H.A. Servais family. Pablo disappeared Monday and Mrs. Servais immediately inserted an ad in the paper.

Thursday morning, Mr. A.R. Bobbitt called her to say that he thought Pablo was resting in a tree outside his house. Armed with bird seed and Pablo's cage, Mrs. Servais hurried around to St. David Street.

For a long time she tried to coax Pablo from his perch, but the parakeet would have none of it; his new-found freedom meant too much. Finally, he became bored with Mrs. Servais and tucked his head under his wing.

Mrs. Servais was frantic. In desperation she called Dr. H.A. and asked his advice. The doc remembered that better than anything else in the world Pablo loved ice—ice which tinkled in a tall glass.

Mrs. Bobbitt provided the glass and the ice and Mrs. Servais went back to tempt Pablo.

The ice rattled around in the glass. Pablo was tempted. He pulled his head from under his wing. He hopped around on his tree limb. But he wouldn't come down.

Finally the glass was placed on the ground, next to the cage, and Pablo immediately flew to the glass and began pecking lovingly at the ice. But each time Mrs. Servais tried to catch him, the bird flapped away. At long last the glass of ice was placed in the cage, and Pablo flew and, the door was closed and the Servais family was again happy.

The Battle Avenue water tank is no more. It was cut to the foundations this week by salvage folks, who received for their work not only the metal in the tank but also a fee from the town.

Some folks argue that the town should have kept the tank intact and utilized it. But those folks didn't live in the shadow of the heavy steel which had been looming above them for more than 60 years.

An engineering survey indicating the tank was out-of-line and potentially dangerous. Therefore, it had to come down.

❧

The wife and kids are in Philadelphia for a two-week stay with relatives and while they've been away for only a couple of days, the house is something I just don't want to come home to.

❧

Mr. Cliff Weeks, who is hoping to top the state watermelon title holder (we don't know the official weight), is to produce a number of melons that will pass the hundred-pound mark this year.

We at *The Southerner* wish him the best, provided, of course, he sends us a sizable sample.

❧

Immediately after this week's wind, rain and hail storm I jumped into the car and drove all over town listing damage. Saw wires down, trees down, limbs hanging in trees, front of Long's new building blown down, tv antennas bent double, and a number of other things. However, it wasn't until thc day after the storm that I noticed that my across-the-street neighbor Stan

Liverman had storm trouble. The wind toppled both his antenna and chimney. Sometime you can't see the forest for the trees.

Nothing to do? Tarboro in the '30's was a Great Adventure.

An editorial writer for the New Orleans Item recently expressed concern over the fact that kids apparently don't have as much fun as they use to, suggesting that perhaps the stress of modern living has squelched the old pastimes.

Some of the diversions played by what the writer termed the "Depression generation" included hockey on skates, rubber gun battles, packing case clubhouses on empty lots, the knife-throwing game of Territory and a few others.

During my day clubhouses were not limited to packing boxes. There were groups with an assortment of clubs all over down.

The Webb boys—Corky, Bill and Toby—had a club on Howard Avenue. Claude Hart had an elaborate club over the wood house in his backyard. That club was complete with a spotlight to keep night raiders away. Henry Bourne had a club next to the garage and later utilized "slave labor" (the younger kids) to build a two-story tree house in the cedars along Johnston Street. Ottie Graham had a large clubhouse behind his mother's home on St. Patrick. I believe Bro Hargrove had one in the barn that was about where his house now stands.

All the clubs were involved in a constant feud which ranged from rubber gun wars to direct attempts to demolish the opposing club's house with crowbars and axes.

Hockey games on skates were regularly set for almost every fall and winter afternoon on the street in front of Bridgers School. More than one Tarboro man still carries scars on his shins to remind him of the battered tin can which served as a puck and the turned-down oak plow handles which were used as hockey sticks. I believe Hoke Leggett still has a deep scar on his forehead where someone crowned him with a stick one afternoon.

The coming of rock and tar to cover the smooth concrete put an end to the games.

There was also the time that everyone had to dig a cave to use as a clubhouse. Ed Marrow had a big one containing a half-dozen or more rooms in his backyard. Forest Sledge, Charlie Cullen and I had one in the lot between the Catholic Church and Mr. H.H. Palmer's house. That one worked out fine until one day Forest and I made Charlie mad and he crawled out, jumped up and down on the top of it until the thing caved in on Forest and me.

The sand pit on Gold Hill was another favorite place for digging caves and on at least two occasions we had to dig Ted Morgan out after he had been completely covered by a cave-in.

Other Depression recreation included the cable slide. You don't see'em anymore, but we had some dillies during the Thirties.

There was a famous one in the ravine behind the milk plant, but that one wasn't high enough so we moved out to the sand cliffs which were on the river side of the Riverview Apts. are now located.

From the cedar tree on top of the cliff to the stump which anchored the cable on the far side must have been a distance of 100 feet and from the top of the cliff to the bottom was about 45 feet.

On the cable was a piece of pipe. Usually the pipe was stuffed with lard to make a faster trip. The user would climb the tree, grasp the pipe and shove off for the long swift ride to the bottom.

However, on this particular piece of cable there happened to be a kink, and its first victim, I believe, was Ottie Graham. Ottie was sliding down at what seemed to be express train speed when the pipe hit the kink and stopped dead. Ottie flew through the air, turned a dozen flips and hit the ground flat on his back. He lay there for what seemed to be 30 minutes before he could get breath enough to sit up.

Tarboro weather records—information that lasts forever.

There is quite a bit of interesting information about Edgecombe weather on a sheet printed recently by the Chamber of Commerce. The information was compiled by the state weather bureau and includes average temperatures, rain and snowfall for each year since 1927.

Here are a few facts you might like to file away:

The greatest Edgecombe snow fell in March of 1927 and lay on the ground for four days.

The heaviest amount of rain falls in June, July and August. October has the least rain and the most fair weather.

During the past 30 years Tarboro has not had a temperature lower than 5 degrees above zero; the average winter is less severe with the temperatures dropping to 15 or 20 degrees two or three times during the winter.

The average date of the last occurrence in Spring of a temperature below 32 degrees is March 30; of 28 degrees, March 17; of 20 degrees, February 17.

The average date of the first Fall 32-degree temperature is Nov. 1; of 28 degrees, November 16; of 20 degrees, December 13.

The fact sheet notes that records of both rainfall and temperature were kept in Tarboro as early as 1871, however, there are several entire years missing from the temperature records, and one extended break—1873-1877—in the rainfall records. Since May of 1891, records have been practically continuous.

❧

The town began work this week seeding the Common with winter rye. Ernest Eason, who supervised the job told me they were planting 1,400 pounds of seed.

❧

For the past couple of weeks, and for the first time since I've been married we've had what might be described a serious illness in the family. Pat had a mighty rough bout with pneumonia, then developed a case of hives when she reacted to some medicine. All of that came on the heels of the new baby and a bout with the Asian Flu.

What was so heart-warming was the way folks immediately called and came by with delicious food and offers to let us farm the kids with them. To be frank, I chocked a couple of times at the tremendous goodness of friends who expressed their affection for us by their offers and deeds. Words can never express our appreciation.

Ouch—bad joke—but funny.

My brother Bill arrived with his family late Thursday night from Dallas Texas. Among other things Bill has a sideline of sheep raising and he's also a fabric dealer.

Well it seems that one day his wife Bobbie, became dissatisfied with the color of the living room drapes and ordered him to prepare some blue dye. He made up a big tub of the stuff and after dyeing the drapes, had some left over. About that time a lamb walked by and Bill grabbed it, dunked it in the tub of dye and turned out a beautiful blue ewe.

The next day a motorist stopped by and asked if he could buy the beautiful blue lamb. Bill got a high price for the lamb and an idea. Since that time he has dyed his lambs various colors and has made more money than he ever has in his life.

The truth of the matter is that he now has the reputation of being the biggest lamb dyer in Texas.

The hospital (bond) election is now history, and it seems those who worked hardest to support it could have saved themselves a considerable amount of worry about the outcome merely by having contacted John Price the morning of the election.

Judge Price's prediction of the outcome?

Well, he said t would carry by 250 votes. He only missed it by 24.

Paving crews have patched pavements in Fairview, Cromwell Heights and Forest Acres this week. Paving of Hope Lodge Street was also planned, but the dirt was too wet. Understand it will be paved as soon as the sub-surface is dry enough to make the job practical.

Gas war—just 27.9 cents a gallon.

It looks as though a gas war has started right here in Edgecombe—started by the gasoline companies rather than the individual dealers. Prices in Tarboro are for the most part steady at 29.9, but out on the Rocky Mount highway the price is down to 27.9. I understand that up Scotland Neck way the going rate is 26.9, and the price has at times this week reached a low of 24.9.

Ultra Modern?

W.V. Leggett has purchased the Bridgers property east of Hilma Park and plans to build an ultra-modern motel there in the near future. When complete it will be a much-needed addition to the town and county.

A couple of weeks before the latest addition to the Bass family was born, our five-year-old walked up to her mother, took a good long look at the hatching jacket she was wearing, and finally asked, "Mommie, tell me something about being a mommie."

Pat took a deep breathe, "Here it is. At last the story of the birds and bees is obsolete", she thought. But before she could begin the story, the five-year-old continued "Tell me how to make meat loaf, green beans casserole, and things like that".

A sigh of relief went through the Bass household.

The old town had a lot of brains working in the community.

Politically, is Tarboro becoming the "Shelby of the east"?

Frankly, I don't believe any Tar Heel town of comparable size can hold a candle to Tarboro when it comes to holders of public office. The latest appointment, of course was of W.G. Clark, Jr. to the State Port Authority. Don Gilliam, Federal judge, has been named to the State Probation Commission. We have two trustees of the Greater University of North Carolina—Cam Weeks and Sam Clark Jr. Gene Simmons is a member of the Board of Conservation and Development. Bill Long is a member of the educational foundation.

George Fountain, Jr. is a Superior Court judge. L.H. Fountain is a congressman. C.W. Mayo is a member of the State Board of Water Commissioners. Coming back to Cam Weeks again, he is also a director of the North Carolina Railroad.

Our heartfelt thanks to the town's electric crew for this season's Christmas decorations. While those red candles (which are rented) do look a bit pregnant during the day, they are a decided attraction at night.

Christmas with a bang.

Christmas night, while setting off a half dozen sparklers for the kids I remembered 15 or more years ago when all us kids would save our money for months in order to send for an assortment of fireworks from either Ohio or Baltimore. I favored the Ohio firm and usually manage to scrape together enough to buy what was known as the "Young American" assortment. The mayor usually proclaimed 6 p.m. on Christmas Eve as the legal opening for fireworks shooting and as soon as the clock began striking a barrage of skyrockets and Roman candles could easily be seen.

The boys on Battle Avenue, myself, Clarence Lee Ruffin, Frank Arnes and a half-dozen others were up early Christmas morning, not only to see what Santa brought, but to see who would be the first person to toss a cherry bomb or thunderbolt under Mr. Edgar Harris' bedroom window.

I lost all interest in fireworks on Christmas Eve of 1946, and I still don't care about the darn things.

It was on that date that the firecracker stands on south Main exploded in a blaze of fire, smoke, and whizzing Roman candles. I was behind the stand at Simmons Store when the stand across the street began exploding. A ball of fire shot across the street, setting fire to our stand, and there was only one place to go; under the table. There I stayed while all hell broke loose.

I came out of it with only a few scratches, but Rufus Cromartie, who was also there suffered a painful cut when the plate glass window was shattered by the explosions. Martin Anderson, who hadn't been out of an army hospital too long, also had a rough time of it.

The Christmas Spirit.

Milton Little, our 13-year-old *Southerner* carrier will talk at length about any subject under the sun, so I wasn't surprised the other day when he breezed into the office, pulled up a chair and declared, "The Lord must have willed it. Yes sir, He sure must have."

You see, we sell the carrier boys their papers; they pay for the number they get from us. If a customer fails to pay the boys, it is the boys who lose—not us.

Well, one of Milton's customers, an aging colored woman doesn't always have the money to pay Milton and tells him he'll have to stop bringing the paper for a week or until she gets some cash. But Milton is not one to just let a customer drop, especially when that person enjoys the paper as much as the woman seems to. So the youngster pays for her paper out of his own pocket. And he's not the type boy to do it just to be showing off.

1958

As a rule newspapermen are invited to about every free feed that comes along; barbecues, brunswick stews, rock muddles, fish fries, steak dinners and occasions where fried chicken is served.

We appreciate the invitations and always enjoy the vittles.

But yesterday there came an invitation I just couldn't accept. Tom Bardin called and invited me to join him for dinner. It sounded good, because Monday night I enjoyed the sheriff's hospitality when he and Dinksie Gilliam served law enforcement officers barbecued chicken and brunswick stew.

I realized it was impolite to ask, but I did it anyhow. "What's on the menu?", I queried.

"Oh", came the reply, "we're going to have sweet potatoes and collards."

That suited me just fine.

But the sheriff added, "And baked possum."

I voiced my appreciation, but hastily declined.

A new machine, a stump cutter, was demonstrated last week. Instead of digging a stump from the ground, it chewed its way into it, reducing hard oak to sawdust in a relatively short period of time. It would have taken a crew of men all day to do the same job. The only drawback is the cost—$3,000.

Apparently James Harrell is continuing to make progress at the milk plant. Last year this time the plant was $1,800 in the red. But the semi-annual report shows the plant has made a profit for the first six months of the current fiscal year—$45.

On a navigational lock system for Tar River.

I was talking to town Manager W. B. Howard yesterday and he said he asked the army engineers about the outfall line which is going to be placed in the river behind the Royster warehouse. He also asked about the possibility of having the river dredged (using federal funds).

The letter in reply contained some interesting information about the river, including the fact that the channel from Greenville to Tarboro is supposed to be 60 feet wide, and, get this—20 inches deep. On the subject of making the river navigational from Washington to Tarboro, the writer of the letter quoted a report which was made in 1929. It stated that to do the job properly three locks and dams would be needed and would cost (in 1929) $2,074,000. He said today's costs would be about $7,500,000 and the job could possibly be done if the folks interested could show it was economically justifiable—that is—there was enough commerce on the river. Looks like it's never be done.

I had a birthday this week and received one of the biggest and most touching surprises of my life.

Mother called about 11:30 Thursday morning and offered me dinner and that usually means collards, black eyed peas and cracklin' bread. But when I arrived at 12:30 she and Dad came in with a freshly cooked turkey, dressing, gravy, rolls, candied sweet potatoes, asparagus and my favorite pudding. Mother had gotten up early and cooked the entire meal for me. It was a tremendous surprise and made the day one I appreciated more than any birthday I can remember.

That birthday referred to above was my 33rd and I didn't feel a bit older until our 6-year-old climbed into my lap and said "Daddy, which did you like best; the old-fashion times or today?" I asked what she meant and she then asked if I liked automobiles better than covered wagons.

Despite the rotten weather, there is appearing in many local yards a joyful sign of spring. The jonquils, which have already poked green spikes through the frozen ground, are beginning to blossom. I saw one cluster this week which had already come into full flower.

A crowd of local men just couldn't wait for the herring run on the Roanoke to reach its peak, so they loaded a car with a frying pan, lard, salt and cornmeal and went down to Jamesville Wednesday afternoon.

All the way down they talked about how fine it was going to be for nothing tastes quite as good as fresh herring fried on the bank of a river.

Reaching Jamesville, they had to wait for nine boats before they could buy 18 fish. One boat came in with two herrings, another had three and so on. Fishermen charged a dime each for the fish.

Clock report.

The clock on the Security Bank Building is on the blink again.

About the worst news I've heard in recent years is word that Gilly Nicholson is leaving Tarboro. His moving to Raleigh will be a tremendous loss to Tarboro because he is one of the outstanding young men in North Carolina.

Gilly, as mayor of Tarboro, instituted many changes which resulted in the betterment of municipal government. He was the driving force behind the move which resulted in Tarboro's having a city manager type of government. He devoted long hours to the campaign which made possible construction of a million-dollar county hospital. His other unselfish accomplishments in the civic field are too numerous to mention.

Before the dike.

The health department is still continuing its dirty job of cleaning up the filth left by the Princeville flood. Since the waters receded, the department has spread 2,700 pounds of lime around. In addition, wells have been treated with f100 pounds of HTH, a powdered form of chlorine.

With the cooperation of the town and highway department, 25,000 gallons of fresh water was hauled into Princeville for us by the citizens there.

Have you noticed the unusually large number of squirrels in the Town Common lately? I counted 42 of them scampering around the group late Wednesday afternoon.

Someone (probably Ching Marrow) left on my typewriter a *Greensboro Daily News* story about Toby Webb. Toby, formerly of Tarboro, has been football coach in Albemarle for the past 11 years, but now he has announced he will quit coaching next year to become principal of the junior high school in Albemarle.

According to the article Toby has turn out some unbelievable teams for his school. His 11-year record for 117 games is 93-18-6, and he runs from the single wing.

Shorty Plummer, custodian of the courthouse and avid fisherman, caught a lamprey eel in his net Thursday night., The lamprey was the largest I have ever seen, measuring about three feet long. Lamprey eels are especially destructive to fish. Instead of jaws the lamprey has a circular sucker mouth, set with horny projections like teeth. It feeds on fish, rasping the flesh with its suckers and powerful tongue.

The biggest parade held in Edgecombe County annually is scheduled for May 2. That's when the county's 1,100 Negro 4-H youngsters hold their May Round-up. About 900 youngsters take part in the parade and festivities in the ball park. Floats and approximately half-dozen bands are also featured.

Last year's event drew a crowd of more than 5,000 to town.

Merchants will be for contributions to make the event possible.

Duck Lewis has resigned his job as manager of the Moose lodge in Greenville and plans to attempt to get back into chamber of commerce work.

Duck has managed the big lodge since last August and has made his resignation effective May 1. Says he plans to take a week's vacation—his first in two years—then start looking for a new job. He managed the chamber here for two years, then worked in the Burlington chamber for three years before going to Roanoke Rapids for a period of four years.

Clock report.

Should have mentioned it last week, but with the Easter rush I forgot to say that it's good to have the Security Bank clock back with us again. Repairs were completed last week, and it should be a long, long time before it goes on the blink again.

Trying to save 'Low' School.

The Southerner appreciates letters from its readers and one received this week by Mr. Bernie Price, principal of the high school is no exception. However, I'll differ with him on a number of points.

First, on the issue that Bridgers School is 50 years old with insufficient playground, it should be remembered that just across St. Patrick Street from the school is an entire block of Town Common and by closing that block of the street in front of the school during school hours that particular problem would be solved. As for the condition of the 50-year-old school, the April Grand Jury report reflected close scrutiny of all schools, including Bridgers and there the jury found only that two rear doors needed replacing, additional garbage cans are needed and paint is needed on several plaster walls.

The column extends its deepest apologies to the Hon. Charles E. Clayton of 508 E. Philips Street for inadvertently omitting his name and garden from the list of members of the Gold Hill Gardening and Weeding Society. An inspection of the Clayton premises reveals a fine garden; one unexcelled in all the Gold Hill area and one which is a prime contender for the coveted Eagles Cup. The cup is an award made annually to the society member having the least potato bugs and the largest turnip termites.

❧

The death of Miss Maggie Whitley this week brought back memories of 25 or more years when I was a small boy and spent my pennies at her fabulous candy counter in her grocery store at the depot. She was always patient with while we made our selection. Then the Frozen Delight opened down the street and some of her regular customers went there but we soon learned that stuff melted very quickly and besides, the Frozen Delight never slipped in another penny piece of candy like Miss Maggie used to do.

❧

Buster Wilkerson was beamed like a daddy over the birth of a first child Thursday when the giant new A & P opened. He was smiling from ear to ear as hundreds of folks came up to congratulate him on the big, beautiful (12,000 square feet) new store.

❧

Gus Pistolis is leaving June 15 for a summer visit to the Old Country, his first visit to Greece since the summer of 1952. Genial Gus is taking along some this year in the form of his nephew and niece, Connie and Cris Pistolis, children of Mr. and Mrs. Cris Pistolis.

They will fly to Athens where they'll visit Gus's brother, Dr. Fred Pistolis, who operates the Athens Clinic. While in Athens, they'll also visit the brother of Mrs. Cris Pistolis who is a dentist. Visits to other points of interest in Europe are also planned.

Gus says he plans to return to Tarboro around the first of August.

❧

Long Manufacturing this week started production of its new peanut combine. The combine is the latest addition to a line which reflects progress on the farm machinery front, and the company is a tremendous asset to the community.

New heat pump

Workmen were busy this week installing a combination air conditioning and heating plant in Marrow-Pitt's. The same system which emits cool air in the summer blows warm air throughout the store in the cold months. Those big coal stoves which were formerly used for heating will be stored away.

Weather permitting, this is going to be a banner (tobacco) crop for Edgecombe County, and warehousemen and buyers are already predicting a 60-cent average. Added to the income is the price support which this year will be 90 per cent of parity. That increase represents additional 25 million dollars for North Carolina tobacco growers this year.

The fact that Mr. Boll Weevil hasn't been very active is indicative of an exceptionally good cotton crop.

Mr. Cliff Weeks brought some of his giant watermelons by *The Southerner* office this week and announced that he hoped we enjoyed them. This is to officially report they were extremely good and were much sweeter than many of the small melons we've enjoyed this year.

Local citizens are watching with interest the progress being made at the new hospital site, despite the fact that construction began only last Monday and really isn't much to see.

Several folks have complained recently about the theft of shrubs from plots in Greenwood Cemetery. Not only shrubs, but flowers have also been dug up and removed. In each of the cases reported to this writer the plot owners have said they would gladly have given cuttings of those plants to anyone wanting them. However, some so-called humans seem to get some sick thrill from stealing from a cemetery.

Hurricane Daisy passed us by, thank goodness, but the rains of the past week apparently took a heavy toll of cotton. Several farmers told me their cotton lapped in the row, making it impossible for the sun to dry out the rain-soaked bolls. Those bolls, they say, will rot.

(It is obvious by now that Duck Lewis held more jobs than anyone in Tarboro history.)

Duck Lewis stopped fishing and went to work this week. He is now the executive secretary of the N.C. Motel Association, and organization which has more than 200 members throughout the state.

He has an office in the Capital Club building in Raleigh, but will probably spend most of his time on the road.

Two of the nicest things about this time of year are scuppernong grapes and boiled peanuts. Unfortunately, the majority of the younger generation knows little about either.

For example, just the other day Dick Bryant had a bushel of scuppernongs. I helped myself, and while eating them I remarked to one of the paper boys that Dick had a basket of scuppernongs.

The youngster immediately asked, "I wonder if he would give me a big bunch?"

The kids don't understand how anyone could derive any pleasure from standing under a scuppernong vine, brushing away the wasps and sweat suckers while picking the delicious golden grapes.

Believe me, there's nothing better in the world.

. . . unless it's boiled peanuts.

With just the right amount of salt, you can't beat 'em and you can't stop eating them either.

Prod, prod, pull pull.

Town council meets Monday night and the agenda includes everything from a proposal to make Main Street an avenue of dogwood trees to ratifying bids worth several thousand dollars. Why don't you citizens have interest enough in your town government to attend meetings which affect you?

The item recently about scuppernong grapes and boiled ground peas brought comments from several folks who enjoyed both.

On Tuesday Bob Peters stopped me in the drug store and asked why I hadn't mentioned chinquapins. He went on to say that he had been fortunate enough to obtain some black market chinquapins over the weekend and had "thought about me."

I was indignant.

After all, to me chinquapins rate above boiled goobers and are almost on the same plateau with scuppernongs.

"If I get any more I'll think about you," Bob promised.

"Think nothing," I replied, "Bring me some."

The next day Bob stopped me on the street and forked over a handful of those delicious little nuts. I had almost forgotten how good they were. Many thanks.

Christmas decorations get bad reviews.

Tarboro's Christmas decorations went up this week and less said about them the better. They detract from rather than enhance the beauty of Main Street. Most folks seem embarrassed when they discuss 'em. Someone even advanced the guess that this year's displays are something Bear Grass discarded in 1916.

The cotton crop ain't what it is in California.

I'm always impressed by the autumn line of trucks waiting their turn at county cotton gins and when the U.S. Department of Commerce sends me the ginning report I immediately turn to the page which lists the number of bales ginned in Edgecombe.

This week, however, I took time to read the entire list and was amazed to find that Kern County, California, has already produced 346,097 bales of cotton this year. Three other California counties has also produced in excess of 100,000 bales.

To date this year, Edgecombe has ginned 4,700 bales.

Fitness report.

Following a rumor that everyone on city council would resign, several folks asked me what sort of job Clarence Wickham is doing as Tarboro's mayor.

As one who has attended a lot of municipal meetings over the past nine years, it is my opinion Mr. Wickham is doing a commendable job as the town's chief executive. I have argued with him, cussed him, and agreed with him during his term of office, but whether we saw eye-to-eye or not, he has always done what he believed to be the best for the greatest number of

Tarboro citizens. At the same time, Mr. Wickham has practiced the belief that the individual citizen is an integral and extremely important part of the town. As a result he has done his best to protect the right of the individual in hardship cases where town ordinances could be interpreted one way or the other.

~

Weather and work permitting my family and I will leave Tuesday to spend Christmas with the in-laws in Pennsylvania. It will be the first Christmas since 1946 that I haven't been in Tarboro, but up north there is a grand old lady who wants to see her three great-grandchildren.

Fast photo finishing a new wonder.

Edgecombe Drug Company began using a new film developing service this week and I decided to give it a try.

I carried a roll of color film to the store Tuesday afternoon and got the prints back Thursday. On Wednesday I gave the store two rolls of black and white film at 2 p.m. and they were back the following day at the same hour.

It is hard to believe that extremely fast service can be maintained but it's worth a try if you are in a hurry for your finished prints.

Giving credit where it's due.

This column would like to take this opportunity to wish to Mr. Peyton Beery and family our since best wishes for a very Merry Christmas—his first Christmas as a citizen of Tarboro.

During the past year, Mr. Beery has been pictured by some of us as a year-round Santa Claus who would turn up at any minute with a new industry, new jobs and new payrolls for Tarboro.

1959

Randy Constantine, son of Mr. and Mrs. Randolph Constantine, taught the seventh and eighth grade classes at North Tarboro School for a couple of days last week. From all I hear the students were tremendously impressed with the small dose of nuclear physics Randy gave them. He is currently majoring in math at State College and is a former nuclear physics major. At the close of the classes the youngsters were bandying about such words as proton, electron, neutron and critical mass.

Shad alert.

Hickory shad fishermen are beginning to think about the annual run of that species up the Tar.

For the sake of the record, in 1954 and 1956 the first hickories were landed on Feb. 18. In 1957 the first one was landed on Feb. 16.

An alternative to tobacco?

Edgecombe farmers have been extremely busy this week getting their tobacco plant beds ready. It's the first step in a long time consuming, worrisome job which ends when the cured leaf finally comes to rest on the warehouse floor.

When I think of the months of work that go into the growing and harvesting of tobacco I can't help but recall something that the late Jim Satterthwaite once told me.

Mr. Jim said that if farmers would devote just half of the time spent on tobacco to other crops, corn, peanut, bean and cotton yields would more than double and those increased yields would mean more to the economy than the entire tobacco crop.

Prelude to the Sizzling Sixties mentality.

I was shocked this week to hear from what I consider to be a reliable source that a couple of students at Tarboro High School are deliberately missing questions on tests and are misbehaving in class rooms in order NOT to make the honor roll or principal's list.

It seems they are more interested in being like other members of the "thundering herd" than in being pointed out as superior students.

Reports from down on the Roanoke indicate the annual herring run has started. Understand they are making some sizable catches at Mackey's but things are slowing up at Jamesville. Cotton Guill was down that way Wednesday afternoon and said the fish are forerunners—bigger but not as tasty as the later run of herring.

Mrs. Paul Godfrey, Tarboro housewife, last night was crowned chittlin' queen at a chittin' strut given by the Eastern Carolina Chittlin' Society in Rocky Mount.

Work began t his week on Edgecombe Memorial Park, the new cemetery out on Highway 258. I've seen the proposed layout of the park and it is comparable to such parks in Kinston and Burlington. Sections will be developed as needed. Incidentally, Murray Bullock has been employed as one of the park's three salesmen.

February and the shad report.

The annual migration of shad and herring has started on the Tar River.

Tom Mewborn picked up a couple of white shad, two hickories and a herring one night this week. Shorty Plummer, courthouse custodian, has caught three whites and a couple of herring.

The new Little League ball park behind the North Tarboro School has been surveyed and a heavy wire fence is being erected around it. The field will definitely be ready for this year's crop of prospective Little Leaguers.

The question of just who will seek election as Tarboro's next mayor (not to mention who will be elected) was the major topic of conversation in town this week.

Almost everyone has a favorite candidate. And judging from what I've heard all agree that the candidate should be a successful businessman who has the time to devote to the job.

After all, municipal government is the biggest business in Tarboro and the mayor is more than just a man who sits in a chair and smiles at the eight councilmen once a month.

During his brief two years as Tarboro's chief executive Clarence Wickham has done an outstanding job.

That old question of the distance from Tarboro to Rocky Mount by river has come up again, and Virgil Truitt, manager of the water plant, is the man we turned to for an answer.

Virgil says the distance is 30 miles and he also provides the following distances for those who might be interested:

Rocky Mount falls to Dunbar—16.5 miles.
Dunbar to Bell's Bridge—11.8 miles.
Bell's Bridge to Fishing Creek—4.5 miles.
Fishing Creek to red iron bridge—2.1 miles.
Red Iron bridge to Tarboro bridge—5 miles.
Tarboro bridge to Sparta bridge—7.5 miles.

Recently Henry Britt, Jr. was browsing through some old family papers and came across something titled, "Receipt for cold, coughs and consumption."

While I don't advise that you try it, here 'tis:

"One quart of good corn whiskey, one quart of apple vinegar, one quart of honey. Alum the size of a blue bird egg and one-half as much bluestone. Mix and boil down to one-half the quantity (a brass kettle is best). Then add one tablespoon of fine beaten brimstone and bottle up tight.

"Dose—one teaspoonful four times per day."

Discovery of a couple of old cannonballs buried in front of the Coca-Cola plant set some folks to wondering how they got there.

Old timers say that the old depot use to be where the Tarboro Gulf station is now and that the area where the Coca-Cola plant is located was a marsh. It could have been that a wagon loaded with the cannonballs got stuck in the swamp and was unloaded in order to get out. Perhaps when the wagon was re-loaded, the recently discovered balls were overlooked.

The title of the town's most honest man this week certainly goes to Mr. A.L. Holloman of 1005 Marlboro Street. Last Saturday afternoon Mr. Holloman found the diamond ring which Miss Emma Parker lost on Main Street.

Census Question

I can't help but wonder what the 1960 census will show the population of Edgecombe County is. A large number of houses have gone up in Tarboro, Rocky Mount, Whitakers, Pinetops and Macclesfield during the decade since the last nose count was made. But there's another sign on the other side of ledger. Perhaps you have noticed it.

Throughout the county there are hundreds of tenant houses that are vacant. Porches sag, doors are missing and windows are broken. The yards, once kept swept clean with a bundle of branches, are only a mass of weeds.

Crop cuts and farm mechanization are responsible for the exodus from the farms. Where have the people gone?

Perhaps the census will answer that question.

Construction of the new hospital is ahead of schedule and it now appears it will be completed by mid-August. Transfer of equipment from the present hospital, plus installation of new equipment may be finished in time for the hospital to begin operation by mid-October.

It is an impressive building. I learned that last week when Mr. Francis Jenkins, chairman of the hospital advisory committee, took me on a guided tour. Ceramic tile is used extensively throughout and I didn't see a single piece of wood used in construction and that probably will keep down cleaning and maintenance costs. However, just what the cost per day will be has not yet been determined.

Still nothing new or official about the rumor of changes in the Hotel Tarboro property, but a couple of the stores now housed there have made arrangements for new locations.

Two bulldozers were at work this week clearing new building sites on t he east side of Canal Street in Forest Acres. The old town continues to grow.

For everything except sin.

Next week marks the beginning of my tenth year as a scribe for "The Second Oldest Newspaper in the State." Sometimes I have felt as old or older than *The Southerne*r, particularly during the past couple of years, but in looking back I've found there are things in the past to compensate for those frustrations.

For example, almost a decade ago *The Southerner* was soundly damned for constantly raising its editorial voice for new industry. Today, several of those people who demurred are out rounding up money for a new plant.

The Southerner stood solidly behind bond issues for schools, for an East Tarboro swimming pool, for expansion of electrical and water plants, for a sewage disposal plant, for a new hospital, for the city manger form of government, for married students to be able to attend the schools of Tarboro, for reforms in the police department, for construction of a new library. In fact, it appears that editorially we were for everything except sin.

Hotel going?????? Just a rumor.

There isn't anything official on it yet and the principals involved will issue no statement, but in downtown Tarboro this week the chief topic of conversation has been the pseudo-official rumor that the Hotel Tarboro building from Teele Hardware to the Edgecombe Drug Store corner will be torn down and replaced by a modern two-story building.

The Wildlife Resources Commission in Raleigh will build a boat ramp at Bell's Bridge and it will probably be ready for use by next year's rock and shad fishing season.

The ramp has long been sought by the Edgecombe Wildlife Club and State approval of the project is the direct result of club action. Funds for ramp construction will come from excise taxes and hunting and fishing tackle.

Still nothing new on what will happen to the hotel building. The cigar store and the pool room are closed. Dock Teele and Bip Carstarphen will probably move within a month, and Edgecombe Drug Company "has made other arrangements."

If and when the old building comes down, it will mark the end of an era which, believe it or not was directly responsible for the Carolina Telephone and Telegraph Company's locating in Tarboro.

But that's a story which will be retold next year.

Police Court Judge Martin Cromartie completed his move this week into the offices formerly occupied by Federal Judge Don Gilliam. A number of his friends dropped by Thursday afternoon along about bull bat time to wish him well.

It is heartening to see Tarboro natives come home to roost, and that has been particularly true in the legal profession in recent years.

First Chandler Muse came back, and after several months he became associated with Cameron S. Weeks, then Martin was followed by George Britt, and Creighton Brinson and Joe Bourne.

A brief news release from Annapolis tells us that Midshipman Carl L. Doughtie, who is as fine a youngster as Tarboro ever produced, is receiving "intensive indoctrination" before the Naval Academy's regular academic year begins in September.

In short, it means Carl is catching a lot of preliminary hell.

Midshipman Curtis Norfleet was in town from Annapolis this week and looks like a million dollars. He told me he saw Carl

Doughtie recently and Carl is rapidly getting the hang of things at the Naval Academy.

With the caliber of boys at the Academy now, as well as the type Tarboro has sent there in recent years, I believe we'll yet produce another admiral.

The old hotel is still alive—not well—but alive.

There's still nothing new on what will be done with the hotel building. The future of the building is still the main topic of conversation on Main Street since the property is some of the choice down-town real estate.

Chief Warrant Officer Charles Proctor, Jr. came home for a few minutes Thursday. Charlie landed his big helicopter on the field adjacent to the armory. His father met him, took him home, and brought him back. The big "bird" cranked up in a big cloud of dust and tornadoed into the air.

The kids and some adults (me among them) got a king-size charge out of it.

The weather was cool but municipal government activity was extremely hot—boiling—in town this week.

It started off with the issue of extending Panola Street across the ACL railroad tracks in t he vicinity of the armory. That proposal died when practically all the residents of one section of the street protested, and six councilmen voted against it.

The biggest surprise of the week came when the town manager fired the chief of police with two councilmen and three police officers looking on.

There are those who say pressure politics will be brought to bear and the chief will be re-hired within 30 days.

However, I haven't heard of anyone willing to bet on it.

News of the old hotel is buried in an avalanche of breaking news stories.

This has been quite a week for news, some of it good, some bad, some horrible.

On Monday came the story that local police solved eight burglaries with the arrest of two Negro youngsters who concentrated on the homes of Negro school teachers.

On Tuesday we were holding our collective breath, hoping that Gracie would veer away from our homes and our crops. Then came the announcement that the old hotel building will be torn down to make way for a two-story combination store and office building. The same issue of *The Southerner* reported that Patrolman Floyd Owens hit the jackpot when he nabbed a man who was transporting 141 gallons of white lightning.

On Wednesday came brief details of the real shocker: seven people killed in an Edgecombe wreck.

Thursday's paper carried all the details of the collision, plus a picture. It was the kind of story you hate to have to write.

Yesterday brought news that a new industrial plant wants to locate here.

Today's fare—at this writing—seems mighty slim.

On the more pleasant side, friend Julian Hyman came in the office this afternoon and left me a large bag of chestnuts. The flavor is wonderful and about as near to chinquapin as any other nut. Many thanks to Julian.

The grass which was planted in the Common last week really came up in a hurry. Of course, those two showers during the week helped tremendously.

The City Barber Shop (in the hotel building) is scheduled to move to 103 E. Church Street on November 1. Tom Stokes tells me the ceiling there will be lowered and the interior will be completely repainted.

The Tarboro Tigers wind up the season here next Friday night after one of the most successful years in THS history.

At the start of the season there was plenty of moaning and groaning from the fans because of the tough Northeastern Conference schedule, plus a non-conference contest with Rocky

Mount. But the Tigers did what many considered to be the impossible. Last week's game saw the Blackbirds score fewer points against Tarboro than at any time since the early 1930s.

Hog killing time—ugh.

This is the time of year when the weatherman starts talking about the possibility of the season's first hard freeze. That's the traditional hog-killing time when folks use to have some extra tenderloin and spare ribs.

The freezer locker changed all that and now I learn that Charlie Rogers of Colonial Frozen Foods has gone so far as to prepare a masterpiece designed to discourage home butchering. He calls the piece "The Gentle Art of Hog Rasslin'." Here it is:

Do you, once a year, turn the whole family out at the crack of dawn, freeze your feet, burn $8 worth of cord wood, mess up $40 worth of clothes, pans and kitchen floors, get salt in a split finger, and a sniffle in your nose, just to "rassel" a hog?

Do you blast away with the old rusty-trusty, burn up six bits worth of mail order ammunition, break three axe handles, slip twice in the slooplolly of the pig pen, and ruin two perfectly good pork shoulders trying to get one poor shoat struck somewhere between the snout and his fourth rib, in the hope that he will bleed clean?

Do you annually ruin the rain barrel, poke a hole in the family boiler, spill a boot of boiling water down your pants leg, and sprain your back, trying to get a pig scalded—only to have the hair set tighter than in a Fuller brush, and have the finished carcass look like a case of leprosy?

Then Charlie goes into a pitch for the slaughtering facilities at his plant, pointing out that the present price of pork being what it is Sir Hog deserves some consideration as to the dignity and surroundings at the time of his departure. All in all, I think it's one of the best sales letters of its kind I've ever read.

The Rocky Mount Chittlin' Society will hold its first chittlin' strut of the season Monday night at 7:15 at the Rio Restaurant.

On the menu are collards, cracklin' bread, sweet potatoes, blackeyed peas, and you-know-what.

An item in the Evening Telegram stressed the fact that ladies are "especially invited." I suppose that means that last year's Chittlin' Queen, Mrs. Paul Godfrey (she was crowned with a garland of collard leaves), will be in attendance as a highly honored guest.

Photographer Charlie Killebrew has promised to provide appropriate photos of Tarboro chittlin' fans in action.

Prosperity rears its head in the form of tax collections.

While businessmen generally still complain of a lack of business for the past couple of months, the sales and use tax collection figures tell a different story. Things are better than last year and September business was better than August.

For example, August collections for Edgecombe were $57,578.49 while in September they jumped to $61,734.05. In August of '58 collections amounted to only $54,066.50.

Those two cannonballs which were stolen from in front of Spencer Dancy's house Wednesday night were unusual in that they were extremely large—too large for use in most of the guns of the Confederate artillery.

The cannonballs were shipped to Tarboro by rail in preparation for the Battle of Plymouth. They were to have been used in the guns mounted on the ram Albemarle. Arrived too late.

During the past week everyone has been talking about last Saturday's Christmas parade and all agree that it was by far the best Tarboro has had in several years. The town's Christmas decorations have also come in for their share of favorable comment during the past week. They are far superior to those beat-up candles which were used for several years.

The value of tobacco on the American economy.

I read this week that excise taxes on tobacco last year amounted to $100,000 more than all the federal taxes on all the automobiles sold: 10 times the excise on all trucks and buses.

They were 47 times the government's excise collections on all refrigerators, freezers and air conditioners.

For every one dollar the tobacco farmer received for tobacco used in domestically consumed cigarettes, $3.23 was collected in taxes by federal, state and local governments on cigarettes manufactured from this tobacco.

And still people talk about how much money tobacco farmers make on a crop they have to baby 13 months of the year.

Progress and prosperity.

Rode down to the sewage disposal plant site Thursday. There's a tremendous amount of work going on. Much of the concrete has been poured for the settling basins, and the force main has been installed from the plant site to the pumping station site directly behind the circus grounds. The main will roughly follow the river bank, except for the area behind Royster's warehouse, where it will rest upon cement pilings in the river.

What were Edgecombe County's top news stories of the year?

That's a question I asked a number of people this week, and I just about consistently got the same answers: Edgecombe's success in getting two new industries; the collision which claimed seven lives; and completion of the new hospital.

One of the resolutions I made last New Year's and which I intend to keep is that there'll be no Christmas presents at the Bass household this year which have to be assembled on Christmas Eve.

For the past eight Christmases I've had to put together tricycles, doll houses, sliding boards and a number of other items which just didn't want to fit. The ordeal with the sliding board became so great that I ended up by dumping the whole thing out the back door and telling the kids the next morning that Old Santa was in too big a rush to put it together.

That'll do it for this week. There still some last minute shopping to be done. So I'll take this opportunity to wish each and everyone of you readers a Merry Christmas.

1960

(The year opening year the decade of the Sizzling Sixties was exhilarating for Tarboro and Mabrey Bass. Everything was going the right way. Prospects were never better for Tarboro's explosive industrial expansion. New jobs, new attitudes, new leadership and the upcoming bicentennial celebration made living there wonderfully exciting. Approaching 35, Mabrey's level of professionalism was still expanding and despite salary limitations he and Pat were tasting the delicious joy of raising a family surrounded by good friends. The sweet smell of success was in the air and Ramblin's reflected it almost every week. He approached the bicentennial celebration with zeal and enthusiasm.)

More expansion.

Looks as though Tarboro moved into the big league this week when it comes to attracting some of the state's top industrial brass. Monday the Glenoit officials were here. On Thursday leading ACL officials came to town for a looksee and liked what they saw (there were 15 freight cars on the plastics plant siding). Then yesterday a large number of Burlington Industries officers came to town for an inspection trip of Hart Mill.

What'll happen next week is anybody's guess.

A large prehistoric shark's tooth—about half as big as a man's hand—was found in the fossil bed near the sewage disposal plant site recently.

Repairs to the sagging courthouse roof are well underway, but much remains to be done which isn't included in the present work.

For example, at this week's county board meeting, Auditor Allen Lee Harrell said, "This work will keep you from getting crushed, but it won't keep you from getting wet."

The work needed to repair the leaky courthouse roof would cost an estimated $20,000 or more.

Several wives called this week to know if their husbands had a right to grow beards just because our bicentennial celebration has tentatively been set for the fall. The answer, as near as I can determine is that the men folks can start growing beards anytime they wish, bicentennial or no bicentennial. However, there will probably be an official starting date if such chin growth is to be eligible for judging in the celebration. In short, what the spouse may do in the way of whisker-growing won't count this fall. However, he may just want to practice . . . .

The demolition of the old hotel underway.

The Fordson Wrecking Co. is making good progress on demolition of the hotel building, although you can't tell from looking at the front that anything at all is being done. Nearly all of the work has been done at the rear of the building or inside the building.

Incidentally, the mortar in the old building has given way to time. It's so rotten that three workmen, using a two by four are doing the majority of the wall topping.

Town officials seemingly are doing their best to save every possible penny. At least that's the way it seems at the Town Common where a couple of huge garbage cans are painted a screaming yellow. It's apparently the same paint used to mark off-limits parking areas.

Dark green would have been much more appropriate. Oh well, a penny saved . . . .

J.H. Fortson, who is wrecking the old hotel building, pulled out a number of huge old timbers from the roof yesterday. The 6 by 12 timbers, apparently heart pine, are 36 and a half feet long!

Last week's crack in this column about those unattractive yellow garbage cans in the Common, brought a Monday morning telephone call from Town Manager W.B. Howard. He explained the can are strictly temporary. They were placed there while the regular green containers were taken to the town hop for repainting and repairs.

~

Congratulations to Wayne Flye on being chosen Tarboro's first Morehead scholar! It is a tremendous honor for a truly outstanding young man.

Graphic details of death are not for the faint hearted.

A streak of blood was smeared for about 50 feet down the middle of the s street, ending with a glob of congealed red on the curb. On the floorboard—driver's side—of the smashed car was a shoe. The driver's foot had apparently been knocked out of it by the crushing impact of steel on steel.

Under blankets lay the bodies of two boys. Four other boys battered but still living had been rushed to the hospital.

That was the picture in Macclesfield last Saturday night.

The police called me and I crawled out of a warm bed, called my picture-taking cohort, Carl Rosenbaum together we went down to get the story.

It was another one of those times when I felt all twisted inside. I wanted to cry and at the same time I wanted to fight and scream. Won't they ever learn?"

A constable who was helping direct traffic at the scene say the boys like a number of others in the area had a reputation for fast and dangerous driving. He also said that on Friday night he and some highway patrolman were hoping to trap the boys while they were speeding on the county roads. But somehow the boys got word of what was going on and cancelled their plans.

Apparently they tried it Saturday night, for the car, which was in a residential area, was certainly traveling at an extremely high rate of speed when it went out of control.

Speed is like a narcotic; if not controlled it will kill. And this is proven time and time again on our highways. It was the case Saturday night.

If newspaper men are supposed to become hardened to sights such as those which I saw Saturday night and have witnessed far too many time during the past ten years of newspapering, then perhaps I had best start seeking another job.

Fishing will probably the chief source of recreation on Easter Monday. The rock are biting, but some folks are still fishing for hickory shad. Yesterday, fishermen casting just above the bridge were really pulling them in.

About Easter and his biggest worry, the bicentennial celebration.

The question being most often asked around town these days is, "What is being done about Tarboro's bicentennial celebration?"

Frankly, I don't know and can't find anyone who does know. However, if something isn't done soon it will be too late. Only five months remain before the tentative date of October. As one man said yesterday, "It will take me at least that long to grow a respectable beard."

Many folks described last Sunday as Tarboro's most glorious Easter. Nature put on a spectacular display of color which made even the finest, most colorful attire of humans seem dingy by comparison.

Shrubs are still holding their color. Particularly beautiful is the old town cemetery behind the Presbyterian Church. Memory Chapel is framed by lacy garlands of white wisteria.

The tentative census figures published elsewhere in today's edition will come as a shock to many people, this writer included.

While there may be some later revisions by the bureau of the census, it is extremely unlikely that the growth figure of 269 will vary greatly. Of course Tarboro's town limits haven't been extended to any great extent during the past decade, but there have been many a baby born to families within the town limits.

In discussing the situation yesterday, we discovered that the staff of *The Southerne*r has contributed almost ten per cent to the growth of Tarboro in the past ten years.

Why the girls' dressing room was painted that way.

I was up at the community house Wednesday afternoon when Town Manager W.B. Howard asked me to look over the basement dressing rooms which were being cleaned up in preparation for the swimming pool opening Thursday.

As we walked down the steps he reminded me that the rooms had been freshly painted last spring and normally no additional paint would be required.

In the boys' dressing room most of the doors had been ripped from the lockers. Emblazoned on the wall was a big red "Z" and on the side of a locker was a smaller "z" with the reminder, 'Zorro Strikes again."

While I didn't see where that was too much to worry about, I wondered what was up when Howard said, "Now let's look at the girls' dressing room.

When I walked in I was astounded. Every wall from the entrance to the private dressing locker, the bathroom, even the light fixtures were covered with all of the obscene words in the English language. Some were repeated a dozen or more times. Both lipstick and heavy black crayon were used to do the job and the "handwriting" wasn't the same in every case.

It was agreed by the manager and me (and two ladies who made the inspection trip) that the walls would have to be repainted. But it was also agreed hat white could not be the color, since it would undoubtedly encourage more lipstick smears.

The dressing room is now painted the brightest shade of red that can be purchased in town.

Contests for aging black fireman something of a problem.

Announcement today that the Negro firemen of North Carolina will hold their annual convention here brings back pleasant memories of the days when such a meeting saw the entire town turn out to watch the races.

The events were usually held, as I recall, on St. Andrew Street between Park and Wilson. Ladder wagons stationed at one end of the street would race for a pole located about midway the two streets. Teams would speed to place the ladder against the pole, with the object being to get a climber to the top and down again in the shortest time. Some of the feats were fantastic, and citizens both black and white, of the various towns loudly cheered their colored firemen.

Now time has claimed the ladder wagon and hose wagon used by members of the Fulton Hook and Ladder Company. Time has also taken a heavy toll of the colored firemen, and with a wagon, it's difficult to create any interest.

Some of the senior colored firemen such as Columbus Beamon and Nelson Parker will soon be out attempting to round up funds ands to pay for their company's share of the convention expense.

Yesterday when Beamon was telling me about the convention he said it was a rough job for the old firemen to undertake, but at last year's convention the other colored firemen from throughout the state said that because of the outstanding hospitality and unusually good time they had here seven years ago, they wanted to come back.

Please keep in mind when Beamon and other "old" members of the Fulton Hook and Ladder Company ask for a contribution to make their convention a success.

Summertime and Pat is visiting her family in Pennsylvania.

Newspapers are scattered over the living room floor. Discarded typing paper is piled beside the ironing board which I use for a typing table. The nearby desk is covered with folders in which I keep notes for stories that are to appear in the bicentennial edition of the paper this fall. On the sofa is a huge stack of reference books which provide the material for notes.

There is a ring in the bath tub. The laundry hamper is packed so full of dirty clothes that the top refuses to close. In the kitchen sink are four frying pans begging to be scoured.

The bed hasn't been completely re-made since Saturday.

The bird dog is howling and the kittens are yowling for supper.

The wife and young'uns have been out of town since early Sunday morning.

Looks like it's going to be a long, long two weeks!

The dates for the big event are set—one big birthday party.

Tarboreans are showing a great deal of enthusiasm for the 200th birthday celebration that is scheduled for the week of Oct. 30-Nov. 5.

The directors made excellent choices in Col. Louis Knight as general chairman, Peyton Beery as executive vice-president, and Mrs. Mary Ellen Forbes as finance chairman. Don't forget, they have tremendously important jobs and need the full support of hard working committees.

~

Town water plant crews, installing a water line to the new Farrar Building last week were down about five feet when they struck one of the old fat lightwood logs which use to serve as a curb on St. James Street. It took a long time to get through it so, naturally, a day or two later they cut sharply into what appeared to be another log. It turned out to be a telephone cable, and it required a couple of hours hard work by the cable splicers to get *The Southerner* and the WCPS teletypes, plus telephones, back in operation.

~

I regretted to learn of the closing of General Plywood, one of the "home grown" industries which started as the Red Gum Veneer Mill. I'm sure the community joins me in hoping that the development board can find a replacement that will give preference to those who lost their jobs when General closed down.

August and preparation to open the tobacco market.

Crews were at work this week cleaning out local tobacco warehouses, painting up, and getting everything ready for the opening of the sales season on Aug. 23.

With approximately 90 per cent of the crop housed, farmers and business men alike are keeping a close eye on prices being paid on the Border Belt. While there is talk of the quality here seems to indicate that it is good, that certainly isn't the impression gained by tobacconists, who drove through the Border while the crop was being housed. They say the tobacco was badly in need of rain and appeared to be far below the Eastern Belt in overall quality.

Inflation report.

The price of haircuts being what they are ($1.25) brought the suggestion that for the bicentennial celebration local men should quit getting haircuts and continue to shave.

Good News from THS.

One extremely encouraging fact revealed with the opening of Tarboro High Thursday was that the physics class had the largest enrollment since the course was first offered. It's another indication of the progress possible when local schools have a guidance director and a principal who stresses the fundamentals rather than the frills.

~

This week Julian Hyman brought me his first Chinese chestnut of the season. He said his trees are bearing heavily this year, but the flavor of the nuts is not nearly as good as last year. Julian said it's probably because of too much rain.

Serenade in the night.

A number of local folks were shocked awake at 3 a.m. Tuesday by the chimes of the First Baptist Church.

One man openly admitted, "I thought I had died in my sleep. However, I was consoled by the belief that I had apparently made it to heaven."

It seems the timing device on the chimes was knocked out when Hurricane Donna slammed its way through town. When the electricity came on the clock hadn't been re-set and it was 8 a.m. instead of 6 p.m. when Tarboro was serenaded by hymns.

A week later.

All Tarboreans can rejoice in the fact that the bicentennial celebration is now a reality, thanks to the tremendous amount of work done by the finance committee and the generosity of local citizens.

The excellent celebration that is planned will certainly redeem the lack of a 100th birthday celebration in 1860. Although the citizens then certainly had just cause not to celebrate.

Abraham Lincoln had just been elected President, and the blue cockade—symbol of secession—were being worn on Tarboro streets, in the words of *The Southerner*, "by both men and boys and even ladies." War clouds were rising.

But the editor and publisher, Cris C. Callan, in *The Southerner* of Dec. 1 still found time to insert the following item:

"A Century Old—Yesterday (Friday) was the Centennial Anniversary of Tarboro, and yet it passed away unnoticed. Not a single demonstration was made, not a sign was manifested to distinguish it from any other day. How many the changes since one hundred years ago the Colonial Assembly of North Carolina granted a charter to the town of Tarboro. Where now are its founders? Gone, all gone!"

⁂

Fall is here. The birds are silent and the only sound in the late afternoon is the constant and lonely chirp of the cricket. At no time during the year is the sky as blue as in October. Although the calendar tells me it's too early to mention a brilliant blue October sky, it is just that. Football is entertainingly with us. Frost isn't far away.

⁂

Several of the local ladies are hoping bicentennial officials will "enact" proper legislation making it unlawful for females of the village to appear in public without a bonnet. Tentative plans call for those who do not choose to be thus attired to purchase a permit, or be sentenced to either a jail or stocks which will be set up on the courthouse lawn.

⁂

The idea of burying a "time capsule" on the Common appears to me to be one of the best of the entire series of special events planned for the celebration.

Just think how fine it would be if the same had been done in 1860, with instructions that it be opened this year! A letter from great-grandpa to generations yet unborn could be an important thing in the life of any family.

The cost is practically nothing—one dollar per envelope of reasonable size—but be sure to use quality paper with a high rage content. Civic clubs and churches should certainly immediately plan to place accounts of their activities in the capsule.

The Farrar Building is now complete, having passed its inspection by owners and tenants this week. Telephone Co. folks have moved in the second floor and Rose's people are fast getting the first floor ready for the opening during the first week in November.

After Bicentennial—extra copies are available.

Persons who reserved copies of the bicentennial edition can pick them up at *The Southerner* office. There are also a number of extra copies available for those who wish to purchase them.

Christmas Eve and history bubbles over into the present.

This is, always has been and always will be the best of seasons, a time when men extend themselves to give comfort to those less fortunate and to enjoy themselves and their families to the fullest.

An account of Christmas in Tarboro in the year 1787 appeared in the historical edition that was published in October. Since then, however, I have found a brief account of what went on here at Christmastime of 1858. Here it is, taken from *The Southerner* of that year:

"The Christmas holidays brought about the usual gaieties of the season. The streets were thronged from morning until night. All the stores were densely crowed with customers, and the town presented a very busy appearance. The merchants reaped a golden harvest.

"On the evenings of the 23rd and 24th Mr. H.S. Lloyd, owner of the hotel known as Mrs. Gregory's, furnished a grand ball.

The Pennsylvania band was secured for the occasion. The ball was very largely attended. Many of the fairest daughters of the old North State, as well as one of the fairest of Vermont, honored the occasion. Never did an affair of the kind present happier faces; every thing passed off as pleasant as the human heart could desire."

In the edition of the paper the advertisements tell much about what was taking place in Tarboro.

Mrs. M.E. Bond was advertising for a dress maker to work in her millinery shop. She offered to pay wages of $14 per month.

George Howard, publisher of *The Southerner* and Tarboro postmaster, served noticed that he was taking his son William as a copartner in his drug store, located opposite the courthouse.

The Tarboro Hotel (formerly Mrs. Gregory's) advertised that the hotel was remodeled and the following rates were in effect:

Board and lodging, $20 per month, for guarantee of three months; $25 per month, for only one month; $15 for half-month; $8 per week; $1.75 per day.

Town commissioners served notice they would as approval of the legislature to sell that portion of the Town Common lying between Tar River and N.M. Terrell's coach shop, fronting 150 feet on Water Street from the bridge "and running 100 feet towards Tar River".

The trustees of the Tarborough Academy announced the next school session would begin on January 3, 1859 and continue for five months. Mr. Frank Wilkinson was employed as principal of the male department. Misses Ann L. Dodge and Sarah P. Harris continued in charge of the female department.

William A. Thigpen informed the public that the new Conetoe Academy would open on Monday, January 17, 1859. Board was $7 to $8 per month, while tuition in the primary branch was $10 per session. Tuition for "higher English and mathematics" was $12.50 per session and cost of learning the classics was $15 for the same amount of time.

To take advantage of the Christmas trade R.T. Hoskins and Bowditch advertised a new stock of "new raisins, Languedoc almonds, Zante currants, Havana sweet oranges, pecan nuts, Turkish prunes, Smyrna figs, chocolate, sardines, sweet oil, cranberries, citron, dates, Heidick champagne, Madeira and port wines, French brandy, London porter, and Edinburg ale.

James Mehagan put in a plug for "new and fashionable goods" which were offered "Cheap for Cash".

For Tarboro 1960 was a wonderful year.

New industries made more jobs available. House building boomed. An attractive new store-office building replaced the old Hotel Farrar. The tobacco market average was excellent. The local motel was enlarged. The bicentennial celebration was tangible evidence that Tarboreans—rich, poor, and in-between—can accomplish anything under the sun that we put our hearts into.

And 1960 passes into time.

Regardless of what the bank statement says, the new year will find each one of us richer than we were when the curtain came down on 1959. We are richer because some event during the past year no matter how trivial it may have been at the time has given us added knowledge and understanding, perhaps without our even realizing it at the time.

1961

Legendary George Earnhart returns to Tarboro.

The Honorable George N. Earnhart and his fine wife Katy returned to Tarboro this week after spending more years living in Florida than they care to talk about. They plan to again set roots in Tarboro where George was for years as much a local landmark as the old town hall.

For those of you who have moved here since genial George left, I'll attempt to fill in a few of the high spots.

For years he was town clerk, unofficial town greeter, baseball mentor fund raiser deluxe, swimming team promoter, editor of an outstanding newspaper—The Home Front News. At various intervals he was connected with local banks. He's a champion story teller with a catalogue of jokes that fill a five-foot shelf. He is one of those rare individuals who has never met a stranger.

Tarboro is richer because George is back.

The editor is not moved by a new conservative —Jesse.

A local man this week suggested that I make a point of watching the Jesse Helms news commentary on a Raleigh television station each evening at 6:25.

Had I not known this man personally, I would have immediately marked him for a bachelor. Any married man with chill'un knows that particular time of day is strictly for the kids and their assorted friends—Deputy Dog, Huck Hound, Yogi Bear, Chief Rain-in-the-Face, and countless others.

If Jesse wants to get through to me, he will just have to find another time of day for his program.

A congenital environmentalist—born that way.

Someone at Hart Mill apparently goofed up Thursday and dumped a mess of oil sludge in the storm drainage system. As a result, Hendricks Creek, which is backed up because of the high level of the river, became coated with oil. As late as noon yesterday patches of oil could still be seen drifting down the Tar.

To prevent a recurrence, the mill, I understand, has made arrangements to have any future deposits of sludge carted away and burned.

Woody Anderson says the herring run is getting underway on the Roanoke now. He went down to Jamesville Wednesday to get enough for a fry at his oil company, but the Jamesville fishermen didn't have enough. Woody was finally able to get a fishbox full by driving on down to Mackey's.

February warm spell is intoxicating.

This wonderfully warm weather can't last, but even with rain it gave me a feeling of power to turn off the old floor furnace.

The camellias, jonquils, japonica and crocus are blooming. The fish at the Wildlife Club are biting. The spring frogs are croaking in roadside ditches and pasture ponds. Hand-holding is back in vogue at THS.

Wouldn't it be nice if we could tear March off the calendar and go directly into April?

The question of a new courthouse for Edgecombe is one which looms like a mountain over many of the other problems which confront the county commissioners.

A new courthouse or renovation of the present one would certainly require a bond issue, and it is extremely unlikely that a bond issue for a courthouse or for anything else would meet the approval of voters this year.

Historic milk plant limping along towards oblivion.

MILK PLANT—It now appears that the Town Council will take no action Monday night to close the milk plant, but a price increase of a penny per quart will be recommended. Should that fail to produce a profit then it is highly likely that the plant will be closed.

It is difficult to predict just what course the councilmen would take Monday if a showdown vote should be taken. But from folks I've talked with, I'd be inclined to say that the dear people don't give a hoot whether the plant stays open another year or is closed day after tomorrow.

COOL weather during the past week has served to hold back blossoms and leaves without damage and without causing any real discomfort to us mortals. However, the weather has caused a growing impatience among fishermen who go by the old axiom that rockfish really begin biting when the dogwood is in full bloom and the white oak leaves are the size of a squirrel's ear.

Political activity spurted this week when Dr. Ed Roberson announced that he is a candidate for mayor. The doctor has plenty of experience in municipal government via the old board of commissioners and the present town council. He's rated the most capable member of the council. Yet rumor has it that he will not have the active backing of what is considered the town's most potent political machine.

In town last week for a pre-Easter vacation from Annapolis was Carl Doughtie, Jr. He still thinks the Naval Academy is the finest thing in the world and has a full summer of intensive training ahead, including amphibious training at Little Creek, Va., a tour of Cape Canaveral, and aviation courses at Jacksonville, Fla. However, there's a break in June that will mean Carl will have several weeks vacation here.

Town politics heating up.

At the rate politics picked up this week the municipal election on May 2—a Tuesday, by the way—promises to be a whiz bang. It appears that Mayor Herbert Bailey is successfully getting some of his supporters to run for office against incumbent council members. This week Perry Pitt, staunch Bailey supporter and business associate, announced he would oppose Wat Smoot in the Sixth Ward. The same day Hill Hale, also an associate of Mayor Bailey in the used car business paid his filing fee to oppose Curtis Leggett in the Seventh Ward. Whether Bailey had any influence in S.J. Brewer's decision to oppose Ira Jenkins in the First Ware is not known in this corner. However, when Jenkins was chosen to fill the unexpired term of M.M. Shepherd, he did not have the mayor's support.

A few days later, Bailey withdraws from town race.

The biggest political surprise of recent years occurred Wednesday morning when Mayor Herbert Bailey withdrew from the campaign. Some of those close to the mayor say that the reason for the action was the fact that the money which he felt was needed for the campaign was not available. And campaigns can be expensive.

Maybe Herbert is bowing out of all politics, but I doubt it.

Genial Gene Simmons' advertisements for a cigarette, Kentucky Kings, is currently being shown on the "Naked City" tv program. 'Tis impressive, still, but as something of a veteran of the steaming Georgia and Eastern Belt markets, I doubt the authenticity of Brer Simmons' crisp white shirt.

The open house at Glenoit Mill Wednesday is an event which I hope very citizen will try to attend. With my limited knowledge of the textile industry I found the operation there to be fabulous. How can people take a raw material which looks similar to a cigarette filter and turn it into a finished product which a mink can't tell from his own mama or a seal from its sister. It is very impressive.

Love of history continues to blossom.

Earlier this week I typed out a short article about the 100th anniversary of the Edgecombe Guards leaving for the Civil War. I got the May 9 date from Bridgers and Turner's History of Edgecombe County. Later in the week I was reading an autobiography of Brigadier W.G. Lewis and in it he stated the Guards left Tarboro for Fort Macon on April 21, 1861, and stayed there ten days mounting cannon, storing ammunition and drilling. Lewis wrote that Fort Macon the Guards were ordered to Raleigh to be incorporated into the First Regiment of N.C. Troops.

Maybe that difference in dates is accounted for by a layover in Tarboro before they went to Raleigh.

Anyhow when you start delving into history, you're asking for trouble.

Much traveled Duck Lewis keeps job.

From Raleigh this week, came word that Tarborean Duck Lewis has been re-elected executive secretary of the N.C. Motel Association. He's credited with being a wheelhorse in a campaign which brought his association a large number of new members during the past year.

Drive carefully!—a regular Ramblin's feature showed concerns for everyone in town.

Middle Street is probably one of Tarboro's shortest streets and it isn't heavily travelled. However, folks there suspect there will be serious accident in the neighborhood. Because of the light traffic children are inclined to play in the street more than usual, despite the warnings of working parents. Knowing that Middle Street is not heavily travelled, a driver or two each day will speed around the corner of Office Street or Cedar Lane into Middle. There is a squeal of brakes as youngsters scamper quickly to the side.

Perhaps someday brakes won't hold quickly enough and there'll be a tragedy. Residents suggest that a couple of warning signs should be erected by the town. I'm inclined to agree...in the meantime . . .

A few days later, the squeaking wheel was greased.

Thanks to the town for installing warning signs on Middle Street.

The tax on food goes into effect while Sanford vacations.

Today is the day we begin getting our Sanfordrized grocery bills. It goes on fat back and corn meal, lard and grits, salty crackers, sardines and cheese.

Don't feel badly, though. You can still buy a crate of Pepsis and a carton of smokes without paying the additional tax. What makes it so nice is all that money is going to give our children that intangible something called "quality education".

The Sanford program resulted in town and country governments paying sales tax on all their purchases which heretofore were exempt. If you live in Tarboro you should realize that 7 1/2 cents of your $1.10 tax rate (per $100 of property valuation) will go to finance the Sanford program. There's also something in the county budget which will go for a similar purpose.

A modern patriot sings out.

Chances are that the real significance of the Fourth of July will pass unnoticed by most Tarboreans. It has come to pass that the anniversary of the signing of the Declaration of Independence is a day for doing almost everything except recalling the birth date of the Republic.

But it wasn't always that way.

Buried in Old Town cemetery in a grave marked only by an American Legion insignia and a small American flag is one of the State's great patriots. Some scoffed when Mattie Shackleford saw to it that newly born Tarboreans were presented with a flag and a copy of the Declaration. Some thought it foolish when she insisted that ceremonies be held on the Common or at Memory Chapel on the Fourth, Flag Day and Memorial Day.

Some, but not all.

However, as the years pass, the One World crowd and the ultra-liberals have seen to it that we have been fed a diet of political pablum. It increases with each passing day—fewer and fewer people are brave enough to express their individual convictions about the greatness of principles on which this nation was founded. To be a patriot, to be openly proud of the American flag, to admit that your skin tingles when the Declaration is read is "corny". That is what they try to tell us.

But it isn't true.

~

A couple of weeks ago I noted that few people now call that section of Main between Walnut Street and the railroad "the depot". The statement brought an immediate retort from Tom Knox and Johnny Carpenter, who said "It's been the depot for a hundred years, and it always will be known as the depot".

Well, I ain't one to argue.

Watermelon champ runs afoul foul weather.

Mr. Cliff Weeks isn't making any claims to fame as a watermelon grower this year. For the past several seasons he grew melons which weighed in excess of 100 pounds, and the flavor was excellent. This year, however, he planted and replanted four times, and each time some form of disaster struck. Weather, disease, insects and animals wiped out the crop. Seems like we should take up some kind of a watermelon collection for Mr. Cliff. After all he has been mighty generous with his past crops.

The hero of an era yet to come seeks support.

Quite a few folks around the State this week received personal letters from Senator Sam Ervin, Jr. in which he asks support in his bid for re-election next year.

In my opinion, Sam Ervin has done a magnificent job of representing North Carolina, and I can think of no other person of his caliber in the State.

~

The past week brought considerable interest in the proposed essay contest, "What's Right and What's Wrong With Tarboro?"

Should *The Southerner* receive entries from all those who have announced their intention to enter, you readers will have a treat in store, and a lot of us will have some sincere soul-searching to do.

During the decade that this column has appeared each Saturday, some bouquets have been tossed in various directions, and brickbats have been hurled with equal vigor. Both extremes usually brought the desired action.

Let's have some entries next week.

~

PROGRESS NOTE—In 1860 the population of Tarboro and Greensboro were the same—1,050.

INDICATIONS—All indications are that this autumn will be the most colorful old Edgecombe has enjoyed in many a year. All the ingredients are here: warm days and cool nights, and it has been dry.

Perfect cotton picking weather.

OVERTIME—Tarboro ginners are working overtime to keep up with the constant stream of cotton-loaded trucks. Perfect picking weather is responsible. I can't understand why farmers don't demand that cotton sheets be tightly tied. The shoulders of highways throughout the county are littered with cotton. Money thrown away!

HOPING—Folks over at Marrow-Pitt are apparently hoping for a quick change for a mild fall to a hard winter. They had sleds displayed in front of the store Thursday afternoon.

The display is an excellent advertising gimmick. When the first snow of the winter falls, your young'un will come flying over and demand, "Pop, get me a sled, right now."

PROBLEMS—When our young'uns went north for a visit with Pennsylvania relatives this summer 5-year-old John had only the highest praise for his grandma's flowers. As a result, greenfinger John returned to Tarboro with eight large potted orchid plants. It was all right this summer when the pots could be kept in the yard. But with the coming of cold weather, the plants have come to constitute a king-size headache.

When the sun begins sinking, I have to tote the durn things into the kitchen. Ma has to step over and around them while preparing supper. It's the same story at breakfast, for at that time of day it's still too cold to take'em back outside. We still haven't decided what course we'll take when it becomes "sure-enough" cold, for the house is too small for two adults, three children and eight orchids.

Senator Sam coming to town.

OPPORTUNITY—Local folks will have an opportunity to hear an excellent speaker Monday night when Senator Sam Ervin holds forth in the Tarboro High auditorium. The meeting is jointly sponsored by the PTA and the local chapter of the N.C. Education Association.

HULL—Former THS football star Al Hull made quite a name for himself at Castle Heights Military Academy, Lebanon, Tenn. during the past season. The academy newspaper had this to say about Al in summing up the season: "Coach Stroud Gwynn has three fullbacks, any of whom could handle the position aptly by himself. Jimmy Gamble, Harper Ruff, and Al Hull form a formidable threesome at the fullback slot that makes the position at Heights the strongest in Mid-South.

Prod, plead, pull for citizens to do their duty.

COUNCIL—The Town Council meeting Monday night will probably be a routine affair—most of them are. However, every single form of business that is transacted—no matter how insignificant is may seem—is important for it has some bearing on the town and YOU.

Take time out Monday night and drop in at the meeting. The councilmen will be glad to know that folks are interested in the kind of job they are trying to do FOR Tarboro.

Christmas

LAST DAY—The last hectic shopping day is at hand and supposedly we can sit back and enjoy watching the excited youngsters open their gifts. But there is still tomorrow night when Pa has the chore of helping Santa set up his presents.

A book could be written about that task. However, portions of it probably wouldn't pass even the most liberal censor. The still night air of the eve of Christmas has been blasphemed blue by frustrated fathers attempting to put together some toy or trinket.

WORST—The worst of all the things to put together on Christmas Eve are those tin houses and airport and service stations, etc. When you buy 'em the clerk says it's a simple matter of just putting the little tabs in the small slots.

It just ain't so.

On the service station, slot B has to go with part Z after you have found and inserted part 2-Ab. Some how the gas pump ends up in the grease pit and the ladies rest room is next to the tire rack with a sign over it which advises, "Winterize Now".

1962

Boat licenses and other important reminders.

LICENSES—January 1 was the time to begin buying auto licenses. T'was also the date on which your fishing and boat licenses expired. Like everything else that were subjected to the scrutiny of the last legislature, license fees are higher. Resident statewide licenses are now $4.25, county licenses are $1.65, a one-day permit is 85 cents and a combination license if $6.25. Persons who own boats powered by motors of over ten horsepower must renew their registration.

John Glenn orbits the earth.

YOUNG'UNS—I made a point of getting up early Saturday morning and calling off a bird hunting trip in order to see the launching into global orbit of Col. John Glenn, Jr. Also made sure the children were up in time to witness what would have been a history-making event: a real first for the United States. But then came a halt in the count-down and the announcer advised the launching would not come off until 10:30. The boys immediately went into a frenzy.

I finally got 'em calmed down enough to ask the trouble, and they both shouted, "If they shoot him up then, we'll miss Mighty Mouse."

I gave up.

Semper Fidelis

NOTE—Former fly boys, dog-faces, and swab jockies are reminded of the indisputable fact that it was a member of the

U.S. Marine Corps who orbited the earth this week. New recruiting posters will read: "Join the Marines and See the Planet".

CONGRATULATIONS—To Gus Andrews on becoming the first Tarboro High football player ever to be chosen for All-American honors. For two years Gus played terrific ball for the Tigers, never complaining when the honors went to others. Now it's Gus's time to strut.

The Milk Plant problem.

MILK—The current milk plant controversy is viewed with mixed emotions by this writer. Even with the terrific advantage of being completely tax-free it is unable to compete financially with a privately owned distributorship that came to being here six years ago.

As to public opinion, the councilmen have their answer to that in the fact that so few citizens are using the municipal product. Apparently, the majority does not care what happens to the plant.

On the other side of the ledger, the plant currently is responsible for bringing about $100,000 into the community. It has a payroll of about $25,000 and pays milk producers in the neighborhood of $62,000. The remainder is spent for goods and services bought locally.

The number of employees at the plant is at a minimum, yet that number could process twice the amount of milk that is now being turned out.

The last Federal milk survey, made in 1959 by the U.S. Public Health Service, showed that the average daily distribution of milk in Edgecombe County (excluding Rocky Mount) was:

Tarboro plant—248 gallons.
Sealtest—733 gallons.
Maola—118 gallons.
Gardners—210 gallons.
Meadowbrook—7 gallons.

Sanitation-wise the local plant stacked up with the best. Its rating was 96: Sealtest was highest with 97.

It could well be that advertising would do much to increase the sale of Tarboro's product.

The heartbreak of Viet Nam Comes home to Tarboro in April.

SAMMY—Shortly after I returned to Tarboro 12 years ago I joined a group of hard-noses who gathered at Sam Womble's service station in the late afternoon when our work was done.

While we talked of everything under the sun, Sammy Womble, a skinny, wide-eyed youngster scurried about helping—in his way—his father operate the station, When Little League baseball came to Tarboro, Sammy went for it in a big way. After he "aged out" of the league, he helped little brother, Mike, prep for a spot on one of the league teams.

During high school he was a good athlete and after school and on weekends from college, he continued to help at the station. He joked with the older men, but unlike many youngsters, he knew the meaning of respect—he knew when to stop. He was quick to smile, easy to know. He made countless friend for himself and his father's business.

Then Sammy joined the Marine Corps. From boot camp at Parris Island, he returned home on furlough as straight and tough as a young hickory. He inherited the sense of humor and judgment of his father and the gentleness of his mother. And a sense of fairness from both. His tragic death this week saddened the community.

He will be missed.

Love, Marriage and God.

12 YEARS—Today marks the 12th anniversary of my marriage to a girl from Wayne, Pa. and including all the trials and tribulations they have undoubtedly been the best years of my life. Arguments have been few and when they occurred they usually concerned finances, nothing more. She's a good cook, good mother, fair housekeeper, keen observer, excellent writer, good sport and, above all, is never one to complain that, "We never take a vacation" or "I haven't a thing to wear." The truth of the matter is that "we don't" and "she doesn't." But we make out.

Over the years we have learned that friends are actually the dearest possession and that you feel closer to God while looking at a sleeping child than at any other time.

Each day is in some respect an adventure unto itself. We've been happy, sad, elated, depressed, ill, well, and have experienced an assortment of other emotions.

But never bored.

And I thank you, the former Miss Patricia Lobb Shoyer.

SERVICE—It is fitting that Edgecombe folks will gather tomorrow to dedicate a headstone on the grave of Miss Mattie Shackleford in Old Town Cemetery.

Throughout her life she fought a never-ending battle for the poor, the lonely, the forgotten people of the county. Her constant prodding of county officials and the public conscience resulted in the building of the present county home which, although now more then 20 years old, is still far superior to similar buildings in other counties.

Her love for her country was intense and she never missed an opportunity to remind us of our heritage.

When members of the American Legion asked me to write the epitaph for her headstone in "not more than 100 letters", I thought the task would be impossible. After several days of writing and rejecting, I dug up an old story about Miss Mattie which I wrote back in 1951. In it was something she said many, many years ago. Those are the words which we chose for the headstone.

FEVER—John Hanner, formerly with the Edgecombe Bank, got a terrible case of rock fishing fever last Thursday, got two of his friends and drove non-stop from Troy, Ohio, 640 miles to Tarboro. Within an hour after arriving here they were fishing above Bell's Bridge and managed to catch a single rock.

A fourth Ohioian flew into Raleigh-Durham Saturday and joined the expedition. But nary another rock did the foursome catch.

When it came time to leave Monday, they were a mighty discouraged group. However, a local fisherman came to their aid by giving them 15 rock, the largest of which weighed better than eight pounds.

The fish were iced down for the trip back to Troy where they probably will provide material for some of the biggest lies ever told in that part of the nation. Within the next week we will very likely see an interesting number of cars with Ohio licenses parked along the Tar.

Local boy makes real real real good.

HULL—This week Bill Hull completed what is very probably one of the most distinguished college careers to be achieved by a Tarboro youth in recent years.

According to Russell Brantley, publicity director for Wake Forest, when Bill received his degree in business administration, he also was commissioned a second lieutenant in the army reserve and was cited as a distinguished military student. In addition to his prowess at football and basketball, Bill was voted one of the ten most outstanding seniors, was elected to Omicron Delta Kappa, intercollegiate honor fraternity, and is listed in Who's Who Among Students. He was president of the senior class.

Bill has been assigned to the Military Police Corps and will take an orientation course at Ft. Gordon, Ga. before going on active duty. After his military obligation is filled, he plans to play professional football.

Quite a record!

(The Daily Southerner was ready to embark on the most ambitious capital improvement venture in its history—converting to the new off-set printing process. It required a new press, new technology and new training for the printers.)

BACK TO SCHOOL—Son Creech and Fred Sanderson left today for New York where they'll go back to school for a week. Purpose of the trip is to learn to operate the new Fairchild press which is scheduled to be shipped here in the next couple of weeks.

Except for wiring, the new building that is to house the press is complete and ready for the new equipment including a $3,000 camera which is needed to take full-page pictures.

Last weekend Billy Evans was in Elizabethtown, Tenn., studying the operations of the offset newspaper there.

Town Hall is the next victim to the God of Progress.

TOWN HALL—Keeping the Town Hall on Main Street rather than putting up what one man described as a 'pea dinky building on a pea dinky creek bank' is certainly good for Main Street.

But it's expensive and before it's over John Q. Public is going to be handed an ultimatum.

In the first place there is the purchase of the parking lot adjacent to the Colonial Theatre. That's $28,000.

Then there's the demolition of the old building. That's estimated at about $8,000.

Next is $450 a month rent for the Benton Buick Company property owned by V.E. Fountain. For rent and renovation, add about $12,000.

Suppose the new Town Hall had been built at Wilson St. That would have meant the present property could have been sold to private interests for maybe $35,000. The town would have had that money and the property would have been returned to the tax books

But that ain't all.

The new Town Hall will not have quarters for the fire department, and $60,000 in refunding bonds (which can be issued without a vote) which would have been used to get matching federal funds (We aren't eligible for such grants now) will now be used to pay the increased cost of the new building.

All of this means that when the Town Hall is built and occupied the fire department will still be housed in the Benton Buick property. It will likely stay there until the voters of Tarboro approve a bond issue to provide the money for a new station. And what if the voters don't approve the bonds?

Well, the fire department will stay in the Benton Buick property, the rent of $450 a month will still be paid, and it is likely that fire insurance rates will go up. The council would have to drastically increase the tax rate to get the money needed for the new station.

All this because the new Town Hall will go on Main Street.

Me? I'm one of the people who argued like the devil against putting it at Wilson and Popular. I wanted it on the site of the present building. Still do. *(And that is where it was built.)*

Diverse history and comments on the Town Clock.

CLOCK—Announcement that the Town Hall would be demolished called to mind several stories concerning the old clock.

The clock tower was part of the original structure but the responsibility of putting in the clock was not undertaken by the commissioners.

Citizens of the town staged benefit suppers, barbecue and other events in an effort to get the needed money to buy a clock, but somehow the money—according to legend— went to sources other than the special clock fund. Finally, in 1909, 19 years after the Town Hall was completed, Mayor Paul Jones told the commissioners that $400 had been raised and he would be responsible for soliciting for the $200 still needed. Mr. Moses Heilbroner was the largest single contributor since he gave up the commission he would have received from selling the clock to the town.

For years, Mr. Heilbroner would climb the steep stairs of the clock tower each Sunday to wind the clock—a task made obsolete when electric works were installed.

Ching Marrow recalls the old story of one man stopping another on Main and asking, "What time is it?'

"Look at the town clock", came the answer.

"That's for poor folks. You got a watch."

For years Cap Wooten has been mighty secretive about his fishing spots in Edgecombe. When asked where he caught a fine string, Cap traditionally replies, "I don't fish anywhere that I can't hear the town clock."

The old clock bell was used for the town fire bell before being hung in the belfry, but it will probably be too big and too loud to use when and if Edgecombe gets a new courthouse.

However, if it is used in the new courthouse, it will serve as a loud reminder each Sunday to Preachers Brodie and Hobbie of the traditional time to end the service.

Famous Edgecombe politician Cousin Willie Clark passes on.

Friends, political associates, and acquaintances from all walks of life and all parts of North Carolina called at the Clark home or attended the final rites of Cousin Willie Clark Sunday afternoon.

Heading the list, however, were widows of three of North Carolina's governors, Mrs. O. Max Gardner, Mrs. H. Melville Broughton and Mrs. Luther Hodges.

(A look at the new town hall and a brief history of the Edgecombe County Courthouse are offered. The account of the Courthouse is an example of Ramblin's use of exquisite historical details. He had become a complete, thoughtful and intelligent historian of his home town.)

TOWN HALL—A man asked me Tuesday if I had seen anyone who liked the design of the new town hall based on the architect's drawing we published last week.

The answer is a flat "No".

In answer to the question, "Don't you think the $450 a month rent for the Benton Buick property is to high?" my answer is, again, no.

The property will house the fire and police departments along with the clerk's office. To locate these departments in separate building over town would probably cost just as much, and having the jail next door is an important factor to consider.

COURTHOUSE—In more than 200 years, Edgecombe County has had only a few courthouses and while the next is entirely up to the voters on December 19, even from the first there was controversy about location.

When Halifax County was formed from Edgecombe 1758, this county was left without a courthouse. In fact, there was a single incorporated town in the entire county.

Realizing that when the division was made, Edgecombe would have no seat of government, the General Assembly designated a place known as Redman's (or Redmond's) Old Field as the place for court to be held in this county.

No one is certain of the exact location of this field, but from a map drawn in 1777 it appears that it was in the vicinity of McKendree's Methodist Church, about six miles from Tarboro.

That site was the subject of controversy for in 1759 a Mr. Johnson presented the Assembly with a petition from the principal part of the free holders and inhabitants of the county.

It charged that "Thro" mismanagement and in a Secret and Clandestine Manner and Act was passed last Session of Assembly to fix the Courthouse of said County at Redman's Old Field on Tyoncoca which is found to be near the verge of said County and inconcentment to the Inhabitants to attend said County Courts".

There is no record that the Assembly took any action at all on Mr. Johnson's petition, and four years later, in 1762, a Mr. Palmer petitioned the Assembly again on behalf of Edgecombe residents.

He claimed that the act designating Redmond's Old Field as the place for building a courthouse, a prison and stocks was wrong. He contended, "Redman's Old Field is an obscure place and greatly inconvenient to the inhabitants to meet and transact the public Business of said County . . . ."

Palmer asked legislative approval for building the courthouse at Tarboro which had been incorporated two years previously. Later the same year - 1762 - a Mr. Howell and a Mr. Ruffin appeared before the Assembly to protest the Old Field site and to ask the courthouse be located in Tarboro. This time they got action and Howell was told to prepare a bill setting forth a place for the courthouse.

His bill, which was approved, designated Aquilla Sugg, William Haywood and James Hall to contract with workmen for construction of a suitable courthouse, clerk's office, prison and stocks on lots set apart by the town commissioners.

The same act authorized a poll tax of two shillings to be levied on each taxable resident of the county for a period of two years. The money was to be used to pay for the building.

The assembly put teeth into the act by declaring that from its passage until such time as the new courthouse was completed, there would be no court at Redman's Old Field. It was stipulated that court would be held in Tarboro at some convenient house until the new facilities were available.

Whether this was the courthouse that was in use 23 years later when William Attmore, the Philadelphia merchant, visited here, is not known. But he gave the only known, though brief, description of the courthouse that was standing in 1778. He wrote, "The courthouse is a large wooden building of two apartments . . . and standing on brick pillars".

The building must have been a large one for it was ample enough to accommodate the 180 members of the General Assembly who met here that year.

It is believed this courthouse remained in use until 1835 when the walls and foundation of the present structure were built. Probably with minor additions, the 1835 courthouse continued to serve Edgecombe until 1912 when it was remodeled and enlarged.

In 1911 the county commissioners retained the architectural firm of Wheeler and Stern of Charlotte to submit plans for the work. In May of that year the commissioners authorized the sale of $20,000 in bonds to provide money for the work, and the bonds were purchased by E.H. Rollins and Sons of Boston.

During the remodeling period, county court was held in the opera house, located in the second story of the town hall.

County commissioners held their first meeting in the "new" courthouse on September 4, 1912, and one of the first items of business was to authorize W.O. Howard and George A. Holderness to solicit funds to purchase portraits of outstanding Edgecombe barristers. Those are the portraits which now hang in the present courtroom.

Miss Sally Staton's will made history.

WILL—The will of the late Miss Sally Staton was scheduled to be a topic of discussion at a meeting of Vassar College trustees this week. However, the meeting was postponed until October 20. That information came to us by way of the Associated Press.

Ramblin' discovers Rachel Carson's famous book.

SHOCKER—I wish every thinking citizen would take the time to read Rachel Carson's "Silent Spring." It is both illuminating and disturbing to all concerned with the future.

Imagine a spring season without bird song, Miss Carson says, "On the morning that had once throbbed with the dawn chorus of robins, catbirds, doves, jays, wrens and scores of other bird voices, there was now no sound; only silence lay over the fields, woods and marsh.

"On the farms the hens brooded, but no chicks hatched. The farmer complained that they were unable to raise any pigs—the litters were small and the young survived only a few days. The apple trees were coming into bloom but no bees droned among the blossoms, so there was no pollination and there would be no fruit."

Such a sterile world, of course, does not exist. But some day it may. Miss Carson warns, because of careless and indiscriminate use of insecticides and other chemicals. It is not her contention that such chemicals should never be used. She argues only that their ultimate effect upon the land must be thoroughly studied and understood. Many of the insecticides which we use around the farm and home can and have destroyed the enzymes that protect the body from harm, of blocking the oxidation process, of causing malignancies.

The book is in the library.

Another local boy makes good.

GOING UP—According to press release from Nashville, Tenn., a Tarboro native is on his way up in the entertainment world. Bill Brock, son of Mr. and Mrs. William Brock of 835 Sunset Avenue, recently made his first appearance on the "Grand Ole Opry", singing "Black Cloud" which he recently recorded on the Crescende label.

COMMUNITY HOUSE—A couple of folks wondered aloud this week what will happen to the community house when a new Town Hall is constructed. I'd like to see the building used as a museum of local history. After all the house is 152 years or more old and is certainly attractive, and certainly as the bicentennial proved there are hundreds of items of interests which could be deposited there.

What's your thinking?

Goodbye to clock bell?

MISSED—Well, the old town clock's booming of the hour is now a thing of the past unless, of course, we approve the courthouse bond issue. On the proposed courthouse a modest dome will house the clock and its clapper will again remind citizens of the passage of Tarboro time.

It was bad enough when the chimes on the N.C. Bank's clock stopped working several years ago. But when the old town clock came down it was a tragedy. There's still time, however, to ask Santa for a new watch.

QUESTION—During the past week I was asked why I favored a new courthouse rather than having the present building enlarged and remodeled. The questioner pointed out that I have probably written more local and county history than anyone in the present generation. The insinuation was that I should have some sense of history and tradition and a love for "Antiquities".

Remodeling and enlarging the present courthouse would destroy the present lines which, incidentally, are only 50 years old; The cupola would be a thing of the past. When completed no vestige of the present building would remain.

As for the portion of the courthouse build in 1836, no one under 50 years of age has ever seen it, except in photographs.

1963

The old girl comes down—death of a Town Hall.

SORE—Quite a few sore necks developed in Tarboro this week as folks looked skyward to watch the wrecking of the old clock tower. There were the usual wisecracks, such as, "I understand they're gonna call the new building the Captain Howard House".

About the best sentiment I heard was expressed by an elderly colored man who observed, "They sure have left a great big hole in the sky!". Come to think of it, they certainly have.

LANDMARKS—To me it seems there was something symbolic about the events of a cold Wednesday afternoon in Tarboro.

As the old spire of the old town hall was toppled into dust, friends of Harvie Ward (Sr.) were on hand for his burial in Greenwood Cemetery. Both Harvie and the old spire had been on the local scene for more than 70 years. There was a certain dignity about the old spire and Harvie Ward that was what we younger citizens respectfully refer to as "a gentleman of the old school".

I considered him a friend, and I believe the feeling was mutual.

A landmark on Main has gone.

SHAD—The hickory shad are here again. First report came late last Saturday afternoon from Kate Edmondson at Old Sparta who said a Wilson fisherman landed the first one reported in the area. Several were caught Wednesday at Fishing Creek in the vicinity of Mabrey's Bridge.

Water levels and weather permitting, things should pick up over the week end.

Food critic.

I'm a Brunswick stew fan and I've tried about every variety available in local stores. Yet I have never found a brand to my liking, and others I've talked with seem to agree. The stuff they sell in restaurants tastes more like soup than stew.

For my money the best mass producers of Brunswick stew in these parts are the boys at the fire hall. It is always thick and flavorsome, always good, the quality is consistent. What more can you ask of a food product?

Food critic in trouble.

STEW—This column's remarks about fire hall Brunswick Stew last Friday got me in a stew - literally. Irvin Staton brought me a quart cooked by the members of the Church of Jesus Christ of Latter Day Saints with the reminder that "Our church has cooked and sold over 20,000 quarts of stew so it must be good". I agreed. Then the seniors brought by a quart which the wife had ordered. It was cooked by members of the Moose Lodge, and it also was very tasty.

Still, both offerings lacked something that is inherent in the stews cooked behind the fire hall. Maybe it is the flavor added by the well-seasons hickory paddle which Ike and Jesse use for the stirring. Regardless of what the "something extra" is, it imparts a delicate flavor to "fire hall" stew which is apparently unobtainable elsewhere.

I certainly appreciate the samples and will volunteer to continue as the county's unofficial stew sampler.

POLITICS—Well, the old political pot may not be boiling yet, but at this writing it's is certainly simmering smartly. Two of the incumbents already have opposition and there's talk that more of the present Town Council members will have to face opposition at the ballot on May 7.

Scrap Green's entry into the race was surprising to this writer in view of the fact that less than 24 hours before he filed he told me that under no circumstances would he consider running for the council seat he once held.

What happened during that interval is anybody's guess.

The big contest for mayor has yet to jell, but rumor has it that Herbert Bailey, unsuccessful the last time around, is getting his ducks in a row. Pledges of firm support have already reportedly come from the heavy-voting First and Eighth Wards. However, Dr. Ed Roberson remains one of the most popular men in Tarboro and a political power to contend with.

OHIO DELEGATION—Those three anglers from Ohio duplicated their last year's performance during their non-stop trip here last week end to fish the Tar.

John Hanner, Bud Eberwine and Dave Galbrith drove the 675 miles from Troy, Ohio, to Tarboro without stopping. Changing clothes at the William Vance they immediately headed for the river where three and a half days of hard fishing produced only a single rockfish. Some who saw the lone fish the boys caught said it could more properly be classified as a pebble rather than a rock.

On the bright side of the picture, however, was the fact that frog gigging expeditions on farm ponds produced about 60 pair of fine legs for the homeward trip.

Before leaving Monday afternoon, John asked that this column express appreciation for the traditional hospitality shown him and his friends.

What about next year?

The trio is already making plans to return.

No. 82—Monday marks the 82nd birthday of a fine Tarboro gentleman who hasn't been able to get around too much since an illness last May.

I'm referring to Mr. Sidney Brown, a man who was an artist with a paint brush during the many years that he did paint contracting work in Tarboro. In fact, at the age of 80 he and a helper painted the exterior and interior of both Edgecombe Acres and Edgecombe Meadows boarding homes.

A man who moved to Tarboro just a few years ago employed Mr. Brown to paint the interior of his home and was amazed when he showed up for work in his business suit. Mr. Brown removed his coat, donned a pair of coveralls, set up his drop sheets and ladders and went to work.

Recalling it, the man said, "Mr. Brown didn't need those sheets. He didn't even spill a drop of paint on them."

Since his illness Mr. Brown has for the most part been confined to his home on Wilson Street, but is able to take short rides with his family. He spends a good deal of his time drawing and painting excellent pictures of birds which he gives to his friends.

This column joins his hundreds of friends in wishing J. Sidney Brown a happy 82nd and many more birthdays.

SCALES—Getting a big fish weighed in Tarboro can get to be a long and frustrating process. Take what happened Wednesday night for example.

Jim-Boy Simmons caught a big rock in his net and on our return to town, Jim, Cicero Price and I attempted to find out how much she weighed. The scales at a service station said 14 pounds the ones at Harry Hull's store took our penny but didn't provide a reading. Scales in front of Jack Mobley's said the fish weighed 20 pounds. The ones at McCrory's said the weight was 16.

That averaged out about 17 pounds.

New press means more local pictures of local citizens.

GRADUATES—Monday's *Southerner* will feature photographs of every graduating class in the county - Tarboro High, Pattillo, Conetoe, Carver, Phillips, West Edgecombe, South Edgecombe, and North Edgecombe.

On young love, young man's fancies and Southern belles.

PERSONAL—Ah, summer . . . the turning of a young man's fancy . . . a time for the gals to set their collective caps for a beau during the months before school.

These thoughts, traditional for this time of year, combined with observing the hand-holding of the younger generation, plus the fears of some parents about "young love" and its supposed consequences, set me to thinking about the events of many, many years ago.

Be it true confession or not, and with malice toward none, here are a few notes on the early loves of the editor which (and many a local mama will say "Thank God" for) came to naught.

So far as I can recall, the first girl I ever went out with lived on St. Patrick, just a couple of blocks from the downtown business section. Her folks had the best refrigerator in town for raiding.

I remember taking her to a murder movie called the "Florentine Dagger" in the old opera house. It (the movie) scared me so badly SHE had to walk me home. I didn't think the incident had any bearing on what I considered a romance until a couple of weeks later when we were invited to a party. In the course of the evening post office was played. She sent me only a post card as a token. But she sent Joe Bourne about a dozen air mail special deliveries and two parcel posts.

Somehow or another I got the hint and kicked the toe out of my shoe on my lonely way home.

Junior high brought a summer courtship with a beautiful gal who lived on Baker Street and each night I wended by way from my home on Battle Avenue, by the swimming pool, past the home of the late Mr. Martin Carstarphen. More times than not, he would stop me and chide me about courting. "Take her a flower", he'd say, and I'd pluck a cape jasmine from the bush by his porch. It proved to such a great aid in courting that when Mr. Martin happened not to be around, I'd swipe a handful. The gal was a fool for the sweet fragrance so the theft was worth the gamble.

One of my best friends in those days was Ed Bond and he was the bashful type. So one night I asked him to with me to the house on Baker Street.

In an atmosphere that seems to be unfortunately absent today, the threesome enjoyed its collective self to such an extent that the gal suggested we get together more often. I should have realized what was coming.

A couple of nights later Ed and I met at the corner of St. Patrick and Bridgers to go to the house on Baker Street. As usual I had swiped some of Mr. Carstarphen's flowers. Ed had gotten his courage up and helped himself to a handful of talisman roses from Mrs. Carlisle Moore's back fence.

Arriving at our destination, the girl accepted my flowers as if they were something to be taken for granted. While my offering wilted on the coffee table, she proceeded to ooh and ah over Ed's roses. Said they were the prettiest she had ever seen.

Suddenly I realized I had been done in again.

I swore off all women . . . vowed to live as a hermit on the banks of the Tar for the remainder of my life. And I kept the vow, too . . . for about a week.

Then came utter infatuation with a girl who lived in what is now the country. Her pa had built the first house in what is now Glenburnie, and it was surrounded by a cotton field. The open spaces were refreshing. There was a porch swing, a record player and for the moment, no serious opposition.

Then one starlit night when her folks were visiting friends, the old swing creaked as I sought the right words to convey my thoughts. Suddenly there came a scream like a jet clawing its way through the sound barrier. I flew inside the house and locked the door. But I had to unlock it when my date begged to be allowed to enter her own home.

The howling continued, along with scratchings on the screen. Rocks were tossed on the roof. I kept telling the girl I wasn't a bit scared as she tried without success to get me to come out from under the sofa.

Finally, her folks came home. And as I tried to tell her father how I had protected his daughter, the scratching came once more. Pa grabbed a revolver, piled outside and fired six shots into the air. As it turned out the noises were made by a couple of my "friends", who were scared so badly by the hail of bullets that they clawed up four rows of cotton in the present vicinity of Curtis Leggett's house.

RIVER—The Tar River is lower now than in many years and this is good news for the contractor who has the job of snagging the stream from Rocky Mount to Tarboro. Work has now progressed to a point below the Dunbar bridges, but it's still a long, long way to Tarboro.

History

100—It was one hundred years ago today that the only Civil War clash of any consequence occurred in Edgecombe. And that one was only a skirmish.

The site of the fight was just a few miles from Tarboro on the Oak City road, then known as Daniels School House. There the Yankees of the Seventh New York Cavalry were ambushed by Confederates under the command of Major John T. Kennedy.

The Yankees lost 17 horses, two dead, 15 wounded and 16 prisoners in the brief battle. In their retreat they set fire to the river bridge in a successful effort to delay the advancing Confederates.

Whether it was before or after the ambush, I don't know, but the Union troops set fire to the jail and Confederate commissary here and also are said to have applied this torch to two river boats.

The raid came only a day after Edgecombe lost one of its most illustrious sons. William Dorsey Pender died in Staunton, Va. of a wound he suffered during the second day of the battle of Gettysburg. It was the fifth wound sustained by Pender during the war.

The battle was Pender's first after being promoted to major general - the youngest (29) officer in the Confederacy to hold that rank.

IT—Well, the new town hall is taking shape such as IT is. Those baby blue panels which were inserted this week are really something. The only comforting thing about the structure is that we who live here know what IT is supposed to be. To the tourist it could be a glorified fruit stand, a Holiday Inn, a rejuvenated Hotel Tarboro, a two story Colonial Store (all it needs is a red rooster on the corner). To keep the visitors from having to stop and ask what purpose the building serves, I hereby suggest that once IT is completed a large sign in pastel neon (pink, perhaps?) be placed outside proclaiming IT to be a town hall.

Earnhart back to Florida.

LOSS—The doctor who ordered the George Earnharts to go to Florida for the sake of their health, may have done them a service, but he surely did Tarboro a disservice.

George took over the Merchants Association on an extremely small salary and built it into a well-functioning organization. The tours of local industries and near-by Armed

Forces bases he arranged did much to build fellowship in the association. Furthermore, he assumed an active role in civic affairs that reminded us of the old days when he served as a spark plug for every venture to promote the good of Tarboro. At the same time he was holding down the job of town clerk. *(Earnhart died a few weeks later and was buried in Tarboro.)*

FISH—The unusual is never forgotten.

This week I received a letter from a free lance writer in Jackson, Mich., who wanted details of the time it rained fish in Edgecombe County. Yep, it really happened on May 18, 1928.

The fish fell from the sky on the farm of Mr. Will Doughtie near Mayo's Crossroad during a heavy rain and thunder storm. When the storm passed, hundreds of small fish were found swimming in puddles and flopping on the ground. Where they came from was and is a mystery. The nearest stream was a mile from the farm. There were no tornadoes reported.

Ugh! City Hall getting very bad reviews.

IT GROWS—One local wit this week made the following comment about the new town hall:

"You know, it kinda grows on you . . . . like cancer."

Really though, it isn't all that bad. Now that they've got that shiny strip of metal around the top and are ready to put the glass in the front, it looks more and more like a Tappan gas range.

BRICK—They started laying rick at the new courthouse this week - handmade Williamsburg-type brick that is. The architect estimates the structure is ten days behind schedule mainly because a considerable amount of concrete poured in the jail section of the basement had to be done by hand. Completion of the building is scheduled - tentatively - for May 23.

-0-

FILES—Mrs. Hal Liles stopped by the office yesterday and left us a copy of *The Southerner* for September 28, 1916. The copy was of special interest because our files do not contain any issues of the paper from that period.

Here are some of the items from that day's *Southerner*:

Cam Morrison who was later to become governor "delighted a rather small audience" in the courthouse.

George Pennington, Jr. celebrated his sixth birthday Wednesday.

Miss Kate Cheshire entertained St. Catherine's Guild.

Two dozen Republicans met to choose candidates for the "approaching election". W.G. H. Leigh, L.D. Brown and W.J. Taylor were nominated to run for commissioners, W.L. Stallings for sheriff, and Raiford Liles for the legislature.

Misses Elizabeth Mercer, Virginia Sledge, Willie Wilson and Nannie Mae Brown left Tuesday for the Eastern Carolina Teachers Training School in Greenville.

Thad Thigpen, a Confederate veteran, died at the home of his daughter, Mrs. B.F. Shelton at Speed.

The movie "Ramona" was showing at the Opera House.

Town commissioners passed an ordinance requiring that sidewalks be paved on St. Patrick from St. James to Battle Ave.

Thanksgiving and the death of John Kennedy.

THOUGHT—Despite the food and family fellowship, Thanksgiving was sad because our thoughts kept wandering to the tragic event in Dallas last Friday. However, Thanksgiving was a most opportune time to offer God our eternal gratitude that this great United States is a nation of laws and not of men. Thus, we are able to survive the most trying of times.

In many nations this would not be possible. Assassination of a leader would have been followed immediately by civil strife and bloodshed, a struggle by opposing forces. In this nation, however, such a tragic occurrence served to unite, not divide.

PHOENIX—Peyton Beery tells me the new Phoenix Trimming Company plant on Highway 258 is far ahead of schedule and will probably be completed well in advance of the date machinery is scheduled to arrive. That's excellent news, especially in view of the tobacco acreage cut which will leave a tremendous hole in our economy.

All right, Brer Beery, it's like the man said, "I know you've done a lot for us, but what have you done lately?"

How about getting us a nice new industry for a Christmas present?

Initials in trees—signs of the times.

CREEK—Our children make a weekly habit of exploring the Hendrick's Creek low grounds and on a recent trip I suggested they look for an ancient beech tree. I explained that I had carved my initials on it when I was a boy. They returned home in about an hour and I asked them if they had found it.

"We sure did", was the reply.

"Did you find my initials carved on it?"

"Nope, just dirty words", came the disgusted reply.

Well, times change.

The old Town Hall came down and new offices were in one year.

MOVING—Some town offices will be moved into the new town hall this weekend. Included are the town clerk's office and the police department. That will leave the fire department alone in the old garage building on St. James Street until such times as the new fire station can be build.

HEROES—Certainly the unsung heroes at this season are the town's garbage men who were on the job bright and early yesterday removing boxes of discarded paper, ribbon, and turkey bones from local yards.

FIRST—A record was set at our house Christmas morning. It was the first time in memory that I didn't get a single necktie or handkerchief.

BIRDS—We don't go in for extensive bird-watching, but it was something of a triumph last Sunday when a pair of evening grosbeaks spent most of the morning on our feeder. They were the first we had seen this year, however, they haven't been back.

1964

CARD—We received a Christmas card from the three Italians who visited Glenoit Mill last fall, and they asked that we extend the following to our readers:

"Best wishes to all the wonderful people of Tarboro".

The card was signed by George Curtis, Alfonso Caffino, and Comonico Bosehind.

POPULAR—The most popular calendar in town this year is the Tarboro Savings and Loan's offering which features a handsome picture of the old town hall. Demand is said to surpass even that for the perennial favorite - Currier and Ives.

Incidentally, it was just one year ago yesterday that the demolition crew ripped the top from the old structure and started toppling the clock tower.

COURTHOUSE—The new courthouse appears more massive each day as huge sections of steel are hoisted into place for the roof. I don't know if the weather has set the construction back too much, but to the casual observer it certainly seems the building will be ready on time.

Rosenbaum's Closes.

IRONIC—There was something ironic about Tuesday's issue of *The Southerner*. On the front page was an article about a new industrial plant, but elsewhere in the paper was an ad announcing that two of the town's long established businesses were calling it quits.

Peter Pan, Inc. was established after World War II and has done a splendid job of providing the clothing needs for the younger set.

The history of Rosenbaum's goes back much further, it became Rosenbaum's Inc. on Feb. 15, 1933, but for 25 years prior to that time the business had operated as Rosenbloom-Levy. The business was named in memory of Mr. Julius Rosenbaum who served many years as manager and part-owner of Rosenbloom-Levy. Generations of Tarboroeans have been customers of this fine old firm.

A new neighbor comes to town and two old friends leave. Somehow it doesn't seem right . . .

CROWDED—Trustees of Edgecombe General have a long range plan already mapped for hospital expansion, with the only stumbling block being the shortage of funds. Edgecombe General is severely overcrowded. It has a capacity of 75, but the head-count yesterday was said to be 92 patients bedded down in the halls and waiting rooms.

With the weather we've been having, there's no reason to think the situation will improve before the spring thaw.

The nicest part of covering a political campaign.

ROTARY—Regardless of the outcome of the Democratic primary, I'll always have a warm spot in my heart for Dan Moore, Richardson Preyer and Beverly Lake. Because of these gentlemen I was invited to be the guest of the Rotary Club to cover their speeches. As a result, I enjoyed three excellent meals at Lloyd's.

CANDIDATES—If the Democratic Primary were held tomorrow, for whom would you vote?

The Tar Heel State has three high caliber men seeking the post which can go to but one. But the image which these candidates project on television is horrible. The Richardson Preyer ad agency folks take the smart way out by using the "This is your Life" approach. If Preyer speaks at all, it is briefly approving motherhood and condemning sin.

Someone in the Dan Moore camp should be hanged for allowing the TV film I viewed last week to be shown. Judge Dan looks like some kind of monster from the twilight zone than a man who says he'll make more jobs available. From the way the judge "projects", I'd say the jobs would be offered to apprentice undertakers and junior grave diggers.

While this column has yet to see a Beverly Lake TV pitch, I'd be willing to venture a guess that the good professor would only succeed in projecting an egg-head image.

A cold lonely night, trying to help a friend.

DIXIE—The night was cold and for the most part Main was deserted when I stopped in at the Dixie for a cup of coffee. I asked Cris the usual question, "How's business?" and got the expected answer:

"It could be better".

We then proceeded to talk about the cafe of days gone by when it was the chief gathering spot for the men of town. The cafe came into being during the Depression and successfully weathered that storm. But in these prosperous times, business at the Dixie, "Could be better".

The next time you think about it, stop in. The food is good and the coffee is second to none in town.

And Cris would appreciate it.

Still in February.

SIGNS—Sure signs of spring—girls getting out their jump ropes and boys chalking dirty words on the pavement.

HEARING—The public hearing on the US 64 bypass, scheduled for March 24, promises to be the most spirited event held in the new Town Hall since it opened. Of course, the owners of all the property involved will want to be heard. Some will benefit, and others will lose, but that's the price we must pay for progress.

HALL—When town workers unloaded jack-hammers and went to work busting up the pavement at the Town Hall last week, one local wag took a look and suggested that town officials had finally admitted their mistake and had decided to demolish the new building and restore the old one. But no such luck. They were just replacing the sidewalk.

Peaches or fish?

RUINED—Not only did this week's freeze ruin the peach crop, it also had an adverse effect on this year's crop of largemouth bass. Harry Cornell, chief of the Wildlife Commission's Division of Inland Fisheries, said yesterday that the early spawn of bass has been ruined by the cold weather. In hatcheries as well as in farm ponds the fish had already scooped out spawning beds and females had deposited eggs. Cold water temperatures drove the fish away from their spawning urge and beds and the eggs will be eaten by other fish or destroyed by fungus.

Cornell also said the run of such migratory fish as shad, herring and rock will be delayed somewhat by a surge of colder water downstream.

FLOOD—The high water during the past week caused carp from the Tar to migrate to the low ground in Princeville. In one stretch of flood water behind the old river road they were rooting around like hogs.

FRIENDLY—Hubert Parks, a long-time fixture at G.T. Thorne's Drug Store, has purchased the Friendly Grocery on Howard Avenue from Sam Taylor and will manage that neighborhood establishment. Sam will continue to work for Hubert at the store. Hubert said Friendly will continue to offer a premium line of fresh seafood, plus the usual complete line of grocery items. Planned hours are from 7 a.m. until 9 p.m.

AUDITOR—County Auditor Allen Lee Harrell was hospitalized by a "light" heart-attack last weekend. If there is anything at all good about it, the attack will at least make him take a much-needed rest. He is one of the hardest working individuals we have at the Courthouse, the very core of county government. Not only does he make up the annual budget—a tremendous task in itself—but he is the overseer of all other department where county funds are involved. The new courthouse paperwork alone was enough to occupy the time of a ordinary man, but he shouldered that responsibility along with his regular backbreaking load.

Here's wishing him a speedy recovery.

Hanner Report.

NO LUCK—Well, the three fishermen from Ohio drove nonstop 700 miles just to fish the Tar for rock, and it was the same old story—no luck. They fished hard for four straight days and not even a catfish did they have to show for their efforts. But the trip wasn't a total loss. For John Hanner, it was another opportunity to renew friendships of the days when he worked in the Edgecombe Bank. For Bill Shields, a dentist whose hobby is architecture, it was an opportunity to inspect and admire our new courthouse. He even delayed the first day's fishing to go over the building which he described as "magnificent." Someone at the courthouse told him about Calvary Church, so the trip was further delayed while Bill reverently inspected the church.

For Dave Galbreath, it was simply an opportunity "to get away for awhile." All three are already planning to return next year.

CARTER—Russell Carter has served notice that he is quitting as manager of the Edgecombe Agricultural Fair which is to be held here this fall.

Russell has served the fair in some form of management capacity since it was started here about 13 years ago, but says that the demand of his other jobs make it necessary that he step down. Russell claims he has told the Lions Club, fair sponsor, a dozen times that he is quitting, but they won't believe him. "Put it in the paper", Russell said, "Maybe that'll convince them I'm not kidding."

Justified praise for the Wildlife Club

RODEO—Parents and youngsters who enjoyed the fishing rodeo Wednesday afternoon owe a debt of gratitude to a couple of Tarboro men who have taken the Wildlife pond as something of a personal project since retirement from their respective jobs. They are Howard Alford and A.C. Hughes and while they are helped by other club members they have been the leaders in the shrubbing and clearing work that has made the area surrounding the pond most attractive.

Runoff Election in June.

PRIMARY—Well, at least it's about over. All the politicking and name calling that has gone on for so many months is at an end. We were disappointed rather than surprised by the events of the past ten days. The publicity boys tried hard to picture Richardson Preyer as an expert on tobacco. Dan Moore said he knew nothing about either the state's Good Neighbor Council or the Ku Klux Klan. Confusing to say the least, and not too creditable.

On the other hand, the various campaign managers in Edgecombe have conducted their various efforts on a high level (as far as this writer knows) and for that we can be grateful.

WATERSHED—Edgecombe fishermen are expressing concern over possible construction of a dam across the Tar. While the Corps of Engineers hasn't yet even conducted a flood control study of the river basin the very mention of dam brought expressions of concern of what such a structure would do the traditional spawning grounds of rock and shad. Judging from a map drawn after a survey was made around 1947 the dam as then proposed would be between Tarboro and Shiloh and would flood a vast portion of lowgrounds for quite a distance above the mouth of Fishing Creek.

NOVEMBER—Speculation that Hubert Humphrey will be Lyndon Johnson's running mate in November is causing an increasing number of old-line Edgecombe Democrats to declare that if it happens, they will vote unhesitatingly for Goldwater. Even some of the die-hard Democrats are conceding that Goldwater may carry Edgecombe and the Second Congressional

District as well. And that is something that didn't even happen in 1928.

TREES—Ed Clayton provided the good news yesterday that the oaks around the post office would not be taken down because of the expansion which is slated to begin Monday. meanwhile, around at the new courthouse, Knox Porter was busily preparing to set out trees to beautify the handsome building. An extra touch at the courthouse this week was the installation of an underground sprinkler system which will be used to water the lawn.

RUSH—The rush is on to attend to the countless details which will lead to the completion of the courthouse. Furnishings for the new building are scheduled for delivery on August 24.

Meanwhile, most of the old tax records have been moved out of the old building, the many shelves have been repainted and installed in the tax supervisor's new office.

The county commissioners took giant steps toward solving parking problems in the vicinity of the new courthouse. The old ravine on the Zoeller property at the corner of Granville and St. Patrick has been filled in and within a year will have settled enough to permit paving. Until then it will be usable in good weather.

Summer is fading but life is sweet.

AUGUST—In many ways August is a month I've never been able to make up my mind about. I just don't know whether I like it or not. The days are hot and humid, but the nights give cool promise of Indian Summer. You realize almost suddenly that the days are becoming shorter. The frantic activity of children seems to indicate a burning desire to put as much summer playing as possible into the few weeks that remain before the opening of school.

In the late evening—If you close your ears to the other sounds—the crickets and other small insects chirp away as if to make the most of every second until the coming of first frost.

Tobacco market opens and something is missing.

TOBACCO—The opening of the tobacco market next week promises to bring to the warehouse floors something that has been missing for the past couple of years - AROMA! Numerous farmers have told us that when you go into a curing barn this year, there is a powerful, pungent and pleasing old-time aroma of flue-cured tobacco. After the past couple of years farmers were beginning to think aroma had been bred out of tobacco.

Figures show Bill Long's contribution to local economy.

LONG—Many of those who took part in the Coastal Plain Planning and Development tour this week were surprised and impressed to learn the size of Long Manufacturing Company—Tarboro's largest industry. The company now has 1,100 employees, 900 of whom work in Tarboro. There is also a plant in Davenport, Iowa, and branch offices in Dallas, Texas; Tifton, Ga., Columbus, Ohio; and Florence, S.C.

The annual payroll is in excess of two and a half million dollars.

HERONS—Immediately after the heavy rain Wednesday afternoon I rode down to the municipal boat landing and there wading in the shallow water just off the sandbars were six stately herons. It's an unusual sight so close to town.

Siding with underpaid, overworked garbage collectors.

WALKOUT—At this writing the walkout of the town's garbage collectors seems to have fizzled out and apparently no action has been taken on their demand for more pay. I'm inclined to side with the collectors. In the past this column has commented on the diligence of these men. I've never seen one loafing on the job, and they perform one of the dirtiest tasks in town and are at the bottom of the municipal pay scale. It is difficult for a man and his family to exist, let alone live on 86 cents an hour.

Sense of history grows.

RELICS—When the time comes to sell the old courthouse, I hope the commissioners make arrangements to keep title to the old bell, the cornerstone and any items of historic interest which may be found during demolition. No telling what could be up in the attic.

LADY BIRD—Will Mrs. Lyndon Johnson make a whistle stop at the depot here next month?

It certainly seems possible. Congressman Herbert Bonner's office has said she will make a train stop in Ahoskie on the afternoon of October 6. This morning the *Greensboro Daily News* stated that a stop in Rocky Mount is tentatively included in her tour as well as one in Norfolk. The only way to get from Norfolk to Rocky Mount is through Tarboro.

Scuppernongs and romance.

AROMA—I spent a goodly portion of last Sunday afternoon under a scuppernong vine and while stuffing myself I suddenly wondered why some scientist hasn't succeeded in distilling the aroma of those wonderful grapes into a perfume. Even the homeliest gal using the scent on a winter night would be absolutely irresistible to a country boy.

Yawl or you all?

SPECIAL—We are glad the "Lady Bird Special" managed to work in a brief stop here Tuesday and the Politicking seemed to be fully enjoyed by all. However, it seemed to me the First Lady and her daughter bandied the expression "You all" or "Yawl", about too much. However, as one spectator put it, "When in Rome . . . ."

Soak in the beauty.

TIME OUT—Sometime this weekend drive around town or in the country and just take time out to look. Look at the magnificent colors. Soak in the beauty of autumn in Edgecombe. It's mighty invigorating.

AUTUMN—Thursday's wind just about ended the autumn color in Edgecombe, but it certainly was lovely while it lasted, and it lasted a long time. A local man dropped by the office

Wednesday and said some folks like to go to the mountains but he preferred to get his family together on November Sunday afternoons and ride slowly on the back roads of old Edgecombe.

"The woods here are just as pretty as anywhere else in the state", he argued, "It's just a matter of opening your eyes to the fact. Last Sunday, we fully enjoyed the color, and in addition, we saw a deer, a dozen or more rabbits, and a couple of coveys of quail."

I suppose he has a point there.

PUPS—I'm now taking reservations for folks who would like a puppy in a couple of weeks or so. My bird dog has a litter of eight—six of 'em males. I'm not sure of the papa's identity, but the heads of the pups look something like Bubu—Yogi the Bear's little buddy.

The line forms on the right.

SNOW—Snow flurries Monday put an end to any hopes that Indian Summer would linger into December. One observer said he thought it snowed more Monday afternoon than it did all last winter, and no one took issue with him.

What's ahead?

Well, folks who watch such things say the caterpillars were unusually wooly last summer; squirrels stored away extra large supplies of acorns; quail are said to have a heavy layer of fat; rabbits have heavier coats of fur; and Bruce Russell's coal supplies are tremendous. Looks like we're in for along, hard winter.

LIGHTS—Tarboro's Christmas lights are most attractive, but they make the river bridge seem darker than ever. In fact, I can't even remember the last time the bridge was lighted. It seems to me that I read in the town minutes than when t he bridge was built, the town agreed to keep it lighted at night.

WINDOWS—Even if you do your Christmas shopping during the daytime, it is worth a special trip downtown at night just to see the windows. Many merchants have gone all out to make them more attractive than ever.

WEEK—Just a week from today - Christmas! Where in the world did the past 12 months go? It seems like only last week that we were going to graduation, taking the kids swimming, mowing the lawn and buying school clothes. Now it's time again to buy and find suitable hiding places for presents. But come to think of it, the youngsters have already found all the possible hiding places.

COMMON—For years we've campaigned for better treatment of the Town Common. So I hesitate to criticize.

This year the town heavily disked the Common, after first applying a thick coat of sludge from the disposal plant. Then grass was planted. It should eventually be real pretty. But the work is the reason we won't have our excellent Christmas and New Year's display on the west side of Main this year.

1965

New Year and a hint of a rate reduction.

VEPCO-The Virginia Electric Power Company announced yesterday that it is reducing rates to its customers and since Tarboro purchases a tremendous amount of current from VEPCO we wonder if any of the reduction will dribble down to the customers? It is estimated that Tarboro this fiscal year will be $400,000 from VEPCO.

CLUBHOUSE—Members of the police department are putting the finishing touches on their clubhouse, and it's about the most handsome do-it-yourself project I've seen. The 20 by 50-foot building has a well-equipped kitchen and a large fireplace with a raised hearth.

The officers did most of the work on the structure during their off duty hours which makes it even more meaningful to them.

WILDLIFE—The Wildlife Club got its new year off to a good start at Conetoe last night with Bobby Helms taking over as president from Dinksie Gilliam. The club also made history by installing its first major female officer. Miss Velma Bottoms fills the all-important job of secretary-treasurer, taking over from Dick Denton, Jr.

BOMB—This week one of the television networks again attempted to make much of the "moral issue" involved in dropping the first atomic bomb on Japan. Thank God Harry Truman decided in favor of dropping it.

That decision saved the hide of many of us out in the Pacific who were scheduled to make the initial landings on the mainland of Japan.

40—I've always heard that life begins at 40. Tomorrow I'll begin finding out if it's really true.

Shad Prediction on February 5.

HICKORY—Jim-Boy Simmons says he'll catch the first hickory shad from the Tar this month and he claims he'll do it within the next ten days. Maybe he can pull it off. After all, the first one to be landed with rod and reel is usually picked up around Feb. 18. Whether Jim can get ahead of those fellows at Old Sparta is another matter.

Prod prod, nudge, nudge.

COUNCIL—Monday night's meeting of the Town Council is an important one for all citizens. The council will have public hearings on the proposed fire code and also on the establishment of a parking authority for Tarboro.

A scene that became familiar in America during the mid-60's.

MOB—A mob of from 50 to 60 Negroes taunted, cursed and belted our ABC officers with sticks and bottles Saturday night.

An axe was thrown at one of the men. Only a faulty 12-gauge shotgun shell saved one of the officers from death.

All of this transpired during a relatively brief period Saturday night with the officers arresting a Negro couple for possession of non tax-paid whiskey.

One of the veteran officers said he heard the name of Martin Luther King chanted more during those trying minutes than he had in six months of watching television. By these same people there was also countless threats of "Kill those white s.o.b.'s".

It would appear that a certain segment of the population believes the civil rights bill gives them the right to break any law they choose. In any society, rights demand responsibility.

What happened on an Edgecombe farm Saturday night was that for the second time in four months an officer was threatened with death because of some individual's wanton disrespect for the laws which govern the society in which we live.

With the situation apparently going from bad to worse, it is only a matter of time before one of our officers will have to kill in self-defense. Then there will no doubt be wails of "police brutality" and "rights violations".

Those responsible for the continuing threats to the men we pay (or should I write "underpay") to protect us had better get the word and quickly.

February 19: Iwo Anniversary.

IWO—It was a long 20 years ago today that I struggled ashore with the third wave of marines to land on a rugged piece of Pacific landscape called Iwo Jima. The big brass predicted it would take 10 days at best to clean out the Japanese and then we could go back aboard ship and sail for a new landing at Okinawa. It turned out we were on Iwo for five long weeks in a battle which claimed a third of all the Marine lives lost during the entire war. When the fighting ended we were so badly shot up we had to return to Hawaii for replacements. It was a frightening experience because some still re-live it in nightmares. Among the other local folks who remember the black volcanic sands of Iwo are Albert Walker, Vinson Bridgers and Lawrence Morris.

SQUIRRELS—Charlie Cooper says Tarboro has a pair of unusual squirrels in the block of Common in front of Bridgers School. He and Johnny Webber spotted the pair Thursday afternoon. He says they are a light gold color and have a silky fur that out sharply against the ground and trees there.

Like Alabama? A dirty slander.

REGISTRATION—In this day of violent "non-violence" movements, I've had a bellyful of blanket indictments of registration procedures in the South, and in spite of what has happened in Alabama, I'm not yet ready to consider North Carolina a northern state.

I have never heard of a serious complaint being registered with the county elections board. All applicants hae been treated fairly and without discrimination, yet because a portion of the population hasn't taken the time to register, Edgecombe finds itself classified in the same category as Dallas County, Alabama. That is, subject to having a federal registrar. That, sir, is a dirty slander.

SPRING—The calendar says spring will officially arrive tomorrow afternoon, but the weatherman doesn't promise first-day sunshine for those of us who are itching to begin scratching in the dirt. Last Saturday's mild temperatures gave me the planting fever, but I was smart enough to start a couple of indoor seed beds. Last year I planted outside too early and a late frost wiped out all my seedlings.

April 2 and Will Alderman offers his garden—free.

GARDEN—Mr. Will Alderman came in the office yesterday and said that because of ill health he will not be able to tend his garden this year. He was generous enough to add that the 80 by 100-foot fenced in garden is available to anyone who'll cultivate it. He doesn't want it growing up in weeds this summer. Mr. Will may be reached at his home on Howard Avenue.

DIKE—I'm in full sympathy with Princeville officials in their efforts to secure rights-of-way for the proposed dike. Apparently, the Corps of Engineers got snarled up in its own red tape, failing to provide needed information in a reasonable length of time.

The project not only will provide flood protection for the town of 850 but also for about a thousand others who live outside the town limits. As Mayor Ray Matthewson pointed out, the $300,000 for the work will largely be paid out and spent right here in Edgecombe County.

EASTER—If the weather continues to cooperate Sunday should be the prettiest Easter we have had in many a year. The trees literally turned green overnight. Dogwood burst into blossoms like popcorn. Against that background, this old town's thousands of azaleas, quince, cherry redbud and wisteria give us a panorama of color equal to any section of the United States. You can have Wilmington and Charleston in the spring.

I'll take Tarboro.

Hanner expedition returning again.

VISITORS—Via telephone last night I learned from John Hanner, an Ohio banker who still has deep roots here, and a couple of his cronies will arrive early next Friday morning for their annual rockfishing trip to the Tar. Sherman Winchester is again expected to provide a suitable boat for nightly frog gigging expeditions while the Ohio trio is here.

POISON—The big chemicals accused Rachel Carson of over dramatizing the dangerous uses of insecticides in her book, "Silent Spring". But now comes damning proof of just how deadly and contaminating these pesticides can be. The latest discovery is that penguins and seals in the Antarctic—thousands of miles from any known use of pesticides—have measurable amounts of DDT in their bodies. These animals spend their entire lives feeding mainly on shrimp and occasionally fish.

Annapolis graduate Carl Doughtie pays the price.

CARL—The terrifying undeclared war in Viet Name was brought tragically home to us last week with the news of the death of young Carl Doughtie.

He was one of our most enterprising carrier boys a decade ago and liked to wait for his newspapers by sitting in the editor's office talking about things that happened in school, in town or along his route. Sometimes the talk would turn to hopes and ambitions. More than anything else, Carl wanted to fly. When the chance came for him to attend the Naval Academy he studied diligently for the exams. During the years of Annapolis he always found time during his leaves to drop by the office for a talk. But as the years passed his love for flying was tied to his devotion to the academy and its traditions and he developed a strong sense of obligation to his country. He died filling that obligation. In talking of Carl the other night a graduate of the academy recalled a couple of lines of verse recited in Bancroft Hall many years ago: "He lived as mothers wish their sons to live. He died as fathers wish their sons to die. For his country."

COURTHOUSE—J. H. Fortson is cleaning up what little remains of the old courthouse and around Sept. 1, the N. C. National Bank will begin construction of its new building. Last week the bank purchased the old law office building on St. James to further enhance its holding at the town's major intersection.

Tarboro's first City Manager retires.

HOWARD—Bill Howard lost no time after retiring in moving to his home at Kerr Lake and he will be missed in our government. As Tarboro's first manager, he did much to put the old town on an even keel and give it good government second to none in the state. He accomplished much and he made quite a few people mad in the process.

The nectar from the gardens, as good as life itself.

VEGETABLES—This is one month of the year when I can get along without eating a single piece of meat.

Snapbeans, butterbeans, tomatoes, new potatoes, onions, beets, squash and corn really make July a month to look forward to, especially when you have generous relatives and neighbors with gardens.

(Charlie Clayton, known to almost everyone in town as "Charlie Boy" was afflicted all his life with a horrendous speech impediment and the lurching walk of a drunk even though he did not drink. The name "Charlie Boy" was used tauntingly by those who did not realize his broad intelligence and how much he was tormented by his affliction. Ramblin' understood and rarely ever used the nickname. When Charlie could bear it no more and his loneliness overwhelmed him, he parked his station wagon in a field and took his own life. The incident was reported in Thursday's edition on July 15. Here are Ramblin's comments on a friend the next day.)

CHARLIE—The town was stunned this week at the news of the tragic death of Charlie Clayton, a young man who became something of a legend in his own time. Despite a handicap which would have disheartened a lesser person, Charlie undertook as a means of making a living the most difficult of all professions—

sales—in the highly competitive business of printing. He did not limit his efforts to Edgecombe, to the contrary, he traveled thousands of miles each year throughout Eastern North Carolina successfully seeking business for what he proudly termed "Edgecombe's oldest printing house." He loved his town and had tremendous pride in his garden and the quality of the work his business produced.

In discussing the town's loss of Charlie one businessman remarked, "Certainly he was handicapped but he never let it bother him. He was an aggressive salesman and a shrewd businessman. He was a Tarboro institution. We will all miss him."

We most certainly will.

Only in a small town do we know how many chickens were eaten.

FRYERS—Everybody in town must have eaten chicken at least once last week.

Buster Wilkerson says that last weekend the A&P sold more fryers here than at any time in its history. A total of 6,600 chickens weighing more than 17,000 pounds were sold by the store during the three-day period. Buster says it was because of the high price of pork and beef.

POOCH—The family dog is quite a character. His mama was a pointer and his papa is unknown. He was unlike any of his litter mates. While they were all short haired, his coat is a long wavy jet black, except for his tail which is tipped with white.

The critter's main joy in life is stalking and pointing bullfrogs in Dail Holderness' pond, and on a couple of occasions this summer he has managed to catch several which he proudly brought home and deposited on the front steps.

Tuesday the pooch hit a new high, or maybe it was a low. Anyhow he came trotting down the street with a box turtle in his mouth, carefully holding the tail end in his mouth.

What he'll tote home next is anybody's guess.

Changes threaten the tobacco market.

SUMMER—Where has the summer gone? The tobacco market opens next week and school soon afterwards. Bad weather means bad crops and then bad sales and things have changed so much for the bad that it's hard to get any good out of the market.

Courthouse problem.

PIGEONS—Well, I suppose it had to happen. The pigeons have finally found the top of the new Courthouse to be an ideal place to perch. Somebody said the birds were frightened off the Masonic Temple by a dummy owl which was installed there. Hope a solution to the new problem is found before the copper roof is badly stained.

COMMON—The Town Common has received its annual discing prior the seeding of winter rye grass. But in the area between Main and the sidewalk the sand and topsoil was completely removed. Unless it is replaced the young dogwoods there will die because they have a shallow root system. Seems a shame.

New trees are coming to Main Street.

TREES—The Town Council took action Monday to "dress up" downtown with its approval to plant 64 trees in the sidewalk.

It hasn't been too many years since Main Street was lined with trees—mainly graceful elms-from the Common to the river. But the trees interfered with power lines and there was also the problem which will confront the new trees—concrete.

A nurseryman has told the town he'll guarantee the life of the new trees for a year. Once the town takes over their care, it will probably be another story. The trees will require regular watering and fertilization. And if past history, the trees are practically doomed even before they are planted.

And the Common oaks are being neglected.

The big oaks in our Common are sadly in need of care. But even at that they aren't as neglected as the long row of oaks in the center of Howard Avenue.

Now that we are talking about planting new trees, let's stop and take stock of what we already have and then resolve to do better by them. Our trees are a tremendous asset. If you don't believe me, just ask some of our visitors.

AUTUMN—Fall officially arrived yesterday afternoon and few pastimes more enjoyable than reaching upward to enjoy the fruits of a tangled scuppernong vine. This will probably be disputed by the folks whose main joy in September is eating boiled goober peas and sucking the salty juice from the hulls. Some will say it's six-of-one and half-dozen of the other.

TREES—The Rotary Club has undertaken the responsibility of raising the funds needed to purchase trees for planting in the downtown business section.

Plans now call for live oaks at corners and American hollies neatly spaced along Main.

It's an extremely worthwhile undertaking to dress up the very heart of Tarboro.

DIKE—Robert Barnhill's construction crew is providing plenty of entertainment for sidewalk superintendents as they build the Princeville dike. It seems only yesterday they started work but a portion of the dike upstream is already higher than the river bridge.

CONGRATULATIONS—Best wishes for many happy birthdays to the Rev. M. M. Weston, retired rector of St. Luke's Episcopal Church. He will be 94 this weekend.

A couple of years ago someone got the bright idea that the traditional red wasn't the right color for our fire plugs, so they were painted with a "reflective" shocking pink or was it a bile green? About the only purpose served was to scare the canine population half to death. Anyhow, during the past week or so the hydrants have been given a coating of firehouse red, which is as it should have been all along.

Russell Cater does it again.

PARADE—Last Friday's Christmas parade was another feather in Russell Carter's cap and we're all grateful for his efforts. He wasn't too pleased with the late (five minutes) start or the fact that several entries failed to show up.

Several folks remarked that the size of the crowd seemed equal to or larger than the one which turned out for the Bicentennial five years ago. Whether or not that's the case the crowd last week caused a traffic jam of epic proportions. One report said incoming traffic on US 258 was backed up all the way to Shiloh. Shucks the excellence of the parade was worth the trouble.

BELL—The old courthouse bell has found a new home. It has been attractively mounted on a brick stand adjacent to the courthouse parking lot.

PRESENT—In retrospect, it seems that the biggest and best Christmas present the town and county received in 1965 arrived early. It was Peyton Beery's announcement that Anaconda would build here a multi-million dollar plant which, when finished, will provide jobs for about 250 of our fellow citizens. To all involved to make the location a reality—again, many, many thanks.

Ending the year around a hot coal stove with sweet memories of fellowship.

STOVE—What with all the modern conveniences nowadays, I had forgotten how conducive an old-timey coal stove glowing on a cold night can be to conversation and fellowship.

The other night I stopped in a local store which still relies on such an stove for heat and two of the town's top net fishermen were sitting there enjoying the warmth. They invited me over to join them. They talk immediately turned to past nights on the Tar and it continued for more than an hour. They recalled a spring night more than 15 years ago when the river literally erupted with rock. After catching all they needed, they went to the ball park where a Coastal Plain league game was in progress, spread the word of what happened and almost caused a stampede.

All the talk of pleasant spring nights brought back names of men, now gone, who were members of that special fraternity of netters who not only enjoyed the netting but also the sights and sounds and smells peculiar to the Tar—Dick Hyatt, Gray Harrell, Mack Ruffin, Dudley Sherrod, Bill Worsley, Jesse Guill, Bob Pender, Henry McNair and numerous others. Those fishermen and other like them spent a good deal of their time on the Tar seeking to outwit Milford Haynes, the county game warden for many, many years.

1966

Crisis

WORLD—Shortly after 2 o'clock Wednesday afternoon the office phone rang and an almost tearful voice asked to speak with our female foreman of composition and typography.

She answered and the side of the conversation I heard went something like this:

"Oh, no!

"She couldn't have!

"Is she hurt bad?

"Well, is she dead?

"Oh, no. That's terrible!

"I just can't believe she'd do a thing like that.

"It's just terrible, terrible.

"Weren't they to be married Friday?

"It's just terrible.

"Oh, poor Ellen, But I never did like Franny very much.

"Oh, what will happen to her and David and the boys?"

Those of us who heard the one-sided conversation got mighty upset. One rushed over to Dr. Bass' office for some smelling salts. Other went to Rose's for some fortifying coffee, and still other hurried next door to Me-Ma Creech's establishment to place a "to whom it may concern" order for flowers.

Finally the gal on the phone slowly replaced the receiver and as we waited to share her grief, she tearfully announced that Ellen Cole had crowned Dr. David Stewart's housekeeper, Franny, with a blunt object when Franny threatened to tell the doc's adopted son that Ellen was his real mama . . .

Of course, she was relating that day's happenings on "As the World Turns" which everyone knows is the world's most popular television program. The female population of this community is admittedly addicted to watching the daily happening of the Hughes and Lowell families. Even some of the males, when questioned closely, will confide they catch a quick snack in front of the boob tube from 1:30 until 2.

A couple of years ago Jeff Baker, Penny's first husband, died, and we held up the press run for a few minutes so we could run the obit on the front page. Folks hereabouts appreciated it and we even received a nice letter from CBS. We also stuck in a social item making note of Grandpa Hughes' birthday, and everyone knew about whom we were talking.

I lost contact with the program when my lunch hour was changed from 1 to noon. But with this new crisis unfolding (and a year-long murder trial seems certain), I just might revert to my old schedule.

PARKER—Tarboro native Jim Parker today leaves Siler City where he has served as news editor of the Chatham News for more than 15 years. On Monday, he becomes part owner of the Sampsonian, a weekly paper printed in Clinton. We join with his many friends here in wishing him the best of his new undertaking.

BUSTED—a check at Edgecombe General reveals that seven broken arms resulting from the snow and ice, plus an uncounted number of sprains. And the old folks say the current mess is just waiting around for another one to come.

SEASON—Of course, it's still a long, long time before we're frost free, or even snow-free, for that matter, but during the past week several things have happened which makes it seem that Spring isn't so far around the corner as it was two weeks ago.

In the first place, the Burpee folks sent me their annual gift of sample flower seed, complete with glowing descriptions of what gorgeous blooms would result if I "plant outside after the soil has become warm."

Within hours after the snow melted in our yard, the yellow crocuses bloomed, and a walk around the house disclosed that the tender green spikes of jonquils and tulips had broken through. In many yards the warm days of the past week brought out the japonica and first-breath-of-spring bushes.

All are false signs, however, for as one local resident remarked long ago, "The only sure sign that Spring has arrived is when school boys start chalking dirty words on the sidewalk."

DIKE—Barnhill Construction is more than 80 per cent finished with the Princeville dike. The section from the railroad bridge north to the Legion building has been seeded and covered with a protective coating of straw and asphalt to prevent erosion.

Never more beautiful—again.

COMMON—Every spring about this time we remark that "the Common has never been more beautiful". So we say it again, but this time, without a doubt, it seems more lovely than in any of the more than 40 years I've lived here. I'm sure a lot of folks will join me in expressing appreciation to Town Manager David Taylor and all others responsible. The planting of Kentucky fescue certainly seems to have been a tremendous success, and the ample quantity of fertilizer applied appears to have had a marvelous effect on the dogwoods and other trees. This spring the Common is surely a joy to all of our town's citizens.

END—That's about it for this week. The fish are biting.

Ohio Expedition headed west to Hawaii.

OHIO—Those three fisherman from Ohio who have driven to Tarboro each spring for the past four years to fish for rock aren't coming this year. It seems that former Tarborean John Hanner, who spearheaded the annual trip, got so high and mighty he's going to Hawaii for a week.

JIM—Glad to see Little League is honoring Dr. Jim Branham, our local Casey Stengel, for his contributions. He retired this year after many seasons of hard work, a career marked by hundreds of friendships with his boys and their parents. Someone said he had more team's in the cellar than anyone on record—but I doubt it.

BYPASS— Tarboro folks are mighty glad that Robert Barnhill got the contract for the bypass. Over the years most of his contracts have been outside North Carolina-in Virginia, D.C. and Maryland-but lately he has been low bidder on several major jobs in this section of the state.

The only bad thing about it is Barnhill's crews go to work so early that the noise of those huge earth movers even wake up the roosters.

A nice country place to live and the arrival of a wood duck.

COUNTRY—The old town is growing. Annexation swelled the population to almost 11,000. But, brother, Tarboro is still a country town. You can still stand in the western Common and hear quail whistle. Gardeners still complain about rabbits nibbling their crop. But something which happened in the Marrow-Hussey-Horton block of Main last Sunday afternoon really put the icing on the cake.

The young'uns came running in to report there was a crippled duck in the yard. The grown folks investigated and sure enough a wild wood duck was pretending to be hurt in order to lure the kids away from a flock of her ducklings. The mama and ten of her young were rounded up and placed in a pen made from old window screens, but wood ducks are climbers, so cardboard was rounded up and placed over the top.

Finally, in desperation, the mama and her flock were boxed up and taken out to Leggett's pond where, at last report, they were doing fine.

POOLS—Like a lot of other parents I'm mighty glad the swimming pools will open tomorrow. Our youngest has already "accidently" fallen into Hendrick's Creek a dozen or more times.

TREES—The newly planted trees on Main are lovely and most seem to be thriving. We are appreciative of the efforts which led to the successful completion of the project, but isn't the placing of the name of the project sponsor at the base of each tree overdoing things a bit?

July 4th and it's later than you think.

DEADLINE—It is only three more days until the most glorious of all our national holidays, but it still isn't too late for you to plan your observance, whether it be the neighborhood or family type.

All you need is a Flag, a lunch, a copy of the Declaration of Independence and someone who can recall the courage of the men who signed it, and the valor of the men who fought and died to make it a reality.

Perhaps, this year more than ever before the story needs to be retold.

In the past 12 months Old Glory has been ripped to tatters, ground into the dirt, spat upon and even urinated upon. These desecrations happened not behind the Iron or Bamboo curtains, but right here in the United States.

The shame of it all!

Come Monday, let's remember the Flag and all that it stands for! It is later than we think.

SEASON—This is a good time of the year because of the way gardens are producing. Corn, cukes, tomatoes, new potatoes, snaps, onions, butterbeans, okra, squash are available in abundance. One of my favorites is squash but only when it's cooked down with plenty of onions.

And the next week—a whole lot of eating lost.

STORM—That terrific storm Wednesday afternoon left a lot of folks without power for varying periods of time. But worse than that, it made a lot of gardeners cry. Young corn was blown over, bean vines tangled and tomato plants broken off. A whole lot of good eating was lost.

TRIP—In spite of the long drive involved, the family vacation in Pennsylvania was extremely enjoyable. We spent most of it visiting the various national shrines which abound around Philadelphia and I believe our two youngest were truly impressed. I know I'm still old-fashioned enough to get goose bumps when I look at the Liberty Bell, when I stand in the room where the Declaration of Independence was signed, and when I look at the old church where I signed away my independence 16 years ago.

Rain needed very very very very much.

DRY—Of course, it is no news that the need for a soaking rain in Edgecombe is critical, particularly in the northern section of our county. Some say they can't remember when the streams of Edgecombe were so low. In fact, it is possible to walk across the Tar and Fishing Creek at some points without having the water come over the top of your shoes.

This week marked the first time that I've seen farmers use irrigation equipment on their peanuts and on a number of additional water holes are being rushed to completion.

And the rains came the following week.

RAINS—The rains of the past week meant millions of dollars to the farmers of our county. They also meant I had to have my shoes half-soled.

PORCH—With summer waning, dog days here, and school opening just around the corner, I have suddenly realized that we have spent less time porch-sitting with neighbors this year than for the two summers past.

A prime reason is that one neighbor has installed central air conditioning, so what's the use in sitting outside swatting mosquitoes when you can sit inside and stay comfortable.

Another neighbor has used his porch less because the nights this summer just plain haven't been conducive to outside sitting. Too hot and too humid, and also too cloudy for star gazing and satellite-watching.

Still ahead, though, are the usually delightful nights of September and October.

MARKET—As in past years, the opening of the tobacco market was THE big event of the week in Tarboro. But this year it was different.

For as long as I can remember, it was the first market opening accompanied by cool weather, and what a pleasant change it was! The weather also lightened the chores of "Wild Bill" Coley, who totes the cold water bucket to the usually perspiring buyers and warehousemen. The opening marked the beginning of Squinch Lindsey's 42nd year as tobacco buyer and was probably the coolest one he can recall.

That was some pot of soup.

FIRST—Autumn isn't officially here yet, but for some reason Distaff decided the other day the time had come for putting together a pot of homemade soup.

There was a bit of grumbling about it being "too early", but as it turned out the decision was an excellent one. The soup proved to be the most popular dish served up in a long, long time.

In fact, it was so good that our youngest consumed four bowls along with a half-loaf of garlic bread, then announced he wanted another bowel for dessert. At breakfast the next day he warned me not to finish off the soup at lunch because he wanted it for after school.

PAVING—Back in July we wondered when repaving of Main Street would be completed, and were told it was just a matter of the contractor setting up his asphalt plant. Well . . . the plant is up, winter is coming around again, and old Main still bears the scars of last fall's shaving.

BANK—Yesterday's Nuisance and Disturber gave notice of the one-million-seven-hundred and fifty-thousand-dollar and 00 cent North Carolina National Bank building in downtown Raleigh. The building was filled with dignitaries.

NCNB also owns an eighty-five thousand-dollar and 00/cent lot in downtown Tarboro. The lot is filled with weeds. And it has been for a long time except last summer (1965) there were several watermelon vines and wine bottles mixed in.

PROGRESS—Old Edgecombe is in a state of constant change and if you don't believe it, think back to just a year ago.

Earth movers were piling up the Princeville dike. Now the dike is completed, but the huge machines are still at work, this time building the roadbed for the bypass and within another year that job will be completed. Just a year ago the sides of the McNair Crossing road were fields of corn and peanuts. Now what was once a farm is the huge Anaconda plant. Near Pinetops, a former piney woods is the site of the new Puritan sportswear plant. Residential building has been steady throughout the town and in the suburbs. And the new bypass is opening up additional areas for development.

Old Edgecombe stood still for a long, long time but that's history.

LOT—Many thanks to NCNB for making the courthouse lot available for parking, for cutting the weeds and filling the hole at considerable expense. The 50 spaces provided will do much to relieve downtown parking problems.

KNIGHT—Somehow it was ironic that the careers of Mr. Bob Knight and the power plant he operated for so long and so well should end so nearly on the same date. Mr. Knight devoted 41 of his 77 years to operating the plant with its two old McIntosh and the Nordberg generators, and, later, the temperamental Worthingtons.

Mr. Knight's efficient operation enabled the plant to make many a million. He was also generous in passing along his practical wisdom to young men who had the technical but not the practical know-how of power plant operations.

The plant ceased operation Saturday. Mr. Knight passed away Monday.

We are grateful for his many years of service to our town.

CROSSINGS—Several people have called during the past week to express disbelief that the new bypass road will not have overpasses or traffic lights on Howard Ave., Wilson Street and

W. St. James. But it is true. While it is too late to do anything about additional overpasses, perhaps a letter to the Highway Commission might aid in getting traffic lights.

But I seriously doubt it.

Tribute to a long-time Tarboro supporter, Coca Cola Brown.

M.S.—M.S. (Coca Cola) Brown is a patient out at Edgecombe General, and I'm sure his thousands of friends wish him a speedy recovery.

The words "public servant" are among the most abused in the language, but not when they are applied to Mr. Brown. In his four score and two years he has devoted more of his personal time and money than any Tarborean in our history. It would take this entire page to list all of the things Coca Cola Brown has done for our town.

For more than 20 years he was president of the Chamber of Commerce, and on hundreds of occasions he passed out thousands of free Cokes to people from neighboring towns who came here for swimming parties, home demonstration and farm meetings. As a town commissioner, he was in charge of both the swimming pool and the milk plant and devoted as much time (perhaps more) to them than to his own business.

When Tarboro was a red hot baseball town, Mr. Brown's plant crew provided the first grass infield and he was a solid supporter of the team.

Through his hobby, photography, he saw to it that old Tarboro received top publicity in the *News and Observer*, *Greensboro Daily News,* and the *Virginian Pilot*.

He also provided *The Southerner* with hundreds of dollars worth of pictures, never charging us a dime, asking only a credit line (which I, too often forgot to include). At one time or another he took photos of just about everyone in town and gave the pictures at no charge.

For many years, Mr. Brown personally carried the THS band, staging fund raising suppers (at his own expense) and providing a place for members to practice when none was available at the school.

Hurry up and come back to the "depot," Mr. Brown. We miss you.

Salute to the Rev. Mr. M. M. Weston.

REV. WESTON—Although he was 94, the death of the Rev. M.M. Weston came as a shock, probably, I suppose, because I thought he was indestructible. In all the years that I knew him and enjoyed his friendship, he looked the same-erect and immaculate.

The Rev. Mr. Weston was truly as much a part of the Tarboro scene as the Town Common.

It must have taken him hours to make the daily trip from his home to the post office, for he would stop and chat with dozens of friends along the route.

Another real gentleman is gone and the community is poorer because of it.

LEAVES—Since we've had only one frost of any consequence, I hadn't paid any particular attention to the changing of the leaves until yesterday. But it's worth a drive around the county just to see the fall color, and there is a maple in front of the Charles Pillow home on St. David Street that is especially pretty.

On historical accuracy—or inaccuracy.

HISTORY—As one who is interested in history it is mighty frustrating when responsible organizations continue to publish false "facts." Three recent examples come immediately to mind.

The telephone directory—for the second straight year—lists the community house as the "old Foxhall residence." No Foxhall ever owned it so far as know and no Foxhall ever lived there. A recent town publication featured a handsome sketch of the community house, but dated it as having been built in 1850. It has been documented as having been constructed about 1810. The third instance is the Hill Directory which dates the formation of Edgecombe County at 1731. It was the legislature of 1741 which confirmed the formation of our county.

Rotary tree program a success.

TREES—Some folks are upset because the young trees planted along Main have died and have not been replaced. The Rotary Club, which sponsored the planting, has a guarantee on the trees. They will be replaced and guaranteed to live, but there is a proper time for planting, and - we are told - it isn't now.

December 23.

TIME - Yep, it's that time again: Time to say thank you to the boys in the electric department for the long hours they spent changing thousands of bulbs to give us the attractive arches of light across Main instead of the usual hodgepodge of color, and also for again giving us the "Merry Christmas" sign in the Common. Thanks also to the many folks who took the trouble to set up outstanding outdoor displays for all of us to share with them. Thanks to the churches for the Christmas plays, and to the choirs for the beautiful carols which they let us share with them. Thanks also to the hundreds of citizens who shared their Christmas with the less fortunate in our state hospitals by contributing to Operation Santa Claus. Thanks from all go to the Jaycees and all who aided them with their annual Goodfellows project. Thanks to Russell Carter for giving us one of our best Christmas parades and to Bobbi Jean Collins for seeing to it that nearly all of our local beauties were riding the floats for all to see. And last but certainly not least, thanks to Joe Grayiel for again playing You-Know-Who to provide thrills for thousands of young folks.

1967

(January: The Roses store that replaced the Farrar Hotel is a new shopping experience. It is selling fishing equipment cheaper than local stores could purchase the same goods wholesale. It had deep implications.)

EARLY - Over a cup of coffee yesterday morning I commented that Roses certainly believed in modern merchandising since they already had Valentine candy on display. One wag in the crowd looked out the window and observed, "That ain't nothing. Tarboro already has its decorations up for next Christmas.

LITTER - One thing about a dusting of frozen stuff like we had yesterday, it doesn't cover everything with a "blanket of white." It just seems to emphasize the ugliness. Out of place things look even more so. Beer cans, abandoned cars and trash in general look even more out of place.

BACK - The most hated of all birds are back - the grackles, cow birds, starlings and all the other black robbers. Last Sunday afternoon between 4:15 and 5:20 they swarmed over Tarboro in what seemed to be an almost black river against the clear blue sky.

From west to east they flew toward their roost, the stream flickering out only as twilight came.

Monday I talked with Extension Service folks about the black birds and was told that in addition to being pests, they spread disease among cattle and eat up an unbelievable amount of grain around feed lots.

SCOUTS—This being National Boy Scout Week, the question arose this week as to who was Tarboro's first Eagle Scout.

The first person I remember as having been mentioned as an Eagle winner was Mr. Bill Mahler, but he won his long before moving to Tarboro. The first Tarboro boy I remember winning the highest honor was Frank Ballard, but I was a Johnny-Come-Lately on the local scouting scene. Herman Creech tossed out the opinion that perhaps the first local winner was Dan Iverson, or perhaps Tom Bass. He also thought perhaps Marvin Ruffin was an Eagle.

The discussion ended without the question being answered. Any help from readers would be appreciated.

MARCH - Well, we missed it again.

A couple of snows were predicted since this time last week, but I haven't heard anyone express regrets. While February is almost a memory, there still could be plenty of rough weather ahead.

Folks hereabouts still recall the blizzard which blew into this area on March 3, 1927. The night was warm when they went to bed, but when they awoke, the ground was covered by about three feet of the white stuff.

COMMON - Work has been underway for a couple of weeks on the annual beautification of the Town Common. Leaves remaining from autumn have been removed, the ground disced, fertilized and seeded. While they are about it, I wish the town would move those dogwood trees between the street and sidewalk. They have grown to a point where they screen the Common and Wyatt fountain is all but obscured.

Roses takes its toll. Bip can't compete with in the price wars.

BIP - Amazement, shock, disbelief, you name it. Those expressions and more were registered by local folks Monday when the "Going Out of Business" ad appeared over the signature of Martin's Home and Auto. That was the official name of the store but few people ever used it. They always referred to going to "Bip's."

Around the turn of the century there was a crowd gathered in the rear of Mr. Whit MacNair's drug store, calling themselves the "Sandpackers Club." Topics ranged from the events of the day, hunting, fishing and in the course of the discussions, some magnificent lies were told.

Bip provided the setting for latter-day gatherings of that type, especially in the days when his store was in the old Hotel Tarboro building. The cast of characters had changed, but the topics were the same - fishing the Tar, hunting the fields of old Edgecombe, what was doing in town and who had been caught at it. The lies told were just as big as those told by the Sandpackers.

From a business standpoint Bip was a pacesetter. He introduced aluminum boats to this area, and offered a line of motors which were to radically change the entire outboard industry:

The store was the birthplace of the present county wildlife club and because of the loving care and hard work of Bip and the ever-faithful Archie Eleanor, the club has prospered. Both men were instrumental in the development of the club's 12-acre pond.

I don't know Bip's plans for the future, but with the shad season here and the rock season fast approaching, a long vacation would seem to be the first order of business.

After all he has only had three days of vacation since 1946.

TAR—Thus far I have heard of only one rock being caught in the Tar. That one was landed by a man casting for shad last Saturday at the pumping station. Netters this week began catching large numbers of shad, particularly white shad. However, some rock action can be expected shortly, for the water temperature as of this morning was a warm 64 degrees.

The editor as television critic.

GO GO - The television "spectacular" this week, "World of Pleasure," featured motorcycle trash, bare-bosomed waitresses, naked bathers, LSD, kooks and other way-out fads had the most down-to-earth conglomeration of sponsors possible.

They included a couple of sleeping compounds, something for tired blood, something for bad breath, something for scaly skin, and a couple of denture fasteners. Only the inclusion of Preparation H could have made the list any earthier.

ADLER—Over on Church Street, Moore Lumber Company crews are rapidly renovating the old Royster office for a new store which will be operated by Irvin and Carol Adler. Named Irvin Adler Shoes, Inc., the store will specialize in women's and children's shoes, millinery and accessories. The building will be of Colonial design, in keeping with the theme set by Edgecombe Homestead and Loan Association.

Irvin says the new store will be opened in July.

FIRST—Several weeks ago this column wondered who had the honor of being the first Eagle Scout in Tarboro and expressed the thought that it was Frank Ballard. A note from Frank, who now lives in Orangeburg, S.C. confirms this. He had it in 1937.

ROSES—The rose is by far my favorite flower and for the past several years I have enjoyed stopping about once a week to look at the magnificent blossoms in the backyard of Mr. and Mrs. Harry Newsome. Last week I found a new stopping place. This one is at the home of Mr. and Mrs. Arthur Pharr on Middle Street. Their roses are some of the most beautiful I have ever had the pleasure of seeing.

The Pharr yard is certainly worth including on your Sunday afternoon drive around town.

JINX-Did you ever have a jinx that followed you?

Since the arrival of Daylight Saving Time a mockingbird has raised pluperfect hell with my early morning sleeping. He perches outside the bedroom window and mocks away for about 15 minutes - just long enough to awaken you to the point where you can't get back to sleep.

Last weekend we were the guests of friends at the beach and after sleeping until a welcomed 8:30, he and I were sipping coffee on the porch. I mentioned how nice it was to get away to a place populated only by such feathered creatures as gulls and terns. No mocking birds at the beach, I said. At that very moment what should land and strut sassily along the seawall but a mockingbird.

Main Street a long way from being dead.

STORES - The old town continues to improve. Irvin Adler's new shoe store on West Church is nearing completion-the glass front was installed yesterday-and he hopes to open before mid-July. An attractive new front is being installed on W.S. Clark and Sons men's store. Both these will be tremendously attractive to downtown Tarboro.

On the other end of town, Winn-Dixie is about ready to open for business in the Tarboro Shopping Center, and further out Bill Moore's new Edgecombe Drug Co. is fast taking shape adjacent to the clinic.

Churches, too, are expanding. The folks at the First Pentecostal Holiness Church hae already started adding to the sanctuary, and the contractor has set up the tool shack for the major expansion at St. James Methodist Church.

GARDENS-This is the season for "first" and "biggest" in the vegetable line. Sam Mayo had his first ripe tomato from his garden last week, and over at Marrow-Pitt Miss Mildred Worsley was displaying a cooked beet from her garden which weighed a pound and a half. She bragged that she had one at home which was even larger.

WEATHER—Dog days are almost upon us, but thus far summer has been unusually pleasant. Cool nights are the rule rather than the exception, and with only a few exceptions the days have been enjoyable, weatherwise.

The cool spring was recalled the other day when I was reading some of the Tarboro newspapers for 1849.

The issue for April 15, a Saturday, reported, "Pleasant weather for some two weeks back grew cold Saturday night and it was snowing Sunday morning . . New Bern paper reported eight inches by night . . . . the oldest inhabitant remembers snow as late as May 20, but nothing like the present severity . . . It extended south as far as Alabama.

Some issues just never become issues.

STREETS—Today's edition carries news of street name changes which will be proposed to the Town Council at its August meeting.

I doubt if it will be a world-shaking issue, arousing the ire of the populace, but I could be wrong. After all, I thought the Howard Avenue tree-cutting issue would bring howls of resentment.

It didn't.

I didn't think Councilman Lum Mayo's proposal to pen local pooches would create much interest, because it was a last-minute sort of thing.

It brought out a full house of irate citizens.

On the name changing proposal, I refuse to make a prediction. But I'm sure the service station people and the policemen will welcome the changes. They're the ones who have to direct visitors and sometimes have to answer, "You can't get there from here."

The proposal to change the name of Main Street to the original St. George Street is something I can live with. However, I sincerely hope the powers-that-be don't get uppity and try to return the town to its original Tarborough. The present spelling is easy to work into headlines, and besides the name of the town was changed to Tawboro back in the 1850's. That led to all kinds of problems. But that story will be told in a future "In Olde Edgecombe."

Late summer leaving its mark.

TIME—Have you noticed how the seasons have already begun changing?

The nocturnal insects have started singing lustily as if trying to give their all before the end of their brief life span.

Leaves have taken on a deep green tired look. Fruit is falling. Grapes are fast ripening. Kids are beginning to get apprehensive about the opening of school.

To put it mildly, this has been an odd summer. There have been few mornings when we awakened to find the sun shining. The fog or haze usually obscured the sun until around 9 a.m.

For the most part nights have been overcast, but not uncomfortably warm.

We are about midway through the hurricane season and strangely there haven't been as yet any reports of even a tropical depression.

Does all this point to an unusually cold winter?

STREETS—The proposal to change the name of a number of local streets holds the top spot on the agenda for Monday night's meeting of the Town Council. If you have any sentiments about it one way or the other, you'd better plan to attend.

Incidentally, the Planning Board has withdrawn its proposal for changing the name of Oakland Avenue. It will remain the same.

And just how hard did it rain?

RAIN—Last night's rain was the heaviest of the summer, dumping 3.38 inches on us by 7 a.m. There are a good many ways to describe such a downpour - sod soaker, frog strangler, gully washer, and trash mover. What happened last night was a combination of all.

Cliff Weeks brings by one of his 106-pound culls.

CLIFF—Mr. Cliff brought us a 106-pound watermelon this week and conceded that it would likely be the largest from his current crop since his vines had begun to fall. His nephew, Edward, is reported to have some melons in the 130-pound or better class.

Another small business bites the dust.

PATE—Some of the saddest business news of late comes with the announcement in today's edition of the closing of Miller's Food Store. Pate has been at his present location for the past 21 years and no nicer, more courteous gentleman can be found in our community. The closing will be deeply regretted by his many friends and customers whom he has served so well for so long.

Nothing could be finer than to be in ....

FALL - this week's northeast winds and last night's first frost brought the first real golden days of autumn.

For folks who complain of "nothing to do" on weekends, I'd like to suggest a Sunday afternoon family walk through the fields and woods of old Edgecombe. It can be an extremely pleasant experience.

Against a background of fall foliage, there are purple possum berries to be picked, rabbit tobacco to be stripped and crushed for its aroma which is peculiar to autumn. Big orange persimmons lie scattered under tall trees whose leaves are still deep green. Beech nuts, hickory nuts and walnuts are there for the taking. But best of all are the chinquapins—those delicious little burr-guarded nuts - which we use to gather by the bagful.

A bit of diligent searching in freshly harvested fields just may yield a few arrowheads or other artifacts of the Indians.

Yep, Sunday afternoons can be much more enjoyably spent at places other than in front of the television set.

SMOKES - The above mention of rabbit tobacco brings to mind old days when as boys we use to roll the stuff in strips of newspaper and smoke it. But rabbit tobacco wasn't the only material we utilized for smoking. Some preferred corn silk, and then there were those who liked stogies—Indian cigars—which we obtained from the catalpa trees in the Common. Others liked to puff away on dried grape vine.

Getting a last look at "old" Howard Avenue.

HOWARD—During the next couple of weeks the color in the oaks along Howard Avenue will be at its peak. Ride along Howard often and enjoy the color for the final time. More likely than not, the trees will be felled long before next autumn's frost and what is now a boulevard will have become a five-laned freeway.

Dog's best friend, a noble, loving man....

DOGS—Nearly every family in our neighborhood has a dog and they range from the purebred to just plain pooches. The aristocrat of the crowd is undoubtedly Pace, a handsome silver-gray Weimariner which has for 11 years been a member of the family of Rudy and Margaret Schaab. Once a day Pace would roam the neighborhood, showing either respect or disdain for dogs and cats alike before returning to her home.

Last Saturday night Pace was struck by a car and in a combination of pain and fright she disappeared. Neighbors joined the Schaabs in the search but it was fruitless. Rudy placed a classified ad in the paper, but admitted it was a last ditch effort.

Late yesterday afternoon the boys at the FCX called the paper to say they found a dog with an odd-colored coat limping along Albemarle Avenue. I went down, and sure enough, it was Pace. She obeyed all the commands and was stretched out on the floor when Rudy arrived.

Folks who say dogs can't talk should have been there for the reunion. Rudy called her name and Pace's tail began beating the floor like a trip hammer. She struggled to her feet, moaning and making other noises which can't be described as barking. Rudy expressed his thanks to those who found his dog. He didn't say much else.

He couldn't. And the fellows at the FCX didn't expect him to.

Before Medicare and Medicaid.

BILL—Of course, all prices have risen tremendously in the past 40 years, but it's still pleasant to recall prices which prevailed in bygone days. As an example, there's a 1925 Edgecombe Hospital bill which State Trooper Floyd Owens found recently. Mr. Willie Everett was billed for seven days at $3 per day, an operating room fee of $15 and a lab fee of $3 for a total of $41.

Incidentally, there was an extra charge for the use of the electric fan.

Santa Claus is coming to town.....later.

DECORATIONS—Christmas decorations went up along Main this week but the town is exercising some measure of restraint and will not light them until the night after Thanksgiving. For small favors we are thankful.

Parking needs brushes history aside.

HOUSE—Beginning Monday, another of the town's old homes will be demolished. This time it's the home of Mrs. D.D. Taylor on East Church-a house which dates back into the 18th century. The demolition work will be done by J.H. Fortson of Wilson, the man who tore down the old hotel and the courthouse. All of the material will be offered for sale. When cleared the lot will be used for Carolina Telephone parking.

HAWK—In North Carolina, all hawks are protected by law. And that's causing considerable concern for the fellows up at James Taylor's service station. It seems that for the past couple of days a big hawk has been feasting on the squirrels in the Town Common, and there is apparently nothing the friends of the squirrels can do except keep a watchful eye and chase the bird away as he swoops down on the little animals.

WEATHER—All summer Ramblin commented on all the signs pointing to a cold - extremely cold winter. The mornings were foggy, the nights overcast, and a couple of record low temperatures were recorded in July.

It would seem the prediction has already become a reality, for this morning Joe Overshoes said that the November just ended was the second coldest on record. Freezing or below temperatures were recorded on at least half of the nights last month. Several people have said their camellia buds have already been killed by the cold.

And the official arrival of winter is still three weeks away.

1968

The year opens with a postal rate increase.

STAMPS—To sell the obsolete five-cent stamps the Post Office needs to produce an extra one billion penny stamps. To enact the new postal increases and to change stamp machines, the department will have to spend 22 million dollars. The increased rates won't mean any better service since most of it will go for pay increases to postal employees.

And the Great Society rolls on.

BUILDING—It was a simple ceremony which marked the beginning of construction of the new telephone building this week, but actually it was an historic occasion for this old town. It is hard to believe, but the three tallest buildings in town - the Masonic temple, the "original" telephone building and the Bridgers building - were all constructed more than 50 years ago.

On Ground Hogs.

SHADOW—For those interested in such things, the groundhog couldn't see his shadow this morning. Everyone knows this means we'll have an early spring. But don't take any bets on it.

At any rate the weather this week has been unusually pleasant. Sam Mayo reported that his bees became active, making numerous trips from the hive. But what on earth is blooming at this time of the year other than camellias?

STRIKE—For the first time since the infamous Hart Mill strike 15of the late 1940s, pickets made an appearance here this week. Several showed up briefly at the depot soon after the Seaboard was struck. All was quiet, of course, but somehow it made me shudder.

RAISE—The town's hard working garbage collectors have been given a raise. On February 1 they were increased to a minimum of $1.41 an hour. Other upward adjustments were made in the fire and street departments.

And the shad report.

SHAD—First reports of hickory shad being caught on rod and reel came from the Old Sparta area this week.

With a warm weekend currently being predicted some should be caught in Fishing Creek.

Still a proud Marine.

IWO—I, along with about a half-dozen others in Tarboro, have a personal interest in an eight-square-mile place of Pacific real estate called Iwo Jima. Back in February and March of 1945 22,000 Japanese and 5,000 Marines died there in what was one of the bloodiest battles of the war.

A short AP news item today noted that next month the U.S. State Department will give the island back to the Japanese. The transfer will mean the hauling down of the American flag from Mount Suribachi, where the raising of the Stars and Stripes by a group of Leathernecks from the 28th Regiment was recorded as the war's most famous combat photograph.

Garbage report in early spring.

DUMP—The town garbage dump, known in municipal circles as the "sanitary landfill" and among those familiar with it as a "municipal disgrace" has been improved considerably since the last meeting of the Town Council. The scavengers who were outlawed by the council were still active last weekend, but for the first time in years, it appeared that the town was at least making some effort to maintain the place as a landfill rather than a dump.

REMINDER—The U.S.S. Pueblo and 83 Americans were seized by North Korea 66 days ago.

And the Great Society rolls on.

Local boy insults Kennedy.

TAYLOR—Former Tarborean Roland Taylor, son of Mr. and Mrs. Sam Taylor, made national news last week. Rollo is editor and publisher of the Welch, W. Va. Daily News and when he learned that Bobby Kennedy was planning a surprise visit to Welch he wrote a front page editorial which stated:

"THAT'S WHAT BOBBY IS: Uninvited, Unwanted, Undesirable, Unethical, Un-American, Unfit, Unprepared, Unshorn, Unpopular, Unloved, and Over Rated."

Because the editorial and the shaggy senator's remarks about it appeared on network television, Rollo has received hundreds of letters from practically every state in the nation. From the ones I've read, it would seem the majority of the writers agree with the editor.

One fellow wrote, "Please send me two copies of your Bobby Kennedy editorial; one of which will be hung on my living room wall and the other to show friends.

Primary results.

DEFEAT—The darkest spot in the election to us was the defeat of Vinson Bridgers by the overwhelming vote for Vernon White in his home county of Pitt. In what records I have been able to check, the next two years will be the first in our history that an Edgecombe man has not been in the State Senate. And the blame lies in the apathy of Edgecombe "citizens" who did not vote in the primary. To some extent, I believe the blame lies with those who did vote, but didn't take the time to see whether our friends and neighbors had fulfilled their obligation of citizenship. As a first-term senator, Vinson Bridgers did a creditable job, not only for Edgecombe, but for the other three counties of his district. We hope he has another opportunity to serve again in the years ahead.

What voter discrimination?

SLANDER - How long will our officials continue without protest to let federal bureaucrats slander old Edgecombe? That is a question which deserves answering and the sooner the better. The first case was a couple of years ago when we were placed under some sort of voter registration regulation because of alleged discrimination in registering. This action came despite the fact there was not and is not a single case of any discrimination or intimidation involving registration in the entire county. If any protest was aired, I don't recall it and if any effort has been made to have Edgecombe removed from such regulations, it also has escaped me. The latest slander on Edgecombe by bureaucrats is even more damning. Some Great Society hack included Edgecombe in a list of "starvation" counties which makes year-round distribution of free food mandatory.

TREES - It appears that this year is going to be one of the best in a long, long time for fruit trees. While the season is still young, folks report their trees are already groaning under bumper loads of apples, peaches, cherries, plums and pears.

THANKS - The citizens owe a standing ovation to Chairman George Britt, members of the Historical Commission and the Historical Society for their outstanding work in securing a suitable house for a small county museum. At present the structure is a terrible looking thing, wrapped in fake brick tar paper and minus its chimneys. However, restoration plans are already well underway and when the work is completed the early Edgecombe house will be something of which we can all be proud.

No demands to close schools for Bobby Kennedy.

IRONIC - We heard no wise guy remarks Thursday morning after the horrible, tragic and useless death of Robert Kennedy.

There was only sober reflection over the conditions which led to the second time in as many months that a public figure was shot down like a dog.

The various movements afoot in this country, aided and abetted by the Supreme Court, have created an atmosphere conducive to violence. The expression "If you don't like a law, it's all right to break it," has become more than a slogan - it's now accepted as gospel.

Robert Francis Kennedy was probably the best white friend the colored people of this nation have ever had. Yet on the day of his death there was not a single request or demand that schools be dismissed, stores closed or special memorial services be held.

This would certainly seem to completely refute the frequent charge that only the whites are bigoted and "race-oriented."

The friends of Ralph Caldwell.

SERIES - In speaking of the series, Mike's dad, Ralph, will be in stands in Omaha for the opening game. He is going through the goodness of his many friends and he certainly has a host of them.

It all started earlier this week when up at Long's Bill Dupree, Jr. got the idea. He passed the world around the plant (Ralph also works there) and the dollars and dimes began to pour in. A cigar box on the counter at Paul Noble's service station was quickly filled.

As a result Ralph now has a round trip ticket to Omaha and motel reservations, and all because Bill Dupree had an idea and because Ralph Caldwell has more friends than he ever dreamed of.

Summer doldrums brings out horse talk.

HORSES—Somehow the conversation shifted to horses one day this week—not the kind you see at the horse shows, but the kind that were an important part of Tarboro's everyday life not too many years ago.

Almost everyone in the crowd recalled the days when Mr. Wynn drove the milk wagon, pulled by a stalwart animal who didn't need the tug of reins to tell him when to start or stop in making the rounds from house-to-house. A check with the town's senior employee—Luke Sheffield—failed to disclose the name of the horse. However, Luke recalled that Mr. Wynn was last man to drive the town's horse-drawn milk wagon. He also remembered that Sherman and Claude Winchester were probably the first to drive milk wagons when the municipal plant first opened.

Luke and Henry Leggett drove the wagons in the early 1920s.

Another famous horse-driver team was the ice wagon. James Davis, that cheerful, beloved colored man with the unforgettable laugh, had only to whistle at his horse to have him move from house-to-house while James ambled along the sidewalk. James was the town's best-known ice man from the pre-World War I days until shortly before his death in the 1950s. During the summer, his wagon and later his truck, were constantly followed by crowds of small boys who clamored for shavings or chips of ice. James always obliged and probably gave away as much ice as he sold on hot days.

Another well-known team was jovial George Worsley and Mr. DeBerry's vegetable wagon which was an important part of Tarboro's summer months. George would drive his horse slowly around town ringing a bell whose sound was as familiar as the town clock.

Housewives who could hear the bell a block away would be waiting on the curb when George arrived.

Equally well-known but little mentioned was the "honey wagon" which was driven by Jule Barrett. In the days before widespread indoor sanitation facilities, Jule and his tank wagon provided an indispensable municipal function. Because of the nature of his work. Jule was the highest paid wagon driver on the town's payroll. He received $23 a week, compared to $12 for the others.

The site of the town's stables is the present location of an electrical substation, but the stables still exist. When the town went out of the horse business, the stable was purchased by Pug Bass, dismantled and taken to his farm where it was reconstructed.

Horse's name was "Pete"

HORSE—Last week's column about the town horses of years back caused Sam Register to recall the name of the milk wagon horse was Pete, and he said that Forrest Register, not Mr. Wynn was the last driver of the horse-drawn wagon.

Cotton blossom time.

BLOSSOM—The race this year to see who could get the first cotton blossoms was the closest in many years. The first blossom, which came from C.T. Meeks, reached the office at 8:30 a.m., and one of the girls remarked:

"I'll bet Jack Tripp and Jodie Edmondson are in here before the day is over."

Sure enough, Mr. Tripp arrived a couple of hours later. But not with a cotton blossom. He came in to renew his subscription. About an hour later after that, Mr. Edmondson came in with a blossom, and before the day ended, Bill Eason called to say that he also had found a blossom.

More important than the mayor.

GARBAGE - The brief walkout by local garbage men last weekend caused one man to say he thought they were already making enough money because some of them "can't even read or write."

I'm strongly of the opinion that literacy has nothing to do with the matter. We can get along without the mayor, the town council, the town manager, or any department head for 30 days or more, but how would you like to have to get along without the services of your garbage man for that long?

The importance of the collectors is made even more meaningful because this is the time of year when cans are brim-full of corn husks, cucumber peels, butterbean hulls and watermelon rinds.

~

RECORD—Cliff Weeks has broken his own record as a grower of giant watermelons. His previous big one weighed 117 pounds and yesterday he brought *The Southerner* folks one which tipped the scales at 105 pounds, announcing that it was the largest he would grow this year.

This morning, Mr. Cliff said he checked his patch and found one which weighed 125. "That's the biggest one I've ever grown," he said.

~

DELEGATE—Bill Clark, III, leaves Sunday for Chicago where he will be a delegate to the Democratic Convention. I don't envy him a bit. It is heart-breaking to think that this nation has disintegrated to the point where those charged with the responsibility of nominating a presidential candidate must meet within the confines of barbed wire, guarded by police and troops.

C.B. - Announcement that C.B. Martin has resigned as superintendent of both the town and county school systems comes as a numbing shock. He is recognized as one of the best school men in the state and has up-graded our systems tremendously during the time he has spent here. We regret to see him leave, particularly at a time when a merger of the two systems is under study and when the town system is under a threat from HEW. However, we wouldn't blame him for getting out of the education business even if his new job paid only $10 a week. Constant harassment of federal officials more interested in integration than education have shortened the life of more than one school administrator who acted in good faith, thinking only of the future of children and the wishes of parents, regardless of color.

Colonial Theater gets another breath of life.

COLONIAL—In less than a week the Colonial will reopen and it is unbelievable just how much Roy Champion has done to the old building. "Splendid" is perhaps the best way to describe the beautiful interior, from the lobby to the screen. It is sincerely hoped that the faith Roy has in the potential moviegoers in Tarboro is justified.

September Tribute To Martin.

C.B.—After attending several events honoring C.B. Martin this week, a man said, "Well, it looks like we've given him everything except a halo!" To which another answered, "C.B. won one of those on his own a long time ago."

Defending the new museum.

MUSEUM—The Historical Society folks are pointing with pride to the old house now awaiting repairs on the community house lot. To all the doubting Thomases we say "Keep the faith." Visualize what it will be when the underpinnings are back, the white weatherboard is in place and the roof shingled, blinds, doors and windows are properly hung. In the meanwhile, society members are asking citizens to consider giving or loaning the society any pre-Civil War treasures they may have for display in the museum when it is complete.

The house is an excellent example of early 19th Century architecture in Edgecombe. After all, this old county had very few houses which could be called mansions and what we had were built before the Civil War after cotton became king. There were darn - few magnolias here, scarcely a trace of Spanish moss and it was corn whisky and water, not juleps, which was sipped at bullbat time.

Dilapidated house of today, my friends, qualified the Historical Society (for museum) for $12,000 under the terms of the will of the late Miss Katherine Pender.

Keep the faith.

More surveys.

SURVEY—Readers have only today and next Saturday to contend with the great bumper sticker poll. This week's survey disclosed two pickup trucks without the customary Wallace stickers. One of them had sideboards which bore the neatly-lettered proclamation, "I'm For Hubert Humphrey and Bob Scott." The other had no signs at all. It was driven by a colored gentleman. An increasing number of Humphrey stickers was noted during the week, but none of them were on pickup trucks. And in the municipal parking lot, one car carried two stickers on the rear bumper. The top sticker said, "Jesus Saves." Directly below it was "Nixon-Agnew."

In other political doings this week, one wag said the Democrats went too far when they got Jackie to marry Onassis in an effort to lure the Greek vote away from Spiro Agnew.

One bigoted vote for Wallace.

VOTING—It was an established fact throughout the county Tuesday that while the white folks split their ticket, the colored folks went down the line for the Democrats. In Rocky Mount's all-Negro Precinct 4, Humphrey got 1,418 votes. Somehow five votes were dropped in for Nixon. Apparently the single vote cast there for George Wallace was placed in the box by a Negro bigot.

RUSSELL—Again we thank Russell Carter for the splendid job he did once again in staging the annual Christmas parade. Until Russell (then aided by the Lions Club) took charge of the parade, they were pretty much rag-tag affairs. One year the parade included two Santas, much to the confusion of the younger folk. Those days are now gone, thank goodness, and Tarboro's parade would be a credit to any town.

Last flap of 1968.

VISIT—While riding around town last Sunday, Mrs. Oscar Page noticed a car and camper with Michigan plates circling around the Common. She stopped and asked if she could be of assistance. The Michigan man explained that he was trying to find the Civil War cannonballs which were supposed to be embedded in concrete and displayed there. Mrs. Page allowed as how she knew nothing about any cannonballs on the Common.

The gentleman, a Mr. Brooks (or was it Mr. Shaw), explained that he was an owner of the Brooks and Shaw Construction Company which installed the natural gas system here in the 1950s. He said some of his crew unearthed the cannonballs near the Coca Cola plant. Town officials confiscated the find, and the man said he still had a letter pledging that the town would embed the balls in concrete and place them on the Common.

He was upset that the promise had not been kept, for he had detoured on his trip from Michigan to Florida just to show the relics to his family.

In an effort to find out why the town had not kept its word and what had happened to the cannonballs, I called Ruth Ballard at the town hall. Ruth said the relics are in the community house and will be kept there until the Historical Society museum is completed. They will then be placed on display there for all to see.

1969

Flu exposes daytime television.

FLU—So you've got the flu. Welcome to the club. This season it is about as exclusive as a public school under a federal court order. The fever, the chills, the assorted aches reduce all of us to the lower common denominator, and to make matters ever worse, there is daytime television. If you think nighttime television is bad, you just wouldn't believe what goes on along the soap opera circuit. Some of the doings make Peyton Place pale by comparison. On a noon show there is a pregnant teen-ager who is about to put the finger on the school principal, although he's as pure as the driven snow. On the same show a dowager is attempting to lure to her millionaire son, the sexy but brainless wife of a struggling young student.

This week was the first time in eight years that I watched two straight episodes of "As the World Turns." In fact, the last time I saw it Ellen had just married Dr. Stewart, who had adopted her illegitimate son. In those days, the wood's colt was just starting elementary school. This week I discovered the kid had become a doctor (just like his real dad), but still didn't know he was a bastard. That is, at least, until on Tuesday an evil M.D. told him in no uncertain terms what he was and who his mama was. That's right strong stuff.

Even stronger, however, are the daytime commercials. Somehow, the Preparation H commercial seemed to come at the same time I sat down to eat. This was usually followed by some woman who tells a poll-taken that she prefers "the milk-type" laxative over the oil or candy kinds.

And if that wasn't bad enough, then along comes a fellow who says, "You've probably never seen this before." This is a picture of excess fat in the lower intestinal tract. Probably?? Darned few folks outside the doctors and nurses of the community have seen that particular type of "excess fat" and I doubt they do it as a hobby.

Equally obnoxious are the "anti-perspirant" commercials. In the past the hitch has been aimed at armpit musk. But now they have gone even further and offers something which "guards against wetness."

Another bright, patriotic Tarboro man gives his life in Vietnam.

VIETNAM—The name of Lt. Hugh E. Best, III, is now on the list of the more than 31,000 Americans boys who have been sacrificed in Vietnam. Butch was only an eighth grader when the leaders of this nation committed to "defending Southeast Asia against Communist aggression." And in Paris, the diplomats continue to sip tea after bickering for months before reaching a decision on the shape of a conference table.

The most meaningful Christmas card our family received last year came from Butch. It was only the end of a cardboard K ration container on which was scrawled, "Merry Christmas and Happy New Year." But it made us recall other Christmases spent on alien soil when we, like our fathers before us, fought what we believed to be a war to end all wars.

Butch Best was a member of a patriotic family in town from the standpoint of military service. During World War II, his father served as a B-26 pilot in the Air Corps. His grandfather was in the Navy and served in the Fleet Post Office at Norfolk, and his grandmother was in the Woman's Army Corps.

Shad nets—the sign of spring.

SIGNS—While we've been extremely lucky in missing out on icy weather thus far this winter, the law of averages would indicate that our luck cannot hold.

However, there were some encouraging signs of the season ahead in town this past week.

Jonquil spikes have pushed through the frozen earth, and in some yards crocuses are already blooming. The robins arrived in numbers during the past ten days, and despite overcast skies and frigid winds, a number of kites were being flown over town last weekend.

The surest sign of approaching spring, however, came not from nature, but from our friend, James Plemmer. He has already purchased his shad netting.

JAIL—Someone told me they read this week that the state is outlawing the serving of fatback in Tar Heel jails, claiming the inmates should be served more "red meat."

That's a dirty shame. The quality of the fatback served in the county lockup is the finest in the nation. While I don't recommend it as a steady diet, there is something heavenly about the crisp fatback and hot cornbread as served by Jailer Gil Hollis.

The occasional patrons of jailhouse cookery should demonstrate.

Howard Avenue trees get yet another reprieve.

HOWARD—The Howard Avenue trees will live to see another spring, and very possibly, another fall. There is no money available. It seems the state bonds earmarked for the project can't be sold because of the current interest situation. So, the folks along Howard have their town-provided new water and sewer lines and the street has its muddy-now, dusty-later, shoulders.

SPRING—God gave us a perfect day of spring yesterday. Wiping away the gray of a very cold winter, we looked around and suddenly noticed our First Breath of Spring bush had been blossoming for several days, the Japonica by the front door was magically more open that which was brought in-doors to be "forced" a week ago.

Finally the DDT alarm went off.

DDT—Not too many years ago a few local citizens became concerned over the county health department's use of DDT in the insect control program. They contended the chemical harmed more than just mosquitoes. The health officer declared there wasn't anything wrong with the use of the insecticide, and he even called in a state health official who backed him completely. The use of DDT continued through last year. But this year, it's a different story.

The DDT is being replaced at the "suggestion" of the State Board of Health. The insecticide now used is a combination of malathion and lethane which dissipates and breaks down more rapidly than DDT.

ROCK—Where, oh, where did the rockfish go? That's a question members of the Wildlife Club are asking, but they aren't getting any answers. In the days when the Tar was polluted and choked with log jams, rock were plentiful. Then we built sewage disposal plants and snagged the river from the falls to Greenville. Then came Texas Gulf Sulphur. Then the rock left. Questions have been asked of the Wildlife Resources Commission, but the answers given aren't too satisfactory.

Pump jockey.

TAYLOR—Roland Taylor, son of Mr. and Mrs. Sam Taylor of Tarboro, is the president of a new West Virginia corporation. Since 1963 Roland has been editor and publisher of the Welch, W. Va. Daily News, and has now purchased the West Virginia Daily News which is published in Lewisburg and serves Lewisburg and the White Sulphur Springs area of Greenbrier County. The new corporation will publish both the Welch and Lewisburg papers.

I'm getting old. I can remember when Rollo pumped gas for Murphy-Jenkins.

Cronkite and the moon flight.

TV—Throughout the journey of Apollo 11 I have been about as impressed by the stamina of Walter Cronkite as that of the three-man crew. It took a most unusual person to sit before an audience of millions, talking almost constantly, but never becoming boring. We watched the Huntley-Brinkley only briefly before becoming more convinced than ever that the pair can be impressed by nothing, except themselves.

The remainder of our viewing was via Channel 9.

Sworn at.

BILL—We appreciate Gov. Bob Scott's appointment of Bill Clark to the State Highway Commission, and we commend Bill for accepting it. After all, it is one of the toughest jobs in state government since everybody wants some asphalt on his particular road, and countless arguments are constantly offered as to why one road should have higher priority than another.

About the best advice Bill has been offered thus far came from the man who said, "Get yourself an unlisted telephone number."

Wednesday Bill was sworn in. From now on he's going to be sworn at.

True recreation.

MEMORIES—Somehow the conversation got around to "recreation", today and all yesterday. Recreation hereabouts is a big thing today. And it's organized. One could say it's regimented. The kids are uniformed, coached and criticized. Parents are expected to become avid fans. The big thing is to win. I'm in no way critical of our recreation program. But my mind wanders to the days of the 30's. Even if the people wanted an organized recreation program, there was no money for it. But we didn't mope around the house complaining about "nothing to do".

There was an uptown gang, a downtown gang, a Runnymede gang, a West Tarboro gang, a Hart Mill gang and an East Tarboro gang.

There was an integrated baseball game every summer day on the grounds of the low school. And you became a big boy when you could knock the ball from home plate by the persimmon tree over the telephone line on the Common side of St. Patrick St.

A common meeting ground for all the gangs was Hendrick's Creek, even after the WPA crews finished building the swimming pool. There was just something about plunging stark naked into the deep hole back of Keechtown. The creek water was always cooler than the pool even though Tarboro has "The Only Refrigerated Swimming Pool in the United States". On more than one occasion we emerged from the creek in hues of red, blue, green, purple or yellow, depending upon what type of dye Runnymede was dumping that day.

When we tired of baseball or swimming, the chicken yard (nearly everybody had a chicken yard) provided a plentiful supply of worms. And it seemed that the perch and catfish would always bite where Hendrick's Creek entered the river. Whether they bit or not didn't really matter, for someone in the crowd usually had purchased a cigarette for a penny from the downtown D.P. Store. We'd pass around the butt, taking puffs and talking big.

On the way home there was always the possibility of jumping into the boxcar of a slow-moving freight at the cotton yard and riding it to the depot. There was the laziest of all summer pastimes—fishing for a doodle bug. For the unenlightened, this consisted finding a doodle bug colony, usually in dry sandy soil. All the equipment needed was a piece of pine straw and glob of spit. The latter was placed on the former and then the former was inserted into the doodle bug's hole. The first boy to catch a bug was declared winner and we didn't care if it took 15 minutes or even longer for a bug to bite. In those days, time was of no consequence.

Saturday was a very special day. For a dime you could go to the Colonial at 2 p.m. and stay until 11 o'clock if your folks would let you. There was the granite-jawed Buck Jones, who always rode a huge white horse; Ken Maynard, who always wore a hug white hat; Tim McCoy, who always wore a huge black hat; Hoot Gibson, the homeliest cowboy on the silver screen; there was Johnny Mack Brown, the cowboy with the Southern drawl; Bob Steele, who wore black gloves, but still looked like a sissy; and lastly, there was the greatest of them all, Tom Mix.

There was none of the violence so prevalent in the Westerns of today. In fact, today's Westerns are usually rated for mature audiences or as being unsuitable for anyone under 21. In the 30's the horse was the only critter that got kissed.

On the way home there was always the opportunity to knock out a street light and we knew that we could run faster than Police Chief Berry Lewis, Jack Spruill, Mark Ruffin, Jesse Martin or Reddin Pittman. But no one ever knocked out a street light in his own neighborhood. The street light which dangled over the intersection was the neighborhood recreation center on hot summer nights. It seems "kick-the-can" was one of the nightly favorites.

Summer in the 30's, and the living was easy. And un-organized.

Men from the moon.

APOLLO—In watching and listening to those three matchless moonmen in New York, Chicago, and at the banquet in Los Angeles, I could not help but wonder if the 24 billion tag wasn't a cheap price to pay. It took a year and 24 billion bucks and a trip to the moon to do it, but at last the good guys had their day. All across the country there was a feeling of fellowship, a renewed respect for the flag, a sense of rededication.

On Wednesday, the majority ruled. And it was about time.

Little town—big town.

CITY—Tarboro is basically a country town. A mama wood duck raised a brood of six ducklings at one end of the Common this spring, and a covey of quail hatched out at the other end. A couple of times a year someone reports finding a possum in a garbage can. But if town officials have anything to do with it and if one-way streets are any indication, we are fast on our way to becoming a city. The one-way streets, we are told, "will end downtown traffic congestion." That, I don't quite understand. The merchants do their darndest to get folks on Main Street, and the town does its best to get them off.

About the only time I notice any real congestion on Main is when the telephone company lets out, and on Friday afternoons when the eagle flies at local industries.

A measly 99 pounder?

MELON—Thanks to Mr. and Mrs. Cliff Weeks for sending the office crowd a 99 pound watermelon. We cut it last Friday and it was enjoyed by all.

MUSEUM—The Pender Museum is virtually completed, and the big job now is finding suitable furnishings and items for display in time for the October dedication. Noting the $27,400 price tag, one wag termed the restoration, "the most expensive tenant house remodeling job ever done in Edgecombe."

MISSING—This column has been missing for the past couple of weeks, mainly, I suppose, because of frustrations.

Local news was at a premium when the computer broke down. A repairman came from High Point, fixed it, left, and couldn't have gotten further away than Belvedere when something else went wrong. Two more were called. They worked on it all day and night Friday and Saturday (including a two-hour phone call to St. Louis). Work on the machine continued Sunday and by Monday the thing was gutted. Late Monday the cause of the trouble—a dead power transistor was found. Since then, the computer has been blinking and printing enough for us to get a fairly decent paper out, but it still keeps us on edge.

HISTORIAN—Kelly Turner, who died this week, was the only man to have written a history of Edgecombe County. The vast majority of his research was done while he was a student at Duke University. Other material came from the files of Col. John L. Bridgers, who shares with Turner authorship of the volume.

When he lived in Speed, I talked with Mr. Turner frequently about Edgecombe history and he once said, "There's an old trunk upstairs that I'm going to let you dig through one day. It's full of Edgecombe history, including some that I haven't showed anyone in a long, long time."

I asked for an explanation and he continued, "I call it forbidden history. It's stuff I found about some of the county's so-called great men of yesterday, who actually weren't great at all."

He wouldn't elaborate, and he never did get around to letting me dig through the old trunk. However, I hope some of the powers that be in the Historical Society make an attempt to see this material - if it still exists - isn't thrown away.

We'll never know how much in the way of historical interest has been lost to us by way of the trash pile.

A nation divided: the other side of Vietnam protests.

MORATORIUM—This is the weekend when thousands of Americans will give more aid and comfort to the enemy than Benedict Arnold ever thought of doing. They'll march (and likely riot) and read the names of the many Americans who have given their lies in Southeast Asia.

Out in Las Vegas last month the father of 18 year old PFC Gregory M. Thompson, who was killed in Vietnam, wrote his newspaper taking issue with the peace demonstrators who have been reading the names of war dead in public places.

Here are this father's words:

"When the peace demonstrators read my son's name, let them know how he felt about the Vietnam war and how the parents who shaped him felt about it.

"It is we, the parents, who wrote long, anxious letters to him during his three months almost continuous combat—not the agitators.

"It is the ones who saw his body returned in a flag-draped coffin who first should be heard—not the protestors.

"These transparent propagandists were not there to see my son buried, nor do they accompany me on my trips to lay flowers on his grave.

"My son was killed while fighting for his country.

"America cannot be permitted to perpetually persuade its citizens to instill in their sons a sense of patriotism, loyalty and a determination to defend the oppressed and then, after the sons have died, suddenly change her mind and yield to those who killed them.

"Most of the peace demonstrations and name-reading ceremonies across the nation are an obvious propaganda device designed to influence the President of the United States into surrendering South Vietnam to an enemy which admittedly and openly seeks to conquer it by any and all means.

"When they read my son's name to advocate peace at any price—the price being defeat—let them remember that he whose name they read did not surrender.

"When these pretentious mourners read my son's name, let them realize that their grief would be better served if applied to the Viet Cong whose flag they wave even as they burn the one which graced my son's casket. Let them apply their bogus sorrow to those aggressors felled by my son as he won his posthumous Silver Star for heroism in combat.

"And when they read the name of my son, let them know that he advocated an increase in the bombing of the ammunition depots in North Vietnam—not a cessation so that his enemy would receive unlimited war supplied with which to kill him.

"Whey they read the name of Gregory Malcolm Thompson, let them realize that they are proving before the world the truth of the oft-repeated Communists claim that many Americans have become soft, decadent and yielding to any determined force which opposes them.

"And when the weak, gullible ones read his name in their avowed pursuit of peace, let them remember that a peace purchased at the price of surrender is but a brief Munich-type peace lasting only until the aggressor's appetite demands more victims.

"Finally when these hypocrites read the list of the dead who defended South Vietnam, let them know that they have reached the ultimate low in the world record of human infamy, in that they willingly and cunningly utter a dead man's name to achieve the defeat of the cause for which he died."

A response the following week.

CALL—Last week's column quoted the father's objection to the "peace" marcher's using the name of his dead soldier son. Friday night my telephone rang and a voice said, "My wife and I just want to say thank you for publishing what you did in tonight's paper. We don't like to think of that crowd of people using our son's name, either."

Their son was the first from Edgecombe to give his life in the Vietnam War.

1970

(Entering the new decade, Tarboro was blessed with rapid industrial expansion and growth. The drug problems of the permissive sizzling '60's lurked in the background but had not been addressed openly by Ramblin'. Watergate, Nixon's resignation and Jimmy Carter lay ahead. In the meantime, it was business and politics as usual and Tarboro's Gene Simmons was almost always in the political picture.)

GENE—Bob Scott did a good day's work when he named Gene Simmons as state chairman of the Democratic Party. I suppose Gene has as many friends and knows as many people as any man in the state. He has magnetic personality and a gift of gab which has served him well since he won his first oratorical contest while in high school.

Helping Princeville pass the hat for a new fire truck.

TRUCK—The Princeville Fire Department will soon launch a campaign to raise funds for a new fire truck, and the campaign will be an important one for many citizens of our county. The Princeville truck's vintage dates back to the 1940s and it is costly to operate as well as undependable. Yet the Princeville volunteers have accepted the responsibility of answering fire calls for a wide area of the county. This responsibility was shouldered when Tarboro stopped answering out-of-town calls except on a mutual aid basis. Technically, this means the Princeville department must get to a fire, determine they cannot handle it alone, then call other departments for aid. Thus, precious time is lost.

Leggett, a relatively prosperous community began making plans for a fire department before the Princeville volunteers organized. Yet, Leggett still has no fire trucks and in the event of fire, it's Princeville that is called and responds. In fact, a couple of years ago the motor on the Princeville truck burned out while it was answering a call to Leggett.

A lot more people than those living in Princeville lean heavily on that community when it comes to fire protection. That's surely something to keep in mind when the hat is passed.

After all, a new fire truck costs about $18,000!

Banana pudding mystery solved.

BANANAS—In case you're wondering why banana pudding has been on the menu at Roses so much recently . . . they ordered 30 bananas and the wholesaler delivered 30 pounds.

In February, the ugly news of drugs is in the open.

POT—Discovery in a local home this week of a package containing a large number of marijuana didn't surprise this writer as much as it would have a week ago. During a casual conservation over coffee, a friend remarked that his minister was currently counseling three local teenagers who had drug problems. Since then, I have heard that another local minister is also involved in such counseling in his church.

I have also been told by several young people that marijuana is relatively easy to get at Tarboro High, and the going price is 50 cents per cigarette. Other drugs are also said to be available if you know the right person.

As the years passed, Ramblin's revisited the hell of Iwo more often. This was the 25th anniversary.

MEMORIES—I don't usually have dreams, but at this time of the year, I can generally count on a couple of nightmares. Responsible for them is a four-week hell on earth which began 25 years ago on a God-forsaken place of real estate called Iwo Jima. There are others around town who probably also have bitter memories of the place—among them Vinson Bridgers, Albert Walker and Lawrence Morris.

You try to forget, but you can't.

There was "Manila John" Basilone, leader of a machine gun platoon in the 28th Marines. He was killed by shrapnel within hours of landing. Holder of the Congressional Medal of Honor for extreme heroism in the Solomons campaign, Basilone didn't have to make the landing. Because he was a hero, the Marine Corps public relations boys tried to get him to stay in the States and appear on band tours. He wanted to get back to where the action was.

He did. And he died.

There was the "old man" of the company—a 36-year-old private who was practically decapitated by a mortar the first night. He left a wife and four kids.

There was the 18-year-old Italian who, at our first mail call, received a letter telling him the girl to whom he was engaged had been killed when a water heater exploded. An ammunitions carrier in an artillery battery, he asked and was granted permission to join a casualty-shattered infantry company of the 27th Marines. There he volunteered for the dangerous job of flame thrower man. He got four pillboxes before they got him. Those who saw it called it the bravest thing they had ever seen.

Those of us who knew about the letter called it suicide.

Then there was a young corporal—member of a forward observation team—who lay pinned down by crossfire for three hours with the body of his sergeant and best friend before he could be rescued. He didn't speak to anyone for three days. And it was weeks before he smiled again.

There were these and there were thousands of others a quarter of a century ago on a black volcanic island in the Pacific.

But at this time of year, it screamingly seems like only yesterday.

ECLIPSE—Next Saturday March 7 is the day of the total eclipse in this area. It hasn't happened in the Tar Heel State since May 28, 1900, and there won't be another one visible in our area for the remainder of this century. We'll have more about it next week, but under no circumstances should anyone even peek at the sun during the eclipse without taking special precautions.

Move is on to restore the old cotton press.

PRESS—More than one citizen has wondered aloud just how long it will be before the town or some interested group will take steps to restore the old cotton press in the Common. After all, well over $20,000 was spent to completely re-build a little house described as "typical of the early f19th century in Edgecombe". The old press is something which was unique in Edgecombe in the 19th century, yet is rapidly rotting away. There are still plenty of old houses around the county, but there is only one cotton press here and probably less than a dozen left in the entire South.

April and new industry keeps pouring in.

YEAR - This year is only three months old but in at least one way, it is already a record one for Edgecombe; Monarch Mills hadn't begun operations before ground was broken for Polyok; and before the first block was laid for Polylok, ground was broken for the Black and Decker operation.

This, of course, means job opportunities for 600 or more people—jobs which didn't exist a mere three months ago.

Even more frosting on the cake came in the form of an announcement that approval had been given a federal grant of a million and a quarter bucks to bring houses in a portion of the West Tarboro area up to standard. Then came word that a half-million dollar permit had been issued for construction of United Manor Court which will provide much needed housing for low income families. And, finally, it was announced that a 35-bed nursing home will be built on Western Boulevard.

Even if nothing else along these lines happens for the remainder of the year, 1970 has already been a banner one for us.

Marker tree threatened.

TREE—In an effort to "rehabilitate" the river bank along the John Price Boulevard in the vicinity of the river bridge here, the town is going to kill about the only historic tree we have.

The tree in question is the "marker tree" on the downstream side of the bridge. In it are iron spikes marking various high water levels of the Tar, including the record "Noah's Flood" of 1919. That marker spike was reportedly driven there by Pug Bass.

The town has covered the base of the cypress and its neighboring tree with fill dirt which dooms them as surely as if they were downed with a chain saw. Numerous other trees along the road have been killed in a similar manner.

The newly dumped dirt should be removed immediately.

Disaster averted.

MARKER - During the past week the town has removed some of the dirt and broken pavement from the "marker tree" just downstream from the river bridge. Several people remarked this week that they looked for the iron flood crest markers in the old cypress but couldn't see them because of the dense poison ivy vines. The lowest marker was placed there during a flood in the 1870s by Isaac Palamountain, who was a local gunsmith and blacksmith. The middle marker was driven in around 1908 by Dow Pender, and the high marker was placed in 1919 by Pug Bass.

The final fatal, terrible blow that destroyed Howard Avenue.

TREES—It took man days to plant them and it took God years to grow them, but it only required a few hours for a chain saw to bring down the oaks which line Howard Avenue.

Someone remarked yesterday that there is now enough oak wood available on Howard to barbecue every pig in Edgecombe County and half of those in Nash.

Just think of what the future holds for the folks who live along Howard— beautiful five-lane asphalt speedway!

June 26

BLOSSOM—This was the week of the great cotton blossom contest. Will Godwin brought in the first one of the year Tuesday afternoon, and even before the news got in the paper two others were reported. Wednesday afternoon a farmer called to say that he had found a blossom two weeks ago. But that didn't count with us. for the prize of a year's subscription goes to the first person who reports and brings us a blossom.

Incidentally, this is probably one of the longest running contests of record for while looking through some of the 1850 issues of *The Southerner*, I came across a report of a year's subscription being given for the first blossom.

On gnats and lightning bugs.

ECOLOGY—One of the porch sitters remarked last night, "I saw a number of lightning bugs tonight", and another added, "And I saw two butterflies today." Small talk, to be sure, but fireflies and butterflies hae become so rare as to rate comment. A third said, "We won't have them for long; the bug machine is making the rounds this week."

And that's the tragedy of our times. We rid ourselves of the nuisance of mosquitoes and gnats we also destroy delightful little creatures which add sparkle to God's world.

Memories.

RETROSPECT—You're getting along in years hereabout if you can remember:

The Coastal Plains Fairgrounds with church bazaars, nightly fireworks and sulky races . . . the 10 cent Saturday matinee at the Colonial which entitled you to sit there until 10 when A.M. Smith ran everyone out . . . movies in the Opera House . . . Tom Mix, Buck Jones, Lash LaRue, Hoot Gibson, Charles Starret, Johnny Mack Brown, the Three Mesquiteers and their backup comics, Fuzzy Knight, Al St. John and Gabby Hayes . . . .

You're moving on in age if you can recall Mr. Marcus Bridgers and Mr. Almond Hart, trailed by a dozen or so small boys trudging along the hot, dusty shoulders of the Leggett road to Collins Hole on the Tar for swimming lessons . . . . When the St. Andrews Street swimming pool was built by the WPA . . . when the pool's wire fence was draped with wire each morning to provide privacy while Nelson Howard conducted the 7 a.m. "Fat Ladies Swimming Class" . . . .

When James Davis delivered ice for the Atlantic Company; Mr. Wynn delivered milk for the municipal milk plant and George

Worsley hawked vegetables for Mr. DeBerry—all from horse drawn wagons . . . .

When baseball was king . . . . the wooden grandstand . . . Henry Webb was in charge of the concessions for "Coca-Cola" Brown . . . The Coastal Plains League with such notable managers as Snake Henry, Bunn Hearn, Peahead Walker and Jim Tatum . . . And did any fan in the history of the game ever give an umpire a harder time than did Helen Cheshire and Mabel Fountain? . . . Miss Minnie Williamson's boarding house for ball players . . . the Tarboro House and signs which read, "Tourist Accepted" . . . .

You're getting up there if you remember . . . .

The Frozen Delight, the 97 Wine Store, Miss Maggie Whitley's Grocery, the Turrentine Motor Company, the Thomas Company, curb service at drug stores, the tent factory, The Sunday Call, excursions to Ocean View . . . .

When any young Tar River rat could pinpoint the location of Hem Island, Eagle Ridge, Chapel Spring, Pope's Hole, Collin's Hole, Blue Banks, Shiloh, Dicken's Seine Hole, Green Banks, Poor Boy's Swimmin' Hole and Rattling Springs . . . .

When your mother knew how to wring a chicken's neck, how to bake bread, darn socks, turn shirt cuffs and collars . . . .

You're on the far side of 40 if you recall Dr. L.E. Norfleet's Franklin . . . Ben Fenny's Stutz . . . When Miss Sally Staton boarded her horses in Miss Sally Norfleet's stable and what happened when Miss Norfleet presented Miss Staton with a board bill . . . When Henry McNair and Bob Pender always called each other "Ike" . . . when Lawrence House always called everybody "Bo" because he never could remember names . . . when Fitz ran the hotel and it was widely advertised as the "Worst Hotel in the World" . . . Fitz's Boston Bulldog and his Airflow Chrysler . . . Tom Farrar's cigar and diamond ring . . . Clarence Johnson's vast expanse of stomach, spanned by a gold watch chain, which to a small boy, looked substantial enough to anchor a battleship . . . Mr. Johnson's annual remark concerning the arrival of spring . . .

Matty Matthews grocery on St. James and his cooking skills at outings on the Roanoke and Pamlico . . . Batt Moore's barbecue place . . . Mack Abrams drive-in at the depot . . .

You've had it if you remember when risque reading consisted of the Police Gazette, Film Fun, Spicy Detective, Spicy Mystery and when you really wanted something "way out" five of you pooled your nickels and bought a copy of Sunshine and Health. The youngest of us never could understand why the nude male pictured didn't look like us . . .

And you're getting good and gray if you remember Jules Barrett's "honey wagon", Sammy De Rosa's "Fortune", the vanishing parking meter bases, the old iron horse trough on the Common, the proposed municipal hotel bond election . . . Mr. Babcock's bus line.

And that's it for this week, I have to take my Geritol now.

Restoration opens door to history.

HOUSE—Merkle Pully has completed restoration of the Battle house for Francis Jenkins and Dr. and Mrs. Vic Herring have moved in.

Recently, I came across a bit of information about W.S. Battle, builder of that beautiful home, which some of you readers might like to keep.

He was born October 4, 1823, the son of James Smith Battle and the great-grandson of Elisha Battle, one of Tarboro's founders. When his father purchased the Rocky Mount Cotton Mills, he turned over the management to young William, who gave up his extensive turpentine business. William also became manager and part-owner of the Rocky Mount flour and grist mill.

Several fires, seven of which took place in two years at the Falls and on different plantation, caused a loss of at least $60,000 more than the insurance coverage.

He rebuilt both his cotton and grist mill at great expense and was on the road to success when the panic of 1873 occurred. His failure was due to low prices for manufactured products and the expense of rebuilding when the materials and interest rates were high. He also lost a daughter and several sons at early ages.

Dr. Kemp P. Battle wrote of William:

"He attributed his losses to accident or act of God. No one has ever heard him complain with bitterness of the hardness of his fortune. The same high-tone, equable, kindly temper, the same tenderness of soul, which characterized him in his prosperous days, he retains when his energies are confined to a smaller area and when he is dealing with lesser interests."

Integrated schools open.

SCHOOLS—Well, the first week of school has ended with the net result that members of the Tarboro Police Department spent more time in Tarboro High than did the pupils.

When I was in college the head of the journalism school was a crusty old newspaperman by the name of Oscar Coffin. Over a beer at the Shack on Rosemary Street one fall afternoon, he advised a group of us, "Boys, don't ever get caught in the middle of the road on any issue, because if you do, you're gonna get hit by traffic going both ways."

This paper certainly didn't take a middle-of-the-road course on the opening of schools. We urged compliance with the law, respect for the law and the schools, and cool heads for all.

And as a result I got more threatening calls than the high school. Well, they weren't really threats, but they were extremely abusive, but they came from both blacks and whites. The whites seemed to think I was a member of the Black Panthers, while the blacks thought I was a card-carrying Kluxer.

Those calls didn't hurt half as much as the fact that only a half dozen people took the time to say they appreciated that this newspaper was attempting to work for the peaceful opening of our children's schools.

RETROSPECT—In early July, Ramblin' devoted a little space to memories of Tarboro which those over 40 seemed to enjoy . . In a current column, Associated Press columnist Hal Boyle wrote, "The human memory is like autumn, a season of both recollection and premonition.

"It is also like autumn in that it is a harvest. The reward of the green and g rowing years is the golden sheath of memories one is left with in the Indian Summer years of life".

So, once more, let's see just how bountiful is our own memory crop:

When there was no need for alarm clocks because Tarboro was so quiet the booming bell of the town clock could be heard throughout . . . When Chan Muse came home to practice law after World War II and everybody said he would starve to death because "Tarboro already has too many lawyers" . . . When at least once every ten years you could ride through Princeville in a boat . . . When little boys vainly attempted to break into Solomon Pender's grave on the banks of Hendricks Creek after older boys told them that at one time Pender was the richest man in Tarboro and "they buried his gold with him" . . . When the town water tank was where George Grayiel's home now stands, and of taking a dare to climb it . . .

When the curb market attracted huge crowds each Wednesday and Saturday . . . When the back alleys of the town were filled with mules and wagons instead of wine bottles . . . First Saturday . . .

"Miss Kate" Johnson's recipe for pit tail pie, and what Mrs. Fraley said to Mrs. Johnson on one unusually frosty morning . . . What Mr. Perry Jenkins said he did when the "Squeezer" grabbed him . . . When folks loaded up the car and drove to Rocky Mount to see the "Streamliner" whizz through town . . . When nearly every home had a woodshed . . . When mama could bake perfect bread in the oven of a kerosene stove . . . Earning the right to lick the dasher by turning the ice cream freezer between after church and dinner time . . .

When Mr. Cliff Ruffin owned more mules than now exist in the entire county . . . When folks "sat up" at the tobacco barn . . . When folks gathered outside Marrow Pitt to bear the World Series broadcasts . . . Remember?

The brass pole at the fire station . . . Sitting outside the town hall on hot summer nights . . . Playing kick-the-can under the street light . . . digging backyard caves . . . building camps in the "woods behind the ball park" . . . launching a homemade raft in the Tar only to have it sink before you could get aboard . . . getting up courage enough to walk across the "Red Iron Bridge" . . . When our churches were cooled by cardboard fans, "Compliments of Carlisle Funeral Home" . . . Mr. Ed Winslow's huge

Fourth of July barbecues at the Cromwell Place . . . Cypress tubs filled with real lemonade . . . When soda-jerking was an art and many of the syrups used were concocted right there in the drug store . . .

When cotton warehouses burned frequently . . . When Simmons' fireworks stand exploded . . . When ladyfolks went into barber shops only reluctantly . . . When bank tellers worked in cages . . . When bankers were the most awesome men in town . . . When the major night time entertainment was window-shopping Main . . . When gasoline pumps were hand cranked . . .

November 6.

SNOW—Several people have said they saw snow mixed with rain as the cold front moved through about 10:30 Wednesday night.

~

DRUGS - Parents are concerned, and the kids are the first to tell you, "You can get any drug you want in Tarboro, except heroin."

The drug scare apparently started here in February when about two kilos of marijuana were brought from Vietnam packed in the back of two stereo speakers. Another shipment from Vietnam was intercepted by postal inspectors.

Since then, drug use, particularly marijuana, is said to have increased, but only six cases have been made by enforcement officers. These involved 11 persons, all boys or young men.

The most publicized was the arrest of four men after tablets found on the premises they occupied were tentatively identified as LSD. In district court last week the state declined to prosecute the quartet, reportedly for two reasons. The first was that the search warrant was faulty, and the second was that the tablets contained not LSD but something the SBI had subsequently identified as "Hawaiian rosewood seed", the possession and use of which is not illegal.

In two of the pending cases, the marijuana was so contaminated with foreign matter, leaves and sticks, that its possession constituted a misdemeanor rather than a felony.

In another case tried this week, the grass involved was potent enough to rate a felony charge and as a result, the young man now has a criminal record and it will remain with him always.

It just ain't worth it.

It should be noted that of the six drug cases, all involve possession - not selling the stuff. And therein lies the major problem. Nobody will name the pusher-man. It's said to be a matter of fear rather than loyalty.

1971

New Year Purgatory?

MISERY—For three days this week I was flat on my back with an ailment of the lower back brought on, no doubt, by lugging a large suitcase which was apparently filled with bricks and pig iron up three flights of stairs to my daughter's dormitory room. I could stand up or lie down in reasonable comfort, but there was no sitting.

There's an old saying about such-and-such being "worst than being in hell with your back broke", if purgatory could make me any more miserable than I was this week, it's time I started mending my back-sliding ways.

STORM—Last weekend's ice storm brought our renewed appreciation for the men we take for granted on a day-to-day basis—the men in the fiberglass buckets and those with spiked boots who work in the wires high above the ground to bring light and heat into our homes. To the local crew, the contractors, to Edgecombe-Martin co-op men go our thanks for doing a wonderful job of repairing the damage done by an irate Mother Nature.

BIRDS—At least two species of birds have apparently marked Edgecombe off their visiting list for this winter. For the first year since Hurricane Hazel blew through a huge flock of sea gulls has failed to shop up in no. 2 township. And thus far there have been no reports of grosbeaks.

FIREMEN—Leggett firemen are jubilant over the result of last Friday night's auction sale. They netted $1,320 for the fire truck fund which now stands at $5,600, which is about enough for a down payment. They expressed appreciation to those who contributed items for sale and to the large number who turned out for the event.

Billy Thigpen comes home.

BILLY—It was more than a decade ago that I stood with a father and watched as his young son, shirtless and tanned, piloted a big tractor across a dusty field with obvious pleasure.

"Do you think he'll grow up to be a farmer?" I asked.

"I don't know", the father replied. "I don't push him. I just want him to be what he wants to be. He'll make his own decision when the time comes."

The years passed and he made his decision. He majored in agricultural engineering at N.C. State, and after fulfilling his military obligation, planned to farm the Edgecombe land as his family had done for generations.

But this week Billy Thigpen returned home from Vietnam in a flag-draped casket, just as have more than 20 other of our fine Edgecombe sons.

He was no flag desecrater, draft-card burner or bomber. Far from it.

Billy was a clean-but young man who knew the meaning of hard work, the deep-down satisfaction of seeing the things he had planted come alive. He knew the fellowship of 4-H, the fun of hunting and fishing the fields and streams of his native county. He knew the thrill of active competition in competitive sports. He knew of the anxieties that accompany the high learning process, and he knew the joy of being a husband and father. Lastly, he knew of the heavy responsibilities of being an officer in the service of his country.

And now he has joined 45,000 others who gave their lives to the first war in history which this country did not fight to win.

Doctors concerned about tobacco effects.

SMOKING—"The terrible ravages which tobacco smoking is making on the minds and bodies of the young seems to be attracting the attention of medical men in various parts of the world. In a pamphlet just issued by Dr. Seymour of London on Private Lunatic Asylums, and cases of insanity in later years, the doctor denounces with emphasis as one of the leading causes the practice of immoderate smoking indulged in by boys and young men at the universities and large schools.

"The doctors remarks are applicable to the youth of this country as well as those of Europe. No one conversant with disease can doubt that excessive smoking, especially in the case of young people, must be highly injurious to both mind and body. Its effect is to depress the circulation - the heart becomes weak, irregular in its action and the pulse can hardly be felt and the mind fills with imaginary evils . . ."

The above sounds like something out of the Surgeon General's report issued this week. However, it is something which appeared in *The Southerner*, 1859.

Jack's is closing.

JACK'S—For the past score of years it has been known as Walgreen's, but to my generation it was simply "Jack's". It has been a Main Street fixture for the past 50, growing from a hole-in-the-wall to its present size through the diligence of the Mobley family.

And now its closing.

Rock gone! Shad too??????

RIVER—The Tar has been bankful for nearly two weeks, so if the hickory shad are coming, they are probably already here. But are they coming? Rock were practically non-existent on the Tar last year, and there were reported declines in both the hickory and white shad populations. Someone said the wildlife people attempted to conduct a fish tagging program last spring, but couldn't find enough rock to carry out the program.

PARK—Some call it City Park and others say Sunset Park, but actually the town's 26 acres out on Western Boulevard have never received an official name.

I would like to respectively submit to the town fathers that the lovely spot be officially titled Brown Memorial Park as a lasting token of respect for a man who gave so much of himself to our town and its young people.

The likes of Milton S. Brown will not likely pass this way again. He gave unselfishly of himself to our baseball facilities and teams, the swimming pool and teams, the county wide 4-11 program, the band and a host of other youth-related activities.

The "Letters" column is wide open for readers who would like to comment.

SPRING—The official arrival of spring is Sunday week, but the harbingers are already here. Of course, the jonquils, Japanese magnolias and a variety of other flowers have already signaled the advent of the new season, but this week we heard the shad frogs squeaking in the early evening. That is said to be an almost sure sign that the season of ice is behind us.

Hickory shad are already being caught in the Tar and now that the Tar is back within its banks, more will probably be caught this weekend. Good news for fishermen is that the wildlife people have removed the log that blocked the mouth of Fishing Creek and are in the process of removing the huge pine which almost completely blocked the river at the bridge here.

PARKING—Two weeks ago, through the courtesy of W.S. Clark and Sons, 100 additional off-street parking spaces were made available in downtown Tarboro. But, alas, the big lot is being utilized by less than a dozen cars per day.

Perhaps the solution to prime parking areas being used by clerks and office workers is to extend the two-hour parking zones.

Son John matures to the N. C. School of Arts.

NUTCRACKER—Son John, who is a student at the N.C. School of the Arts in Winston-Salem has a busy schedule next week. He has a role in the school's sixth annual performance of the Nutcracker Suite.

Four performances will be held at Reynolds Auditorium in Winston, one at Page Auditorium at Duke and one at Ovens Auditorium in Charlotte with the Charlotte Symphony.

POLITICS—As of 5 p.m. today the filing deadline is passed and the candidates are off and running for the May 4 municipal election.

We offer each candidate free space on our editorial page to express his views, his reasons for wanting to be or to continue to be a member of the town's governing body.

What!!!! No Clock?????

NCNB—Work has started on the new NCNB building and on the front page today is the architect's drawing of what it will be. It is attractive, but no clock. How in the world is downtown Tarboro going to get along without the old "Security Bank" clock? If the present clock is disconnected when the new building is occupied Main will have only the "Thing" at the town hall which has no numerals and the Bertram Brown Memorial sun dial in the Common which has no dial.

Of course there's always the courthouse clock, but you can't see it while standing in front of Marrow-Pitt.

Mama Duck Returns.

DUCK—Our wildlife friends seem to like Tarboro as much as people do.

Evidence of this is that the mama wood duck who hatched out a brood in the middle of Tarboro two years ago is back.

She wasn't seen last year, but this morning she was seen strolling down a mid-town sidewalk, followed by nine ducklings. All seemed as much at home as if they were in some sheltered woodland.

Mama duck made her first appearance here three years ago and she stopped traffic on Main as she and about six ducklings crossed the street. This year she is nesting in the same hollow tree as on her first visit.

End of April.

FENCE—The old iron fence which the UDC is planning to install around the Wyatt Fountain in the Town Common will enhance it. The fence once graced to R.B. Peters, Sr. home on 300 block of St. Andrew Street, and it could be that at its new location it will serve to discourage vandals who have been damaging the fountain with increasing frequency.

VICTORY—Victory Warehouse is already being rebuilt (after a devastating fire). Brother Leggett, his sons, and others worked throughout the weekend clearing away tons of blackened debris. By Wednesday the west wall was rising again and the structure should be ready for occupancy well in advance of the tobacco market opening in mid-August.

COMMON—Numerous citizens have remarked that this spring our Town Common seems even more beautiful than ever and few will disagree. Because of the method of fertilization used in recent years almost every citizen of the community is responsible for its current beauty.

Building boom roars.

BUILDING—This might be a time of recession or inflation, but it certainly hasn't put a crimp on building activity in Tarboro and its environs.

In every section there seem to be housing starts or remodeling.

Out on Davis Drive, the new academy is being rushed to completion and downtown the new bank will eventually be completed. Out on Wilson Street final portions of the floor will soon be poured for the new Charlie Hussey building, and just across the street, the lot has been cleared and is being filled for the new Edgecombe Mutual building.

Just off the bypass, a number of modular units have arrived for the new motel, and foundation work has already started.

At Fairview houses are being moved for the new Peoples Bank, and, reportedly, for a parking lot and a new Zip Market.

At Parkhill, the new Belk Tyler store is rapidly taking shape with blocks being laid at an amazing rate.

Why finance company moved.

MOVE—Some folks wondered why a finance company moved its office from the 200 block of Main to the 400 block of

Main, to a place considered by many to be the town's choicest business location. Now the answer is known.

It was a as close as they could get to town hall to provide the financing needed by most to pay their light bills.

BUGS—We were enjoying a neighbor's porch Wednesday night. There were no mosquitoes. Down the street came the infernal bug machine, casting a dense fog and breaking up the conversation. Ten minutes or so later I turned on the porch light and almost instantly it was surrounded by a board of insects, ranging from gnats to moths. If there was any pesticide in the stuff the boys were spraying, the bugs - all varieties - have developed an immunity to it.

It still ain't like it used to be.

MARKET—Everyone agrees that the opening of the tobacco market in recent years has failed to generate the excitement of the past when the warehouses were packed to the walls with farmers and businessmen, all awaiting the opening chant as eagerly as children on Christmas Eve.

It just won't be the same without John Price, nor Slim Johnson, a warehouseman whose word was his bond and was as mannerly to the poorest sharecropper as he was to the biggest grower in the county.

PRESS—This week Merkle Pulley began putting his master's touch on the old cotton press on the west end of the Common. The action on the part of the Historical Society is welcome and it came not a moment too soon. Earlier this summer I stopped to talk with a tourist from Alabama who was taking pictures of the press. "It's a shame," he said, "to let a treasure such as this got away."

AGILE—After having watched my oldest son go through his paces at the parish house dance concert Tuesday night, one of my sweeties of yesteryear came over and said, "I just can't believe he is your boy. When we were that age, you were the only boy in Tarboro who couldn't do the Big Apple."

That's the story of my life, stiff knees and two left feet.

And still more building.

CONSTRUCTION—Building continues at a rapid pace on Western Boulevard. The nursing home is almost completed. Large air conditioning units were placed atop the new Belk Tyler building, while nearby the new A & P was staked off. The foundation was poured for the new Kentucky Fried Chicken establishment, and considerable progress was made on the new motel.

The eternal environmentalist.

WEEKEND—Last weekend was the only one of the summer that our family was able to get together at my favorite vacation spot: Salter Path. And it was the most gorgeous one I have ever enjoyed.

Sunlit days with a gentle southwest breeze sent crystal clear, tot sized wavelets tapping at the strand.

Moonrise Saturday night was something I will always treasure.

Over the whispering surf it paved a path of silver, beckoning one to follow it eastward to the cape Magnificent.

Sunday was something else. I wanted to show Distaff something I had read about near the end of Rogue Banks. To get there we had to pass through the most misnamed place in Tarhellia "Emerald Isle" which is an area pitilessly raped by the bulldozers of over zealous developers. I do not consider myself to be an ecology nut but what they did to that stretch of what used to be termed God's green earth is a crying shame.

Shortly afterwards there loomed into view the prize, the new bridge over the sound. Its low railings afforded a fantastic and spell-binding view of the green and blue marshes stretching endlessly east to west Magnificent.

But we had to go back through the sterile litter-strewn "Emerald Isle."

Sunday night we sat on the cypress steps which led to the still whispering Atlantic at moonrise Distaff took my hand and asked, "What are you thinking about?"

I replied that somehow it didn't seem the same as the night before - that less than a dozen Americans had set foot on that sterling orb which had seemingly arisen from the sea but already they had drilled holes in it, toted away portions of it and had left on it millions in scientific litter.

She patted me on the hand and said, "It's time for you to go to bed, Luv."

And it was.

As fall approaches, downtown gets shot in the arm.

MAIN—Cato's expansion is a pleasant addition to downtown. But the prospect that Tarboro Drug is going out of business one of these days will leave yet another vacancy in t he 400 block of Main. It seems as soon as one vacancy is filled another develops. How great it will be when the time comes that we can view Main from one end to the other and exclaim, "Look, Ma No cavities!"

TALMON—The many, many friends of Talmon Tew will be glad to know that last Friday morning he was permitted to sit up in his hospital bed for the first time in 73 days. Since August 23, when he fell from the top of the new NCMH building, he had been flat on his back in traction.

Talmon called Friday morning with the news and to say thanks for the prayers prayed in his behalf. Incidentally, hospital personnel say Talmon has received more cards than any patient they ever had.

CLOSED—Today was the last day for the Electric Service Shop as Vernon Pitt closed the door which he first opened in 1911.

As Joe Grayiel said, "It's sad because there goes another one of our Main Street managers." He referred to the dwindling group of men in the 300 block of Main who would lean against parked cars to talk about politics, the weather, business and suggest general solutions to all our problems.

We sincerely hope Vernon doesn't abandon downtown altogether because he's one of the good guys.

December.

FRIENDS—I am convinced there is nothing on this earth truer than that old adage about "You don't know who your friends are until you need them."

It came home to me again Tuesday night when more than 20 persons personally responded and about that many more called to volunteer the type of blood which my mother needed at Edgecombe General.

It was deeply gratifying and even more moving to me since the Christmas season is approaching.

All I can say—and I say it from the bottom of my heart—is God bless you, everyone.

GHOULS—At this time of the year more than ever, the ghouls are operating in Greenwood Cemetery.

I'm referring to those sick kids and adults who steal Christmas plants and wreaths from the graves there. It's something that has been going on for years and, unfortunately, I do not believe anyone has ever been caught and convicted.

Equally depressing is the theft of flags which is a year-round occurrence. I know of one mother who placed seven flags in a month's time on the grave of her son who gave his life in Vietnam. All were stolen. Where is also the widow of a World War I veteran who finally gave up in despair after having to replace flags weekly for a year.

It's a shame, a crying shame.

1972

Pooch Town.

DOGS—Elsewhere in today's paper is a copy of the new town dog ordinance which will be proposed for passage at the town council's meeting Monday night.

If adopted as written our pooch population will be grossly discriminated against without regard to race, creed, sex and national origin.

How about that proposal to charge a license fee of five bucks?

During the last six months of 1971, 173 automobiles caused 81 accidents, injured 43 men, women and children, and caused property damage of $36,560 on the streets of Tarboro.

While there is no record of the damage to life or limb caused by the canines during a comparable period, I doubt that it anywhere near approaches what was done by the Detroit creations. Yet, the town fathers propose charging five times more for a dog license than they do for an auto license.

One section of the ordinance requires that dogs be kept locked up and another practically makes it a crime for dogs to bark. Other than a full moon or the fire horn there is nothing in this world that will make a dog bark quicker than penning him.

And why shouldn't dogs have the privilege of treaties? In that way Lady could go in Tiger's yard, provided Tiger was given the same privilege in Lady's yard. The same would hold true for reciprocal agreements between Brownie, Long John, Rusty, Noopy, Fido, Rover, et als.

Under the proposed ordinance even the Nazis and Communists among us would have more rights than our dogs.

Most of the ordinance reeks of the same type bureaucracy which hired a "traffic expert" for $85 a day to advise that certain shrubbery should be cut to make certain intersections safer and employed a college student to suggest changes in certain street names.

The latter effort came to naught, I hope the same fate awaits the major portion of the proposed dog ordinance.

The following week.

POOCHES—Well, the Battle of the Bow Wows is over for at least another month. One pre-ordinance councilman who was on the losing side Monday night said Tuesday that he planned to propose a new ordinance. It would require no license fee and would permit all dogs to run at large PROVIDED they are muzzled and diapered.

The brass monkey and cold weather.

FREEZE—With one exception, damage from last weekend's deep freeze seems limited to shrubbery and pipes. Ferrell Rollins said the brass monkey which adorns his back lawn was severely damaged.

The famous concrete mystery door on Albemarle Avenue.

PROJECT—More houses were demolished in the old Keechtown area this week as progress on the Hendrick's Park Urban Renewal project was accelerated. A bit of local history - the old East Carolina Railway shop on Albemarle - fell before the blade of a bulldozer and was hauled away in splinters.

The work in that area caused one man to speculate about the concrete door in the retaining wall in that area. Several generations of Tarboro boys have speculated about what was behind that door. Some said it was used to store gold during the Revolutionary War. Others said it was an entrance to a long tunnel used by the Confederates.

I recall one dark summer night when a bunch of us got a crow bar, pried the heavy door open and found a bunch of water pipes. That's all.

Dog vote.

VOTE—In nearly 22 years of attending meetings of the Town Council I can't recall anything remotely resembling what took place Monday night.

The three councilmen I have talked with said they had no idea a vote on the controversial proposal would be taken. After all, the agenda noted only that a report of the dog committee would be heard.

The fact that the agenda furnished this newspaper did not include the revised ordinance—a complete turnabout from past policy of the town manager's office—is enough to indicate some sort of subterfuge.

The public was given no notice and, as stated above, neither were some of the councilmen who opposed the action. All in all it was about as rash a display of "the public be damned" as I have ever seen at the town hall.

(The new law severely restricted a dog's freedom of movement and activity. It was hard to take for a true dog lover like Ramblin'.)

SPRING—The fairest season of them all officially arrives Monday at precisely 7:22 a.m., but already the sweetness of flowers is with us again and the elms and maples are beginning to show green. But remember, the only heavy snow of 1972 fell in the last week in March.

April 7.

FRANK—Tarboro native Frank Sanders, who is assistant secretary of the Navy, is scheduled to be named under secretary of the Navy today. He was in town yesterday and Herman Creech and Frank's other boyhood cohorts were already trying to convince him to move the Norfolk Navy Yard to the mouth of Hendrick's Creek and the Great Lakes Naval Training Station to Holderness Pond.

What to call Hart Mill.

NAME—As various development and redevelopment programs have come into being here, names of sections have been changed at the suggestion of residents of those particular areas. A couple of examples: Keechtown is now Hendrick's Park and East Tarboro is designated as Panola Heights.

Councilman Ray King says a number of citizens in his ward want a new name for their area of town which has long been generally termed "the Hart Mill section."

The point is well made, for it has been a long, long time since we had a Hart Mill. Yet, no one refers to that part of our town as the "Burlington Mill" or "Klopman Mill" section.

Residents of the area are asked to send this paper their suggestion for a new name. We will gladly publish them and perhaps a straw vote could be taken.

Anniversary.

TIME—In a way it hardly seems that it was 22 years ago today that I stood before the altar in old St. David's Episcopal Church. Actually I don't remember much about it, except that it was the first time I ever saw it snow in April and I was as nervous as a puppy dog with a peach seed problem. The preacher seemed sort of indifferent, so much so, in fact, that my best friend paid him off with $50 in Confederate money.

How any woman can stand to be married to a newspaper for more than two decades is more than I can fathom. But for it I am eternally grateful.

And that settles that.

NAME—On the informal proposal to change the name of the Hart Mill section, a friend who was born there stopped me this week and said, "It was good enough for my granddaddy, good enough for my daddy and it's good enough for me."

DOGS—Dog Deadline Day is ten days away, but as of yesterday only 144 pooches had been licensed. Someone wondered what would happen if the deadline passed and there were still more than a thousand canines roaming at large. There would be no way to impound all of them. One listener said that Mayor Ed and the four pro-penning councilmen would probably declare a state of emergency and bring in the National Guard.

You just can't fight city hall.

DST!!!!!

TIME—I suppose I could live with Daylight Saving Time if it were not for one thing. The night time changed and a mockingbird moved into the japonica bush directly in front of our bedroom window. Beginning at 3 a.m. he began singing his fool head off. Just when I thought I had become use to it and began to doze off, the critter would change pitch, bringing me wide awake again. It continued until 6 a.m.

There's an old saying that a sure way to get a one-way ticket to hell is to kill a mockingbird. Since there is a rumor that I already have a reserved ticket, I am seriously considering blasting that bird with a load of number 7 shot.

GOURDS—Buck Clark, the Merita man, called Wednesday night to say that he has some gourd seed that he has some gourd seed which he would like to share with those wanting them. These seed are fairly hard to get these days, and there are two varieties—the type used for martin houses and the long-necked kind used for dippers and many other purposes. They are available free on a first-come-basis.

PRESS—Restoration of the town's old cotton press was renewed this week as Merkle Pulley, Russell Brown and Don Corbett began hand-hewing 10,000 cypress shingles. In this day of prefabrication, there is something refreshing about watching craftsmen use their hands in practicing an art which goes back hundreds of years.

ECLIPSE—There will be a total eclipse of the sun July 10, but only about 60 per cent will appear covered by the moon in this area. The event will begin about 3:40, reach maximum at 4:45 and end at 5:45. The sun will be about 45 degrees above the horizon at the time of maximum eclipse.

Dog law was working and Ramblin' was man enough to admit it.

DOGS—Apparently the dog control program is working well.

The police department report for June notes that 54 dogs were picked up and of that number, 21 were returned to owners and 33 strays were destroyed. Apparently the group referred to by the pro-pen councilmen as the "silent majority" are speaking up over the telephone for the warden investigated 163 complaints and drove 1,838 miles in so doing.

It would seem the program has been fantastically successful in one respect. The mayor said in at least two council meetings that hardly a night passed but that someone wasn't brought to the Edgecombe General emergency room with a dog bite.

Last month there wasn't a single case of dog bite reported.

How about that?

MYSTERY—For the past three or four months I have been getting post cards from all over the Northern Hemisphere. They are in the same handwriting, and usually bear a one-line message. Signatures have included "The Green Hornet", "Tonto", "The Lone Ranger" and "The Shadow." They have come from various New England States, Canada, Florida and the West Coast. This week's brief epistle came from Illinois: bore the message, "I ain't lost." and was signed, "The Durango Kid."

I have no earthly idea as to the identity of my pen pal.

Father of the bride—first born leaves the nest.

REFLECTIONS—"Are you nervous?", the young friend asked the Father of the Bride.

"Of course not," he declared and dropped the shirt stud for t he fourth time. The truth of the matter is that I probably wouldn't have made it to the church had it not been for Connie and Celia Pistolis who came to the rescue, nimbly inserting studs, cuff links and hitching up my galluses.

I thought I performed well at the church, only to be later informed that my "I do" sounded as though it came out of a 1906 Victrola with a dull needle.

Afterwards I abstained from partaking of the bubbly water and a friend wanted to know why. "I'm no wino," I snorted.

But the truth of the matter was that I was still shaking so I was afraid I would spill the contents before I could get it to my lips.

Despite the chronic shakes, Wednesday was a grand and glorious day as two young people set out on the journey of life together.

Tar Flounder.

FLOUNDER—Several people have asked if the flounder pictured on last Friday's sports page was a first for the Tar here. While hooking a flounder this far up the Tar is a rarity, it isn't unknown. About 40 years ago Pete Clark caught one at the mouth of Hendrick's Creek, and about ten years ago Cecil Mills landed one while casting below Bell's Bridge. Bill Dupree reportedly caught several very small ones while seining for minnows in the vicinity of the Legion home.

~

FALL— Autumn officially arrived at 5:33 this afternoon but the signs of the changing season preceded it, courtesy of the Postal Service.

For example, the Sunnyside Oyster Bar in Williamston, long a favorite of Eastern Carolinians opens tonight. And from the west comes word that the Asheville Civitan Club is planning to hold its annual Fall Color Rail Excursion on Oct. 21 when leaves are at their peak there. With such news we don't need a calendar to tell us fall has arrived.

Police state.

REPORT - "The fuzz don't know nothing but arrest people for speeding and b bust the kids at the parking lot."

This is a time-worn and baseless complaint, usually voiced by those who have been arrested for speeding or who have been checked because of suspicious behavior.

So for the record, let's look at what the 23 members of our police department did last month, not in order of importance.

They only charged two persons with speeding, one with reckless driving, eight for drunken driving, and five for driving without a license. Fifty other traffic citations were various and sundry reasons.

They provided 43 escorts for merchants, nine for funerals and three for emergencies. They handled 40 wrecker calls, 31 rescue calls and 11 fire alarms.

During their nocturnal rounds they found forgetful citizens had neglected to lock 61 doors and windows and 21 street lights had burned out.

They assisted 216 motorists, answered 5,000 telephone calls, 1,873 radio calls, and conducted 1,281 desk window interviews.

They investigated 11 cases of breaking and entering and solved one. They probed four cases of larceny and cleared three. They recovered the only car and only bicycle stolen during the month.

They investigated 14 traffic accidents in which three persons were hurt and $9,960 in property damage was incurred.

They made 41 criminal arrests, which included four cases of assault with a deadly weapon, six for simple assault, one for carrying a concealed weapon, two for resisting arrest, 18 for public drunk, three for petty larceny, one for trespassing, and one for destroying public property.

They handled 340 complaints of one kind or another, issued 311 parking tickets (and collected 263 of them), issued 22 warning tickets and spent 45 hours of their time in district court.

That's a pretty good batting average in anybody's league.

History lost.

CEDARS—For years I have wondered about the old cedars which until recently lined Albermarle from the Common to Howard Avenue. When most of them were cut to make way for the upcoming widening project, I hoped to get a section of one to determine its age. Unfortunately, the centers were rotten, ruling out a ring count.

I suppose I'll never know.

DISTAFF—The usual Friday offering is missing today. Her 95-year-old grandmother died this week and was laid to rest in Valley Forge. She was a grand lady and one of the most avid baseball fans I have ever known with complete allegiance to Philadelphia with only one exception.

That occurred one night this summer when she was listening to a Phildelphia-San Diego game and suddenly exclaimed, "That boy pitching for the Padres is from Tarboro." It was, of course Mike Caldwell. That night Nana cheered for the Californians.

November 7.

ELECTION—All in all, it was the slowest election night in history at *The Southerner* office. Few calls were received throughout the long, long night.

Russell Carter stuck it out with me, as he always does, tabulating the returns as Distaff called them in from election headquarters.

About 10 p.m. Pres Martin and Lum Mayo came in seeking returns for their candidate, Jesse Helms. Russell showed them the chart with the two lone precincts which had reported by that time. Pres took a look and shouted, "We're ahead. We've already carried Nobles Mill Pond and High Level grocery."

OUTCOME—The final election results came as no surprise to the 5-year-olds at the First Baptist kindergarten. They took a straw vote last Friday, and Nixon won by a landslide.

BOOK—One of the nicest gifts we received at Christmas was a review copy of a book of poems by Tom Walters. For those of you readers to arrive late on the local scene, Tom is the son of Mr. and Mrs. Tom Walters of Conetoe. He now, and always has been, extremely talented as both a writer and artist (his first published drawing appeared in this paper while he was still in high school).

His latest book of poems is what I would call "very loose verse," and is titled, "Seeing In The Dark." It concerns his tender years when he was a ticket-taker and popcorn boy at the Colonial and now-gone Majestic theatres during the time they were operated by Charlie Danderlake.

Tom is a graduate of UNC-Chapel Hill and earned his master's and doctoral degrees at Duke. He now teaches English and English-Education at N.C. State University. Tom is married to the former Ellen Rucker of Tarboro.

Hog killing time.

WEATHER - You may have to read this one twice to get it.

It seems a Florida-born and raised weather forecaster was transferred to the Raleigh-Durham Weather Station in the middle of January. On his first day on the job, a farmer called and asked him, "Will it be cold enough tomorrow to kill hogs?"

The Florida forecaster replied, "It's going to get mighty cold, but I don't think it will get cold enough to kill your hogs."

1973

TAGS—The mention of dogs brings to mind the fact that the town says now is the time to buy new dog tags. But is it really? We were told the tags would cost three bucks per year. The law became effective in May, thus it would seem the tags still have four months to run before they expire. I don't recall if the ordinance refers to the physical year or the fiscal year, but either way it would appear the pooch owners are being gyped.

CLARK—Bill Clark The Third has handed in his resignation as highway commissioner and we are grateful for the service he performed for us during his four-year tenure.

The four-laning of US 64 between Rocky Mount and Tarboro finally got beyond the talking stage. The Howard Avenue project was completed the bids were let for the widening of Albemarle Avenue and North Main, and the Fountain Street project was committed.

He has looked after the home folks, but not at the expense of the other counties of his district.

SNOW—The birds got their signals badly mixed last week. With the yard covered with six inches of snow, a flock of robins suddenly arrived and this is apparently as far south as they plan to go for they were still around yesterday. The robins were soon followed by a huge flock of cedar waxwings which quickly stripped the neighborhood of every berry and then moved on.

The agony in Viet Nam is over and Ramblin' remembers.

PEACE—The Governor and President urged us to mark the signing of the Vietnam cease-fire at 7 p.m. last Saturday.

We left home and headed for Calvary Church, but the church was dark and the old bell silent. However, the bell of Howard Memorial, just around the corner, pealed joyously. Horns were honking, sirens wailed and the fire horn croaked. In the church vestibule, the Rev. Bob Burns was tugging away on the bell rope.

We walked into the dark sanctuary and dropped to our knees. I thanked Him for it being over and the fact that my boys would not be called as four generations of their family had been.

There was a stillness in the church as the outside sounds seemed to disappear and memories of the war came flooding back. I remembered the boys who came home early in f lag-draped coffins and I recalled those who will never come back. There were memories of writing their obituaries with the phrase, "with full military honors", of the honor guard, the folded flag and the sounding of taps.

During those brief minutes in the church I recalled three of my favorites.

There was Carl who began carrying papers for us when he was about 12. While waiting for the old press to run, he would plop down in my office and share his thoughts and ambitions with me. He said he wanted to fly and he wanted to go to a service academy. His twinkling eyes and infectious grin were contagious. I always felt a bit brighter having talked with him. Carl got an appointment to Annapolis and he got his wings. He was our county's first to pay the full measure and he will never come home.

Bobby was also a favorite. He was an extremely dependable carrier who delivered his papers on time and built up a paying route in his hometown of Princeville. Bobby died of wounds shortly after his 21st birthday.

And there was Billy, that stocky, pug-nosed kid, who was a spark plug in our high school athletic contests, a fierce 4-H competitor, to whom the best smelling things on God's green earth were newly plowed ground, July corn, an August tobacco barn and Conetoe barbecue.

Billy "bought the farm" a few days before he was to have come home to continue a family tradition in no. 2 township.

As we left the church Distaff noticed the courthouse bell was silent and said, "It just doesn't seem right", so she went into the courtroom and set off the electronic bell. It sounded artificial.

When we arrived home, she suggested, "Do what you do on New Year's." So, I got out the old shotgun, loaded, stuck it out the back door and fired away. I reloaded, pulled the triggers, Both shells were duds.

⁂

MARCH—A most pleasant month of March has passed the halfway mark with lamb-like tendencies prevailing.

Thus far I have noticed only a few kites soaring aloft. Those being flown were mostly of the plastic variety which required no special effort to get off the ground.

There was no evidence of the old home-fashioned varieties made of split reeds, newspapers stuck to cotton string with flour paste. The balancing tail was usually made from strips of old sheets or out-dated neckties.

Also missing this March is marble shooting. Perhaps it is too early, but the other day I walked over the school grounds at Bridgers and North Tarboro and found nary a sign of a marble ring.

April 6.

CHASE—The Great Chicken Chase was staged in downtown Tarboro shortly after five o'clock Wednesday afternoon. The chicken was first spotted on the lawn of the telephone company office building late Tuesday afternoon. During most of Wednesday the pullet spent its time pecking for worms on the lawn of NCNB. At mid-day, this caused one wag to remark that poultry prices were at such levels that some farmer was apparently entrusting at least one member of his flock to the bank for safekeeping.

I suppose some people considered it somewhat undignified for a hen to make herself at home on the lawn of a financial institution in a progressive community. At any rate, when the bank closed Louis Perry suggested to the employees, "Catch that chicken!" Thus the Great Chicken Chase got underway.

The lady tellers, casting decorum to the winds, took off in hot pursuit of the cackling chicken which fled across the parking lot. They were soon joined by Joe Bourne who probably had visions of free Sunday dinner. At this point the ladies were squealing as loudly as the chicken was squawking and the St. James traffic slowed as motorists watched the spectacle.

Hearing the commotion, Martin Cromartie came out of his office and Louis Perry hollered to him, "Catch that chicken!"

Martin instinctively lit out after one of the mini-skirted tellers and was last seen rounding the Presbyterian Church corner.

The chicken flew over cars and ran under them, finally taking refuge under an auto in front of the Marrow-Pitt Record Shop. Bystanders watched in awe as Barrister Bourne, on hands and knees, prodded at the plucky pullet with an umbrella.

The chicken broke for it, ran through Perry's bow legs, and fled across the street where Joe and Debbie Dempsey finally cornered it in the doorway of Francis Jenkins office.

Only in Tarboro!

BOOK - Julius Sadler, son of the late Mr. and Mrs. J.T. Sadler of Tarboro, is the co-author of a splendid new book, "Mr. Jefferson, Architect", which was published April 13 by the Viking Press. It is an outstanding work of 200 pages with eight color plates and 125 black and white illustrations.

May.

Judge W.C. (Buck) Harris told this one during a recess in the old courthouse:

An elderly colored farmer went to the railroad station to make a shipment. Being a station more often used as a flag stop than anything else, the railroad agent handed the farmer a batch of papers and said curtly, "Sit down over there and fill'em out. I'm busy".

Unable to read or write, the farmer summed up the situation with, "I was always told the littler the station the bigger the agent".

June and a bit of 1908 history.

PAPER—A July 16, 1928 issue of *The Southerner* was brought into the office this week and it is interesting to note that the names of some of the advertisers and individuals are still with us. Edgecombe Drug Co. was advertising exterminating gas insect powders, quicksilver and mothballs. F.M. and S.Q. Carlisle (Phone 129) offered hardwood, metallic, cloth covered and extra size caskets in addition to steel grave vaults and monuments. W.L. and J.E. Simmons addressed their ad to "Mister Husband" and urged, "When you hear it said by your wife or children that they need a nice porch chair or hammock just phone 31". The "Personal Intelligence" noted that Nicholas Constantine, Jr. "left this morning for Ocean View where he will spend the summer."

Elsewhere in the paper Joe Peele informed readers he had "3 fine horses for sale cheap". They were priced at $25, $30 and $40 dollars and could be purchased for $10 down and 75 cents a week.

The Bank of Tarboro informed readers that it had capital of $25,000 and surplus of $16,000. Officers were J.F. Shackelford, president, J.T. Howard, vice president; L.V. Hart, cashier; and E.B. Hussey assistant cashier.

The N.C. State Normal and Industrial College in Greensboro advertised board, laundry, tuition and other expenses, including the use of textbooks could be had for $170 a year. For these who agreed to teach in N.C. schools after graduation the cost was $125 per year.

VISITOR—Mama wood duck has returned to Tarboro for at least the third year to raise a brood of ducklings. A hollow in an old oak tree in the Common is again the home for mama and her brood of ten.

A week later.

DUCK—The mother wood duck we wrote about last week is up to her old tricks of yesteryear. Wednesday morning she stopped both northbound and southbound traffic on Main Street as she and her large brood of ducklings waddled across the street, apparently heading for the Porter's ditch ravine next to Mrs. Stamps Howard's house.

GONE—For those of us who have been a part of Tarboro for the greater part of our life, there is something distinctly sad about the loss of the Seven Up Bottling Co. to Rocky Mount, for the business goes back a long way.

Sometime between 1900 and 1903 T.W. Thrash established a soda water bottling business in a frame building at 1603-05 St. Andrew Street. His territory was wherever he could profitably ship by railroad in Eastern Carolina. During the period from 1909-1912 he had franchises for both Pepsi-Cola and Coca-Cola.

BOOK—Elsewhere in today's edition is a review of Capt. Henry Clark Bridgers' new book, "East Carolina Railway Route of the Yellow-hammer." The captain was good enough to leave a copy at the office, and I took it home Tuesday night, intending to read it at leisure but could not put it down.

Capt. Bridgers has preserved a very important chapter of the history of Edgecombe County.

CLOSING?— For more years than I can recall, the local post office lobby has been open to the public around the clock, but the practice may soon become a thing of the past. The reason? In recent weeks not only have people been going in at night and covering the floor with litter, they have also been urinating on the floor.

How crass can one get?

32 empty pint jars left over.

PRESERVING—Having come in possession of a mess of bell peppers last Saturday, I decided to devote Sunday to making a winter supply of pepper relish using an old Pennsylvania Dutch recipe which I have found to be one of the best.

I rose with the sun and immediately sterilized three dozen pint jars. While they were bubbling away I chopped and ground the peppers and onions, got the other stuff together, after about three hours, I had my relish ready to go into the jars. My labor produced only four pints. The only consolation is that I have on hand 32 very clean pints jars.

MOVED—The old cotton press was moved to its new home this week. It is now located at the corner of Albemarle and Porter Streets, across from the Boykin residence. Restoration work which began last year will be resumed.

THANKS— Appreciation is hereby expressed to Mr. and Mrs. Glen Bennett of Conetoe for the bountiful bag of tomatoes they brought me. The bag was topped by a huge one which weighed two pounds, two ounces.

CLEAN UP—The old Confederate on the Common got a chemical cleaning this week and while I can't see where it did much good, at least it apparently did no harm.

For such small favors we should be thankful, especially in remembering the "Big Ugglies" still span Main at downtown intersections.

When the scaffolding was first erected I heard plans were afoot to dress the old fellow in permanent pleat pants, a double-knit coat and, perhaps, a pork-pie hat.

MAIL—It has been said that a return to Pony Express would be a tremendous improvement over the existing mail service. In light of what I have heard this week, even a return to the days of the mule train would be better.

One local gentlemen mailed a letter to a local lady, placing the letter in the box outside the post office. It was delivered to her home, six block away, eight days later. An attorney told of how it took him 13 days to get an important letter which had been mailed from Rocky Mount. Another local man sent three to Rocky Mount Monday. They had not been received Thursday morning.

"Neither snow nor sleet nor dark of night may stop the postman from his appointed rounds". But something surely is.

September 28.

PUG—Somehow attending Town Council meetings in the future won't be the same for me without the presence of Pug

Bass as a member of the governing board. It is amazing to think that for more than half of his life he has been an elected representative of the people of Tarboro, and I am incline to believe that 46 years of such service must be some kind of a record for the state.

Throughout his career of public service he never hedged on an issue, and whether you agreed with him or not, you had to admire his frankness and his fairness. He never was one for straddling the fence.

DOC—Dr. Spencer Bass had another birthday this week: Number 90.

He doesn't know how many babies he brought squalling into the world during his long years of practice. I know the last one was our oldest. Some claim first ones were a couple of kids named Cain and Able, one of whom went astray.

The environmentalist suffers again.

LOGGING—A couple of weekends ago Distaff and I took a Sunday afternoon ride and ended up at Eagle Ridge. It was the first time in about ten years that I had been there, and I was looking forward to the magnificent show of color from the variety of oaks, beech and hickory which covered the high ridge between the river and Swift Creek.

Alas. The loggers had been there since my last visit, and the once-beautiful had been stripped. Only a few scrub hardwoods remained. It was disheartening for to me for the ridge was one of the most beautiful spots in the county during the spring and fall.

December 28.

FIRE—There was a sincere sense of sadness among spectators as smoke mushroomed from the front windows of Marrow-Pitt Wednesday morning. The better part of the work of 60 years was being consumed by flames.

One man remarked, "I feel like a part of me is gone" Another said, "I have been trading there for 50 years. I'm gonna miss it". And a third added, "Except for food and clothes when you thought of buying something, you always thought of going to Marrow-Pitt first". One lady who had worked there in past years stood silently, tears streaming down her cheeks.

Just how old the building was isn't known, but Dr. Spencer Bass recalls when it was occupied by D. Litchenstien who used the first floor for a store. Doc says the second floor was the town's "Opera House" used prior to the time the old town hall was completed, around 1890.

For years Marrow-Pitt has been a "customer generator" for downtown Tarboro (over 700 buying customers went through the store Monday). Will the store be rebuilt or relocated downtown or will it be moved to the out skirts? Those are decisions which face the owners and ones that are anxiously awaited by a large number of citizens.

To the Pitts we express our deepest regrets at their loss for it was a loss, not only to them, but to the entire community.

LEAVING—The pending retirement of Willie Harrell and Mrs. Virgie Cummings from NCNB takes two more of the "old crowd" from downtown Tarboro.

Virgie, in her 21 years with the bank, was about the only person who could "put down" the late Luke Cherry in some of his more ribald moments. Her ready smile and always pleasant manner will be missed.

As most of us know, Willie is something of an institution. In years past, Willie was the person assigned to call and tell you that you were overdrawn or that your note was delinquent.

When he called, Willie would personally apologize to you for your own mistakes in either your checkbook calculations or those of your spouse. He would cheerfully say in effect that if you couldn't make a deposit that particular day, then the next day or even the next would be perfectly all right.

1974

SALVAGE—There will be no fire sale of damaged merchandise at Marrow-Pitt. The store's insurance company has sold the entire damaged inventory to a salvage firm which today began moving it to the western part of the state.

Billy Pitt said a decision is due early next week as whether to rebuild at the present site or to relocate.

WEATHER—Look for bad weather Wednesday. That's my birthday and nearly all of the January 9's for the past 48 years have brought bad weather. Usually it brought rain, snow or sleet.

ELECTIONS—It's hard to believe, but the filing deadline for any candidate for political office in the general election in November is almost upon us - at noon on February 25.

The date for the primaries is May 7 with any runoffs scheduled for June 4.

Voters will be called on to decide on office holders ranging from the board of county commissioners to the U.S. Senate.

Thus far, at the county level, there has been speculation only concerning only the office of the High Sheriff. While no official statement has been forthcoming from Tom Bardin, it has been rumored for the past couple of months that he will not seek re-election.

At this writing there are at least seven candidates rumored to be interested in the office. They are Deputies Enoch Sawyer Jr. and Mac McLin, County ABC Officer James Johnson, Magistrates Horace Ward and Jack Harrell, State ABC Officer Al Felton and Fred Mueller, a former highway patrolman.

Based on this one race alone, the events between now and May 7 could be very, very interesting.

SUNSET—Perhaps it was because the sun has been seen so seldom thus far this year, but Wednesday evening's sunset was without a doubt one of the most beautiful I hae ever seen. With the exception of green, the colors were more vivid than a rainbow.

SENTENCES—One of the major tv news networks Wednesday morning made a big deal of interviewing the inmates on North Carolina's "death row". The prisoners told of how horrible it was "to know or not know if you was or wasn't gonna die." Not once was mention made of the crimes which put them there, nor was there any mention of the victims.

The infamous gasoline shortage hits home.

SHORTAGE—Because of the gasoline shortage and because our regular service stations are unable to supply us, we are having to turn to the so-called "discount" or "convenience" stations.

But what about those men we bought gas from over the years before the big suppliers came along with what I consider to be a contrived shortage?

These men still have to pay station rent, pay their employees, and provide for their families. Because of the quotas, their profits have been drastically cut. In short, they are hurting.

These station operators are the men who, over the years, came to our houses on frigid mornings to get the family car started. They are the ones who willingly went out in the rain when the wife had a flat.

They are the men who washed our windshields, vacuumed our cars after a trip to the beach, checked the oil, the water, the battery, the brake and transmission fluids - all without charge.

You can't find many, if any, of these services at the "convenience" stations.

BIRDS - The warm weather of January was a disaster for the family bird feeder. Around Christmas, we had orioles and a couple of flocks of grosbeaks, but they have disappeared along with the chickadees and juncos.

CHECK—Dr. Spencer Bass came into the office yesterday morning, sat down and pulled a letter from his pocket. It was from a lady he didn't remember and contained a check. She wrote that when she moved from Tarboro, she owed him $3.50 and the check was in payment for the debt, plus six per cent interest for 40 years. That's right, she moved from Tarboro in 1934.

FISH—Lovers of fried herring and rock stew will be jubilant to learn that the Cypress Grill on the banks of the Roanoke at Jamesville opened for the season last night. This year it is under the management of Leslie and Sally Gardner.

MOVING—The Boss came in this week and told to write a story about our future plans to build a new plant on W. Wilson Street and asked what I thought about the site between the motel and the whiskey store. I told him I thought it was just great for the younger members of the staff, but for me it was 20 years too late.

March 15.

VACATION—Distaff will be vacationing in Pennsylvania next week. The reason for the late-winter trip is so that she can take her mother to see our son John perform at the Philadelphia Academy of Music Monday night. John, who is a senior at the N.C. School of the Arts, is back on tour with the Agnes De Mille Heritage Dance Theatre group.

FUTURE—Those of us who have special place in our hearts for downtown Tarboro were elected by two events this week.

Exactly three months from the day it burned, Marrow-Pitt reopened a door on Main Street not far away from what the oldsters use to refer to as "The Old Stand".

The following day ground was broken for a 21,000 square foot supermarket smack-dab in downtown.

These are certainly two firmly set anchors to hold our downtown in place.

HAPPENING—Thanks to all responsible for the third annual Happening which has always been excellent, but seems to get better with each passing year.

And this one even featured streaking but with clothing. I refer to the wholesale take off by the crowd when the skies opened up at 4:30 p.m., cutting an entire hour from a most enjoyable afternoon.

ACTIVITY—Albemarle Avenue was the scene of much activity this week as crews began pouring the foundation for the new Harris Supermarket, and workmen began erecting more of what Bob Harper refers to as "big uglies". That are, of course, traffic signals being installed at the intersection of Albemarle and Battle and Baker.

TOMATOES—From N.C. State comes the best reason yet for giving up smoking-at least during the spring and summer months.

It seems that smokers who touch tomato plants before first washing their hand, transmit some sort of mosaic disease which kills the plants.

June 21.

SUMMER—It hardly seems possible. All of a sudden spring has gone and summer is upon us. It officially arrived at 2:38 this afternoon.

The azaleas, wistaria, japonica and camellias have been replaced by the less attractive, but more productive blossoms of tomatoes, squash, snaps, and corn tassels. And many gardens are already putting forth summer's bounty.

Distaff and I went "cropping" in a relative's garden late Wednesday afternoon. After filling a couple of sacks with snaps, onions and squash, we were invited to climb a barbed wire fence and dig some new potatoes.

On her knees and with sweat dripping from her nose, Distaff looked over her shoulder and said, "If you had told me 24 years ago, when I married you, that I would be grubbing for potatoes and enjoying it, I would have said you were crazy."

During the years she has also developed a liking for frog legs and grits.

~

SUMMER—This is the most bountiful of all seasons and appreciation is hereby expressed to Mr. and Mrs. Glen Bennett of Conetoe for the generous supply of corn and squash they thoughtfully brought by the office last week. Also, thanks are in order to the unknown friend who left a large bag of new potatoes and onions at the office for us.

This is the blessed time of year when I could exist without meat, except for seasoning.

~

DAIL—Dail Holderness yesterday ended 41 years of active service with Carolina Telephone. For the past 16 years Dail and Nancy have given a May barbecue.

It hardly seems possible, but not once during those 16 May days has the annual event been rained out. There were days when dark clouds have hovered at what seemed to be tree-top level, but the rains held off until the guests had gone.

I was reminded of the time when Distaff and I were going to one of Mr. Sam Clark's outdoor birthday parties and as we dropped the children off at my parents' home I remarked that it seemed certain the celebration would be rained out.

My father smiled and said, "Son, don't you know it only rains on the Clarks when they want it to."

It would seem the same applies to the Holdernesses.

Nixon Resigns.

NATION—I suppose the majority of us breathe easier now that the Obstructor is in exile and our new president has declared that he will make a sincere effort to bring us together.

After hearing President Ford's speech Monday night, one local teenager said to his father, "That is the first presidential speech I have ever heard that I understood every word of. I believe in that man".

PRESERVING—I ran smack-dab into the jar and jar lid shortage and the galloping inflation of sugar prices last weekend. Because of the prevalence of bell peppers in the backyard garden plot, I decided to put up some pepper relish. The only jars I found in town were in Ma's basement. Lids were equally hard to come by, but finally I rounded up 15 of each and sterilized them carefully.

After seeing the staggering price of a five-pound bag of sugar, I tried, without success, to find a way to substitute saccharin.

After grinding for what seemed like an hour, I was certain that I had produced a winter's supply of relish. But when I finished cooking and ladling, I found I had produced only five pints.

I haven't done any per unit figuring yet, but I am certain that for the cost of a bottle of my relish I could buy a pint of the finest on the shelves of any Aunt Betsy Clark store.

Ugh! Coffee creamer.

DOSE—What would you do if someone tried to give you a dose of hydrogenated vegetable fat, sodium caseinate, disodium and monosodium phosphates, emulsifiers, sodium aluminosilcate, and tricalcium phosphate?

You'd probably take it, for they are part of the ingredients of a popular non-dairy product used in coffee and tea.

GONE—Whatever happened to May, June, July and August? It hardly seems possible that summer has ended, and the kids are back in school. Superintendents C.B. Martin and Lee Hall say the openings were uneventful. Lee even went so far as to say, "It was the smoothest opening in years".

COWBOYS—I was watching an old tv movie recently and it turned out one of the extras was a fellow named Dick Foran.

As I recall, Dick was one of the "singing cowboys" of my childhood, and I never could stand singing cowboys. Gene Autry and Roy Rogers were not for me.

Sissy! Pure sissy!

As a boy, I don't recall having played Cowboy and Indians, because everybody in the crowd wanted to be a cowboy. So at our Saturday morning get-togethers something developed which could best be called, "I Bid To Be".

The oldest boy present would say something like, "I bid to be Tom Mix".

In descending order by age, others would "bid to be". Some said Hopalong Cassidy, Ken Maynard, Kermit Maynard, Buck Jones, Charles Starrett, Tim McCoy, or even Bob Steele or Hoot Gibson.

I always wanted to be Buck Jones, but by the time my time came, I was usually limited in choice to being "a trusty side-kick" such as Andy Devine, Fuzzy Knight, Al St. John or Smiley Burnette.

Once I even had to settle to "bid to be" the Great Horse Silver". But my youthful pride would never permit me to stoop so low as to "bid to be" a singing cowboy.

Dick Foran, I hate you.

DOC—One morning more than two decades ago a gentleman with a neatly trimmed moustache and wearing a red corduroy coat came into the office and introduced himself. After chatting a few minutes, he asked, "Do you think Edgecombe County can use another veterinarian?"

I allowed as how I thought there were enough critters in the county to go around, but suggested that he go see Mr. Jim Satterthwaite and his boys at Shiloh for an expert opinion. Some lasting friendships were established that day with a man named Dr. H.A. Servais.

The Satterthwaite clan sort of adopted Doc, taking phone calls for him at their Shiloh office until he could open an office of his own.

As it turned out we were to become neighbors. Distaff and I were living in the basement of the Norfleet Apartments at the time and the Servais moved in on the first floor. Both families later moved, but we became neighbors again eleven years ago on Peach Street.

A gentleman who has a special fondness for small animals came into the office Monday morning and while here expressed sorrow over Doc's death.

He said, "I reckon he was about the nearest thing to an old-timey family doctor we had. No matter what time we would call him about one of our cat or dogs—day or night—Doc would always tell me to meet him at his office". Doc was that way, Many are the nights when I have heard him back the Ford from his driveway, on his way to help some cow or mare in trouble.

Doc loved the outdoors whether it was downing doves at the Mayos in September or trying for rock at his favorite spot between Shiloh and Blue Banks in April and May.

On spring, summer and autumn nights, the Servais' porch was something of a neighborhood forum where we gathered to talk about whatever came to mind and a decade or so ago we were excited as kids as we eagerly awaited the nightly passage of the "moving star" - the Echo satellite as it made its sweep from west to east. Small talk would go on for an hour so, unless we were rudely interrupted by t he infernal bug machine. On such occasions, Doc would flip away his ever-present cigar butt, and we would scatter homeward.

Nearly everyone I know called Harold Albert Servais either Doc or Doctor Servais. The only exceptions were his children who called "Dad," and his beloved "Rube" who called him "Silver".

Some poet once wrote, "God gave us memory so that we can have roses in December".

For that we should be eternally grateful.

December.

SHORTAGES—You can add wild rabbits to the constantly growing list of shortages.

Herbert Powell was in the office this week and said the West Ridge Beagle Club needs rabbits for their field trials, but haven't been able to trap many bunnies. The club is willing to pay two bucks each for trapped bunnies, but even that offer hasn't brought any results.

So how do you hold field trials with the main contestants missing?

WALK—A couple of Sunday afternoons ago the family did something we hadn't done in years: we went for a long, leisurely walk in one of the prettiest woods in Edgecombe County and capped it off with an arrowhead hunt.

The woods is, I believe, one of the largest stands of hardwoods still standing in the county. Beeches, oaks, birches, sycamores, and hickories abound there, and while most of the trees were bare, the ground was completely covered by a plaid-carpet of Autumn leaves. Around the base of rotted pine stumps were deep beds of moss, trailing cedar and what we use to call turkey berries.

The arrowhead hunt shifted from the hardwood to a harvested peanut field a couple of miles away. We drifted, heads down, along designated rows. The search produced a couple of broken points, some pieces of pottery and, finally, one perfect point.

It was one very satisfying afternoon.

Tribute to a one-time Yankee.

DIXIE—Twenty-five years ago this week I brought Distaff to Tarboro for the first time. She was a product of Miss Agnes Ervin's School and was raised on Philadelphia's Main Line. Her mother was somewhat distrustful of her daughter's trip to Dixie, since she believed everyone who lived south of Washington wore bed sheets and peaked hats and had hookworms.

By the following June we had managed to change her mother's opinion of Southerners, had married and moved here. Over the years her eating habits changed. First she came to like grits. Her doubts about barbecue changed slowly and that item suffered a severe setback when she discovered a hairy piece of gristle in her plate at a luncheon in the parish house.

With the passing of the years, she became fond of quail and frog legs, turnip greens cooked with fat back, baked sweet potatoes and other Southern staples such as backbone and spare ribs.

But this week, on the 25th anniversary of her first visit to Tarboro, Distaff went all the way.

At 7:15 a.m. Tuesday I was shaving, when an aroma which certainly had no business being around at that time of day, reached me. Dropping my razor, I went into the family room and wonder of wonders there sat Distaff, *The News and Observer* propped in front of her, a cold biscuit in one hand and a bowl of left-over collards in the other.

She looked a bit shamefaced, but threatened, "If you say one word about this, I'll kill you!"

Farewell friends!

1975

GARDEN—Most people think of home gardens in terms of spring and summer months, but a former Tarboro resident recently made news in the Decatur, Ga. paper because of what's going on in his backyard this winter.

Harl Newsome, the son of Mrs. Ethel Newsome and brother of Mrs. Leroy Holland, both of Tarboro, has a 70 by 70 garden in his backyard and in that garden this winter he has 1,200 collard plants growing. What's more they are whoppers, measuring three feet across and weighing from seven to nine pounds each.

I don't know what Harl plans to do with all those collards because there couldn't be much room in either his pantry or freezer. He put up 600 quarts of vegetables from his garden last summer.

YEARS—A number of years ago, a reporter friend from the Evening Telegram stopped in and said he wanted to write a feature article about our Town Common. He added that he wanted to "humanize" his story with accounts of events which happened there in the past and needed a source. I sent him to see Dr. Spencer Bass.

The feature appeared the following Sunday, and I thought it was especially good. Monday morning Doc came into the office. I commented on the article and the quotes attributed to him, and Doc seemed a trifle miffed.

"Why", he questioned, "couldn't that boy just have stated that I was 75 years old instead of saying I had been around here for three-quarters of a century?"

At the time it seemed to me that Doc was nit-picking, but today I know better. Yesterday I turned 50, and regardless of how I say it, 50 doesn't sound one bit better than half a century.

Friends who had gone over the hump before assured me Wednesday that I would feel no different Thursday. But it didn't seem that way. My morning coffee didn't taste right, and I seemed to be having hot flashes. At the office, I remarked that my elbow was sore, and Jessie really helped things when she casually remarked, "You're now at the age where it's probably arthritis".

Bright and early yesterday my mother called to wish me a happy day and remarked that skies were clear and the sun was shining. She reminded me that of all my 50 birthdays, the sun has shone on only ten. The others were marked by torrential rains, cold drizzles, and blizzards.

The other kids got measles, chicken pox, mumps and croup. Not me, I had ground itch, hoof and mouth disease and what was once believed to be a terminal case of dandruff.

A stone buddy and I joined the Marines together, swearing to stick with one another come hell or high water. He spent the war packing parachutes. I got shot at.

After the war, I considered studying medicine. I went up to Chapel Hill and after an interview, the gentleman suggested that I take an aptitude test. I did. While we were waiting, the fellow next to me said he wanted to be a writer. We took the test and it was turned out that the recommendation was that I was suited to the writing business and he was suited to science. Today he has a PhD and is a top chemist with DuPont, and here I sit pecking away at a typewriter which is only 20 years younger than I.

Oh, well, there is considerable consolation in the words of Robert Browning's Rabbi Ben Ezra, who said:

"Come grow old along with me.
The best is yet to be."

I certainly hope so!

❧

(News reporter Rogers Hall was one of the first full-time reporters on The Southener Staff.)

BLAHS—Early yesterday afternoon Ms. Hall bounced into my cubbyhole and announced that she was afflicted with an early case of spring fever. The Newsperson said it would be an excellent time for some pre-spring photos and asked if I had any suggestions.

Since I also had premature visions of fishing poles, lady slippers and violets, I had already done some after-lunch scouting around. I suggested she get pictures of folks fishing along John Price Boulevard, and one of the season's first kite tangles in the power lines on West Johnston Street. I told her where to find a field of jonquils and suggested she drive down to Old Sparta and check with Karo Edmondson about the shad situation.

Camera in hand, Newsperson Hall ambled out of the office (she always ambles whether it be by foot, car, truck, bicycle, jet, skateboard, or slow boat to China) to record on film what at the time was a beautiful day.

Ms. Hall hadn't been gone 30 minutes before the clouds moved in, the temperature fell and a miserable, cold drizzle set in.

It wasn't too long before the front door slammed. It was Newsperson, totally dejected. She ambled over to her desk without speaking to anyone and began angrily punching away at her typewriter.

It was the most sudden recovery from spring fever I have ever seen.

A few weekends later—again enchanted by the renewal of life.

SPRING—Today is the first day of spring, and while I feel certain we have some severe weather ahead, the greenery doesn't know it.

Riding around town yesterday, I was surprised by the large number of azaleas already in bloom. A dogwood in Calvary Churchyard is making a valiant effort to burst into full-flower before the early Easter. Of course, jonquils and tulips are rampant.

⁂

STATISTICS—Edgecombe, which has a population of around 53,000, according to the 1970 census is woefully lacking in indoor plumbing and standard housing. But according to figures released yesterday by the Department of Motor Vehicles, Edgecombe has a car or truck for almost every man, woman and young'un in the county. There are 41,280 cars and 10,263 trucks registered here.

Rape of cemetery continues.

GREENWOOD—The ghouls are still at it, in Greenwood Cemetery.

A friend called yesterday afternoon distraught that someone had taken all of the beautiful potted plants from the grave of a friend and former co-worker who was buried Sunday. She also said she had just learned that such thefts were common and asked if something couldn't be done to prevent them or to arrest those responsible.

Sadly, Greenwood thefts aren't limited to potted plants. The mother of one of our Edgecombe boys killed in Vietnam tries to keep a small American flag on his grave, but to no avail. Last November 11 I placed a flag on my father's grave. By the next afternoon it was gone.

Admittedly, this is being written in anger because for the past 25 years I along with a number of others, have expressed concern over the continuing thefts from Greenwood and the apparent apathy on the part of our local police over such thefts.

THEFTS—Last week's column concerning the continuing theft of plants from Greenwood brought a surprising number of calls from readers. Some even complained of thefts of plants from their own gardens. One lady complained, "First they stole my peonies, next my lilies and now they have taken my two white azaleas".

June 1.

ANNIVERSARY—Come next Wednesday and if The Boss doesn't change his mind, I'll be beginning my 26th year with this newspaper.

If research serves me correctly, no person in the 149-year history of *The Southerner* has held down this spot for that length of time. I mentioned that fact at the Wednesday morning meeting of the Downtown Society of Bigots, Back-Sliders and Back-

Biters and a fellow—known as a 32nd Degree Spine-Snapper—snickered and said, "What's so great about that? The rest of them had sense enough to move on."

Office gossip has it that The Boss is planning to give me a timepiece to mark my quarter-century of service. I asked Ballyhack Billy Evans if he had heard the rumor, and he confirmed it. He allowed as how he had even been with The Boss when the anniversary gift was purchased. "And I'll tell you this," he confided, "he bought you the most expensive three-minute egg-timer in Williams' Dime Store."

BUILDING—The first section of floor for our new building is to be poured today, and the steel should be going up by the latter part of next week. We are still shooting for a mid-August move.

June 13.

FRIDAY—Until today I never really believed that bad things happen on Friday the 13th. But Rogers is leaving us today. I would write more, but my typewriter keys are wet and that is not just because the roof leaked during last night's rain.

CENTER—This week's progress report on construction of the town's two new recreation centers noted that the center in the park on the west side of town is as yet unnamed.

That is good, for it means that some of us still have a chance to have something devoted primarily to young people named in honor of someone who unselfishly gave of his time, his talent, and his pocketbook to Tarboro recreation for over 30 years.

I refer to course, to the late M.S. "Coca-Cola" Brown.

A number of years ago, I suggested to the Town Council that a park on the west side of town be named in honor of Mr. Brown, but the suggestion fell on deaf ears.

If the council would consider a petition, I feel that are still a number of us around who still fondly remember "Coca Cola" Brown and his many contributions to provide such a document.

WEATHER—There's an old saying among farmers that "dry weather will scare you to death, but wet weather will ruin you".

While I haven't yet heard of anyone being ruined, such could well be the case if all of a sudden the rains stopped and a bright, hot sun took over the weather. It would be the ruination of the tobacco crop.

At this writing, Tarboro has had over nine inches of rain this month, while some of our rural areas have received well over a foot.

Celebrating the noble collards.

FESTIVAL—Some how or another I am just going to have to make arrangements to get to Ayden on September 13.

The good people there are going to devote a full day of activity in honor of the collard. There'll be rides, a street dance, games, a concert and even a "Miss Collard" pageant.

I am particularly interested in the latter and have written to the publicity chairman to find if there is any upper age limitation for contestants. If not, I just might be able to field a winner. Testimonial must count for something, and I feel certain that few if any of the younger entrants could attest to having (on at least one occasion) eaten a brimful bowl of cold collards for a 7 a.m. breakfast.

GONE—The Siamese cat which owned Joe Grayiel and Mrs. Maude Leggett for 13 years passed away this week. Joe fashioned a coffin out of old pine boards, lined it with the cat's blanket and laid him to rest in the flower garden.

AUGUST—It hardly seems possible that August is already here and soon the kids will be returning to school. But for the past couple of weeks I've noticed signs of the coming of Dog Days.

I get up about 5:30 in the morning, brew a cup of coffee and sit before our picture window while awaiting the arrival of the N&O girl. Of late I have become aware of the buzzing and chirping of crickets and other small creatures that inhabit the grass in the backyard. Those are sounds not heard on early morns of June and July. The little critters have begun singing their swan songs.

This week also marked the arrival of the pair of neighborhood humming birds, who put in their appearance at 6:30 Tuesday morning. This marked the fifth straight season they have favored us with a visit at this time of year.

The infamous Brunswick stew story.

STEW—Lew's (Heilbroner) story last week about the brick that was supposed to cure a scorched Brunswick stew took me back to the late 50s or early 60s.

In those days, a couple of Wednesday evenings a month, a bunch of us would gather at the late John Cheshire's log cabin for some nickel and dime and for supper.

While John, Dr. Bud Moore, Big Jim Simmons and other regulars sat around a couple of blanket-covered tables to shuffle and deal, Archie Eleanor, the late Gene Clark and I would be in the kitchen tending to the cooking.

One particular Wednesday the three of us went out early to cook a brunswick stew. We were doing pretty well, but as the shadows lengthened, Arches suddenly squalled, "IT'S SCORCHED."

It was, but not bad.

One of us remembered or thought we remembered what Lew had written some years earlier about using a brick to take the burned taste out of stew. Archie said, "All we've got to do is find a brick and drop it in the pot."

John's cabin was built of logs and had a concrete block foundation so we had little hope of finding a brick. Gene remembered "Rico's house."

Rico was an egg-sucking quail-eating bird who had been owned by John and Dock and had died several years earlier. His abandoned pen was located a short distance behind the cabin.

Without thoughts of how many times the old dog had stood three-legged over the bricks which supported each corner of his house, we pulled two of them out, pumped some water over them, scraped off the moss, washed them again, plopped them in the pot of scorched stew and started stirring.

After a couple of nips we tasted what we told ourselves was a resurrected stew and announced that supper was served.

At previous sessions we had chipped the poker pot so that night's feed was a free one and the boys loaded their bowls, some taking second and nearly all remarking that the stew had a certain "smoky taste."

Archie explained that by saying we had decided to double the amount of smoked ham we used.

One local businessman came in and dippered out his third helping when something went "clank". He dipped again and again heard "clank."

He asked, "What in the world is that?"

Archie rose to the occasion and said, "Mr. Clark, that is the ham bone from all that good old smoked meat."

No more questions.

In cleaning up the kitchen that night, we used the brick to scrub the bottom of the pot, something which—I learned from Lew's more recent column—we should have done in the first place.

August 22—History discovered in the back of an old drawer.

MOVING—Today is moving time for us, so since Wednesday I have been cleaning out what I thought was just my 25-year collection of junk from the top and innards of the old desk.

It turned out the contents of that old office fixture go back much further than that. For example, stuck to the back of one of the drawers was a check on the Bank of Tarboro in 1896. It was made out to "J.H. Bryant or bearer" and signed by Paul Jones, who was a long-time editor of this newspaper.

Still another find was an envelope containing a scrap of silk left over from the flag which the ladies of Tarborough made for Col. Louis D. Wilson and the Edgecombe Guards when they marched away to the Mexican War. Until I found it yesterday, I had forgotten it had been given me by the late Miss Vera Keech, one of many items she gave me from the collection of her father, the late Dr. J.P. Keech.

Still another find was an ancient pair of eyeglasses, identical to the ones worn by George Howard in the only painting I have ever seen of him. Mr. Howard brought what is now this paper from Halifax to Tarborough in 1826 and published his first issue here on August 22 of that year. And that is exactly 149 years ago today—the day we move into our new building!

The old desk yielded many things utterly useless. Like the share of stock in the old wildlife pond, a company life and health insurance policy which the company dropped for a much better one, an arrest warrant, a certificate naming me a "Country Squire" by Governor Kerr Scott, some "Umstead for Governor" campaign pins.

There was also a letter to the late Mr. Jim Satterthwaite from a former German prisoner of war who was imprisoned here during the war and had worked digging peanuts on Mr. Satterthwaite's farm. The writer wanted to know if Mr. Satterthwaite could offer employment.

One heck of a lot of Tarboro's past has been written on or near that old desk here on St. James Street, and this afternoon it and I will move out to West Wilson.

Things will never be the same again.

SHORT—This column is unusually short this week. The reason that I vowed I wouldn't write anything about my new grandson. But that is the only thing on my mind.

October 3.

HARDWOODS—One of the last and largest stands of hardwoods in the county has been sold, and we are hoping to be able to take a couple of Sunday afternoon walks through them before the chain saws arrive. Portions of the woods are carpeted with a half-dozen or more kinds of mosses and wildflowers abound there.

TUESDAY—It was really quite an election night.

Because of the low key campaigning, we had no idea there would be such an interest in the returns. But *The Southerner* office was crowded with the largest turnout of citizens than at any election in 15 or more years. Our phone lines were jammed by incoming calls to such an extent that Distaff, who was at the board of elections office sending us the returns, had to drive over to the office with the last two precincts.

DAY—This Thanksgiving was an extra special one at our house. It was the very first such day for young John Aubrey, and great-grandma, grandma and grandpa doted mightily.

1976

FRIEND—It was only yesterday that I learned of the death Monday of Father Kenneth Parker in Edenton. He was a former pastor of St. Catherine's Catholic Church here, and was the finest friend a lot of Tarboro youngsters ever had.

PRAYERS—After my mother fell and broke her hip last week, we were determined to keep the news from Distaff. However, Friday morning the phone rang and the nurse in ICU told me that somehow the patient had found out about it and was upset.

I rushed to the hospital and found Distaff not only upset, but downright mad—with me.

I told her that mother was going to be all right, and that, after all, with all those tubes and wires connected to her there was nothing she could do. To further reassure her, I added, "Jim Bramham has the Presbyterians praying for her and Catherine Smoot has the Methodists praying for her".

Distaff looked me dead in the eye and asked quietly, "Don't you think just one little Episcopalian's prayer might help some?"

I don't believe I have ever felt quite as small.

COMPACTS—During my stint of hopping between two hospitals I have come to have a black hatred for compact cars. Parking is nearly always at a premium in parking lots and it seemed as though when I thought I had found an empty place and began turning in, there would be a compact of some sort cuddled up at the curb.

Frustrating, to say the least.

OPEN—Folks hereabouts who hanker for fried herring, roe and rock stew will be glad to know that the famous Cypress Grill at Jamesville is now open for business.

WEATHER—The flowers are blooming and the shad frogs are singing at dusk dark. Everyone is commenting on the extremely mild weather—but with reservations.

The usual comment is, "We're gonna have to pay for it". Then they recall last year's snow at the end of March, and the oldsters remember one of the heaviest snowfalls of record came in early March in 1927.

Let's enjoy it while we can.

THANKS—Our open house was a great success and The Boss was pleased at the turnout by the more than 300 visitors who came to see the results of his planning.

I got up early Sunday morning and rode over half the county picking jonquils and pear blossoms from the yards of deserted tenant houses so that the building would be properly decorated for the occasion. When I drove up to the back door of the building and began unloading, the boys in the pressroom began laughing. "Go look up front", one of them advised. It turned out the contractors and other friends had sent us an array of flowers and plants which would have been the pride of any first class funeral parlor.

My meager offerings were arranged in an out-of-the-way corner of the backshop.

April 2.

SAM—Wednesday afternoon Sam Womble pumped his last gallon of gas, washed his last windshield, spent several pleasant minutes with friends in the grease pit and went home. It marked the end of more than 30 years in the service station business and the beginning of his retirement.

It must have been with mixed emotions that he drove westward on Wilson toward home in Speight Forest. The two stations which he operated during those years were the favorite meeting spot for many local men, particularly those who had retired. As a result more lies were told there than in place in the county, with the possible exception of the courthouse. And more fish were caught there than in all of the rivers in Eastern Carolina.

I wish Sam many happy days and full fish boxes during his retirement, and I suppose a chorus of local voices will join me in saying, "It's been a pleasure doing business with you".

As time passed, Ramblin's remembered how good years had been.

FUN—Do kids in this electronic and pot-puffing age have as much simple fun as kids did when I was coming along 40 or more years ago?

I doubt it.

It has been years since I've seen hop-scotch squares chalked on sidewalks or, for that matter, dirty words scrawled on a board fence, and it has been almost as long since I have seen small boys playing "Territory" on the school grounds.

I seem to recall that latter game involved flipping a pocket-knife into an opponent's marked square and carving out a piece of his "territory" if your knife stuck in a particular direction.

That game will probably never be revived, because they'd call out the National Guard if a bunch of kids toted Barlows on the school grounds today.

I can even remember how long it has been since I have heard the clatter of a tin can on the pavement when boys gathered under a street light on a summer night for a spirited game of "kick the can".

When I was a kid, obliging police would rope off the street in front of the low school for the young skaters in town. Using hooked sticks or shaved-down plow handles, we would engage in lively games of roller skate hockey. As a matter of fact there are still some scarred shins and crooked noses around to attest to what a beat up tin can puck could do.

BRIDGERS—The demolition of Bridgers School Friday was a sad, sad day for many, many Tarboreans—both for those who attended and those who taught there during its 66 years.

While watching the huge claw eat away at those solid brick walls I vividly recalled the days I attended Miss Sturgis' first grade in the front room on the Park Avenue side of the building. There were no electric bells, and each morning Columbus, the janitor, would come out of Principal Mary Bridgers' office with a big brass bell. Little boys would crowd around him, clamoring for the "privilege" of announcing the taking in of school by running around the building a couple of times while clanging away.

I hadn't thought about the bell in years but Friday the memory of it was as clear as yesterday.

MELON—Edgecombe's champion watermelon grower, Ed Weeks, has made the national spotlight twice in as many weeks. A photo of Ed and his two sons, Van and Ken, along with their 197-pound melon is featured in the current issue of the newspaper. "The Family Food Garden", and last Sunday there was a sketch of Ed and his melon in Ripley's "Believe It Or Not."

FACILITY—Tarboro had a genuine public toilet last weekend.

It seems a commode fell from the back of a pickup truck at the intersection of Main and Wilson Saturday and someone thoughtfully removed it from the street and sat it on the corner of Sam's 66 station.

The police department was called and asked to remove it, but the caller reportedly was told the police weren't responsible. The task was the duty of the garbage department, but that was closed.

In the course of the afternoon, someone placed a roll of Charmin by the john, and there it stayed until Monday.

June 4.

TOMATOES—For several years V.B. Anderson has been the first to call in the spring to announce he had a ripe tomato. V.B. called Wednesday, but this year he was a week late. Lew Heilbroner had already produced a batch.

FREEBIE—This newspaper got a nice helpin' of free publicity on the front page of last Sunday's evening Telegram.

Charlie Killebrew took a picture of a man who used his chain saw to fashion an easy chair from a stump. The photo showed the fellow sitting on his stump-chair reading a newspaper, and the paper was ours. I hope Telegram publisher Carl Worsley won't be too harsh on Killebrew, since they are both displaced Tarboreans.

Happy Birthday, America, July, 1976.

BIRTHDAY—Down through the years I have said some mighty harsh things about television, but after last weekend I'll think twice before uttering an ugly.

For most of the time from 7 p.m. Saturday until late Sunday I sat glued to the tube, and it wasn't just that I was being entertained. I felt as though I were omnipresent. The majesty of the tall ships and the power of the gray cruisers, the marching, the singing, the cheering.

I joined the huge crowd in Boston and hollered "Encore" for the Boston Pops, and I'll admit to having shed a tear when the Marine Band broke into "Semper Fedelis" as it marched toward the Iwo Jima Memorial.

Problems with hi tech living.

PHONES—I still haven't gotten use to having to dial the full three digits before dialing the number I want. By the time I finish the 823, I forget the number I wanted in the first place, and while I try to remember it, the system kicks in the original buzz. I have to start all over again.

Eventually, I'll get use to it, but I don't suppose I will ever get accustomed to that new ring, because it is a rude ring, one which seems to demand that you drop whatever you are doing and answer the thing immediately. Sort of like a young'un screaming that he wants to go to the bathroom—right now!

With regard to phones, I heard a phrase the other day that I hadn't heard in years. The thing rang and someone in the office answered it. Instead of saying something like, "Just a minute", he said, "Hold the phone". That one goes back a long ways.

HELP—Despite their best efforts, the volunteer firemen of Princeville are having a difficult time raising money for their operating expenses. Perhaps many don't realize it but people outside the Tarboro limits who live within a four-mile radius of Princeville rely solely on the Princeville firemen for fire protection. They are really hurting for money so mail those contributions to Box 1274, Tarboro.

October 15.

FINALIST—Congratulations are certainly in order for those who compiled the material which led to the selection of our town as one of the 18 finalists in the All-American City competition.

Tarboro was the smallest municipality on the list and the only one in this state, which, even if we do not make the final list, is a signal honor.

However, if we are one of the chosen few to be announced next spring, I wish some arrangements could be made to have us designated an "All-American Town". Because that is exactly what we are and what I wish we always will be, the "progressive" element to the contrary.

DISHES—Over the years Distaff and I have taken turns washing the dishes each night. However, a couple of weeks ago she announced, "Anything with tomato sauce on it makes my hands break out".

Being the kind of person I am, I offered to do the dishes any night the menu included anything having tomato on or in it. That has proved to be my undoing. The nightly fare of late has been spaghetti, pizza, meat loaf with tomato sauce, barbecued chicken, pork and bean casserole, and stewed tomatoes. I don't believe I'll ever have any relief.

Tarboro—The All American City.

PRESENTATION—As the result of what happened in Williamsburg Tuesday, David Taylor is floating around way up there on Cloud 18, and the town manager has plenty of company.

The fact that about 75 of our fellow citizens cared enough to make the trip was worth a great deal, for when they arose to show their support for the town's 10-minute presentation, the members of the All-American Cities jury gave them a full round of applause. It was the only such show of any emotion by the panel during any of the presentations by the 18 contesting municipalities.

My only regret about the proceedings is that one person who should have been sitting on t he front row in Williamsburg wasn't able to because of illness.

Since the transition nearly two decades ago from the commission to the council mayor form of town government, Ruth Ballard has been an active participant in every single facet of municipal progress. During the years since the federal goose began laying golden eggs, Ruth was the one who sifted through the reams and reams of rules, regulations and guidelines in the quest of those eggs. And she found them, millions of dollars worth, and in at least one instance found, prepared the application for, applied for an received for the town, a grant that no other community across the nation had even sought.

Ruth had to miss what went on Tuesday, but her friends are confident of two things—that the town will win the coveted award come springtime, and that Ruth will be there for the final presentation.

December 17.

MEMORIES—I suppose it was a combination of last week's snow flurries, and the unusually cold weather that brought back memories of something which happened about this time in December 34 years ago.

Joe Bourne and I were freshmen at State College. It was the day of the last exams and the beginning of the Christmas holidays. Others from Tarboro—Billy Manning, Billy Powell, Forrest Sledge, and W.C. Ranes had already departed for home, probably by bus. But Joe and I were going home in style.

You see, Joe had come into possession of an open Model A Ford truck through a swap (I believe it was with Little Brother Leggett), and Brother got the best end of the deal. That truck was open from the tailgate to the windshield.

About the time we were loading up our dirty laundry, it began to snow heavily, and it looked as if it would be a long, long 72 miles from Raleigh to home.

At the time, Joe was a member of the freshman wrestling team, so he went over to the gym, talked with Mr. Doak and came back with a piece of sweat-stained canvas cut from a discarded wrestling mat. We tacked it over the top and left some of it hanging down the sides. It was around noon when Joe pushed up the spark on the Model A, and we were on our way.

As we chugged out of Raleigh, the snow began to stick. That's when we remembered the Model A didn't have any windshield wipers. We solved that problem by reaching out from under the canvas and clearing away the snow by hand, but since we had no gloves, we were candidates for cases of frostbite by the time we reached Zebulon.

At this point, we realized something had to be done, so we stopped and got a stick about four feet long, got a towel and wrapped around the end of it, and for the rest of the trip I would reach out and clear the windshield with it so that Joe could see.

It was in Zebulon that we made a bad mistake. For some unknown reason we took NC 97 instead of US 64 to Rocky Mount. And from that time on we were trailblazers. There were no tracks to follow, just a sheet of snow. I mean it was real bad!

It was pitch dark when we finally got to Rocky Mount and it was still snowing. We had gotten on the Edgecombe side of the tracks when Joe looked at the gas gauge. It was dead on empty, so we pulled into a filling station.

Joe asked me how much money I had (he was always doing that). I turned up 25 cents. Joe had a dime, so with 35 cents worth of gas in the Model A, we started those long, cold final 16 miles.

It was 8 p.m. when we finally arrived home, and our parents were about frantic because they had checked with the parents of the other local boys and all had arrived home by the early afternoon.

I suppose that's what you would call a numbing memory.

1977

WEATHER—Two snows this week and January, February and March are still ahead. In doing some checking yesterday I was shocked to discover that I have already purchased as much fuel oil this winter as I did all of last.

Fraley weather, indeed!

TAR—Broken sheets of ice floated down the Tar last week, and while ice on the river is rare, it is by no means unheard of. My uncle drove across the river at the end of Trade Street in the teens, and Col. John L. Bridgers wrote of skating from Tarboro to Shiloh in the mid 1880s.

At the rate we're going some such skating may be possible again before spring.

FUEL—Of course, hindsight is always best, but wouldn't it have been wonderful if we had taken some of those many trees which were cut from Howard Avenue and Fountain Street and the wood from those demolished Urban Renewal houses and stockpiled them. The old rehabilitated garbage dump would have (and could still) made a perfect place.

With coal practically nonexistent, that wood would have curtailed a lot of human misery this winter. But sadly, most of it has been buried.

Perhaps it could be done in the future.

OPEN—Lovers of fried herring and rock stew will rejoice to learn that according to the Williamston Enterprise, the old Cypress Grill in Jamesville was scheduled to open for the season last night.

February 18.

CLOSING—During the nearly 27 years that I have been on this job, I have written stories of good things which made my spirits soar. I have written stories of tragedies with tears in my eyes. I have written of happenings which had made me mad as hell, at the same time fighting to keep my objectivity.

In retrospect, I truly believe the story which hurt me most down deep inside as I typed the words, was not one written years ago. It was one which I wrote at 4 o'clock Tuesday afternoon. I headlined it, "Burlington Cut Here To Cost 300 Jobs".

Lord, how it hurt!

I know a lot of folks who work in that old mill just up the street from us. I knew a lot of their daddies and their granddaddies. They also worked in the mill.

Of course, the story made note of the fact that those folks who will be getting the word, "will be interviewed about possible transfers to other local jobs or Burlington plants".

Three hundred folks? Other local jobs?

Just ride by the unemployment office on Albemarle Avenue any Wednesday morning. And then there's that old thing about teaching an old dog new tricks.

Jobs at other Burlington plants?

Perhaps for some of the younger ones. Maybe. But a lot of those 300 have spent most of their adult lives in that mill. Over yonder in Greenwood Cemetery they have kinfolks who also worked in the mill. They never knew what a 40-hour week was. More likely it was a 50 or 60 hour week. Maybe more. And the only times they were able to get all of the lint out of their hair was for Sunday church, weddings or funerals.

Talk about roots!

WEATHER—The wonderful weather-including Thursday's rain of the past week will probably lull us into a false sense of security.

"Ballyhack Billy" Evans, our fearless folklore forecaster, reminded us that there have been two periods of thunder since last Saturday. That, he says, is a sure sign that it will snow within ten days. That prediction in past years has proven more right than wrong.

BREAK—I gave Distaff a CB base station for Christmas and she gave me a camera. She uses the camera and I use the CB. However, since I haven't gotten my license yet, I mostly listen. But by and large the Cbers are a great group-always cheerful, even at 5 a.m. and always seeking ways to help out needy channel breakers.

JUDGE—The bench's gain was the coffee crowd's loss this week with the appointment of George Britt as a district judge.

For at least 15 years George has been one of the group which met from 20 to 30 minutes to enjoy coffee and conversation, so hence forth things just won't be the same.

A masterful story-teller, George could stretch out details of his two-hour visit to the circus in Raleigh over a period of at least a week. After a visit to New Orleans where he would see Sweet Emma Barrett and the Preservation Hall Jazz Band, his stories could dominate the morning conversations for as long as six months.

ANNIVERSARY—Distaff and I marked 27 years of marriage yesterday and as a present she didn't ask me to do the dishes last night. This means I will have twice as many dishes to do tonight.

OFFER—Last Friday I announced that in my zeal to be a part of the All-America parade, I would cheerfully don a clown costume and grease paint, shoulder a shovel and follow the horses in an effort to protect the environment.

On Monday, the mail brought a letter which stated, "Buy a shovel at Marrow-Pitt and charge it to me. As for the clown costume and make-up, you don't need them. Come as you are."

The epistle was unsigned, so I suppose I'll have to supply my own shovel.

June.

FARSIGHTED—Edgecombe lost one of its real leaders this week with the death of Mr. S.B. Kittrell in Pinetops.

I suppose not many people know about it, but Mr. Kittrell is directly responsible for the location and well-being of at least two industries in Edgecombe.

When Bill Long attempted to go into the farm machinery business, he found it impossible to get his much-needed financing in Tarboro. I don't recall whether Bill sought out Mr. Kittrell or vice versa, but Bill got the money he needed to go into business from Mr. Kittrell's small Bank of Pinetops.

RETURNS—After an absence of two years, our hummingbirds have returned. I spotted the pair hovering around our camellia bush about 6:30 Tuesday morning and they were back again Thursday.

SAM—Several years ago, Sam Mayo, our former circulation manager, suffered a stroke which left him partly paralyzed, and robbed him of most of his speech, but it took nothing of his spirit or his love gardening.

He hobbled into the office Tuesday, cane in one hand, a sheet of paper and a bag in the other. He had brought me some onions and peppers from his 1977 crop, and quite a crop it must be!

On the paper he had written that he had spring onions in March, garden peas in April, cukes and lettuce in May, hot peppers, Kentucky Wonders, fresh corn and tomatoes in June.

VOW—Throughout this week, and particularly on Tuesday, I have been sorely tempted to break a solemn promise I made early one morning last February when the furnace went off, and the mercury was flirting with zero.

"Lord," I promised, "I'll never complain about hot weather again".

JIM—Some of the best news I have heard in a long came Monday when I learned that Jim Parker is now the owner and editor of Clinton's daily paper, the Sampson Independent.

Largest egg purchase in the county.

RETIRED—Irvin Taylor, who has made weekly egg deliveries in Tarboro for more than 20 years, called it quits last week.

We will certainly miss his Thursday visits which provided us with the goings-on around Conetoe and Mayo's Crossroads.

I suppose I have the dubious distinction have having indirectly made the largest individual purchase of eggs from Irvin, and I didn't get to eat a one of them.

It was eight or ten years ago as I was driving the company van home to lunch. As I neared the intersection of St. James and Albemarle, I saw my daughter drive the family car through the Albemarle stop sign, slap dab into the side of Irvin's egg-laden station wagon. Fortunately, no one was hurt.

The bill for the damages included 96 dozen eggs!

August 12

POOL—I suppose it happened around 40 or so summers ago when cooling was provided only by front porch rocking, accompanied by the flutter of woven palm or pasteboard funeral parlor fans.

About all the entertainment the kids had was the "washed air" cooling at the picture show and the swimming pool. The pool closed at 9 p.m. and after that things got deadly dull in Tarboro.

On one particularly hot night about 10 o'clock five or six of us were getting tired of riding our bikes around town and throwing rocks at street lights, when someone said, "Let's go swimming".

We pedaled up to the community house, shucked off our clothes, hid them under the bushes and went over the fence—buck naked.

We had been paddling around happily from about 30 minutes before someone decided to do a "cannonball" off the high diving board. Thinking (correctly as it turned out) that the noise of splash would cause one of the area residents to call the police, we headed back over the fence.

We had just cleared the fence when a police car rounded the corner and pulled into the pool driveway. Still naked, we scattered like a covey of quail.

I couldn't get to my bike, so I headed for the bushes where the clothes were hidden and dove under them. The bushes, it turned out, were Japanese hollies. Talk about hurting! It was pure torture to crouch there naked amidst a million thorns as the police probed about with their flashlights. Finally the light went away and the police car started up. I had endured all I could take, so I crawled out of the bushes and began picking off hundreds of dried holly leaves. I got into my clothes, got my bike and headed home; hurting real bad.

I learned the next day that all except one of us had evaded the police. The officers stopped this unfortunate naked lad as he was pedaling furiously past the high school.

When asked to identify his companions, he replied, "Sir, they were perfect strangers. I had never seen a one of them before in my whole life".

FILMS—In the middle of the Depression a commercial film company came to town and filmed a comedy which featured an all local cast, plus scenes around the community. When completed, it was shown, in conjunction with a talent show, to packed house for several nights at the Colonial.

After the initial showings the film was forgotten until it was found in the early 1950's. As I recall, the film was in pretty poor shape, but the late W.C. Ranes spliced and restored most of it.

In the early 1960s, the powers-that-be decided the old town hall had no place on the local landscape. No one mourned its demolition more than the late Charlie Clayton. But he did something.

Charlie made a step-by-step filming of the demolition from the time the first beam was removed until the clock tower was toppled and only an empty lot remained. He sent his color film direct to Eastman Kodak with special instructions that it be treated to last forever. Kodak guaranteed its processing for a hundred years.

When the film came back to town, Charlie made arrangements to show it to a meeting of the Town Council which was then meeting in a temporary town hall next to the old jail on W. St. James Street. At the conclusion of the showing, Charlie made a formal presentation of the film to Mayor Ed Roberson with the suggestion that it be put in the town vault "for safekeeping" so that the destruction of a landmark could be viewed by future generation.

The last time I inquired at the new town hall, no one knew anything about Charlie's film.

DEER—My friend, Mrs. Helen Bennett of Conetoe had what must have been something of an unnerving experience last Saturday morning.

About 10 o'clock a doe deer, being chased by dogs, jumped headlong through the window and into Mrs. Bennett's dining room. The badly wounded creature created general havoc before it was removed and destroyed.

SUPPER—If I ever had any doubts about my mother-in-law caring for me, t hey were fully dispelled Tuesday night.

Distaff was in Zebulon this week helping to care for our new granddaughter, so Polly invited me to her apartment for supper. Now, that lady was born, bred and until little more than a year ago, lived all of her life on Philadelphia's Main Line. I just couldn't believe it when I walked into her apartment and smelled - of all things - COLLARDS.

That lady had made the supreme sacrifice to cook up that pot of greens just for me to go along with the ham and sweet potatoes.

CUE—Old friend Lee Gooch called Monday morning, and he was somewhat irate. He wanted to know if I had read a feature in the Sunday N & O about Eastern Carolina barbecue, and when I said I had only scanned it, he let it fly.

At no place in the entire article was any mention made of Tarboro or Edgecombe County. Rocky Mount, Goldsboro and even Kinston were praised for long tradition of quality cue, Lee said somewhat disgustedly.

He recalled that in years long ago the most popular eating spot in town was Don Sherrod's barbecue stand which was located on Granville Street, behind what is now the City Seafood Market.

"Don Sherrod was a black man and he cooked the best barbecue in the whole county. His wife worked there with him and her pan-baked corn bread was something everybody bragged about".

Lee also recalled the many years the late "Cap" Wooten operated what started out as a barbecue stand in the old Creek Bridge Store building on W. St. James. There is no way to even estimate how many hundreds of succulent pigs were slow roasted to perfection in the adjoining pit by Cap. Gray Harrell and Tom Walters.

Well, Lee, so what if the N & O article excluded Tarboro and Edgecombe? You remember, and I remember and that is what counts.

(Rambling ended 1977 with a re-telling of the great firecracker explosion on Main Street on Christmas Eve of 1946 at Simmon's furniture store. The event resulted in a statewide law banning the sale and shooting of fireworks. He ended this column with a heretofore unknown item: What happened immediately after the explosion.)

.... As the Simmons' window shattered, a long sliver of glass embedded itself in Rufus (Cromatie's') back. For Martin and me those minutes amid the rat-a-tat of the strings of firecrackers interspersed with the explosions of the aerial bombs meant re-living the hell of our personal experiences in World War II.

I really don't recall too much about what happened next, suddenly it was quiet and the firemen were there extinguishing the burning stand and a mattress or two and a pall of acrid smoke blanketed Main from the river bridge to the present site of NCNB.

Mr. Jim ordered his entire remaining stock of fireworks dumped into the river that night, and at the next session of the general assembly fireworks were banned statewide.

1978

GREETINGS—Shortly after 8:30 Monday morning the phone rang. It was my mother who wanted to know if I "had looked outside".

I allowed as I had. The strong northwest wind was hurrying soot-colored clouds southeastwards at tree-top level, and those clouds were spitting snow. A truly nasty morning.

She chuckled and said, "Happy birthday".

Over the years, the weather on my birthday has become something of a family joke.

February 3.

SNOW—Yesterday's snow was just right. Most of it fell when we could see and enjoy it, and most of it had melted off the street by the time we were ready to go home. The best thing about the day was provided by one of our favorite "short people" Margaret Newsome—one of our typesetters. She came back from lunch armed with a saucepan and all of the necessary ingredients and provided to whip up enough snow cream to feed the entire shop crew.

⁂

GRILL—The best news of the week for a lot of folks in this part of the state is that the Cypress Grill opened for the season last night. For the uninitiated, the grill is a board shack which sits on the bank of the Roanoke at Jamesville. To say the grill is "nothing fancy" is an understatement, but the food there in the late winter and early spring is something else. The limited menu consists principally of the harvests of the Roanoke and Albemarle Sound. Crisp fried herring and herring roe, fried rock, steaming bowls of rock stew, all accompanied by french fries, slaw and hush puppies."

It's too early in the season and too cold to interest me now, but it gives me a warm feeling to know the old grill will be in operation when dogwood begins to blossom and the white oak leaves are the size of a squirrel's ear.

March 3.

SPRING?— I saw my first crocus this week and my first jonquil buds. So what? I also saw February to out with snow and march come in with snow and ice. According to the calendar, spring is only 18 days away.

I don't believe it!

CICERO—Jim Simmons was in the office Monday and said he caught a five and a half pound roe shad in Swift Creek Sunday. He told me he was on his way to take the delicacy to Cicero and Ozelle Price.

That brought back memories of nights when Jim, Cicero and I along with Preacher Luther Brown, Frank O'Neal and several others would net fish spring nights at Ruffin's Landing. One night when the fishing unusually slow a voice from the darkness declared, "I think Cicero Price would trade off Ozelle for a fresh caught roe shad". From along the river came laughter and words of agreement, not one disclaimer was heard-not even from Cicero.

CLEAVAGE—Every time one of those lovely lasses, wearing a low-cut gown, jiggles across the TV screen and shimmies down next to the talk show host, I am tempted to go over to the set an peer leeringly downward. Of course, I know that such foolishness would be to no avail, but then there is always hope, like something that happened at Zoeller's Drug Store 20 or more years ago.

A bunch of the telephone boys took their morning and afternoon breaks there and most of them were Coke drinkers until the day Mr. Harvie Ward, the owner, changed soda jerks.

She was short, pretty, exceptionally well-built and just loved to wear those low-cut peasant-type blouses.

I don't recall which one of the telephone crowd first noticed it (perhaps "it" isn't the right word), but probably it was the fellow who ordered the five-cent ice cream cone. That little gal leaned way over, reached way down brought up a single scoop, and handed the cone to the fellow with the bulging eyes. He cleared his throat and said, "I think I'll take a ten-cent-er." He elbowed the guys on each side of his and the soda jerk went through her leaning and reaching routine again. They, too, stared.

Well, it didn't take long for the word to get around and on days when she wore one of those low-cut blouses, they gave up their Cokes for ice cream, flavor made no difference and they ordered their cones one dip at a time. Every time that girl leaned over one side of the counter, the telephone boys stood on tip toes to lean over their side and ogle. Before the week was out the soda jerk had gone through more exercises than the entire high school football team and the telephone boys were beginning to put on weight what with eating double and in some cases triple, dip cones twice a day.

I don't recall whatever happened. The girl probably wore herself plumb out and the telephone boys likely drifted away to Weight Watchers.

Like me and my tv set, they knew their ogling was useless, but as a very wise man once said, "An evil mind is a great comfort".

GOOF—Perhaps I just didn't listen closely enough last week after asking Distaff what she wanted for an anniversary present.

"Just something green", she replied.

Well, knowing she has a big thing going about house plants, I went out and bought the biggest hanging basket I could find—real, real green, accented with clusters of tiny pink flowers.

When I presented it to her Friday afternoon, she thanked me, gave me a sort of understanding smile, and said, "But I was thinking of something in jade".

Maybe next year I'll get the message.

May 5.

DUCKS—For Tarboro's wood duck in-residence and her brood of 11 ducklings, one odyssey ended last week and another began.

Mama duck first made her appearance this spring in Calvary Churchyard. The ducklings were caught in hopes that the mama would follow the catcher down Panola to the river, but she would have none of it. She waddles about, clucking and fussing until her children were returned to her and they were left in the green silence of the churchyard.

Her next appearance was smack dab in the middle of downtown Tarboro at 3:30 in the morning. She had a brood of eight at the time and they waddled (ducks can't do anything but waddle) across the intersection of Main and St. James on the red light, turned west on St. James and disappeared, probably in Miss Ellen Walston's backyard.

Last week Mrs. Gina Jenkins found mama duck and her brood, which now numbered 11, had somehow trapped themselves in the screen side porch of her home on E. Park Avenue.

After due discussion it was decided that perhaps urban living just wasn't the thing for mama wood duck and her ducklings, what with our dogs and cats and cars and kids. So they were all boxed up and taken out to Fishing Creek, freed and were last seen paddling happily upstream.

After all the years, still concerned about traffic safety.

OBSTRUCTIONS—A reader recently wrote to complain that the low, bushy trees which the town had planted along the south side of Howard Avenue were creating a traffic hazard. It is necessary, she wrote for, motorist to drive half a car-length into the intersection of Howard and Peach to see if the way is clear.

I checked out the complaint and if anything, it is understated. The situation at Peach is bad, but at Cherry it is worse. Perhaps some of those trees could be transplanted before something bad happens.

~

NIPPERS—I am among many who cussed the county's old "bug machine" as I retreated from the front porch when clouds of noxious fumes rolled in. But at least we thought the old machine was getting the job done.

The new mosquito-control machine hardly utters a hiss. One of the neighbors slapped one of the nippers off her arm after the machine passed, and muttered, "They are probably spraying with diluted water".

June 2.

STAMPS—The advent of the 13-cent stamp certainly didn't improve service. If anything it made things even worse. Two-cent stamps weren't available and the one-cent-errs were available only in sheets. That works something of a hardship on folks like us who use a hand-operated stamper that requires rolls of stamps. No need to worry about it, things are bound to get worse with the Postal Service. Haven't they always?

June.

RETROSPECT—This week I began my 29th year with this newspaper, and in retrospect I can think of only two of my stories which made the international news.

The first was when I discovered that Lew had inadvertently married 43 couples during the period his license as justice of the peace was expired. It took a special act of the legislature to clear that one up.

The other was an effort of the local school board to ban married pregnant students "because of what they might tell the other girls." That one never got through after the public finished laughing.

One of the sad times was when wrote the story that 300 employees at Burlington Mills were being laid off. And some of them didn't know they were losing their jobs until they read about it in the paper.

PARKER—In Pinehurst last weekend, Jim Parker was elected president of the North Carolina Press Association. Jim is a native of Tarboro and the brother of Mrs. Louise Davis and Mrs. Rosalie Thompson, who still reside here. In addition, he is editor-publisher of the Sampson Independent, the daily newspaper published in Clinton.

MEANEST—It took Mrs. Joe Neal a long, long time to save enough of those grocery store stamps to redeem them for a lawn mower.

Over the weekend the town's meanest man stole the mower and in the process of dragging it away, tore down a row of carefully strung butterbeans.

CROP—Brer George Grayiel reportedly harvested the potato crop last week from his garden at the intersection of Albemarle and Johnston. My source said George dug three pounds more than he planted.

SIDEWALKS—When it comes to the prevailing issue of brick versus concrete sidewalks, I joint the ranks of the latter.

Some years ago the town planted trees along downtown Main and the county did the same around the courthouse. Once the plantings were complete, the planters were filled with small, white, water rocks which were very, vary attractive.

Then one day the rumor got out that Tarboro was targeted for racial trouble. To every merchant looking out his plate glass window, those rocks suddenly seemed the size of baseballs and basketballs, and it wasn't too long before town trucks and crews were working the street, scooping up every available rock. About the same time, the county was duplicating the operation at the courthouse.

Of course, the rumored trouble never developed, but those pretty little rocks never reappeared.

I suppose we've come full circle or something because now some folks to want to line both sides of Main from Wilson to Walnut with loose bricks!

WEEKEND—What's to do this weekend?

Well, the fair is in town, there's a big ball game tonight, and there's the big Spring Hope Pumpkin Festival tomorrow. This is also the weekend of the 13th annual Wilson Antique Show and Sale and our sister city is now advertising itself as "The Antique Capital of the East". It's being held in the recreation center and hours are from 11 a.m. until 10 p.m. Saturday and 1 until 6 p.m. Sunday.

October.

MELON—We are somewhat red-faced about an Associated Press "filler" which slipped into the paper this week. Under a Springfield, S. C. dateline, it stated, "Ken Sanders, 33, has grown a 95-pound watermelon believed to be the largest, field-grown edible melon of its type ever harvested in the state.

"*The Guineas Book of Records* lists a 197-pound watermelon as the largest, but watermelon experts say that a melon that large is not edible and probably not field grown".

That world's record melon happens to have been grown by Edward Weeks, right here in Edgecombe County, while I can't attest to its sweetness, it most certainly field-grown, just like the remainder of Edward's whoppers.

This year wasn't a particularly good one of the Weeks' melon crop. The top one weighed 165 pounds and he had several which ranged from 120 to 140 pounds. "I had one order for 100 melons weighing over 100 pounds and I couldn't fill it." he said.

Incidentally, Edward is now selling his championship seed in every state in the union.

October 27.

REUNION—Our three-class reunion was well-neigh perfect. Some came from California and Florida and expressed puzzlement at why some of their classmates in the immediate area didn't show.

One of my old high school sweethearts was there. We embraced in the middle of the dance floor and then went to her table where I shook hands with her husband. It didn't take long to begin reminiscing. I draped my arm across the back of her chair, sort of against her back. That's when I guess I went too far.

"Remember" I asked, "those summer nights swinging in the swing on your side porch?"

Her husband's eyebrows shot up in a fashion that would put Senator Sam to shame, and she stiffened up as if she had suddenly swallowed an ironing board.

And the lady said, "But our house didn't even have a side porch or a swing".

I smiled and moved on to another table, knowing full well that I pass that house every day and it has a side porch and swing. I suppose that after 36 years you remember what you want to.

The highlight of the reunion for me - at least for a minute - was when a girl I hadn't seen since graduation came over, hugged and kissed me, and said, "Mabrey, I do declare. You look just like you did at graduation?".

She kissed me again and moved on.

I was somewhat elated until I remembered that twice in our senior we had been sent to the principal's office for cheating.

I guess she figured one more white lie wouldn't hurt.

It didn't.

~

RECORD?—Carl Doughtie dug up that giant okra stalk this week and the final measurement was 16 feet, four inches. I don't know what Guiness has to say about it, but the stalk is certainly a record hereabouts.

December 8.

PARADE—Yes, Virginia there IS a Russell Carter and because he exists you and your little friends had a Christmas parade, complete, of course, with Santa Claus.

For a while this fall it seems no group would sponsor the annual event, but the ever-faithful Russell again took the chairmanship, got the bands, the floats, the kids, and the money.

1979

GIFT—Elsewhere on this page Distaff makes much over a bunch of flowers I sent her on Valentine's Day. Actually, I had no alternative.

Last year, she gave me a candy bar with a card which read:

Do you love me or do you not?
You told me once, but I forgot."

OPEN—A half dozen or more people have called to ask about the Cypress Grill down at Jamesville.

The grill has been open for the past two weeks, featuring its usual fine menu of fried herring and rock, rock stew, and herring roe. It's open every day except Sunday.

Mistaken Identity?????

ANNIVERSARY—Tomorrow marks the 29th anniversary of the time Distaff and I checked into the Chalfont-Haddon Hall Hotel in Atlantic City for a one-night honeymoon.

I had never stayed in a swanky hotel before, and I had never been that high off the ground, so it took me a while to get over my awe. By the time I got around to popping the cork off a bottle of warm champagne, the phone rang and it was Distaff's grandmother wanting to know if we had arrived safely. When I assured her we were just fine, she said, "That's nice. What are you doing?" I told her we were sitting on the edge of the bed reading comic books, and that seemed to satisfy her because after a bit of small talk she said good night.

A couple of glasses of champagne later there came a knock at the door, and in answer to my irritated inquiry, a bellhop informed me I had a telegram. I told him to stick it under the door, and I was told something about that being against the rules.

I was about to tell him where else to stick it when I realized he wanted a tip. After a bit of haggling, I told him if he put the thing under the door I would push a tip out. He agreed and I went over and got a quarter out of my pants, and pushed it out as soon as I got my hand on the yellow letter. There was considerable mumbling on the other side of the door.

It was from some of her kin folks in Florida wishing us well.

The champagne was getting low when the phone rang again. When I answered, the operator asked if I was Mr. Bass, and when I assured her that such was the case she told me, "Just a minute for Pittsburgh."

A lady's voice came on the line and said, "Baker, we just wanted to know if you and Nancy arrived safely?" I inquired as to whom was calling and was told, "It's mother". I realized something here was bad wrong.

In the first place my mama doesn't call me Baker. In the second, the girl on the other side of the bed had certainly not signed "Nancy" on the wedding certificate earlier in the day. In the third place, with due respect, I'm not sure mama had ever been north of Richmond until she came to our wedding.

The lady's voice broke the silence, "Is this Baker Bass? I said yes, and she said, "Baker Mabrey Bass? I said yes, and she said, "Baker Mabrey Bass, Jr.? I told her she was right on all three counts. By this time both our voices were getting a bit shaky, so she tried once more. "Are you Baker Mabrey Bass, Jr. of Pittsburgh, Pennsylvania?" When I told her, "No m'am. I am the Baker Mabrey Bass, Jr. of Tarboro, North Carolina", she hung up.

I turned on the light and sat there on the edge of the bed, staring at the phone, wondering if I were losing my sanity. I polished off the champagne straight from the bottle and began looking around the room to see if by chance there just might be a comic book there.

When Distaff wanted to know what the problem was, I explained, and she said, "Don't worry. Everything is going to be all right".

So it was. And tomorrow night in another hotel in another place she will probably be saying the same thing.

DAY—I suppose I've had some memorable Father's Days in my 27 years as a parent, but last Sunday will always be remembered as something very special.

My going-on-four grandson John Broome gave me an entire hour of his time and while we were on our way to the river, the notion struck me to stop in at the fire station.

It was the youngster's first visit there and Leo Fanny gave him the VIP treatment upon learning that John's other grandpa was Jesse Broome, longtime fireman until his retirement a couple of years ago. Leo took the boy over to the old Seagrave pumper and explained that Grandpa Jesse had driven it on many occasions. Leo even rang the bell and cranked the siren for the awestruck youngster who couldn't quite bring himself to climb aboard.

Since returning home to Zebulon he has mustered his courage somewhat and tells his mother he can't wait to get back to "Granddad's fire truck".

RACE—The first Great Tar River Raft Race is now history, but already the participants are chorusing, "Just wait til next year."

There was at least one capsizing, and considerable dunkings as the intrepid rafters poled, paddled, oared and guzzled their way downstream. As expected in any first-time event of such magnitude, snafu areas did develop, but not once did they reach fubar proportions.

Admiral Harvey and Commodore Perry, I do believe Captain "Ducey" Parvin, late of the Steamer "Shiloh," would have been proud.

GONE—Sometime during the past couple of weeks someone cut down "my" persimmon tree. Actually it wasn't mine, for it stood at the edge of a field on what was the Barlow farm near what is now Moderncare.

It was the largest tree of its kind that I have ever found in the county, and on many autumn afternoons, while bird hunting, I stopped by the tree to eat a handful of the tart orange fruit.

Alas!

MYRTLES—Every spring we rave over the beauty of our town's dogwoods and azaleas, our enthusiasm probably boosted because the colors are in marked contrast to the drabness of winter. But this is the time of year for one of my favorite flowers, the crepe myrtles. Their blossoms offset; to some extent, the dog days ahead and their colors span the spectrum.

Dr. Clarence Poe, longtime editor of The Progressive Farmer, called the myrtles "the flower of 100 days" because some of them bloom long after Labor Day.

It's well worth a ride around town to see the wide variety of these colorful trees. Two of my favorites are in the yard of Mrs. Sam Taylor on W. Johnston Street.

TRIVIA—Did you ever wonder where the word "Hilma" originated?

It was coined by Gov. Henry Toole Clark and was the name he gave his home which was located o n the site of the present William Vance Motel. It represents the first initial of the names of his each of his five children: Haywood, Irwin, Laura, Maria, and Anabella.

September.

MISSING—An important bit of Tarboro history was discovered missing this week.

In an effort to aid a researcher, Barbara Boney went to get the minute book for the town's old synagogue from where her father always kept it, but it was not to be found. She believes that perhaps Lew loaned the book to someone who forgot to return it. If one of you readers happens to have it, please give Barbara a call because it is a family treasure.

The synagogue, which was torn down several years ago, was dedicated on Feb. 4, 1897.

RETROSPECT—Most folks keep cherished clippings and such in the family Bible, but at our house we use the Funk and Wagnal unabridged dictionary.

Delving through it last weekend, I came across a letter my mother wrote on Dec. 31, 1945 when I was in Japan. The war was over, but I was stuck with occupation duty while many of my friends were coming home. Here are a few newsy excerpts from her letter which I treasure:

"You know how Little Brother (Leggett, who was also in Japan) loves a dollar and what a trader he is - well he has sent his mother all varieties of table cloths and such. Now, he wrote somebody he had to close his letter because the fleet was in and he and his Jap friend had to do some trading. Don't you know he is a sight!

"Well, Joe (Bourne) didn't get to Tarboro until Christmas Day. He never wrote his mother the whole time he was on the West Coast. Finally, she got the Red Cross to investigate; and they found out he left the coast on Dec. 18 for home. He came all the way from California in a day coach with only one meal a day.

"Joe spent two hours with us Saturday. We thoroughly enjoyed him. He was a tough-looking egg; GI work shoes, wool pants and a dirty T-shirt, but we enjoyed his visit. He has a Yankee brogue like most of the ones who come back home.

"Charley Hussey is home. He went to work at the shop this week. He has been rushing Mamie Lois around, but he invited a WAC whom he went with in Miami to visit him this weekend, so I don't guess he is serious about Mamie Lois.

"Susan (Mrs. Hussey) is expecting a call from Howard any minute, saying he has hit the States. His boat is expected to dock at any time.

"Ashby Wiggins is home from Jacksonville, Fla. on furlough. He brought his girl friend home to meet the family. He isn't but 19.

"Hog Bear (Allen Lee Harrell) and Bo Carpenter leave tomorrow for Chapel Hill. It seems Wake Forest sent Bo to school in Rocky Mount (on a football scholarship) with intentions of getting him later.

"Caruso (Coach Joe) called Bo up last week and cussed him out. I don't know if it will do any good or not.

"The grandstand at the ballpark burned down last weekend. I hear fireworks were to blame."

And that's the way it was in Tarboro on New Year's Eve, 1945.

October. After 29 years, Ramblin' still prodded officials to do their jobs.

CROSSING—I don't know whether the town, the railroad or the department of transportation is responsible for the upkeep, but something needs to be done about the crossing at Howard and Albemarle.

I had a call last week about a blowout caused by an exposed bolt head.

FIRST—We had our first frost of the season this week. One man said it "came like a blanket" around 5:45 a.m. Tuesday, but it was light, so our first killing frost is still ahead.

PARADE—Russell Carter will probably be upset by my writing this, but the next time you see the genial N&O man and credit bureau owner, take time to say, "Thanks".

Why?

Because of Russell, our youngsters are going to have a Christmas parade, and you can be assured it will be a good one.

Several weeks ago I learned that there were no plans for our town to have a pre-Christmas procession for Santa since Russell was no longer associated with the chamber of commerce. No group would undertake the responsibility.

At the time I told Russell that if I had a thousand bucks I would bet that he wouldn't let a year go by without the traditional parade.

"No way," he replied. "It's time someone else took over. You would lose your bet."

But I would have won.

Russell came in the office yesterday and said he had relented. He had contacted the professional float owners, the bands, the industry and business leaders. As a result, we will have our parade.

LIST—Just suppose you could host a dinner party and evening of conversation for any ten people in all of history, whom would you invite?

This of course, comes under the heading of trivia, but you must admit it could be interesting. I pondered for a couple of days this week and came up with the names of Will Rogers, Mark Twain, Irvin S. Cobb, Joel Chandler Harris, Harry Truman, Alben Barkley, Abraham Lincoln, Havalah Babcock, H.L. Mencken, and Al Capp.

I considered including Franklin Roosevelt and Winston Churchill, but I felt those two would certainly hog the conversation.

Of course, I don't expect many, if any, of you readers would like to attend a dinner with my choice of guests. However, I believe you will agree compiling such a list could be intriguing. Any others who would like to share a list are most certainly welcome.

❧

LISTS—There were several more contributors of guest lists of historical personalities this week.

Glennes Weeks listed her choices as Henry David Thoreau, Ralph Waldo Emerson, Benjamin Franklin, John Wesley, Dwight L. Moody, Daniel Webster, Walt Whitman, Abraham Lincoln, Samuel Adams and Robert E. Lee.

Alec Peters wrote from UNC-Greensboro to name his choices as Mary, mother of Christ; Geoffrey Chancer, St. Francis of Assisi, Joan of Arc, Queen Elizabeth 1, Eleanor Dare, William Shakespear, George Wythe, Winston Churchill and J.R.R. Tolkier.

He explained, "It was extremely hard to narrow my list down to ten. So, rather than attempting to name my ten most favorite people of all time, I tried to choose people from different time periods and societies, thinking that the contrast would be interesting. I did, however, choose a couple of them simply because their lives have always fascinated me, and one or two just because they'd be good storytellers."

Jack Hopkins chose Genghis Khan, Lorenzo deMedici, Teddy Roosevelt, George Washington, Bushrod Washington, John Marshall, Richard Henry Lee, Lighthouse Harry Lee, Robert E. Lee, and Simon Bolivia.

Joe Maverick, a former Marine, wrote, "In my lifetime, the United States has been in protracted combat three times. The art of warfare has always intrigued me. I would like to spend an evening with 12 of the finest military minds in the history of warfare; each unique to region, time or circumstance."

His List:

Mangu Khan, Alexander the Great, Julius Caesar, the Alba of Benin, Emilianz Zapata, St. Joan of Arc, Simon Bolivia, Field Marshal Erwin Rommel, General George S. Patton Jr., General George C. Marshall, Admiral of the Fleet S.C. Garshkow, and Mao Tse-tung.

After Christmas.

GIFTS—There was a touch of O. Henry's "Gift of the Magi" at our house early Christmas morning. Distaff and I decided to exchange presents before the rest of the family arrived and things became hectic.

I opened mine first and found a record album. Now, that was real nice because it was Arthur Fiedler and the Boston Pops—among my favorites. But I didn't have a record player. I didn't say anything except I appreciated it very much.

Then she opened her present and found a pair of pretty earrings—for pierced ears—and her ears aren't pierced.

Well, she could exchange the earrings, and I could always go by a friends' house and play my record. That, I thought, was that.

But I was wrong. Later in the morning when the family arrived, I opened my present, and there was a neat stereo.

Among my other gifts was a tape recorder—something I have wanted for a long, long time, but always put off purchasing. I plan to use it to record my stories and those of my father and Uncle Doc to pass on to my grandchildren when they are older enough to appreciate them.

Yep, Christmas 1979 at 1006 Peach Street was a wonderful one for the children, parents, grandparents, and great-grandmothers.

1980

January 2 and an unappreciative guest.

SUPPER—On New Year's Eve, one of my friends was invited over to one of his friend's house for supper.

The menu consisted of ham hocks, black-eyed peas, collards, sweet potatoes, creamed corn, biscuits with "real" butter, pecan pie with vanilla ice cream. With the exception of the pie and ice cream, every item for the feast was cooked on a wood stove and served piping hot.

The guest rubbed his ample belly and reminisced, "It was the best meal I've ever eaten, except for mother's."

RETROSPECT—In looking over the events here at 504 W. Wilson Street for the past year, I suppose our "story of the year" could be called the Ordeal of Fred Sanderson.

Fred, our production boss, suffered a stroke in the early spring which affected his speech and mobility. Perhaps the late Sam Mayo our circulation manager and also a stroke victim, served as a challenge to Fred, because both of them refused to give up. Through therapy and determination Fred overcame his afflictions and is now in complete control of his beloved "Color King" press.

His return to us here at *The Southerner* is one of God's blessings for 1979.

February.

RECORD—It's official, the Blizzard of '80 set a record for Tarboro, despite some who contend it was exceeded by the Blizzard of '27.

Alvin Moore, Jr. has all of Tarboro's weather records, dating back to the 1880s, and they show that the snow of March 1 and

2 of 1927 measured 15 inches compared with 18.5 in the Blizzard of '80.

Dr. E.V. Zoeller, who was the official weather observer at the time, noted that the 1927 snow was the deepest since Jan. 8, 1887, when nine inches fell.

HISTORY—Last weekend's storm caused the Williamston Enterprise folks to go back through their files about storms in this area, and here are some of the facts they came up with:

The blizzard of 1927 began on March 1 and snow fell for 22 hours. It's nearest rival was on March 17, 1886.

Another big snow was reported in midwinter of 1877 and stayed on the ground for almost a month.

The paper reported, "The historic snow of 1857, which began falling on January 1, lasted more than two days and is said to have been deeper than the one in 1927. It was accompanied by one of the coldest snaps known in this section of the county, and it kept everything ice-bound for two months."

STUCK—My heartfelt thanks to the three young men who spent the better part of 45 minute pushing my car out of the snow in a Deerridge parking lot Monday afternoon.

FIRST—The best news for those of us who look forward to annual pilgrimages to the Cypress Grill on the banks of the mighty Roanoke is that Dewey Simpson netted the first herring of the season at Jamesville on Jan. 22.

I'll pass along the date of the opening as soon as I know it.

February 22

RUMOR—Street talk has it that Planters Bank of Rocky Mount will file papers in Raleigh Monday seeking a branch in Tarboro.

It may soon be that Tarboro will have more financial institutions than filling stations.

HOLE—That deep excavation in the courthouse mall site this week resulted in humorous re-telling of a story attributed to the late Charlie Clayton about 25 years ago.

The telephone contractors started tearing up Main Street in order to bury a cable. It seemed as though as least half the folks in town went up the foreman that hot summer day to ask, "Why are you all digging this hole?"

When Charlie ambled over to inquire about the excavation, the fed-up foreman replied, "We're gonna bury every s. o. b. in Tarboro".

Charlie allegedly didn't even blink and asked the man, "Who's gonna be left to cover them up?"

When the story was revived and revised at the mall site this week, someone said, "I thought all the s.o.b's were interred back in Charlie's day."

The reply: "They missed a few and now we've got a whole new crop."

BIRDS—The cedar wax wings arrived in our yard for the first time Sunday after the fresh snow, but found the pickings somewhat slim. The grackles had already denuded the dogwood, the privet, and a couple of other berry-bearing shrubs whose names I can't spell.

HERRING—I was down at Jamesville Wednesday night, and in talking with the boys in the Green Leaf Motel I learned the herring run in the Roanoke has been extremely light thus far this year.

Incidentally, herring roe is selling for $4 a quart.

VISITORS—Thus far, Mama Wood Duck has not made her appearance on the Common, but we did have other winged visitors for a few minutes at 8:45 a.m. Tuesday. That's the time a flight of 36 Canada geese flew over downtown, heading north.

That was one of the few times I have ever seen geese here during daylight, although I have seen several flights as they crossed the October moon heading south.

RETURNS—Last week I wondered if the Town Common wood duck would favor us with another visit this year, just as she has for a number of others.

Fred Howard, superintendent of the street department, came by to report that Mama Duck has already made an appearance.

One of his crews two weeks ago spotted the duck waddling across St. Andrews Street, followed by an even dozen ducklings.

Tarboro always has been a fine place to raise a family.

Push, pull, prod, lead, nag to get it done.

LIGHTS—For more than a year the pet peeve of one of the coffee crowd has been the town's failure to set many of its traffic lights to flash yellow instead of turning red and green between the hours of 10 p.m. and 6 a.m. Certainly, there is something mighty irritating about a red light holding you up at midnight when there is no one else in sight.

The police used to set the lights, but the practice has long since been abandoned.

ROSES—If you're riding around this weekend, stop at the cotton press and enjoy the rose garden. It's a real All-America beauty.

PLAY—This week I came across a yellowed clipping from *The Southerne*r which someone had given me a while back. It pertains to a play which was to be given in the opera house by members of the Wake Up and Live Club, but no date was listed.

That organization was formed here in the Depression by Aubrey Shackle then editor of *The Southerner*, in an effort to give kids something to do. It came at a time when the easiest thing to do was get into trouble. But back to the play.

It was described as a 3-act western comedy and Gene Simmons was listed as being the director. Leo Fanny was listed as being the leading man, but no female lead was included.

Entertainment between the acts was provided by Tom Cordon, who sang, "In the Hills of Old Wyoming"; Ruth Abrams, who sang, "Once In Awhile"; Helen Harrell and James Lee who sang, "You're the One Rose". Other entertainment was provided by Nanny Abrams and Ella Mae Lassiter, who were accompanied by Bert Wells on the guitar.

Members of the cast were Tom Cordon, William Hoard, Stella Keene, Ann Rodgers, Helen Harrell, Lawrence Morris, Bruce

Alford, Otis Taylor, Paul Beech, Jack Hoard, Ruth Abrams, Ruppert Armstrong, James Riley, Estelle Abrams, Ray Alderman, John Brantley, Julian Lee, Irene Parker, Dorothy Harris, Glendora Lee, Emily Long, Margie and Mary Holland, Betty Dowdy, Lula Rogers, William Jacobs, Susie Taylor, Lucy Abrams, Gladys Hoard, Tom Hoard, Moses Abrams, Melvin Hoard, and Ruby Harrell.

I'd be interested in knowing whether or not the offering was a success, but it must have been if the parents of all those kids turned out.

TOUR—For those of you who may have wondered what son John is doing these days, the word is he is mighty busy. The summer schedule for John and others of the New York City Ballet Company calls for performances in Saratoga Springs, N.Y., Washington D.C., Paris, West Berlin and Copenhagen.

The old prison farm takes on a new and dazzling personality.

NAME—By golly, that was really something!

At 9 Monday morning, we didn't have one, but when the county commissioners adjourned for lunch, we did!

Presto!!

Out on the fire tower road there now stands a college where once was an institute. And it was done in one fell swoop.

I suppose the initial cost will be modest. They will have to change the sign—replace it with Old English type. Of course, exterior plywood and whitewash can be used to construct the columns until the alabaster ones arrive. Plastic ivy can be sprigged about until the real stuff takes root. And I suppose we never again will be offered such extra curricular classes as bridge playing, poodle clipping and cake icing.

I reckon the hardest part for me will be getting use to calling Charlie McIntyre "Chancellor".

GONE—Tarboro lost a landmark in last Friday evening's storm, and I didn't even learn about it until yesterday morning.

Bud Shook told me of the loss of the towering old persimmon tree which dominated the north side of what was the Bridgers school ground. It was apparently early in the storm when wind broke off the entire top, leaving only a naked spar.

Bud recalled how we played baseball in the shade of that old tree in the springs and summers nearly 50 years ago and how, after frost came, we enjoyed the succulent orange fruit it bore. He speculated that it was the largest persimmon tree in the county, and I'm inclined to agree.

RECITAL—Several weeks ago, Dennis Rogers wrote an entertaining column about an alleged recital in the old elementary school auditorium. After Miss Susie Pender's pupils had given their best, came the climax. Miss Susie was going to render "Indian Love Call," but, according to Dennis, midway through the lyrics the garden hose which supplied the ersatz fountain got loose. The singer got soaked as did the folks in the first couple of rows.

Dennis wound up his offering with, "I think it would serve Tarboro right if Miss Susie never sang again. That town ain't ready for culture, obviously."

I was going to ignore the Rogers' fantasy, but this week I learned it had been reprinted by at least two Florida papers—West Palm Beach and Ft. Lauderdale. The latter offering was headed, "Tarboro Too Wet Behind the Ears for Culture."

Adding insult to injury, the writer led off his column with, "Tarboro, a sleepy and sunbaked little tobacco town in eastern North Carolina might seem an unlikely spot for a major cultural event. Yet it happened, and all of Tarboro is still buzzing from it if we may believe my colleague Dennis Rogers of the Raleigh *News and Observer*, and I believe we can."

Buddy boy, you can't.

I talked to Miss Susie's contemporaries, other members of Over the Hill Gang and her neighbors. In addition, I talked with the fellow who, as a kid, was paid five cents to gather enough Queen Anne's Lace to decorate the stage for the annual recitals.

Not one of them ever heard tell of the errant garden hose.

OMEN—Mark it on your calendar. Yesterday morning brought the first August fog, and the number of fogs in this month of the year is suppose to portend the number of snows we'll have in the winter ahead. At least we're half-way through the month.

⁂

HOUSE—There's something sad about the Mahler-Powell house being up for sale.

That sweeping front porch with the swing at the south end is certainly a part of our local lore. On summer nights any passers-by were always welcomed to come up and sit a spell with the Mahlers and the Blakes. I suppose more good stories were told, more lies swapped, and more gossip whispered on that porch than any place in town with the possible remote exception of the benches outside the old fire station.

⁂

CHIEF—I'm sure a lot of folks hereabouts join me in offering sincere congratulations to Ernest Ward on his promotion to our town's police chief. I have had the privilege of knowing him and working with him for all of the 27 years he had devoted to the police department. While we haven't always seen eye-to-eye on a few things, Ernest has always been honest with me—always fair.

And in this business, that's all I could ask for.

⁂

NUTS—This is the time of the year—I may be wrong, it's been so long—that I get a craving for chinquapins. I haven't seen even one of those shiny, sweet, acorn-shaped, burr-protected nuts in more than six years.

⁂

PULLERS—I suppose there are few folks now living who know what a "chinquapin puller" is. A chinquapin is protected by a burr which by comparison makes a cuckleburr feel like an egg.

It was a small, tong-like device which quickly separated the burr from the nut. My Uncle Spencer had the only pair I have ever seen, and that was years ago.

NUTS—Last week's item about chinquapins brought back pleasant memories for several readers, but it also revealed that no one at the office under 30 years of age had even heard of those tasty little gifts of nature.

Next week.

My spirits were revived Monday afternoon when Nathan Worsley came in the office bearing a bough with three green burrs attached. He also had a twig on which was a ripe chinquapin, peering from its protective burr.

So the chinquapin still survives in Edgecombe!

JOHN—The best Christmas present of all arrived at our house last Sunday when we learned that son John had been able to re-arrange his schedule so that he can spend five days with us beginning Dec. 22.

EVE—In all of my 55 years, I have been fortunate in that I have missed being with my loved ones on only three Christmas Eves.

On two of them I was overseas in the Marine Corps.

Tonight, I am sitting on the side of my bed in room 225, Edgecombe General. The long hall is quiet and the nurses chat softly by the small white tree at their station. From the TV speaker comes the joyous sound of the traditional service at Duke Chapel.

It is 15 minutes before Christmas.

Much has happened to me since this column last appeared, so tonight I am truly thankful that I can be with my family in spirit if not in person.

I am also thankful for the fellows in the rescue squad, the emergency room crew, my doctor, the ladies in white on the second floor. To those who came and those who called, those who sent remembrances of one kind or another, who prayed.

Christmas is now five minutes old, so as Tim Cratchett put it so fittingly many years ago:

GOD BLESS US EVERYONE!

1981

(Cotton's Restaurant on St. James Street was Ramblin's Combat Information Center. He drank coffee there with his friends, picked up rumors, the latest jokes and local insults. Hardly a week passed that Ramblin' did not give Cotton's a free plug—so many, in fact, and so repetitious that the editors did not include them here. The relationship was warm and wholesome. Cotton's later honored Ramblin' by putting a brass plaque on the chair he occupied every day. The following exchange is typical of the friendship.)

BACK—It was good to get back to the office Monday after a forced absence of a week, and most of the folks seem to have missed me, or at least they said they did.

Wednesday, for the first time in about ten days, I got together with the coffee crowd at Cotton's. When I walked in somebody said, "Well, you're looking good".

Cotton quickly countered, "That's a plain lie. He might be looking better, but he ain't never looked good."

The same might be said of the taste of his coffee . . . It might be tasting better, but it ain't never tasted good.

So there!

HOLIDAY—I was paroled from Edgecombe General in time to join my family at noon on Christmas Day, and the delayed dinner was well worth the waiting.

My doctor's parting words were something to the effect that I could eat as much of anything as I wanted. I think he would have been proud of me. Even had seconds on some, and topped the repast off with huge slices of orange cake and manna from heaven cake, which had been thoughtfully provided by two of my favorite non-resident cooks.

As for the doc's other advice? Well, I didn't even ask for a helping of my mama's famous tipsy cake.

How Miss James Ruffin got her name.

NAMES—I came across a couple of bits of historical trivia involving Tarboro names this week which I believe bear passing along for posterity.

In the first half of the last century, Spencer D. Cotten was a prominent local citizen. In 1833, he was a member of the vestry of Calvary Church, and a newspaper account in 1852 described him as a "a man of wealth and eminence". But he was married to James D. Ruffin!

However, the same article describes James D. Ruffin as being "spoke of in terms of highest admiration" and later ". . . a most splendid creature. . . a gem". The writer continued: "On inquiring as to they why and wherefore Miss James D. Ruffin bore a masculine name, we were told that she obliged to wear it in order to inherit a large estate in land and slaves bequeathed by a bachelor uncle who expressly stipulated in his will that his property be descended to the first born of his younger brother, provided it was christened after him—James D. Ruffin. The old fool had not recollected at the time he made his will that it was possible that the first born of his brother might be a girl."

April 20

VISITOR—Could the mama wood duck who showed up with her brood of ducklings in the courtyard of Tarboro Savings and Loan last Friday morning possibly be the same one who first favored us with a visit eight or nine years ago?

Owen Strickland was the first to tell me about the duck's initial visit. She and her ducklings were nesting in a hollow oak in the Common in front of his home. We agreed, however, that any publicity would be detrimental since children would likely flock to the Common and pester the creatures to death.

The following spring, however, mama duck made news we couldn't ignore. Sam Womble called me from his service station at Main and Wilson to say the duck and ten ducklings had stopped Main Street traffic in both directions as they waddled westward across the street.

Since then mama duck and her ducklings managed to find a hole in Mrs. Sam Jenkins' porch screen and trap themselves. That year Perry Jenkins took the critters out to the small pond at Brinson Chevrolet and freed them.

Last spring, ma and the young'uns turned up in the Mavretic's swimming pool.

Biologists at the Wildlife Resources Commission were intrigued when I told them about our duck.

A wood duck banding program back in the '60s showed the projected longevity of a female wood duck to be 1.95 years. The program also showed that banded female ducklings—when grown—return to the place of their birth to lay their eggs and raise their brood.

Let's be careful how we remove old trees from the Common lest we urban renewal our delightful spring visitor out of house and home.

NAMES—One of life's little mysteries of old Tarboro was solved for me this week when I came across an item in an old *Southerner* in which Mr. Whit MacNair explained why he and his brother Mr. Henry McNair spelled their last names differently.

Said Mr. Whit, "I am Scotch, and Henry is English."

That explains it?

May.

RACE—Tomorrow is the day for the third annual Great Tar River Raft Race, and I'm putting my money on the three-man Black & Decker entry.

Back in April, Eddie Everett, Frankie Gallinoto and Tim Coley won the six-mile Neuse River race against 14 competitors in one hour and 26 minutes. The three use six oars to propel their twin-pontoon craft.

At this writing, the Tar is so low that the oars, at some points, will probably be used as stilts.

Bon voyage to all!

June, beginning the fourth decade as editor.

RETROSPECT—This month marked the beginning of my 31st year in helping to get out this daily family offering, and that's longer by three years the tenure of Frank Powell, the original editor of *The Southerner*.

Nearly every day of those three decades has been interesting, because in this business when you go to bed at night, you have no idea what tomorrow's finished product will herald.

There have been threats on my life and that of Distaff. Telephone harassment has been no stranger, but in all those years I have only once been threatened with a libel suit, and in looking back I reckon that's more of an insult that a compliment.

In all those years, I had two stories which attracted national and international attention.

The first concerned a local justice of the peace who inadvertently married 43 couples from the time his commission expired until the day I learned of it. The "marriages" had been performed over a period of several years and there was no way of informing the couples involved. The ramifications of what had been done were tremendous. Children had, no doubt, been born out of wedlock. A spouse, learning that no legal knot had been tied, could simply walk out on his mate. As it turned out, it took a special act of the General Assembly to undo what he had done.

The Associated Press paid me one dollar for each of the stories I filed on the case. And what about the erring justice?

He got an expense-paid trip to New York to appear on "I've Got a Secret".

My second biggie concerned the Tarboro school board which one spring decided that married teen-agers who became pregnant could not attend school because they would be a "bad influence" on the other students. That riled a bunch of parents somewhat, and I decided to get some mileage out of the story. The story ended with the board looking mighty foolish and the mothers-to-be returning to class.

In the field of government two trivial, but amusing, stories stand out.

Back in the 50s, the county board was composed of Walter Hargrove, Henry Davenport, Ben Mayo, and Robert Lee Dunn. It was a mighty conservative board, one not given to spending the public's money without much, much consideration.

At this particular meeting, an elderly man came into the commissioners' room and sat down gingerly, wincing as he sat. Mr. Mayo, the chairman, interrupted the proceedings and said, "Gentlemen, I think we are familiar with this case, and we agree that $35 is a fair settlement." The auditor then handed the man a check and eased himself up and left the room.

After a few minutes of silence, the board broke into laughter, and I asked what was going on.

As it turned out, the week before, the man had reported for jury duty and during his tenure he had to go the men's room which was located in the basement of the old courthouse.

What he didn't know was that the janitor had swabbed down the john seats with a strong creosote solution, and was called away before he could rinse them off. The result was the juror was scalded around his hindparts. To me, $35 seemed a small amount to accept for the indignity.

The second government story happened one hot summer night as the town commissioners met in the old town hall.

For several years the board had been engaged in dealing with a real estate developer who, at best, could be termed "unreasonable". This particular night the discussion about the developer droned on until it became too much for Mayor Ed Roberson.

He blurted out the developer's name and added, "...is a s.o.b."

A man in the audience sprang up, pointed his finger at the mayor and said, "He is my uncle and I am going to sue you for slander.

Almost tiredly, Commissioner "Pug" Bass said, "Oh, sit down and shut up." He, too, named the developer and added, "is, has always been and always will be a s.o.b."

There was never any lawsuit. In looking back over 30 years of small town newspapering, I believe I can honestly say that I have always tried to be fair. I never deliberately wrote anything to hurt anyone. This job hasn't always been easy, but it has never been dull. Maybe some day I'll write a book.

Maybe.

Killer on the loose.

LOSS—There was a small tragedy of sorts in our neighborhood late one afternoon last week.

For a number of springs, we at the south end of Peach Street have enjoyed the comings and goings of a pair of partridges who paraded across our lawns. Their nest, I presume, is in C.R. Jones' vast backyard. This time of year—mating season—they would fly across South Howard Circle, land in Walter Godwin's yard and walk through the yards of Margaret Holland, Ruby Servais, and Eliza Elliott. They crossed the street at the Johnston intersection, skirted Fred and Josie Davenport's yard and headed homeward through the yards of Mary Kinzinger, Ed and Mattie Hanke, mine, and Clarence and Betty Wickham before returning to their nest.

When they reached my yard last Wednesday, the rooster was strutting and the hen was scuttling along behind. Almost quicker than I could see, a jet black cat sprang from beneath an azalea and grabbed one of the birds. I'm not sure which one for it was just that fast.

I grabbed something to throw and rushed outside, but I was too late. The renegade and its prey had disappeared, and the remaining quail had flown homeward.

Along about dusk dark, I walked out in the hard and from the vicinity of C.R.'s backyard came the call of "bob white, bob white." The whistle also comes in the early morning now and somehow it seems even more plaintive, even more desperate, than it did that first evening.

And the damned cat is still at large.

QUAIL—A couple of weeks ago, I wrote about the black cat which killed one of two quail which were members of our neighborhood. I said I believed their nest to be in C.R. Jones' backyard, which borders Hendrick's Creek.

C.R. called and said the bird which was killed was probably the hen, because he had found a nest containing 14 eggs. The morning after he found the nest, seven eggs had disappeared, so he set a large rat trap nearby. The following morning all the eggs were gone, and the trap had not been sprung.

This week, Jenness Owens came in and said he had seen the killer cat in his yard on numerous occasions. He added that he had found the remains of two quail.

In the late evenings and early morning the cock quail still calls from C.R.'s backyard, and now several young rabbits are frisking around the neighborhood. I suppose it's just a matter of time before the cat begins working on them.

RING—Magistrate Horace Ward probably has the most unusual hobby in Tarboro. He has a metal detector, and he hunts for treasure, mostly in the downtown area.

One of his most recent finds was made on the old Bridgers School grounds near the corner of Park Avenue and St. Patrick Street. His detector beeped or buzzed or whatever, and about six inches down he found a Tarboro High School class ring. It was dated 1921 and marked "10 K". There were no initials.

Horace said he doubted there were many members of that class still around, but I think he's wrong. I know at least four members of the Class of 1916 who are still very much a part of the local scene.

BOOK—I got a copy of Charles Edwards' "The Hell You Say" yesterday. I haven't been worth a hoot for work since.

Edwards, a native of Old Sparta, and, by his own accounting an apparent lifelong job-jumper, is a masterful storyteller. I'm still reading, but thus far it seems there is a chuckle, laugh, or a pure-tee belly laugh on each of its 200 pages. The book isn't limited to events in Edgecombe, but our county in general and Old Sparta in particular certainly have their share.

FRIENDS—There are many tests of what it takes to break a friendship, but none I remember more vividly than one which surfaced during a murder trial here in the late 1950s.

I can't recall whether the questioning was being by Solicitor Hubert May or Cam Weeks and Chan Muse, defense attorneys but it went something like this:

Q—Are you and the defendant friends?

A—No, sir.

Q—Were you ever friends, good friends?

A—Yes, sir.

Q—How close?

A—Well, we bought a lion together when the fair went broke in Scotland Neck.

Q—What did you do with him?

A—We took him out to his place.

Q—And you were still friends and drinking pals?

A—Yes, sir.

Q—Then what caused your falling out?

A—The lion.

Q—How?

A—Well, one day we had been drinking some, and he took my bulldog and chunked him in the cage with the lion.

Q—Is that when you had your falling out?

A—No, sir.

Q—When did that come?

A—When I went in the cage to get my bulldog, and he locked the door behind me.

If there were more questions and answers, I can't remember because the courtroom erupted in laughter, and the judge was among them.

VISITOR—I returned from lunch one afternoon last week to find a large, bearded black man looking at our back issues. Darnell Anderson, somewhat awed, whispered, "He's the Atlanta district editor of "Newsweek" magazine."

Intrigued, I went over and introduced myself and asked if I could help.

He explained his magazine was planning a Veteran's Day article, focusing on the present-day whereabouts of members of a Vietnam infantry company. He said that during several of his interviews, the name of Bobby Jones had come up. He was looking, he said, for the obituary of Bobby.

Bobby, son of the last Police Chief and Mrs. Jim Jones of Princeville, carried papers for us for more than five years, and I considered him to be a personal friend.

We talked for a while and he took notes faster than anyone I've ever seen outside a courtroom. I got Mrs. Jones' phone number for him, and called Ed Bridgers to find out where she lives.

I'm certainly looking forward to the issue of "Newsweek" nearest Nov. 11.

Joe Grayiel has edge in campaign for mayor.

RACE—At this writing there are three candidates for mayor—Leslie Wickham, Joe Grayiel and Billy Stell—which should make for an extremely interesting race.

Leslie has served on a number of governmental committees, Billy spent more than 30 years involved in town finances, the majority of them as finance director. Joe? Well, Joe has attended numerous council meetings over the years, and if there is anyone in the town limits who loves Tarboro more than I do, I would have to say it's Joe.

Actually, Joe has a big advantage over his opponents. He has an identical twin brother, George, but theres a whole lot of folks in town who don't know this. Therefore, Joe can get a heap more campaigning done than Leslie and Billy, and it would be completely honest. George could rap on a door and offer a spiel something like this:

"My name is Grayiel, and I think a Grayiel has a great deal to offer as Tarboro's next mayor. I certainly would appreciate your vote for Grayiel on Nov. 3."

Joe definitely has the edge at this point.

(Ramblin's good friend Cotton Guill, owner of Cotton's Restaurant had become ill the previous summer and had been in a coma ever since. This is Ramblin's final tribute to his old friend.)

OVER—The ordeal of seven long months ended Wednesday morning with the death of Horace Linwood "Cotton" Guill in the Intensive Care Unit of Edgecombe General where he had been since April.

Throughout his life Cotton was independent, almost fiercely so. With the exception of his high school years when he worked Saturdays in a local grocery, there were few times in his life when he took a pay check bearing another man's signature. Cotton, through hard work and foresight, made his own way.

He relished life to the fullest whether it was hunting and fishing in Edgecombe, cooking a stew, frying fish for friends, swapping good stories, or just sitting on the deck of his mobile home at Salter Path admiring the Atlantic.

In retrospect, we are thankful for the years we enjoyed his friendship and his "good company". To say Cotton will be missed is an understatement. We have missed him for the past seven months.

1982

YEAR—I'm of the opinion that one of the best things to happen hereabouts last year was what took place in downtown, excluding the fact that the town took thousands of dollars off the tax books and put several folks out of business.

I'm referring to the face-liftings at Shugar's, Adler's, First Colony, Video, Benton's and Simmons'. The addition at Robert's enhanced the Courthouse Square as well as providing more attractive display space in the store.

To be sure, we still have quite a ways to go, but 1981 marked a fine start. Now if we can just find a buyer for the Farrar-Martin house.

NAME—Several years ago when the town established what is now known as Sunset Park, I suggested in this column that it be named the M.S. Brown Park as a memorial to a man whose public spirit has never been and probably never will be matched.

To update generations not privileged to have known Mr. Brown, he and his brother, Raymond, owned the local Coca Cola plant. If you referred to Mr. Milton Steele Brown, maybe a limited number of folks would know who you were talking about, but mention "Coca-Cola Brown" and the whole county could identify with the man.

At the end of Porter Street at it intersection with Poplar Street there is a new short street which leads to the new swimming pool. Would it not be fitting, even at this late date to name that street in honor of this man? Not just Brown Street, but M.S. Brown Street. I hope this suggestion is given favorable consideration before some member of the local bureaucracy dubs it Very Short Street.

The idea of naming this street did not originate with me, but with a friend of long standing who is also a great admirer of Mr. Brown.

A report from the past.

NOSTALGIA—(From an account written by the late J. P. Keech) "Most of the men who were raised in Tarboro and are over 30 years of age will recall the scenes on Tar River from the bridge to the Black Pond on the Panola Farm.

"There were regular foot paths all the way and every summer afternoon the boys would go up the river and spend an hour or two in Green Banks, the best swimming hole in the world.

"Then, too, all the way on the banks of the river were to be found great quantities of Fox Grapes and Coon Grapes. The trees were often covered by these grapes, and to this day those who have ever eaten these grapes have not forgotten their delightful flavor.

"There are many today who will tell of coming from the river and finding their clothes tied in hard knots, and a few will brag of the fights that often took place.

"Boys would take into the fields of Mr. William Battle (located behind The Barracks) and there helped themselves to Scuppernong Grapes. These trips were usually successful, but often the boy put on a vantage point would yell out, 'A man and big dogs is coming'. Then across the creek and through Mr. J.L. Bridgers' pasture the boys would go.

"We wonder if there are any bad things for the school boys of today can do. There are no grapes to take. They don't bathe in the river. The goats have eaten the grape vines, and the art of fishing among the boys is forgotten.

"The snows have stopped coming. The river won't freeze enough for skating. The boys are ashamed to go barefooted. The fish won't bite. The river is dangerous to health. You can't pick up iron and bones and sell them. Bicycles are a thing of the past. You can't shoot robins, and you no longer build a camp along the creek.

"Who wants to be a boy of today anyway?"

The above was written more than 50 years ago by the late Dr. J.P. Keech, local historian and justice of the peace. I was just growing up at the time, but I swam at Green Banks, fished at Black Pond, and knew the difference between fox and coon grapes. I wore out at least three bicycles that I can remember. I shot robins and cooked then over a smoky pine fire at Lloyd's sand pit, and I camped along Hendricks Creek.

Several generations have come along since Dr. Keech's lamentations, but I suppose that at last it is safe to say that the school boys of today would know nothing of what he wrote and what's more, they couldn't care less.

And that's sad.

March.

PAST—As one of the few remaining local history buffs, I'm always elated when I find a bit of the past about which I know nothing.

Such was the case this week when I come across a column written by Dr. J.P. Keech about members of the Jewish community here during the 1870s and 80s. Most of their stores were located in the 200 block of Main Street, but there were some in every downtown block.

Dr. Keech wrote:

"Mr. A. Spier and family conducted the Gregory Hotel. They were good hotel people, and they were from Boston.

"In those days each Jewish merchant would bring from the North every fall from two to four extra men to use as clerks during the winter season.

"Some of their names follow: Joe Zeistevier, Mr. Chatham from the New York Square, who was the first partner in the grocery with D. Lichtenstein. Blossom Hersberg, Jake and Dave Hersberg, Rosenthal Btar and Jacobs. Charlie Wise, a good theatrical man and singer from Philadelphia. Joe and Meyer Saul, Billy Jacobs, Mr. Rund, Moses Wimberg, Ike Henry, Moses and Joe Litchtenstein, Sol Goodman.

"A. Arnheim and family, Henry, Abe and Joe Morris and families, there were many children. George and Joe Zander and families. George was the father of Gus Zander and Mrs. D. Licthtenstein. Kracker, a man from Prussia and uncle of Gus Zander.

"Sol Luinski, Sol. Whitlock. A. Whitlock and family. Dave Sternglaantz. Sam Schultz. Jim and Joe Odenheimer. Jim Mantel. Miss Julia Feldenheimer, the prettiest woman in Tarboro , a neice of Uncle Jake Feldenheimer. Jacob Feldenheimer and family, who were the first Jewish settlers in Tarboro, and Uncle Jake Hirshbaum."

The Feldenheimers could have been the first Jewish family here, but I'm inclined to believe Tarboro had a Jewish resident in the 1700s. John Schenk came here from the western part of the state and was Tarboro's second postmaster, serving from 1795 until 1807. At some time during his life he amassed what was a fortune in those times. He never married, and when he died he left the majority of his estate to friends here and in other parts of Eastern Carolina. However, he stipulated that a trust be established and a small amount be sent at regular intervals to his brothers in Riga, Russia.

Large numbers of Jews came to this country from that area, so this would indicate to me that Schenk was Jewish.

April 23.

SOLONS—L.H. Fountain's decision to end his long and distinguished career in Congress also means it will be a long, long time before old Edgecombe has another son (or daughter) there.

Throughout its history, Edgecombe has produced only six men to serve in Congress. Thomas Blount was the first, followed by James West Clark, Thomas Hall, Richard Hines, and George White, a black. Fountain is the only one to serve in this century.

(Carolina Tel and Tel had built a huge new office complex on the western by-pass and set aside several acres for employee vegetable gardens. Ramblin's continued love for fresh home grown vegetables shows on June 11 as the gardens were in their full glory.)

GARDEN—For three times a day, five days a week, since Easter Monday I have watched in wonder as the telephone family garden on Western Boulevard grew. At the present stage it can best be described as lush—a sea of varying shades of green. I only wish there were some way to determine the dollar-value of this labor of love to the families involved.

Nowadays, three times a day, five days a week, I am sorely tempted on some dark night to sneak into that Eden and grabble me some new potatoes. Years ago, when my uncles had gardens, grabbling became a seasonal rite for Distaff.

HISTORY—Over the years I have collected a number of items of historical trivia on the local scene, and I reckon now is as good a time as any to share some of them with you:

There is one black buried in Calvary Churchyard.

A stone, erected in her memory near the present All Saints Chapel reads, "Amy, A Good Servant and Humble Christian. Died June 26, 1860. Aged 90 Years".

Amy was a much beloved "mammy" in the family of Hugh Blair Bryan, great-grandfather of W.D. Bryan, Jr.

Today's generation won't believe these items, but in 1879, the police chief was ordered to lay off two baseball grounds on the Town Common.

In 1894, the town board granted permission for a bicycle track a round the Common for the benefit of the bicycle club. It was located on that block occupied by Bridgers School.

At 9 o'clock on the night of Aug. 1886, the Charleston Earthquake struck.

In Tarboro, there came without warning a noise of great thunder in the distance, growing louder and louder. The houses began to tremble, followed by shaking. Dishes were thrown from the shelves, fear gripped the people, and they fled from their houses.

Many were afraid to go back in their homes and remained out all night, but only a few small shocks followed the first severe one.

August 6—a political endorsement.

CHOICE—Well, the town councilmen are hoping to hear from citizens on their choice to succeed the late Mayor Leslie Wickham. I'm sure they will be heard, but the voices of 524 citizens are already on record as having a choice. They're the ones who voted for Billy Stell for mayor in last November's municipal election.

Stell had about 35 years in town government prior to his retirement last year. Most of those years were spent as finance officer and in that capacity he had a first-hand opportunity to know, money-wise, each of the town's departments. He certainly has a working relationship with the town's department heads.

September 17.

FILM—Last week this column sought, without success, the whereabouts of the framed handbill advertising the sale of "The Grove" in the 1850s.

So what else is missing?

How about two films.

The first was a melodrama made in the late 1930s under the sponsorship of local merchants. As I recall, it featured Glennes Weeks being kidnapped right off Main Street. I can't remember who played the villain, but I believe Jimmy Spiers was the hero, and a lot of other local folks got in on the action. The final result played to full houses at The Colonial. A black and white print was given the sponsored and was laid away forgotten until the early 1950s when it was found, brittle and in generally bad shape.

W.C. Ranes, Jr., did a creditable job of restoring it and M.S. Brown showed it before large crowds at the ball park and later at the swimming pool. Mr. Brown stipulated the film be placed in the town vault. And that was apparently the end of that. No more film.

In the early 1960s when the old town hall was demolished, Charlie Clayton took a day-by-day color film of the work, including the removal of old town bell and the spectacular collapse of the magnificent clock tower.

When his filming was done, Charlie sent his film directly to Eastman Kodak with specific instructions that it be developed and treated for preservation as an item of historic significance. Charlie paid the bill.

When his handiwork was returned, Charlie made arrangements to show it to the town councilmen who were then meeting in an old building in the 200 block of W. St. James while the new town hall was being built.

After the showing Charlie presented his film to the town and Mayor Ed accepted it. Presumably, it would have been placed in the town vault, but the last time I asked, no one knew of its whereabouts.

And that's another crying shame.

Things are picking up.

MONTH—September—all 30 days of it—was an especially good time of the year for me.

The scuppernongs were in plentiful supply. I got a note paid off, and only on a few occasions did Distaff feel the need to raise her voice to me.

Hassell Thigpen came in as the days were dwindling down with a bountiful box of boiled peanuts and a half-pocketful of chinquapins.

I took a few of those tasty, shiny, brown acorn-like nuts across the way to Charlie Hussey, who immediately recalled the chinquapin-hunting days of our boyhood.

He remembered the two best places were on the Cromwell farm, now a pine tree farm, and the Sam Jenkins farm. I relied on my supply mainly from a couple of bushes on my uncle's farm, but also made annual visits to the Cromwell Place.

About ten years ago the late Sam Mayo found some of the bushes on a sandy ridge which stretched from the vicinity of the Princeville School to behind Tuck Dew's Garage. We enjoyed them for about three falls, but on the fourth we found the chinquapins had been replaced by a mobile home park.

FOUND—Two of the three "lost" local treasures mentioned here a couple of weeks back have been found.

Charlie Clayton' color film of the day-by-day demolition of the old town hall wasn't lost at all. Rufus Worsley, former town clerk, called to give its precise location in the town vault—it just isn't out on a shelf. In the drawer with it is a tape of the last time the town clock rang from its bell tower.

PERIL—Opponents of the great, green push-em-out trash conveyances chalked up one for their cause last week.

A local lady fell into one of the things.

According to my reliable information, it happened in the Cromwell Heights area when she was loading leaves, and the next thing she knew, she was upside down in the container. Somehow she managed to emerge, shaken but unscathed.

I wouldn't be a bit surprised if she hadn't already told a lawyer about it.

November 12.

HOMECOMING—It seems to me that as this year's observance of Veterans Day approached an inordinate amount of moaning was done about how the vets of our latest involvement were deprived of a proper homecoming. No parades, no speeches, no bands, and because of it some suffered a degree of mental anguish.

Now don't get me wrong. I have only the greatest respect for folks who have been shot at and hit as well as those who were shot at and missed. But I couldn't help but hark back to my homecoming after participating in the Pacific unpleasantness in WW II.

I got my discharge on a late March day in 1946 and paid $25 to ride with seven others from Camp LeJeune to Rocky Mount. I walked from the bus station to Pineview Cemetery and began thumbing home, but apparently the duffel bag to which were strapped a Japanese sword and rifle caused motorists to have second thoughts.

After about an hour, I stopped the first passing Trailways and headed for Tarboro—a place I hadn't seen in more than two years.

I stopped the bus at Main and Battle, got out, shouldered by bag and headed west. In two minutes I was standing in the hallway of 201, and I hollered, "I'M HOME!"

The noise my folks made coming out of the kitchen was better than the best brass band in the whole land. For a few moments there was a whole lot of hugging going on.

Mother stepped back and with tears streaming her face said, "Thank you God". Daddy stuck out his hand and said, "Son, I'm proud of you." That was the finest orating in the world.

The next morning I put on my green pants, khaki shirt and brogans and headed downtown. I had just reached the town hall when an MP came out of the police station and shouted, "Marine, you're out of uniform."

I said, "Buster, you're damned right I am, and it's the best I've felt in three years."

He didn't bother me again as I continued on my way to "Deep Sea" Cosby's Cigar Store and Tom Farrar's Pool Room.

I reckon homecoming was a lot of what you made it to be.

1983

YEAR—I've never been one for making resolutions, knowing it will eventually be a waste of time. Distaff asked me if I planned any resolutions for 1983 and without thinking, I said, "Just one."

She asked, "What's that?"

"I'll try to do better," I replied.

She sighed and said, "You'll break that one before the week's out."

February 4.

SPRING—I am of the opinion that we still have a mess of bad weather ahead, but who am I to contradict the groundhog, the seed companies, and local gardeners?

The catalogs began arriving last week, and the colors would make Technicolor look like black and white. I was intrigued by two offerings of the Thompson and Morgan Co. of Farmingdale, N.J.

The first is a new pot-grown hybrid strawberry called, Strawberry Sweetheart Hybrid F2. Seedmen claim that if planted in April, it will set fruit in late June and continue bearing until October. Seems too good to be true.

The second are New Guinea impatiens, "like coleus with iridescent blooms." The flowers were described as 2 1/2 inches across "with richly painted foliage, cream, white, maroon, bronze, red and many shades of green." That's enough right there to start you filling out the order blank.

Other signs were that the Carolina Telephone garden on the bypass was staked off and farther down the road, a gentleman in West Hills, whose garden backs on the bypass, was running rows.

Who am I to argue with evidence such as that?

February 25.

SEASON—On the calendar, spring is still three weeks away, but the signs of it were plentiful here this week.

But the surest sign was seen by Fred Howard.

Fred said that yesterday, Mama Wood Duck, accompanied by her spouse, turned up in the Common looking for a nesting place. In the many years that the females have returned to the Common from Lord only knows where to hatch their broods, yesterday marked the first time a male had appeared.

But, alas, during the Wednesday morning storm it thundered, and every fool knows that if it thunders in the wintertime, snow will follow within ten days.

VISITORS—It was the earliest arrival of the purple martins that he can remember, but Buck Clark said several of them scouted out his eight gourds on Wahree Street.

Buck said the martins arrived last year on March 31, but their usual homecoming is March 24.

Think of it, those little critters flew all the way from Brazil just to keep Buck's neighborhood free from mosquitoes all spring and summer long.

April 22 and Ramblin's misgivings about the weather bear fruit.

WEATHER—It was snowing heavily Tuesday when the United Parcel Service man knocked on the door. He was delivering some strawberry plants I ordered back in early March and which the nursery promised would be "shipped at the proper planting time for your area."

The following morning my old friend Mr. Lee Gooch called and said, "Mabrey, I am 80 years and 1 month old and I did something yesterday I've never done before and never expect to do again. I was cutting the grass and got caught in a blizzard for a few minutes."

I reckon not.

The Carolina Telephone rice paddie off Western Boulevard seems to have survived the several nights of sub-freezing temperatures.

The only good thing about the weather business is that it prolongs the time for us to enjoy the dogwoods and azaleas.

(May 6, Pat Bass, in her "Distaff" column gives a medical report.)

The Editor is home, and doing well, although a bit weak. Deprived of cigarettes and some of the things that make life more enjoyable, he is eating and sleeping better than in years, and coughing very little.

Of course, a bear with sore paws might be a mite easier to live with but it's still wonderful to wake up in the night and see him sleeping so quietly in his bed.

Friends, prayers, calling, sending cards and flowers (and goodies) and visiting have meant everything to both of us.

May 13—back to the hospital.

HELP—It happened Wednesday two weeks ago.

I was reading some AP copy about 11:45 a.m. when I suddenly discovered I couldn't read the copy out loud. In fact, nothing I would say would come out logically. I could think all right, but couldn't talk.

A few minutes later, I caught the eye of Alfonzo Everette, and used hand signs and grunts to get him to take me home.

My speech was returning when I returned to our apartment, but it was still fouled up enough that Distaff met me at the screen door and ordered, "We're going to the clinic."

I didn't argue.

It didn't take Dr. Dale Newton long to announce that I had a T.I.A.—a mini-stroke, and he was sending me to Greenville "right now" for a Cat-Scan.

At the doctors' office, I was informed that I was to stick my head in a barrel while pictures were taken for two hours. He asked me a few questions and said he wanted me to check into Pitt Memorial for more tests. I didn't argue.

I'm not too sure of what happened that night, except that I was awakened as often as I was asleep. But the all-out tests started early the following morning, continued throughout Thursday, Friday, Saturday and Monday.

There were more brain scans, lung tests, blood tests, disease tests. I seemed to come out all right, but then came the announcement by my doctors they were going to put a satellite or some such in the artery in my hip and send it up the same artery inside my throat. "It's going to burn for a short time going up and coming down," they told me. That was the understatement of the day.

That thing burned like a thousand branding irons of hell going up and coming down. I was greatly relieved when the doctor said the inside of my artery was "rough like a rapids", and he did not plan to operate. Said they could treat my condition with pills. That suited me fine.

Later Saturday, the doctors said they wanted me to stay in the hospital through Monday to take a day-long clock record of my heart. That was a day-long bill wasted Sunday, but I was still apprehensive enough not to argue.

The Monday test was a success and I was sent home Tuesday morning. Only the bookkeeper knows what the hospital stay cost, but I did learn the two hours in the Cat-Scan cost $350.

I would like to offer my sincerest appreciation to those of you who sent calls, cards, flowers, food and prayers. As far as I'm concerned there help can't be measured.

May 20.

FISHING—Jimbo Dupree stopped by the office yesterday to show off a 24-pound rock he caught on a minnow in the Roanoke.

It set my newly medically-thinned blood bubbling and my other juices stewing somewhat. I fished for rock for a number of years, most of them in the Tar, but never ever came close to putting anything that size in the boat, either by way of hook or net.

I keep telling myself I wouldn't really want to catch a fish that big. I don't have a pot large enough to cook it in and it would absolutely dominate any wall it was stuffed and hung upon.

But like Jimbo was doing yesterday, I could have showed it off.

July 1.

MATTIE—I suppose it was predestined or something as the Fourth of July approached that I happened across a yellow *Southerner* clipping paying tribute to the late Miss Mattie Shackelford.

A super patriot and humanitarian, Miss Mattie for years saw to it that Flag Day, Memorial Day, Armistice Day and the Fourth were properly observed by the citizenry of Tarboro, particularly the young folks.

The parades usually formed at the courthouse and climaxed with the reading of her patriotic poetry and a public speaking in the Common.

Miss Mattie was a nubbin of a women whose gray hair was worn tied back in a bun. She was a Red Cross nurse in Europe during World War 1, and her cap and navy and red cape were her uniform until illness struck her down.

A remarkably strong-willed woman, Miss Mattie got the approval of the town commissioners for the cleanup of Old Town Cemetery, also in the Depression, when the hallowed spot looked like a jungle. Mostly with the materials she salvaged from the clean-up, she built Memory Chapel and dedicated it to the veterans of this nation's wars.

The clipping I found this week was titled "A Tribute To Miss Mattie Shackelford". It was dated September 10, 1943, and was signed "Contributed". It follows:

"They gathered there one morning from all walks of life. An eager child who had left her play. Housewives, businessmen, and an aged Negro. They had laid aside their menial tasks and gathered amid the slanting shadows and shafts of light from above, but surely in the sight of God.

"They came to dedicate a simple little chapel in a hallowed spot so that free men might always find a quiet haven for meditation with their God.

They came too, we think, to pay homage to a Christian woman who built something more important than wood and stone. She has builded herself in the very mortar and her loving care is mirrored in the patina of the cedar altar.

"Time will flow on staunchlessly like 'blood from a mortal wound' and when this chapel is but the dust of God's earth, the memory of this great woman will still be a shining light for all men."

(July 8—Another medical report from Distaff.)

Well, when one goes to bed, no one knows what they might wake up to.

Last weekend, I thought we'd have a pleasant Fourth, family get-together, swimming, whatever.

The Rescue Squad took Mabrey to the emergency room early Sunday. He had another low blood sugar attack. So much for the holiday.

He's doing fine. A week of hospitalization is killing me. Once he was out of any special danger, I only felt lonesome.

He's supposed to come home tomorrow. Sure hope so.

(He did come home the next day but only after a week in the hospital.)

August 5

ECHOES—Had a couple of comments on my observations about the new Planter's Bank sign. Don't know if the bank folks had any.

One lady caller said that with a few minor alterations it would be more appropriate outside a dental clinic.

Another caller said, "I'm a Planter's customer and have been for years, even before they came to Tarboro. They don't need that sign. Everybody knows Arthur works in there."

September 16.

HOORAY!—Yesterday morning a large crane removed the plastic logo from the lawn of Planters Bank and Trust Company. I am grateful and hereby express heartfelt thanks to those responsible.

If I recollect correctly this marks the second time in the more than 30 years that a suggestion made in this column has borne fruit. The other was when I asked that a school be named in honor of C.B. Martin.

September 23—crabs in Tar River.

VISITORS—The lack of rainfall and resulting low water in the Tar has increased salinity and has brought us some unusual visitors from the sound—blue crabs.

Bobby O'Neal spotted one near the US 64 bridge about three Saturdays ago while watching a school of small jumping mullet cavort off a sandbar on the other side of the river. I understand both mullets and crabs are numerous in the Old Sparta area. Karo Edmondson, who has lived there all his life, said he has never seen anything to equal it.

Jumping mullet have been occasional visitors to this stretch of the Tar in the past, but never in the numbers that are reportedly here now.

An 1818 dam on Hendricks Creek.

GLEANINGS—Over the years I have collected a number of bits and pieces of local history. If anything happens to me, I'm sure they eventually find their way into the nearest trash can. For those of you not interested in such, stop right here. The rest of you read on. You just might want to clip and save.

W.E. Fountain, the town's first telegraph operator, came here from Rocky Mount in the 1870s. He later served as mayor, was one of the incorporators of Edgecombe Homestead and Loan in 1889 and the same year, he built Fountain Cotton Mills. The telegraph line extended from Tarboro to Washington, N.C.

On Nov. 30, 1895, the F.S. Royster Guano Co. was incorporated with a capital stock of $50,000.

In the 1890s there were large town pumps in the middle of the streets on the east side of Main and Church and Main and Pitt.

The steamboat "Greenville" was commanded by a Capt. Mayo. It left Tarboro at 6:30 a.m. and reached Washington at 2:30 p.m. The return trip upstream required 12 hours.

In 1892, permits for 32 barrooms were issued in the county.

In 1891 Blind Tom gave a musical show in the new opera house.

The same year the grand opening of the Central and Pioneer tobacco warehouses was held. The Central was owned by S.S.

Nash, C.W. Jeffreys, J.F. Shackelford, A.L. Heilbroner, Alex Heilbroner, and F.M. Hodges.

From 1818 until 1820 there was a large dam across Hendricks Creek just to the rear of the Primitive Baptist Church. At the dam was a grist mill and a saw mill. The dam was broken in 1820.

In 1880 the steamboat "Cottonplant" burned at Tarboro.

On Aug. 6, 1880 W.C. Coup's Circus exhibited at a location near the mouth of Hendricks Creek. The next year the same circus exhibited on the Common on the west side of Main.

On Aug. 8, 1880 the town board approval the purchase of a fire bell for $121.57 and $10 for a lamp to be placed at the corner of St. Andrew and St. Joshua streets.

The railroad from Tarboro to Williamston was built in 1882.

October 14.

Son John was on TV Monday evening on "A Salute to Balanchine". The first number was a beautiful series of Vienna waltzes, and John was in three of them.

But only a mother could spot him. The stage was so crowded, and the shots were so long, I could only sit on the floor, find a face who looked familiar, and put my finger on it, trying to trace it through the number.

He got back from Europe Saturday, called Sunday, and told me he would be easy to find in the first dance; he would be wearing a moustache. Forgot to mention all the male dancers wore moustaches.

BROWN—It has been more than a year since I suggested that the lane leading to the new swimming pool be named in honor of M.S. "Coca Cola" Brown, a man who gave greatly of his time, his talents, and his money to Tarboro—particularly its young people.

Within a week a town official called and said the arts commission was proposing a gazebo-bandstand on the site of the old swimming pool. It would be named in honor of Mr. Brown.

I was asked to contact the family to determine if they objected. They were much pleased and the official was so informed. And that was the last I heard of it.

December 16.

MEMORIES—Folks have said that I should write something about Bass Memorial Hospital which stubbornly, but futilely, resisted Barnhill's wrecking crews a couple of weeks ago.

My uncle, Dr. Spencer Pippen Bass, built his hospital because he didn't particularly cotton to some of the folks at Edgecombe. He named it in honor of his father, Dr. Henry Turner Bass.

My first memory of the hospital is not a pleasant one for Daddy took me there for some unexplained reason. We were in the back room which served as Doc's office where he dabbed my arm with a piece of cotton. Then I saw the needle. I squalled and headed for the front door with Daddy in close pursuit. I ran up *The Southerner* office alley and climbed up a cottonwood tree onto a garage behind the present Branch Bank building. I knew Daddy wasn't going to climb that tree.

But I hadn't counted on Alamo Johnson, a black man who was Daddy's right hand man. The bank was then Daddy's office so he just went to the back door and yelled for Alamo who came running.

He had known where Daddy was taking me that afternoon and he looked up at who was on the garage roof and started laughing. Daddy said, "Get him!"

Alamo climbed up beside me and talked. He assured me that the vaccination "wouldn't hurt no more than a skeeter bite". He gave me two choices: "You can climb down and go to your Daddy or I gonna carry you down to your Daddy."

I got the shot and cried some.

My next vivid memory was in the summer of 1935. I was 10 when Dr. Boice from Park View came over and operated on me for a double hernia. I was placed in a rear second floor room which was to be my home for the next two weeks.

My window overlooked the beautiful, fenced garden of Mr. and Mrs. Aubrey Leggett. My only amusement was reading Big Little books and looking out the window on occasions when Aubrey and Maude played leap frog.

I will always have fond memories of the nurses. My nurse during my stay was Lucy Parker who nearly always entered the room singing a line from an Episcopal hymn ". . . shame upon you legion, on this holy ground . . ." She never finished.

Other second floor nurses who bring back fond memories were "Pet" Edwards and Virginia Bass.

Doc's downstairs nurse and bookkeeper was Mrs. Lucy Daniels, who doctored me on several occasions when my uncle was out of place.

I don't remember the year, but it was around Thanksgiving time when my hatchet slipped while I was cutting kindling. "Miss Lucy" applied four stitches to my knee while the doctor was upstairs bringing Frank Carlisle III, into the world.

When Forrest Sledge jumped off the diving board at the swimming pool onto the top of me, Miss Lucy applied two stitches, and when I sliced my right hand while cleaning fish, she stitched in three more.

Perhaps my fondest memories of the hospital are the many, many hours I sat opposite Uncle Doc in his back office during slack afternoons. He told me stories about hunting, about ancestors, about growing up, and stories that I can't share because relatives of the person or persons involved are still alive.

Doc went to the University of Virginia after he was either kicked out or threatened at University of North Carolina for hazing.

At UVA he was captain of the track team and played and on the football team. He was small, but he was very fast.

There was the time Virginia played Carlisle and Jim Thorpe. "I tackled him once", Doc told me, "just once, and he nearly killed me."

This Ramblin' has gone on too long, but the writing of one memory brings more. Perhaps in reading this some of you readers will recall memories of Dr. Spencer Pippen Bass and Bass Memorial Hospital.

I certainly hope so.

1984

January 6.

PEYTON—I admit I am blessed, but Peyton Beery was probably the best thing ever to happen to Edgecombe County.

Our friendship extended from the first month he came here until about two weeks before his death when Jack Barris drove him down to the office where he had a carside chat. It was short. Peyton was tired.

To any area which had only one "outside industry" in its entire history, Peyton attracted plants which provided thousands of jobs for the unemployed, the underemployed, the high school graduates who traditionally had to seek jobs in Tidewater Virginia. The county tax base was increased millions upon millions because of his efforts.

It is interesting to note that his area has attracted no industry since this man retired, despite some of our neighboring counties have been every successful.

In his field, Thomas Peyton Beery was truly one of a kind.

~

SIGN—Well, the groundhog saw his shadow yesterday, presaging 40 more days of uncommonly bad weather.

I don't believe it. I have better omens.

Temperatures were down in the 40s both Tuesday and Wednesday afternoons when the man on the tractor was breaking ground for the Carolina Telephone garden out on the bypass.

April 9.

CHASE—For about an hour Tuesday afternoon the Town Common and several blocks of Downtown was the scene of a chase to rival anything done by Hollywood's Keystone Kops.

The star of the chase was "Jumper", a 6-month-old 4-H project lamb, owned by Perry Jenkins III, 13, son of Perry II and Sally.

As she was being unloaded from a vehicle in the Jenkins' E. Park Avenue yard, Jumper jumped and headed for the Common with the two Perrys in full pursuit.

Jumper crossed, St. Patrick and St. Andrew, bounded over Main and raced to Albemarle where she backtracked. She went back to Main, by Planters Bank, and Sullivans Tire Center on St. John.

By this time news had spread and the hunt was joined by two panting policemen, an ABC officer, and a group of volunteer chasers estimated as high as 50.

Firemen tried to catch Jumper as she turned off St. John onto Albemarle, but to no avail. She reversed her field in front of Braswell Wholesale and headed for the Common again. This time she ended up at the cotton press as the crowd closed in.

But the chase was far from over.

Jumper got her second (or third) wind, took off down Albemarle and hung a right into W. Wilson. By this time the posse had grown by several Town of Tarboro and EMCO pickups and Mary Flanagan's Ticketmobile.

Jumper raced by the ABC store and took a hard left onto Cedar Lane, across W. St. James to the rear of the old Clark Hardware building where she was cornered.

ABC officer Wayne Taylor lunged before Jumper could jump and the two of them ended up in a large mud hole.

They said it was the most excitement in the downtown area in quite some time.

Baseball season evokes memory.

GAME—I don't know how the exhibition game came to be scheduled here, but on April 10, 1940, the New York Giants played the Cleveland Indians in Bryan Park before a crowd of more than 3,000.

The Pullman train carrying the teams stopped beside Clark Warehouse and walked to the hotel which was their headquarters for the day. At 10 a.m. Gene Simmons interviewed some of them for listeners of WEED.

Burgess Whitehead, a native of Tarboro, played third for the Giants and got a double in the eighth as King Carl Hubbell struck out eight to give the Giants the win.

A couple of interesting notes were that Soup Campbell, a former Tarboro player, walked and then scored Cleveland's only run. Johnny Humphries, also a former Tarboro player in Coastal Plain League days, pitched three innings for the Indians.

The final score—Giants 4, Indians 1.

April 27.

BALL—Last week's mention of the exhibition baseball game here between the New York Giants and the Cleveland Indians brought back some pleasant memories for Milford Ruffin.

He still has a ball used in the game, and it is signed by such notables as Carl Hubbell, Bob Feller, and Burgess Whitehead.

Milford served as batboy from the Giants and recalled that Harvie Ward handled the same chores for the Indians.

An extraordinary man.

ROBERT—Clearing for the new apartments off West Wilson at Barlow Road took down the big magnolia which shaded the humble abode of Robert Gibson.

It wasn't much of a house when I first knew of it back in the early 50s. It leaned badly to the east, propped up by several poles. As I recall, Hurricane Hazel wiped the house out.

It was then that Dinksie Gilliam, George Pennington, Bip Carstarphen, Ed Clayton, and some lawyers contributed and an oversized chicken coop was constructed for Robert under the magnolia.

But who was Robert Gibson?

I first met this memorable man on the post office steps one afternoon. He was black with snow white hair and beard, and he was talking in a deep bass voice to no one in particular.

As I passed him, he offered his hand which I took, bowed slightly, and asked, "And who are you, sir?"

I told him, and he replied, "I am Robert Gibson, at your service." With that he left, heading for West Wilson and home.

Robert Gibson was a graduate of Harvard University, and he wrote and spoke both Latin and Greek. He worked for the Washington, D.C., Post Office until he retired and moved here.

Over the years several of us around town received letters from Robert which were mostly far-out clippings, and the envelopes were usually covered with lines of Latin or Greek.

He first appeared in my office one summer afternoon, and announced, "I, Robert Gibson, salute the Honorable B. Mabrey Bass Jr., Esquire, editor of *The Southerne*r."

Smiling, he offered me a fistful of wilted, mostly dead, wildflowers. He would never take a seat. That scene was repeated a number of times over the years, and although I can't recall what we talked about, the meetings were never dull.

Some folks said he was odd and others flat-out said he was crazy, but I can tell you one thing.

I never laughed at Robert Gibson.

HISTORY—Over the years I have often bemoaned the apparent lack of interest in local history by our young people.

But yesterday that attitude changed when I read "A Brief history of Tarboro 1850-1900."

The 30-page booklet is the handiwork of the Tarboro-Edgecombe Academy 7th graders under the leadership of Art Simmons.

Mr. Simmons, if you ever get by *The Southerner* office I would consider it an honor to shake your hand.

June

PARK—On a Sunday morning before the current freshet arrived, I drove down to River Front Park to see how it had survived the last high water.

June 25.

ROBERT—Several weeks ago I wrote some of my recollections of Robert Gibson, the white bearded black man who spoke

Latin and Greek and who lived in magnolia-shaded on what is now W. Wilson Street.

I bemoaned the cutting of that tree by a construction firm, but Linwood Lewis called to say that Robert's magnolia is still standing, but it is further down the street. He also recalled something Robert sometimes did which I had forgotten.

He would line his yard with newspapers and weigh them down with bricks. After varying intervals, he would carry them back inside.

L.P. Hornthal sent me a note recalling Robert and said he still has some of the notes and other items Robert sent him over the years. He also sent me a copy of the program for Robert's funeral which was held in St. Luke's Episcopal Church on April 19, 1970. He had died eight days earlier in the Eastern State Hospital in Williamsburg, Va.

Robert was born Jan. 13, 1889 in Savannah, Ga. and got his early education there. In 1910 he graduated from Hampton Institute in Virginia.

While in Savannah, Robert served as principal of two schools. Later he moved here and worked as principal of a Nash County school.

He and his wife, Josephine, had seven children, but at the time of his death he was survived by only four sons, three in Washington and one in Detroit.

Somehow it's nice to know that people still think about Robert Francis Gibson.

August and Corn Meal Road?

NAMES—Some years ago Mayor Ed and the council approved using a college student during the summer. His job was to come up with new street names to replace existing ones "which might prove confusing."

Well, he labored away all summer doing something and when it came time for his report at the council meeting a goodly crowd was on hand.

The young man began reading off names of "confusing" existing streets along with his suggested changes. There was some muttering, but no one said much until the youth got to North Howard Circle. He explained that this name was extremely confusing because of South Howard Circle and Howard Avenue. That's when he suggested North Howard Circle be renamed "Dogwood Drive".

As I recall, that was too much for Pete Long. He arose rather quickly: Pete was more than somewhat irate, but never lost his cool.

He allowed as how the existing names shouldn't be confusing since any fool should realize that North Howard Circle is north of South Howard Circle and South Howard Circle is south of North Howard Circle. In short, Pete suggested, "If it ain't broke, don't fix it".

Anyway, the council got the message. The young lad went back to college and Pete still lives on North Howard Circle. Incidentally, not one of the suggested changes was adopted.

The above story came to mind one night last week when I looked over the list of county road names and number changes to be proposed at Monday's meeting of the county commissioners.

As a boy, my father, Baker Mabrey Bass, took me fishing many times along the banks of Fishing Creek, just below Mabrey's Bridge. I fished there and I taught Baker Mabrey Bass III to fish there.

The bridge was probably named for Charles Mabrey, who was a large landowner on the upstream side of the creek in the early 1800s, or it could have been for Dr. Baker Mabrey, who served as a surgeon in the Confederacy.

Here's the beef!

For more years than anyone now living can recall, the road from the turnoff the Leggett road to Fishing Creek was (and is) known as the Mabrey Bridge Road. On the list of the names and changes which the county board will be scheduled to approve is one which would change Mabrey's Bridge Road to Corn Meal Road.

The existing name is in no way confusing with proposed changes or names in any other part of the county.

Therefore, I heretofore beseech C.B. and Tom, et al not to Corn Meal Mabrey.

And I'm thankful for small favors.

August 31 and a report from son John.

Was delighted to receive a call from son John from Greece, where he has spent a blissful vacation on the island of Hydra, with friends from New York. Nothing was wrong, he'd just been thinking about us and wanted to know how we were doing. Happily, I could report we were just fine. The only bad part of the call was that I missed him even more than usual after we hung up. Believe I'll have to finagle a trip to the big city this Fall.

OOO-GA!—A couple of weeks ago I mentioned the Dodge touring car owned by the Nicholson family, and at that time I hadn't thought about that style of vehicle in years. Therefore, I was a bit surprised this week to come across a faded clipping from what appeared a 1932 or 33 *Southerner* which mentioned Dr. L.E. Norfleet's Franklin touring car.

The writer noted it "has been giving service for ten years and is in excellent running order now."

I vaguely remembered that old green open car wheeling around town, loaded with young folks. I thought that was really something else.

The clipping struck a spark, so I called my friend, the still honorable former mayor of Princeville, Ray Matthewson. I asked if by chance he had Dr. Norfleet's old Franklin.

Ray told me he had an old Franklin, but not Dr. Norfleet's. He went on to explain that it was a 1925 model which was owned by Miss Lucy Staton. At some point Ray let it be known that if the Franklin were ever offered for sale he would have the first chance at it.

When that time finally came, Ray was serving in World War II, but the long-standing promise was remembered and Glennie Matthewson purchased the old car for his brother.

Years later, Ray was told it would cost an estimated $4,000 to restore the car, a luxury postponed by educating five children. One of his sons once saw the same model car displayed in a Las Vegas auto museum, and the price tag was $65,000. That, too, was a number of years ago.

Today, Ray still has his car, and although it has yet to be restored, it is very definitely not for sale.

Late November and the Phantom is exposed.

BIRTHDAY—Belated birthday greetings to my friend Robert Gooch, who holds the somewhat dubious distinction of playing the longest running trick on me.

It began back in the early 1970s when I began getting beautiful postal cards from all over the country and Canada. The short messages were usually something "Beautiful. Wish you could see it." All were signed "The Phantom."

On Friday afternoon of the week of my 25th anniversary as an employee of this family journal, The Boss called and said, "The Phantom called and said for you to be in your office at 10:30 tomorrow morning. He's coming to see you."

I was there well before the appointed time, and at precisely 10:30 there in the doorway stood Robert, grinning from ear to ear and then some.

I used a few choice words at having been so thoroughly had, and by a person I had talked with numerous times while I was being victimized with never an inkling as to his identity. Certainly, I should have had some idea because I knew Robert was a long-haul trucker for Long Manufacturing, but I never made the connection.

So happy birthday, Phantom, and may you have many, many more.

November.

TOOTS—Over coffee the other morning, Russell Armstrong wondered aloud what ever happened to the whistles scattered over town which marked starting time, noon, and quitting time.

Whistles served such purposes at Hart Mill, Fountain Mill, Runnymede and Mayo, the peanut mill and the laundry. Each had a distinctive sound. It would, indeed, be interesting to know what happened to them.

December.

REMEMBRANCES—The most memorable Christmas? I really don't know, but in retrospect, there have been many, so very many.

Christmas of 1944 was spent on a high wind swept plateau on the island of Hawaii. We knew it was only a matter of weeks before the 5th Marine Division would be committed to combat.

We scrounged enough beer and bologna sandwiches for a party, and shortly before midnight a friend stuck his head in the tent and asked, "Anybody want to go to Mass?"

Several of us joined our Catholic friends and went to a large Quonset hut warehouse where the materials of war had been pushed aside to make room for chairs and a makeshift altar, complete with candles.

I don't recall much about the service, but on the way back to the tent, the stars were never brighter nor were there as many billions of them.

Of the six Marines I prayed with that night, three didn't make it for another Christmas.

1985

FROSTY—I certainly hope you brought in your brass monkeys before the Alberta Clipper arrived. If not they fared some kind of common.

Police reportedly said that about 7 o'clock Monday morning the Confederate statue put down his Sharpe's rifle and crammed his hands in his pockets.

At 8 o'clock there was a report from t he Runnymede area that a dog had become stuck to a fire hydrant.

Californian Steve Pajak's john froze over.

Shades of Mrs. Fraley and her chamber pots!

MOVIE—The word Downtown is that our community may become the site of a Hollywood film later this year.

Two gentlemen were in town Wednesday looking for possible sites of the filming of Louise Shivers' excellent first novel, "Here To Get My Baby Out of Jail".

The writer, who was originally from Wilson and now lives in Georgia, sets her novel in the fictitious town of "Tarborough" in the year 1937. The names of two of the leading characters are Walston and Ruffin.

Hot dog! Just think of it, some of us might et a chance to be in a moving picture.

JOE—I feel sure that an awful lot of us are feeling right proud of Joe Spiers' impending promotion to brigadier general. What's more important, he is the first Edgecombe man ever to earn a star in the Union Army, although we have provided the Navy with four admirals.

TRIVIA—Several weeks ago this column issued an invitation for readers to play a game I called "Good Company". Alas, there were no takers. Maybe it was the weather.

In the early hours last Sunday I came up with an idea for a new game, one primarily for senior citizens. I call it "Tarboro Trivia" and it goes something like this:

1-What role did Catherine Pender play in World War I?

2-Name six Tarboro police chiefs and quote what Leslie Holly had to say about one of them at a reception honoring the first two young black attorneys to being their practice here?

3-Who was Abraham Wooten?

4-Who was Henry Nau?

5-Who was Tarborough's first weatherman, and who has this paper depended upon since?

6-Who was Jules Barrett?

7-How many Edgecombe men served in the Confederacy? How many men and women in World War II?

8-What was the Cotton Valley Farm formerly called?

9-What was the name Editor Aubrey Shackell gave his youth-oriented club during the Depression?

10-Who was Bill Carstarphen's great-grandfather, who was a U.S. congressman from Martin Company and later served as Tarboro's postmaster?

11-Who was Tarboro's youngest mayor?

12-What happened to Harry Hicks, Dr. House and Mr. Koonce?

13-Why did Herbert H. Taylor Jr. strip off his clothes and jump into the Tar in the dead of winter?

14-What was the biggest shad W.F. (Cap) Wooten ever caught?

15-What Tarborean was graduated from Wake Forest Law School at such a tender age that he could not immediately begin practicing? What did he do in the meantime?

Here are the answers:

1-She drove a Red Cross ambulance in France.

2-John W. Cotton, Mr. Pulley, Berry Lewis, Bob Worsley, Otley Leary, and Harry Alderman.

At the reception, Mr. Holly reportedly said, "This is the happiest day for black people since Chief Berry Lewis died."

3-He was a black Baptist preacher who had a string of churches which he called the Primitive Radicue Baptist Church. Dr. Spencer Bass wrote ". . . when he died his funeral procession was five miles long and every plow in the county was idle." There is a monument of white marble which features a ghostly likeness of him in Princeville.

4-Nau was Coach Joe Caruso's assistant at Tarboro High in the late 30s and early 40s.

5-E.V. Zoeller was the first in about 1876. He was succeeded by E. Harvie Ward, who was succeeded by Alvin Moore, Jr. We now rely on Dr. Jack Riley.

6-Jules drove the town's "honey wagon."

7-Edgecombe sent 1,400 men to the Confederacy, and almost 5,000 men and women served in World War II.

8-The farm was formerly called the Parks Place.

9-It was the Wake Up and Live Club.

10-He was Joseph Martin.

11-George M. Fountain, Jr. in 1941.

12-They died in a plane crash while flying to Raleigh.

13-As Scoutmaster, he did it to rescue a Scout in a boat which had gone adrift and was heading for Old Sparta.

14-It was on Jan. 1, 1933 when he and Gray Harrell were skimming. The fish weighed 9 3/4 pounds. It was sleeting at the time.

15-He was W.S. (Bill) Babcock and he went to work as Clerk of Court A.T. Walston. He succeeded Mr. Walston in that office.

If any of you readers would like to play again, please let me know and I'll try to do some more recollecting.

(March: The following item is from Pat Bass's column "Distaff". It is a cheerful, happy little reminder John Bass would be home for a visit. There is not a hint of concern.)

Speaking of sons, John will be here for a mini-visit next weekend. Coming in Saturday, he will return to New York on Monday. Plan to fill him full of barbecue, stew and greens, and send him back with a slightly greasy, happy smile.

April 15 and not all the news is good.

ENDURED—Sunday marked the 35th anniversary of Distaff's having endured my presence in something call the state of matrimony.

To paraphrase Dickens, "These were the best of times and these were the worst of times." But thanks to God, many friends, and local financial institutions, we survived. Two paid mortgages, three children, and two grandchildren later indicates we must have been doing something right.

GRATITUDE—The calls, cards and expressions of concern for son John and his sudden bout with cancers have been almost overwhelming. We have heard from people who know us only through our columns.

All have said John was in their prayers.

Who could ask for more?

VISITOR—Resident wood duck has favored Tarboro with another spring visit.

She was seen earlier this week waddling along St. Andrew near Wilson, followed by six or seven ducklings.

Late in April.

Good news and bad news from New York. John left the hospital Tuesday and went to a friend's home, but had to be readmitted yesterday. Talked to him Wednesday evening, and he sounded very, very weak. His friend called and told us he became quite dehydrated, weak, was having trouble swallowing and running a slight fever, so his doctor wanted him back on IV.

June 14

ENCORE—Once again by request, but perhaps for the last time because I'm running out of items, let's play another game of Tarboro Trivia:

1-What was Bottoms' Special?

2-What was Joe Friar's bill for a 7-day stay in Edgecombe General in February of 1954?

3-Who was Howard Cotten and what happened to him?

4-What is the trivial importance of the large cypress tree on the downstream side of the Tar River bridge here?

5-What is (or was) the record number of cases tried in Recorder's Court.

6-What was still another derisive name for Water Street in the last part of the 19th Century?

7-Who was Doctor Buzzard?

8-Who attended the ceremony of circumcision of infant Gerald Shugar at the home of his parents on E. Baker Street?

9-Who is believed to be the last person lynched in Edgecombe County?

The answers:

1-Bottoms' Special was a tobacco variety developed by Tom Bottoms on his 10-acre allotment on his farm near Leggett in the late 1930s or early 40s.

His seeds produced better stalks and more leaves—from 25 to 30 per plant—and more of wrapper quality.

The variety became especially popular in south Georgia where it was introduced by Sam McConkey, who owned warehouses there.

2-Joe's total bill was $119.50, and it broke down like this: Board and nursing, $57; operating room cost, $25; laboratory, $12.50; doctor's charge, $40.

Joe got a $5 discount by paying cash.

3-Howard was a member of a prominent Tarboro family. He volunteered his service as a Red Cross ambulance driver in France during World War I.

In France, he was severely gassed and was returned home where he died in 1919. He was 38.

His grave is on the left side of the E. St. James Street entrance to Calvary Churchyard.

4-In the trunk of that huge vine-covered tree is an iron spike. It was placed there by A.B. "Pug" Bass to mark the record high water level of the July, 1919, flood.

5-In the late 1930s or early 40s, Judge Lyn Bond tried and sentenced 12 defendants in 90 minutes.

6-Joining Devil's Den and Lousy Leather as names for Water Street was Grab All. I know of no reason for this nicknames, but I have an idea it must have been an unsavory place.

7-Doctor Buzzard's name was Douglas Edwards. He was a "root" or "conjure" man who practiced in his house on his farm between Tarboro and Mildred.

Trailways buses made regular stops at the well-worn path from the road to his house.

8-Among those attending the ceremony were H.I. Johnson, George Earnhart, John Trueblood, J.E. Simmons, Mr. Hopkins, V.H. Creech, Tom Bush, T.O. Moses, L.I. Rubin, Ned Ellis, Mr. Cohen, Mr. and Mrs. Margolis, Mr. and Mrs. Goldstein, Mayor John H. Price,

J. Levy, H. Blackman, Rabbi Cantor, A. Light, J.M. Marks, and Jack Benjamin, who sang.

9-In the 1880s—I believe it was 1882—a black named Ben Hart was arrested for the attempted rape of a 16-year-old white girl near Tarboro.

Because of rumors of lynching, a Judge Shipp, who was holding Superior Court here at the time, ordered that Hart be taken to Williamston for safekeeping.

On a Saturday night, a group of about 100 masked men seized a train at Rocky Mount and forced the engineer to take them to Williamston. Others got on at Tarboro and other places along the line. The group reached Williamston at between one and two o'clock Sunday morning, broke into the jail and took Hart back to Tarboro.

His body was found the next morning hanging from a limb near the place the attempted assault took place, with this note pinned to him:

"We hang this man not in passion, yet calmly and deliberately with a due sense of the responsibility we assume.

"We take executive power in this and hang this man in accordance with the unwritten law of the land, because written law provides no penalty adequate to this crime.

"And be it understood, we who have committed this act will repeat the same under similar provocations.

"People's Committee."

July 12

CLOSING—It was with great sadness that I learned of the decision to close W.S. Clark and Sons, although some had been predicting it for much more than a year.

At coffee last Friday, one gentleman remarked, "Mr. W.S. must be spinning in his grave."

Another added, "If that's the case Mr. Sam and Russell must be in orbit."

MAIL—From time to time this column generates some letters. One example is offered below:

Dear Mabrey:

The June 14, 1985 issue of *The Daily Southerner* carried a piece about the people who were in attendance at my circumcision some 54 years ago. I read the article with interest and quite a bit of nostalgia. After all these years, it is good to learn who was in attendance when so intimate a portion of my anatomy was removed. It was especially good to see the names of so many good friends in print.

The question of what happened to the anatomical portion that was removed should be of interest to your readers.

I believe the part was first given to George Earnhart who used it as a garage for many years. Afterwards, it was donated to the Jewish community in Tarboro to use as a synagogue; however the part was too big for a synagogue. For awhile, it was reported that the rabbi and congregation considered turning it into a stadium for the Town of Tarboro, but the idea was rejected because it was felt they would never be able to fill the thing. Eventually, it was donated to the City of Dallas where, with a few modifications, it was turned into the Astrodome.

Yours sincerely,
Gerald R. Shugar
President & Publisher
Pharmaceutical Communications Inc.
Long Island City, N.Y.

October 4—the greatest tragedy—John Bass dies unexpectedly.

JOHN—Words cannot adequately express our deep appreciation for the calls, cards, flowers and visits from friends, old and new, upon their learning of the sudden death of our son John.

We do not know the cause of his death, but we do know that it was not cancer. Chemotherapy had taken care of the one in his abdomen and his brain. John's obituary in the New York Times stated he died of "complications from treatment of lymphatic cancer."

Friends tell us that during the past three weeks he felt much better than he had in months. His doctor said he was "stunned." Ironically, only 20 minutes before we learned of John's death, his mother had made reservations on Eastern to visit him next week.

When he was 14, John told us somewhat defensively, that he wanted to be a ballet dancer. He expressed disbelief when we didn't disagree.

That same year he sought and won a nearly full scholarship to the N.C. School of the Arts. While there, he was chosen by Agnes DeMille to join her American Heritage Dance Theatre for a nationwide tour.

After graduation from NCSA, John won a full scholarship to the School of American Ballet in New York. In 1976, the late George Balanchine chose him to be a member of the prestigious New York City Ballet Company.

John's death was one of eight "news" obituaries on last Thursday's obit page of the *New York Times*. Elsewhere on the same page was this tribute:

"BASS—John. We deeply regret the passing of our long time friend and colleague John Bass. His artistry and Commitment to professional excellence in dancing and his friendliness and unfailing good humor will be greatly missed. We extend our deepest sympathy to his family. Services will be announced.

Lincoln Kirstein, Peter Martins, Jerome Robbins, and the New York City Ballet."

It is our sincere hope that John's relatively short life will somehow serve as an inspiration to local young people who aspire for a career in the field of the arts.

❧

OPENING—Undoubtedly the best Downtown news of the week is that Sammy Harrell is opening a men's store at the former location of Double S Clark's men's store.

Equally heartening news is that Frank Alford is coming out of retirement to work with Sammy in measuring inseams and such. Frank spent the better part of his adult life in the men's clothing business in the 400 block and with Sammy will do much to make our brick sidewalks more attractive to "personal shoppers."

December

SEASON—Winter made its belated arrival after the record-breaking warmth of November.

Temperatures in the 20's found several azaleas blooming on our terrace. Come to think of it, I can't remember kudzu surviving this late in the year.

Thanksgiving was delightful at the home of Cathy and Mabe, far out in the country. The table groaned with the traditional fare plus several goodies, but a spring-like breeze wafted through the kitchen. Somehow, it seemed more like Easter-time.

Three Labs sat, panting, outside the open door waiting for leftovers.

They fared somewhat common because of what we took home.

Burp! Ah!

MEMORY—This is the time of year for good memories and I suppose one of my best of many was the Goodfellows Club.

It was born in the early 1950s, and its parents were Jaycee Bennie Strickland and Connie Rabin, then superintendent of welfare, whose compassion for the poor is still legendary with some of us.

Anyhow, their offspring, the Goodfellows Club, was quickly adopted by the local Jaycees. At the time, they were mostly veterans, gung-ho to do good and occasionally raise hell.

Anyhow, again, the goal of the Goodfellows was to provide Christmas cheer for Connie's forgotten people.

In that pre-plastic time, the Jaycees began their pleas for used toys and books in October.

On Sunday afternoons, WCPS would broadcast our appeal, asking for call-ins of donors. They Jaycees, listening on car radios, quickly made the pick-ups.

We got a lot of junk, but from it we were able to make useful bikes and trikes. Of course, there were many useful items.

The weekends of late November and early December were devoted to repairing, repainting and remaking.

As Christmas approached, we collected boxes from the ABC stores. The Salvation Army gave us $100 and 100 dolls. The A&P and Colonial Stores sold us meat and fruit at cost or below.

Connie provided us with a list of these in need. The Jaycees never thought of demeaning those families by telling them if they wanted it, come and get it. No, sir! We delivered, and did it on Christmas Eve.

At nightfall on one such eve, "Bro" Hargrove and I loaded his pickup with boxes destined for distribution in the area between Tarboro and Old Sparta.

Our first stop was at the Church Street ABC store where we purchased a pint of Paul Jones for $2, and away we went.

Along the way we sipped and sang. At our stops, many of which two boxes were needed, Bro would shout "Ho, Ho, Ho!" and kick on the door. When it was opened, I would shout, "Merry Christmas!"

Our receptions ranged from squeals from the children to "God bless you" and such from the parents. This was in the days of segregation, but on that eve, the team of Hargrove and Bass was hugged by and hugged back black folks while their children clung to our legs.

With two boxes and a tricycle left, we sipped and sang as we turned up a farm path.

There were a number of cars in the yard, including a late model Cadillac. Bro said, "What's that on the chimney?" I said it looked like a TV antenna. In those days the only snowy channel was Norfolk.

Bro kicked on the door and shouted his greeting.

The door was opened by a man who demanded "What do you want?"

Bro, muscled our way in. There were about six adults around a table upon which were two fifths of Kentucky Tavern that cost $6.50 each.

There were five or six snotty-nosed kids sitting around the walls. They were somewhat awestruck when I said "Merry Christmas."

The man who let us in said, "Put'em down and get out". Incidentally, they were white folks.

Back in the pickup, I said a four-letter word, but Bro countered with "Hell, 19 out of 20 ain't bad." We finished off the last of the Paul Jones and Bro threw the empty on the porch.

We headed back home singing with the realization that, indeed, 19 out of 20 weren't bad.

And that's the way it was when we had caring Jaycees and their Goodfellows Club.

December

SEASON—This has not been the best of years for Ramblin', ex-Distaff et al. But we would like to thank several hundred who thought of us and John, in case we overlooked someone:

May God bless you everyone.

Merry Christmas!

1986

COST—Much has been said and written in recent years about the high cost of dying. But it wasn't always that way. On at least one occasion, the funeral was dirt (sorry about that) cheap.

Friend and author Charlie Edwards of Raleigh, sent me a copy of an old wrinkled billhead from the store of L.H. Wells in Old Sparta.

It itemized the cost L.H. and his sister, Mary Ann Wells, shared in burying their brother John T.

They spent $17 for a coffin, 50 cents for grave digging, 50 cents for a shirt, and another 50 cents for a razor. The total bill—$18.50.

Charlie wrote that John Wells lost a leg in the Civil War. John also lost his father, L.R. Wells, and his brother, Mark B. Wells, in that war.

Unfortunately, the billhead had no date.

~

BIGGIE—Well, after more than 35 years of newspapering, ole B.M. has finally made the Big Time.

I was quoted twice in a front page feature in Sunday's Charlotte Observer. Not only that, but the writer, whom I have never met, spelled "Mabrey" correctly. That's something some folks hereabout don't do.

The story?

It was an excellent feature on Joe Mavretic and his no property tax plan.

~

TOOT—Some of have been wondering why some of the town's various historic committees have done nothing to restore the old fire horn, whose air supply tank exploded and plunged the town into darkness early one morning several years ago.

The device emitted a series of guttural grunts to pinpoint the locations of fires for the town' scattered volunteer firemen, and precisely at noon it gave forth a couple of grunts to announce the hours.

Portable radios replaced the need for fire calls, and, I suppose, the powers-that-be assume each of us has a timepiece. But when that horn hooted twice, we automatically checked our clocks and watches. It wasn't a pleasant sound, but when you've been raised with something, you miss it.

My mother-in-law hated the thing with a deep passion. And with good reason. She was visiting us in the early 1950s when the horn was atop the old town hall.

As it happened, she was driving her convertible north on Main St. very shortly before noon one day. The traffic light stopped her at the Church Street intersection, and then the fire horn went off.

That genteel Yankee lady had never heard such and neither had the car. Before the second blast sounded, both were three-quarters of the way across the apron of Sam Womble's filling station headed for the extension building. Somehow control was regained in the proverbial nick of time.

(Over the years, Ramblin often mentioned Tarboro's legendary nicknames. Finally, in 1986, he somehow gathered up all those funny names and gives Tarboro a classical, laughable look at itself.)

MONICKERS—Good Ole Buddy Bailey has been prodding for a couple of years for another column on Tarboro nicknames. His Monday's offering's closing forced my hand.

I looked in vain for a column I wrote, and a "game" Sam West and Bella Porter sent me back in the 60s. With the aid of "Evil T", and "Shimmy" and my memory, I was able to come up with the following:

Don Gilliam, Jr. was "Dinksie" and his brother, William Farley, was "Boo Boo".

Charles Fisher Clayton was "Vet", his brother Ed was "Buzzard", and their sister, Sarah Tyler, was "Pig".

Gilman Smith was "Deete". Dr. Ed Roberson was "Seek". The senior Lynn Mayo was "Duke". Captain Henry Clark Bridgers, Jr. was "Spicky", Henry McNair and Bob Pender called each other "Ike". C.A. Johnson was "Sporty Deacon".

Tom Bardin was "Evil T", his brother, W.E. Jr., was "Bull". Their sister Elizabeth was "Mink", her sister Beulah was "Dewdy", and her sister Daisy was "Gal".

William Vance Leggett was "Little Brother". Julius Creech was "Son", from Day One. Reginald M. Fountain was "Runt" and his brother Vinton was "The Dance Master". R.A. Lindsey was "Squinch". Nelson Howard was "Shine". James E. Boykin was "Rat".

Postmaster Joseph Martin Carstarphen was "Buzz". His son, Martin Jr. was "Bip", and Bip's brother Manly was "Wop". He married "Woody".

George Earnhart was "Heavy". Walter Knox was "Goat". Henry Irvin Johnson was "Slim". W.F. Wooten was "Cap". M.S. Brown was "Coca Cola".

Walter C. Hargrove Jr., was "Bro". Earl West was "Shimmy" and "Bright Lights". His brother Sam was "Shank". Allen Lee Harrell was "Hog Bear", and Wilbur Walker was "Buster".

Horace Lynwood Guill ws "Cotton" and his brother Irvin was "Monk". William Grimes Clark was "Cousin Willie". W.G. Clark III was "Dubber". William Oliver Clark was "Pete". Henry Staton was "Count". Lafayette Fountain was "Buck". Bill Hart was "Peck", and his brother Claude was "Hunk". Spencer Dancy was "Mank".

"Tish" Jenkins married "Bough" Clark, and those two nicknames are among our town's best-known.

Sorta on the personal side, I don't know that Herbert H. Taylor, Jr. had a nickname. In our too infrequent conversations, I call him either "Judge" or "Colonel", depending on the way the recallings go. These were earned titles.

Hubert Earl Carpenter was "Bo" and Martin Sasser was "Buck". L.G. Shook is still "Bud", but few remember he was also known as "Mohot". Joel King Bourne was/is "Sarge". Perhaps that one is the only one I ever dubbed. Why? I don't know. We spent a lifetime of growing up and attending two institutions of higher learning. Time out for service in the Marine Corps. Still no reason for "Sarge", but that's the way it will be.

One final story comes to mind.

Son John came home after his first day at Mary Wood Heydenreich's kindergarten. We asked him what he learned and he told us her husband's name was "Crackers" and they had a dog named "Biscuit".

With the help of deep mind probing, "Evil T", and "Shimmy", this is the best I can offer.

Fie on you, Radford "Kudz" Bailey.

NAMES—Last week's offering caused the phone to ring more often than usual over the weekend.

The most often asked question was why I omitted the facts that E. Harvey Lewis Jr. was "Duck" and J. Chalmers Marrow "Ching".

I hereby apologize.

Callers and a refreshed memory brought forth some additional Tarboro nicknames.

Daisy Smith was "Ting". Ed Fowlkes was "Bo-Beep" and Frank Grayiel was "Dynamite". Julian Ruffin was "Bully." Julian Evans was "Beans". Julian Green was "Scrap".

David Sugg was "Nut" and his brother Jasper "Phes". A.B. Bass was "Pug". "Doctor" Brooks worked at the Clinic, but he wasn't a M.D. "Tiny" Harrell worked at Hart Mills and later drove a cab.

Carlton Webb was "Corky" and his brother Henry Jr. was "Toby". "Tootsie" Mayo had a brother known both as "Honey" and "Popeye."

"Stonewall" Pittman worked at the Coca Cola plant. Jim Hagans was "Lefty."

Walter Walker was both "Fatty" and "Kid". "Farmer" Cullom worked in the post office.

Mack Ruffin Jr. was "Sook". Henry T. Bryan as "Pop". Mary McCabe Godfrey was "Monk," a name inherited by her son, Paul B. F. Taylor was "7-Up".

Billy Meares was "Wee Wally" and Walter Andrews was "Buzzy". Leonard Noble was "Buddy" and "First Chair". His brother Linwood was "Second Chair" and "Shorty" Hales cut hair in the last chair in the shop.

W.D. Edmondson was "Dink" and his daddy "Baldy" was one of the best farmers in the county. Leslie Wickham was "Shorty." Howard Cosby was "Deep Sea" and Harvey Pittman was "Hot Dog".

Rufus Worsley was "Woo Woo" and James Dupree was "Jimbo." Franklin Winslow was "Dutch" and Harold Shugar was "Bunny". Fred Henry was "Snake."

There was "Biddy Buddy" Pittman, "Flapper" Ruffin, "Red" Bass, "Tip" Wilson, "Nig" Pulley, "Tootsie" Alderman, "Tiny" Aldridge, "Buck" Marrow and "Punch" Whitehurst.

Julian Gatlin ws "Hoss" and his brother David was "Pony". Earl Purvis was "Lum." Martin Cromartie was "Croaker" and Van Martin was "Monk".

George Pennington was "Oogie." Dr. Ed Roberson was also known as "Unk." Columbus Beamon was "Bubba" and Alexander Dancy was "Toot".

In the waning years of the Coastal Plain League, we had "Bull" Hammons and "Gas House" Parker. Clarence Harrington was "Pee Wee" and Billy Evans was "Smoke."

With apologies, all of the above was written in the past tense because I found it awkward jumping from "is" to "was" so often. This two-week compilation has been both a frustration and joy. It was when my recall was exhausted that the phone would ring, and the caller would remind me I had omitted so-and-so and so-and-so.

My spirits soared and I went back to the legal pad and Bic pen to find my recall was refreshed. The result is the above.

And my special appreciation goes to Milford, "Squire of Downtown."

And yet again—more nicknames.

LIST—There just seems to be no end.

The phone range several times and callers somewhat indignantly demanded to know why I didn't recall Mr. Warren Andrews had a son named "Lank".

Deepest apologies.

Of course everybody knows "Buck" and "Poss" Clark resided on the other side of The Creek. There was "Buddy" Griffin and "Little Bud" Griffin. We also had "Buddy Boy" Staton and "Candy" Staton.

Creighton Brinson was "Biggie". Roland Taylor was "The Sundown Kid". Carl Worsley was "Chief", Bruce Fountain, Jr. was "Bugger", and "Doll Baby" Edmondson married Joe Taylor.

Carl Rosenbaum was "King" and "Roscoe". Milton Steele Brown, Jr. was "Sonny". Alvin Moore, Jr. was "the Khaki Kid". Edwin Cherry Jr. was "Buck". George Earnhart, Jr. was "Buck" and "Onion".

Frank Sanders had a sister named "Tut". Mr. and Mrs. R.M. Gaines had a daughter named "Bitty Baby". Edna Moten's boy was "Mutt". "Hot Poppa" worked at Porter "Poo Poo" McNair's filling station. Bill Page was "Bubbles" and Taft Whitehurt Jr. inherited "Red" from his daddy. Alton Page was "Cannonball". "Slick" worked for Sam Womble.

Allen Lee Harrell was "Hog Bear", and "Pea Head" Lehman played third base. Dr. R.W. Moore was "Bud". Horace Kirman called everybody "Cuz". Mildred Alford was "Stump". Spencer Bass Jr. was "Pem". Benjy Trueblood was "Tip".

No doubt there are more, but for three weeks my cup hath runneth over. There will be updates as more come in.

Did I have a nickname? Mrs. Carrie Wiggins dubbed me "Charley Boy".

It was, she said, because as a young'un I had curly hair like Charley Hussey, who was a couple of years my senior. Even as an adult, when I had occasion to talk with "Miss Carrie", it was always "Charley Boy".

And yet again—still more.

MORE—The nicknames continue to dribble in, several remarking on my omissions. For example:

R.W. Long ws "Booney" and David Bunting was "Bolo".

The Summerlin brothers were "Rabbit" and "Squirrel". "Sky" Parker ran a funeral parlor.

"Coonie" Knight was J. Watson Smoot's right-hand man.

Legend has it that once during a poker game at the Elk's Lodge, "Coonie" called for a hold-up in the middle of a round.

He showed his hand to several bystanders, got on his bicycle and peddled off to see Mr. Smoot. There "Coonie" showed him his hand and asked to borrow money on it.

Alas, the outcome of the loan request and the game are forgotten.

Mary Northwood Worsley married James "Bull" Hall. "Fluffo" Taylor had a real bad accident which hurt him privately. "Flapper's" daughter ws "Itzy" Ruffin. Sarah Elizabeth Winchester was "Betty Boop" and her daddy was Lee "Iron Neck" Cummings.

Ella Norris was "Pete" Hale. James Plemmer, chief caretaker of two courthouses and unofficial mayor of the Princeville lowground, was "Shorty".

NAMES—That can of worms I opened here four weeks ago continues to wiggle:

Ed Morris had a daughter called "Dee-Dee". There was "Cookie" Pillow and "Cookie" Carstarphen, "Sis" Ward, "Sister" DeLoatch.

A.M. Smith was "Picture Show" and R.B. Peters Sr., was "Plucky", Jack Mobley Sr., was "Grump".

"Peck" Kornegay still holds forth on the Bethel highway. Clarence "Zeke" or "Zack" Harris left Conetoe to become a big-time car dealer in Wilson.

Early April.

NICKNAMES—The list of also-known-as grew a bit th is week.

"Teeny" Clark married and moved to Wilson.

"Dink" Edmondson's brother was "PeeWee". "B-2" Nash married "Bo" Jenkins and they moved to a house along the Pasquotank. Ted Levy was "Jerk" and there was "Zulu" Lawrence. "Beans" Evans' brother Harry was "Skeeter".

"Boot Jack" Jenkins spent some time around the jail. George "Shorty" Bradley still lives on Howard Avenue. Boise "Crip" Porter probably served as waiter at more barbecues and fish fries than any man in this century. J.A. "Buddy" Everett worked at the police station and Robert Sheffield was another "Bo".

Taking time out from nicknames for the annual duck report.

VISITOR—Word came yesterday that the wood ducks on the Common are back.

Mama Duck stopped traffic on Wilson Street while mama, trailed by seven or eight ducklings, headed for the First Baptist Church.

Seeking water, I suppose.

HARRY—Sincere best wishes to harry Alderman on his second retirement as Tarboro's police chief, and sincere condolences to his beloved Edna for having to "put up" with him full time.

The Alderman-Bass relationship goes back to 1950 when the policing of rural Edgecombe ws done by Sheriff Tom Bardin and deputies Shad Felton, "Bull" Bardin, Charlie Pridgen, and Harry.

I suppose the living and the law-enforcing then was easier than now. But not always. Like the spring morning when Harry stopped a west bound train o the Tarboro side of Speed. Harry didn't plan it that way.

A convict earlier had escaped from the county prison camp and had been raiding rural homes. He had a fondness for firearms and knew how to live in the woods.

But one spring morning the convict ws spotted walking the railroad tracks near the Charlie Lockhart farm.

Harry responded to the call and before long found himself between the tracks with the fugitive about 100 yards away. Both men had drawn pistols, and what followed in the next few minutes was like something from the streets of Laredo.

Thee were the usual words like "Drop it! You're under arrest!" And the two began pacing forward. When they stopped it ws nearly toe-to-toe and eyeball-to-eyeball.

There were two shots, and both men fell between the tracks, Harry with a bullet wound in his leg and the fugitive was over him, dead from a shot to the head.

About that time, help was arriving and when they asked Harry what they could do for him, the west bound train whistled for the Speed crossing.

Harry said, "Somebody PLEASE stop that train!"

Several men went running down the tracks and somehow brought the train to a screeching halt within sight of the stricken deputy.

When he became chief, his door and phone line were always open to me.

Sometimes in answering my questions, he would explain the case and add, "I think it would be better if you held off for a couple of days. But it's up to you." More often than not, Harry's advise was followed and what started as a rumor became a full news story.

August.

FILM—Hot diggity! A moving picture is to be made in Tarborough and its environs. Talk at coffee is that the film will be based on Louise Shiver's novel "Here to Get My Baby Out of Jail". It is also said that the decision to film here was the direct result of the efforts of Wat Brown a couple of years ago.

The story is set in 1937.

September.

FINALE?—More calls came in this week concerning the war bond rally on the Common on a hot day in 1945, and the movie notables who attended.

One thought the actress was Ann Jeffreys, a Goldsboro native who gained stardom on the "Topper" series. Another believed it was Georgia Carroll, who later married Kay Kyser.

Most, however, said the actress was Ann Savage. None could recall having seen her in a film either before or after her visit.

Most callers said it ws Lon Chaney Jr. and not his father, "the man with a t thousand faces", who appeared at the rally.

One said Chaney was "drunk as a lord". Another said the actor was asked to give his "Wolf Man" howl, but couldn't because of laryngitis.

November 21—after another long stay in the hospital.

It hardly seems possible that it has been eight weeks since this column filled this Friday space.

It is here today through the grace of God, Doug Remer, George Hemingway, ICU nurses and many others whose names I'm afraid to list for fear of an omission. And such would be unforgivable in view of what they did for an to me during my 6-week stay at Heritage Hospital. Several friends were also patients.

Some went "up" to the fourth floor; some simply went.

Lost some very, very dear and old friends during those weeks. Didn't have the opportunity to express my condolences then, but I hope Willie Harrell, Frances Walker, Cam Weeks, Vinson Bridgers, Bill Fillmore, and lastly, Herman Creech, know how much I will miss them.

TRIVIA—My get up and go being still in somewhat of a fragile state, this week's offering is again lacking in contemporary commentary.

Instead, how about a potpourri of historical trivia?

In 1891, on the honor roll at the Tarboro Graded School were Florida Foxhall, Mamie Simmons, Sue Clark, Julia Sizer, Kate Nash, Fannie Royster, Abie Arnheim, Robert Foxhall, and Paul Liles.

The first tobacco warehouse in Tarboro was built in 1895.

In 1891, the train for Hamilton left at 4 p.m.

The old cannon which was located on the Common at the corner of Main and Wilson was given to the town in 1926. It was either of German or Hungarian make and was captured by American forces in 1918. It was probably 105mm.

1987

RETURN—A rising fever and what was discovered to be a "spot of pneumonia" put me back in Heritage Hospital for the first part of this week. My brief stay was enjoyable compared to my September-October occupancy there. A number of nurses said they were happy to see me. Another commented on how well I looked as she stuck an oxygen hose up my nose and plunged an IV needle in my arm.

Tuesday afternoon the needle was removed from my arm and the fever had gone. My doctor indicated I just might be going home Wednesday.

~

SUB-RAMBLIN—I suppose the holidays just passed will be the most memorable of all for me.

It was about halfway through Christmas morning, amid discarded ribbons and torn wrapping paper, that I suddenly realized I was being stared at. Could it be that my mere presence was the best present I could give them?

Then came a present to me from granddaughter Jennie. It was a neatly framed crayon drawing of a man lazily stretched out on a sofa watching television. It was captioned "My Grandfather's Living."

Her mother explained that at Thanksgiving her teacher had asked pupils to draw pictures of things they were most thankful for.

At that point there was a bit of eye-wiping.

~

PESTS—Many readers aren't going to believe this, but on several Edgecombe farms, deer are eating tobacco plants at an alarming rate. Farmers can get permission to kill the creatures as crop pests, but the meat cannot be eaten. Carcasses must be left in the woods to rot.

April.

FIRST—Last weekend I put together our first rockfish stew of the season. If I do say so myself, it was fitting. The pot was sopped clean.

CLIPPINGS—This week I came across some brittle, yellowed clippings from this newspaper for the late summer of 1941.

The topic was Coach Joe Caruso's football team, and the starting lineup was as follows:

Allen Lee Harrell, left end; Tom Graham, left tackle; Carlton Webb, left guard; Captain Ed Bond, center; Paul Nobles, right guard; Mabrey Bass, right tackle; Joe Bourne, right end; Pete Clark, quarterback; Martin Sasser and Bo Carpenter, half backs; Julian Gatling, fullback.

Southerner editor Aubrey Shackle had this to say about this columnist:

"Mabrey Bass proved to be a powerhouse on rushing the passer and should give enemy passers a hot time. Mabrey also appears to be the mostly deadly downfield blocker on the squad and should help the backs get away for some long runs."

Who said I was once a 97-pound weakling?

SYMBOLS—Putting first things first, the General Assembly is considering whether to name the collard the state's official vegetable and milk the official beverage.

That is just plain official damned foolishness.

In the first place, the production and consumption of milk is not statewide. I wouldn't be the least bit surprised if the last time some of our lawmakers tasted milk was the day they were weaned.

Always the patriot.

FOURTH—My belated thanks and congratulations to those firms and individuals that staged the Fourth of July celebration.

I didn't get to the mall activity, but greatly enjoyed the music and people watching at the square.

One thing worried me, however, I didn't hear any mention of the meaning of the day, and from where I sat there was a stark lack of American flags of any size.

ADVICE—Dog days are upon us and at this writing it appears it will never rain again. Dogwoods and azaleas seem to be fairing especially common. July flies and other insects make only a half hearted attempt at buzzing and chirping. Tree boughs weigh heavily with dust covered leaves, and seem to be begging passing dogs to pause briefly.

Any relief at all would be greatly appreciated.

(The popularity of old Tarboro weddings, with flowery language and exquisite details, became popular. Here is a typical account of many offered by Ramblin'.)

NUPTIALS—I have never been a reader of accounts of weddings except on occasions when I was called upon to write or read proofs of such doings for this family journal.

However, I thoroughly enjoy reading of weddings which appeared in old issues of *The Southerner.* The style alone makes for much more interesting than the cut-and-dried, fill-in-the-blanks accounts of today.

Take, for example, how Editor Frank Powell described the wedding of Billy Bryan and Louise Barlow in the May 6, 1909, issue of this paper:

"Married Thursday in Calvary Church by the Rev. Bertram Brown, Miss Louise Barlow to William Dempsey Bryan, both of this place.

"The formal announcement of the wedding of the two of our most popular young people tells the story but it does not tell what a pretty marriage it was a 1:15 o'clock.

"Miss Mamie Bryan, the sister of the groom, attired in white messaline empire gown, black picture hat and carrying carnations, was the first to enter God's temple as the wedding march was played. Then marched in the ushers, William Speight, James E. Simmons, Mabrey Hart, Robert Currier, Spencer Hart and Biscoe Howell.

"Charming Miss Sally Barlow, sister of the bride and maid of honor, in white messaline Empire dress, black picture hat and carrying pink carnations, then followed. Then the winsome bride on the arm of her father, W.L. Barlow. Her svelte figure was clad in a gray tailored suit and she carried an exquisite shower bouquet of bride roses and lilies of the valley.

"Mr. W.L. Barlow Jr., brother of the bride, acting as best groomsman, entered alone.

"At the chancel, she was met by the groom, an auburn-haired Adonis, escorted by his brother, Hugh Blair Bryan, of Greenville, S.C., who came from the vestry room.

"With the solemn and beautiful ceremony, they were made man and wife.

"Just before the bridal party entered the church, Mr. J.B. Pennington sang Perfect Love accompanied by Miss Sue Curtis on the organ and Paul McCabe on the violin.

"Both are widely known and esteemed and deservingly so for each has a charming personality that is both gracious and winning.

"The bride is the daughter of W.L. Barlow of this county whose forebears are Edgecombe's best and the same can be said of the groom.

"Of the many presents they were the recipients, but probably the one the two, certainly the male member of the new firm will appreciate the most, is a handsome chest of silver from the "Sandpackers," the nightly habitum of W.H. MacNair's drug store where the groom is chief clerk.

"The bride and groom boarded the 3:30 train for Washington, Baltimore and Philadelphia. They will be at home after May 10th, when it may be said:

"Two B's with a single buzz.

"Two B's they be as one and always will be so."

TV—Last Saturday evening WRAL-TV carried an extremely interesting but all too brief interview with Dr. Milton D. Quigless.

With the interior of his now-empty clinic as a background, the 82-year-old physician recalled some of his trials, tribulations and triumphs. Included were his childhood memories in Mississippi, his medical education in Tennessee, and a stint as a trombone player in a minstrel show band before opening his practice here.

August.

INDUSTRY—Certainly the biggest local news of the current decade thus far is that Sara Lee will build a major manufacturing facility here.

The actual announcement was sort of anticlimactic since rumors of the possibility that Sara Lee would build here began last March or earlier.

Presbyterians get their coverage.

MORE—The question was asked "Didn't anybody in Tarboro ever get married anywhere except in the Episcopal Church?"

Of course they did. Take, for example, the joining in holy matrimony in Howard Memorial Presbyterian in 1924 when Lt. (j.g.) Wilson Durward Leggett Jr. married Miss Mary Chamberlain Howard. Here's how it was recounted in the Oct. 4 issue of this paper:

"A week of gay festivities ended Thursday evening with one of the most beautiful and brilliant social events of the season, the wedding of Miss Mary Chamberlain Howard and Mr. Wilson Durward Leggett Jr., lieutenant (junior grade), United Stated Navy, which was solemnized at the Howard Memorial Church at 9 o'clock.

"Preceding the ceremony, Mr. J.P. Brawly of Peace Institute, Raleigh, rendered several well chosen selections. Mr. Ed Stallings of Wilson played with much feeling Kreisler's 'Old Refrain.' After this the Tarboro Choral Society sang the bridal chorus from 'The Rose Maiden,' accompanied by Mrs. Ashley Speir at the piano, Mr. Robert M. Rawls, organist, and Mr. Stallings, violinist.

"The church with its elaborate decorations of candles, chrysanthemums, smilax, fern and tulle, presented a scene of unusual loveliness. The aisle was a perfect arbor of vine covered arches, and about midway was intersected by ivy-twined gates, which were opened by the little flower girls, Elizabeth Green and Elizabeth Hussey, dainty in frocks or peach georgette and lace. They carried ribbon-embossed baskets of flowers.

"The first to enter the open gates were the ushers, Messrs. Rawls Howard, brother of the bride, Sam Emery, Bisco Howell and J.W. Wiggins Jr. Following them came the beautiful bridesmaids, Misses Mabel Norfleet, Claribel Fountain and Grace Henry of Gastonia, who were gowned in powder blue crepe chiffon trimmed in rings of shell-colored ostrich. Their flowers were Kilarney roses and blue delphiniums tied with ribbon-bordered lace. Then, the groomsmen, Messrs, W.H. Shine of Chapel Hill, Jack McDowell of Scotland Neck, and Allard Battle, followed by Mesdames Sam Emory and Rawls Howard, dames of honor. They were dressed in yellow crepe chiffon with ostrich and carried arm bouquets of Kilarney roses and delphiniums. Following these came the junior bridesmaids, Misses Mary Howard Leggett, and Mary Rawls Jenkins, dressed in powder blue georgette over pink.

"Just preceding the bride came the lovely maid of honor, Miss Lucy Cooper of Fayetteville, attired in peach crepe chiffon, ostrich trimmed and carrying an arm bouquet of Columbia roses and delphiniums.

"The bride, who entered on the arm of her father, Mr. George Howard, was never more beautiful than robed in her exquisite wedding gown of Italian lace and Dutchess satin. The veil of tulle, which was arranged most becomingly, was held at the head with a tiara of pearls and brilliance, and fell in graceful folds to the floor, forming a train. Her flowers were brides' roses, showered with valley lilies and sweetheart roses.

"She was met at the altar by the groom, who entered with his brother, Mr. Tom Leggett, Lieut. Leggett wore the full dress uniform of the U.S. Navy. Rev. Daniel Iverson officiated, using an impressive ceremony of the Presbyterian Church. After the peeling of the wedding bells, the bridal party left the church for the home of the bride's parents, and there waited to welcome the many guests who called to extend to the popular young couple their good wishes.

"The guests were met at the door by Mrs. W.T. Clark of Wilson and were greeted with the graciousness and informality of true Southern hospitality by the host and hostess. Mrs. Howard was lovely in a gown of white cut velvet. Her flowers were orchids and valley lilies. They were assisted in receiving by Mr. and Mrs. W.D. Leggett, the groom's parents. Mrs. Leggett wore a black grown heavily beaded with cut steel and wore pink roses.

"The bride and groom were fortunate in that each had a grandmother to receive with them on this occasion, and it was a pleasure to each caller to be welcomed by Mrs. E.W. Rawls and Mrs. Mary Hester Howard and Mrs. J.D. Leggett.

(The "Auto Club" was copied from a 1910 issue of The Southerner. The Levy-Zander wedding was in 1909. Editor Frank Powell wrote both accounts. The items appeared in the same Ramblin' late in the year.)

Auto Club

"A big crowd gathered at the Post Office yesterday morning to witness the departure of the 'Auto Club' on its first annual picnic, and a merry and delighted crowd filled the cars all gaily decorated with red, white and blue with flags flying and horns honking as they filed in perfect order around the town and then up Main on their 20-mile spin to Coffield's Bridge on the Halifax line.

"Here they found Jim Spraggins, the prince of 'roast pig' caterers, awaiting them in a fine grove of beeches on the banks of Fishing Creek.

"The day opened with showers and gathering clouds and the question on ever lips was "Can we Go?, but the man behind said, 'Go' and when he plans, he executes.

"Nature kindly favored them with a lovely April sun, all dust laid and a fine road not dependent on the 'Good Roads Commission' and the sight was a grand one as the cars sped on in perfect order led by:

"No. 1—Dr. W.J. Thigpen, Hupp.

"No. 2—Henry Clark Bridgers, Hupp.

"No. 3—Dr. J.D. Jenkins, Ford.
"No. 4—Messrs Constantine and Barnes, Mercedes.
"No. 5—W.A. Sherrin, Pope Hart Ford.
"No. 6—W.G. Clark, Buick.
"No. 7—Dr. D.L. Wimberly, Ford.
"No. 8—J.B. Pennington, Ford.
"No. 9—Dr. L.E. Norfleet, Ford.
"No. 10—Dr. J.J. Philips, Ford.
"No. 11—Boaz Gammon, Reo.
"No. 12—Jim Bunn, Maxwell.
"No. 13—W.J. Cummings, Rambler.
"No. 14—Jim Andrews, White.
"No. 15—Durwood Leggett, Mitchell.
"No. 16—T.W. Thrash, Cadillac.
"No. 18—W. Stamps Howard, Buick.
"No. 19—Geo Watson, Buick.
"No. 20—W.E. Fenner, Rambler.
"No. 21—Don Gilliam, 'Georgia Buggy'.
"No. 22—Sam Clark, 'Push Mobile'.
"No. 23—Henry Bagley, 'Peddler."

"A few of these cars were not able to join the party.

"The autoists are indebted to Henry Clark Bridgers for this first annual meet of the Tarboro Auto Club."

Married

(Legend had it that the Zander girls were Tarboro's most beautiful.)

One of the prettiest home marriages that has been solemnized here took place at 12 p.m. Thursday at the residence of Mr. and Mrs. Joseph Zander, their youngest daughter, Miss Gertrude plighting her troth to Dr. Albert L. Levy of Baltimore in the presence of a house full of well-wishing and sincere friends.

The home as tastefully decorated and arranged for the occasion. The parlor where the ceremony was performed, had a color scheme of red which made a splendid setting for the handsomely gowned ladies and their well dressed male attendants. Pink was the predominating color in the dining room, where a more dainty and elaborate collation with cakes and ices, etc., to match, ever graced the mahogany.

Until the presents were displayed in the sitting room, pink was the decorative color, but after the sheen of silver and the glitter of cut glass blended with the original design in restful and attractive harmony. Touches of green and pink added to the attractiveness of the hall, but its real charm was Miss Jennie Hecht who at the punch bowl containing a delightful concoction of Mr. A. Rosendorf, made a Hebe more charming than ever seen on Olympus.

Owing to the indisposition of Mrs. Zander, the mother of the bride, the ceremony was brief and simple, but the conformatory to every requirement of the church of Israel. It was performed most impressively by Rabbi Mendoza, D. D. of Norfolk. To the enlivening strains of Mendelssohn's Wedding March, the bride, on the arm of the fortunate and handsome groom crossed the hall from the sitting room to the parlor, and there while Schubert's Serenade was softly played as Rob Rawls on the piano, Wilson Bell and Paul McCabe violins knew so well how to evoke harmony, they were made man and wife.

The recessional, "The Sweetest Story Ever Told," was more apt, for what sweeter story could be told than a lovely maiden reciting her vows of wifely fealty, plighted by a Queen Rose in our rosebud garden of girls, sweet, winsome, lovely, lovable Gertie Zander, loved irrespective of creeds or race, whose disposition more than matches features and forms.

She never looked sweeter. Her wisteria broadcloth dress, with its exquisite trimmings enhanced a loveliness that we have all admired in the girl.

Dr. and Mrs. Levy left on the 2:30 train to New York, then, for Philadelphia, Atlantic City, Washington and then Baltimore, their home where the groom enjoys a lucrative practice and where we all wish him and his bonny wife and gracious wife, happiness and a long and well-spent life.

1988

Ginger Bishop was now Editor.

YEAR—Many are the events which made major news in our town and county this past year.

One I fear will be overlooked was the naming of Ginger Bishop as editor of this family journal which had its beginnings in this community 161 years ago.

Ginger is the first female of the species to hold the title of editor. I join others in wishing her well, and some have already remarked favorably on some changes.

February

HISTORY—This is Black History Month and much will be done, and rightly so, to cite the roles of Carver, Washington, King, Tubman and others on the national level.

But what have our educators, who stress this observance, done to inform young people of local blacks who made their mark on local history? Why not tell them about:

Frank D. Dancy, a blacksmith who was elected Tarboro's mayor in 1881, and went on to amass enough money to post bond for at least one public official by 1899.

Henry C. Cherry, a contractor who built the town hall which stood on the south side of St. James Street between Trade and Albemarle. He was also a town commissioner and, earlier, a member of the Legislature which adopted a new State Constitution.

The Rev. M.M. Wesson, long-time rector of St. Luke's Episcopal Church and his son, the Rev. M.M. Wesson Jr., who when I last heard, was rector of the largest Episcopal congregation in the nation.

The Rev. J.W. Perry, an early black educator who ran a private school here back in the 1880s and '90s.

Drew Wimberly—a black legislator who cast the deciding vote which provided the money to re-open the University of North Carolina after the Civil War.

Orren James and Camilus Dancy, successful black merchants.

John Dancy, newspaper editor, educator, and federal official who has an historical marker erected in his honor on St. James Street.

Nathan Williams, a black barber here for many years whose son, Nathan Jr., was awarded the barbering franchise for all the steamers of a Chesapeake Bay steamship line.

Fred Cooper, a black restaurateur who donated $140 toward constructing the First Baptist Church in about 1891, and purchased $100 in stock and was one of the incorporators of the Tarboro Cotton Factory in 1889.

William Cook, the contractor who built bridges over the river and creeks of this county in the late 1800s.

And then there was Old William Morgan. I suppose I'm the only one around who knows who Old William was.

When he died in 1837 at the age of 87, the Tarboro Scaevola reported the black man was "much respected by his neighbors, and a revolutionary soldier and pensioner."

I have written the above from memory, and I apologize for any error of an initial or date. If there are any other errors, they are those of omission.

I'll try to do better next time.

March.

CLOSING—Announcement that the Big Star Store will close is sad news for its customers and devastating for its loyal employees.

It was a Tarboro native. David Pender, who started it all, with his D.P. Store, which became Pender's, Colonial and finally Big Star.

Another account of Jewish families in Tarboro.

CITIZENS—Several times in recent years I have been asked what I knew about the Jewish citizens of Tarboro during the 19th century. Unfortunately, I know very little, and it is sad that no one has undertaken a history of these citizens who were an important part of our town.

The local synagogue wasn't built until the late 1890s, but it is regrettable that the minute book has been lost. Lewis Heilbroner told me once in the 1970s that it was in his possession, but upon his death it could not be found.

Possibly Tarboro's first Hebrew citizen was Joseph Schenk, the town's second postmaster. He died a wealthy man and never married, leaving his estate to gentile friends in this section. However, his will provided a modest stipend be sent to his brothers in Riga, Russia, so that they wouldn't think the streets of this county were "paved with gold." That was the early 1800s.

In the years just before the Civil War a man named Odenheimer operated a livery stable and a Feldenheimer ran a dry goods store. Following that war the number of Jewish merchants in Tarborough grew, and it was largely through their support with advertising that this newspaper survived.

Whitlock and Kawalski were prominent names here in the 1870s.

Louis Heilbroner became a merchant in the late 1860s, but his business later failed and he became a manager for S.S. Nash.

Among the most prominent of Tarboro families during the past two decades were the Morrises, Zanders and Lichtensteins.

The head of the Morris family was Henry, a native of England who came here at the age of 26 and was a merchant for 30 years. One of his sons, Arthur, founded the Morris Plan Bank and was known as the father of consumer credit in the United States.

Here is an account of "The Jewish Ball" and its participants here in late January of 1889:

"As was announced last week our Hebrew populace gave a grand ball and supper Tuesday evening. They never do things by halves and this occasion was no exception to the general rule.

"The ladies were handsomely and tastily attired and many were the diamonds sparkling here and there under the brilliant rays of gas. The gentlemen wore the regulation evening dress suits.

"The following is a list of the couples present: H.Morris, Jr., and Miss Sarah Cohen; Carl Kaufman and Miss Mollie Levy;

J.Cohen and Miss Freda Hoffman; G. Gumprecht and Miss Pearl Morris; Gus Zander and Miss Thresa Heilbroner; A.L. Heilbroner and Miss Martha Morris; J. Rosenbaum and Miss Minnie Arnhein; Levie Cohen and Miss Mamie Morris; Mr. and Mrs. Pincus; G. Lowenberg and Mrs. J.B. Lowenberg; Henry Morris and wife; Jos. Morris and wife; Meyer Morris and wife; A. Arnheim and wife. D. Lichtenstein and I. Levy danced as stags.

"Dancing began at 10 p.m. and lasted until 3 a.m. At 11:30 o'clock supper was announced and the participants in the ball—50 in number—proceeded to Cooper's Cafe where there awaited them a most handsome supper seen as only Cooper can prepare and at 12:30 they again returned to the ball room to finish the evening's enjoyment."

A long lost and little remembered poem about the Tar River.

RIVER—Going through old copies of this family journal this week I came across a poem entitled, "Song of the Tar". It was written in 1837 by W.F. Lewis of Mt. Prospect, N.C. It follows:

'Mong Person's spouting springs
I have my happy birth.
Through Granville's grassy glades
I dance in frolic mirth.

Down Franklin's golden sands
I roll my silver tide.
'Mond Nash's barren hills
My flashing beauties hide.

Upon the valley's verge,
Still loath to quit my hills
I pause at man's behest
To drive his thundering mills.

Over huge rocks pouring
In mimicry of the sea,
Rushing, foaming, roaring,
I fall into the lea.

Through Edgecombe's fertile fields
With smooth and gentle flow,
I echo with the Negro's song
As he gathers the autumn snow.

Down Pitt's green vales
On bosom broad and large
I bear the little streamers
And many a freighted barge.

Through Beaufort's gloomy woods
With slow and gentle flow,
I end my lay and merge my life
In broad old Pamlico.

River of health, flow over the sand
Flow on, beautiful river,
Your limpid stream o'er pebbly strand
Flow on—thus forever.

In distant lands your sons
In memory of your pines,
And doth every fondly link
Carolina's name with thine.

When the current of my life
Shall end in death's great deep,
Upon the flowing banks
I hope to sweetly sleep.

REUNION—Some of the most interesting news to come down the pike of late is that the folks across the creek are planning a reunion this fall.

That thing could develop into something of such magnitude that People Magazine and all major television networks will compete for coverage rights.

If this old town ever had an area which was "neighborhood proud", it was Runnymede.

Just let a boy from Fountain Mill or from any other part of town, for that matter, set a foot across Hendrick's Creek in quest of the favors of a Runnymede girl, he was sure to be caught and get the living daylights beat out of him.

I don't recall any other part of town being able to field a baseball team that could beat the Runnymede bunch. I sort of hope the celebration includes a ball game with youngsters taking the names of the oldsters—Lonnie, Poss, Emmett, Ernest, Buck and all the rest.

I wish them well in their reunion efforts and when celebration time arrives, I hope I'll be invited across the creek.

REPRINT—Twenty-seven years ago I asked the readers of this family journal to write letters on "What's Right; What's Wrong With Tarboro?"

No prizes were offered, and the response was slight, but the quality of the offerings were first rate. Here's an example—remember it was written in 1961:

"What is wrong with Tarboro:

"We the people are what is wrong with Tarboro. We are selfish, thoughtless, status seekers. We build new subdivisions with beautiful homes, flowers, lawns, boats and cars. This is to give our children the better things.

"But we have no sidewalks for them, so we curse fearfully and frantically, as our brakes squeal, in our desperate attempts to avoid them as they play in the streets.

"We build swimming pools at the country club in case the Municipal Pool is integrated. Then hire Negroes to keep our homes and our children so that our wives can work to maintain the status quo.

"We have tolerated immoral, dishonest, and inefficient people in our high offices. We have seen justice blinded by money and influence and done nothing to remedy this.

"We tolerate, even encourage, an ABC store located in the midst of the largest group of working men in town. We keep it open night and day, and then shun, deride and deplore our public drinks.

"We wonder why our most talented young people move away. We hire people from all the surrounding towns, but when a native born son of Tarboro, returns home from duty overseas, what happens? We stare him straight in the face and ask, 'Just what do you think you can offer me?'

"We welcome new industry, and new people, promise ourselves that we will be friendly, but after a hectic day's work, we forget everything except our own comfort. Besides, these newcomers might be better material for club presidents than we are. And we have kow-towed, slapped backs, and played yes man too long to let some newcomers walk in and take over our own uncertain positions of leadership here.

"So we pull off our girdles and high heels, our coats and drip-dry shirts, don our shorts, reach for a drink and start the charcoal for the cookout. If the neighbors are also out, we carefully estimate whether they are having steak or hamburgers, if her outfit is new, if his boat and motor and trailer are larger than ours. Then complain to the neighbors on the other side, 'I don't know how they can afford it.'

"We shop in Raleigh and Richmond because the social editor ignores Tarboro shoppers. We watch the newcomers ever so carefully as they so very carefully begin to choose their friends. We watch how skittish they are when some one they know to be just plain folks, tries to be friendly.

"All this proves one thing—we are an average, modern American town, because we do a lot that is right here.

"We respond to every call for help to any disaster.

"We realize we are not perfect and we go to church and ask God's forgiveness and pray for His help to become better citizens.

"We give support to the Little League, Boy Scouts, Girl Scouts, Swimming Team, Red Cross, Easter Seals, civic organizations, churches, some foreign missions and Oral Roberts.

"We make surgical gowns, layettes, and sheets for hospitals in Japan. We ship supplies and clothing overseas for the needy.

"We help needy students to obtain funds to further their education. We call the car dealer and assure him that the down payment for the young minister's car will be taken care of.

"We call the young college student and tell her to select some clothing she really needs and send us the bill.

"We get up in the middle of the night to bail out an employee who has taken our car and wrecked it.

"We look at the children in our school classes and note the ones who need food and clothing. Then we see that they get it, even if we have to pay for it ourselves.

"We provide Christmas cheer for entire families, food, clothing and toys.

"We sometimes do not pay our employees large salaries or wages, but if they get sick or their families are in need, we help catch up their grocery bills and fuel bills.

"We doctor the sick so many times when we know we will never be paid.

"We try to have an honest city government, in spite of people who think no law or city regulation should ever inconvenience them.

"We stand in the pulpit on Sundays and preach the love of God for all mankind and know that some of the congregation live by this. And hope that in the fullness of time we all love our brothers, whether they be native born, newcomers, black or white, high or low on the social scale.

"So what is wrong with Tarboro?

"Why nothing that I can see, and I have lived here for 56 years."

The following week

AUTHOR—The question was asked as to the name of who wrote "What's Wrong and What's Right with Tarboro?" which was written 27 years ago and reprinted here last week. The author was Mrs. Elise Carpenter.

REUNION—Last Saturday I was both proud and honored to be a guest at the "First Ever Runnymede Reunion", which I will long remember as one of the most enjoyable and memorable evenings of my life.

I suppose what made the event even more meaningful was that I was one of only a very few people from the wrong side of the creek to be invited to take part in the gathering of the clans of Runnymede.

Hurdley Rountree recounted sweet memories of Runnymede life when he first went to work in the mill in 1927. The pay was 10 cents an hour for a 60 hour week. "We went to work in the dark and went home in the dark."

He recalled who had the first telephone, the first radio and the first inside plumbing.

In a recording sent from Richmond, Va., Mrs. Elise Carpenter proudly pointed out the various careers successfully followed by those born and reared in Runnymede.

"Runnymede," she declared, "has produced more leaders than any other comparable group in town."

Ronald Butler, a Runnymede native son is now a vice chancellor of N.C. State University, served as Master of Ceremonies.

I don't believe any of my hosts Saturday night thought of themselves as having a guest speaker for their reunion.

Rather, some remarks were offered by Charlie and Elsie Piland's boy Ralph. In the years since leaving Runnymede he has earned a doctorate in Divinity and is the long-time pastor of the Second Presbyterian Church in Waynesboro, Va.

He remembered: "The names of the early inhabitants of Runnymede trip lightly across the golden tongue of memory and continue to weave magic in our lives: Clark, Kent, Taylor, Ellis, Carvin, Felton, Parisher, Fleming, Gurganus, Fussell, And Rogers, Keene, Melton, Collins, Pollard, Eure, Sherrod, Sutton, Little, Rawls, Worsley, Brewer, And Medford, Whitaker, James, Daughtridge, Sims, Johnson, Butler, Everett, Edmondson, Cross, Piland, Moore, Alford, And Owens, Shaw, Fisher, Page, Bishop, Parker, Deal, Harrell, Ward, Richardson, Raynor, Thompson, Rountree, Futrell. And O'Neal, Merritt, Acree, Bowen, Watson, Armstrong, Gooch, Frazier, Hudson. And others!

INVENTION—Over the past hundred or more years Edgecombe men have been granted a number of patents, mainly, I suppose, for devices to ease the drudgery of agriculture.

However, at least one of those imaginative souls came up with a device whose sole purpose was to alleviate human suffering.

This gentleman was Lewis Chamberlain, a watchmaker. He was a native of Trenton, N.J., and came to Tarborough after the Civil War. With a Mr. Rawls as his partner he ran a jewelry store and hotel about where the Hopkins and Allen law office is today.

But Mr. Chamberlain's marvelous invention lay in another field.

What Mr. Chamberlain invented was a toilet seat which, he explained, "is used for the relief and cure of hemorrhoids, internal and external, and all protrusions of the lower bowel.

"The action of the appliance is based according to the endorsement of the leading physicians of the South on the soundest philosophical and anatomical principles of compression."

In advertisements which appeared in his family journal in 1885, Mr. Chamberlain offered his seat in walnut for $6, in cherry for $5, and in poplar for $5 also. He sent samples of his invention to prominent people and in some cases received testimonials which he published in the paper.

If any member of the local medical fraternity would like to see a drawing of Mr. Chamberlain's wonderful invention, one is available in the local history collection at the library.

December

HOLIDAY—I can't remember when Downtown at Christmastime looked prettier. The special touch is provided by the strings of small white lights which outline most of the show windows.

Windows seem more attractively decorated than they have in years. Almost makes one want to revive that long forgotten pleasure of nocturnal window shopping along Main.

To all the Downtowners responsible, many thanks.

1989

(As time was running out on Ramblin', his interest and love for local history was expanding and he found—or remembered—gems of rich but once forgotten treasures that held the city together over the years. His old style of offering little items about a multitude of Tarboro people and scenes had given way to more serious, longer pieces of considerable historic value. The year began with a loss of something good.)

COKE—The announcement last Friday that the M.S. Browns had sold their local Coca-Cola franchise to Charlotte interests came as both a surprise and shock to members of my generation.

To us the names Brown and Coca Cola were inseparable and both were a part of the Main Street business scene since 1912.

That was the year Milton S. Brown Sr., and his brother Raymond opened their bottling business on the east side of the 300 block of Main Street. The present building was constructed and first occupied in 1920.

From the beginning to the present the firm was blessed with devoted employees who took pride in producing and selling a quality product. That in itself is a high tribute to the management.

And a good thing that was still working.

MILESTONE—Tomorrow marks something of a milestone in the history of the local business community, for it is the 50th anniversary of the opening of Robert's Jewelry Company, the oldest business in town still operated by its original owner.

Somehow 50 years ago sounds much better than half a century, but it was then that a former jewelry manufacturer's representative form Huntington, Long Island, new York, named Louis Raskin came town with his wife, Bess, and his 8-year-old son, Bob. He rented his first jewelry store here by taking half the space occupied by Bobbitt Plumbing Company. It was an extremely narrow store, sandwiched in the 300 block of Main between the Edgecombe Drug Company and the lobby of the Hotel Tarboro.

The Saturday, May 13, 1939, grand opening was a great success because 600 people crowded into the little store to register for a variety of prizes.

Just what those prizes were has long been forgotten, but the newspaper listed the winners as being T.H. Harris, J.L. Sherrod, Helen Blake, M.A. Todel, Tommy Thayer, Ruth Lucas, Marie Slaughenhaupt, David Hilliard, and Carl Worsley.

However, he never sought, and, sadly, seldom received any public recognition for his unselfish service to and for his adopted community. Tarboro is equally fortunate in having son, Bob, following the course charted by his parents.

CHURCH—I heard this week that some members of the St. Paul Baptist Church on Lloyd Street are considering a campaign aimed at restoring the lovely old building and, perhaps, adding an education building.

This old church is certainly a gem which pre-dates many projected structures in the so-called "Historic District' of our town. It was constructed at a cost of about $11,000 as the Tarboro Missionary Baptist Church on Main Street, and the first service was held there in the spring of 1891.

There was a debt hanging over the new church and in an attempt to pay it off, a number of "subscriptions" were sought and made. The largest, $2,000, was made by C.J. Austin, one of the town's leading businessmen and a lifelong Baptist. The second largest, $140, was made by Fred Cooper, a black man who owned the best restaurant in town. Perhaps his $140 gift in 1891 was his way of expressing appreciation for the support given his congregation in the building of the original St. Paul.

Portrait of a forgotten lady with special talent and grit.

PUSS—In years past, few people here would argue if you claimed Mrs. Mary Lloyd Gregory was probably the most outstanding woman Tarborough ever produced. Today, however, probably not more than a half dozen local folks even know of this amazing woman.

Her parents had no social standing. She gave birth to a bastard son, later married a scoundrel who abandoned her soon after the ceremony and eventually sued to get a share of her property. Despite this, she amassed a fortune for her day and time, owned a two-story hotel on Main Street, owned farmland and a gristmill.

In his biography, Dr. Clairborne Smith Jr. states Mary Lloyd was born in Edgecombe County in 1768, the daughter of Nicholas and Mary Lloyd.

In an article for this paper, Dr. L.E. Norfleet wrote that she was born near what is now Hobgood and when she arrived in Tarboro, she was known as "Puss" Lloyd.

Nothing is known of her early life here, but on June 30, 1796, she gave birth to a son who was fathered by a Tarborough merchant named Joseph Ross. That September, Ross deeded to Mary the town lot at the southeast corner of Church and St. Andrew streets. Ross never married and in 1803 he moved to Petersberg and seven years later he moved to Raleigh.

In 1807 Mary Lloyd married Edmund Gregory, a smooth talker who just happened to be passing through. "Puss" Lloyd must have misgivings about Ed, because before the wedding, she deeded the lot given her by Joseph Ross to her 11-year-old son.

According to Dr. Smith's account, Mary's venture into matrimony was "brief and unsuccessful as Gregory left almost immediately for Tennessee."

Just when Mrs. Gregory began her career as innkeeper isn't known, but her two-story hotel was located on the west side of the 400 block of Main Street. For years it was the town's social center, the scene of political dinners and wedding receptions. She invested her profits and succeeded as no woman in Tarborough had before.

Her son, Joseph Ross Lloyd, also did well. He was willed the entire estate of his father, Joseph Ross, in 1830. After graduation from the University, he practiced law, and represented Edgecombe in the legislature for one term. He was an attorney for the university, and also served as Tarborough's postmaster. At the time of his death in 1841, he was president of the local branch of the State Bank.

The census of 1850 listed the worth of Mrs. Mary Lloyd Gregory as $25,000. She died on August 5, 1858, at the age of 90, and her obituary in *The Southerner* was the longest tribute ever accorded a woman by the paper to that date.

MEETING—One of the casualties of so-called progress of our times is the annual meeting of some of our churches, particularly those of the Primitive Baptist persuasion. Many of the old meeting houses have disappeared, but for the most part those which remain are well-maintained.

There is a neatly painted church between Sugg's Crossroads and Davistown with a sign designating it as the Few-In-Number church. The full name of the church is the Primitive Baptist Church of God's Chosen Few In Number. In the early years of this century, the East Carolina Railway offered special rates to the Davistown station for the more than 2,000 expected for the Big August Meeting there.

COACH—The name Joe Caruso probably doesn't mean anything to the majority of today's Tarboreans, but to a number of us who attended Tarboro High in the late 1930s and the early 1940s, he was an inspiration—a shining example of one who demanded the best one could give, both on the playing field and in the classroom. Coach Caruso died last week in Florida of bladder cancer and was buried there.

Caruso was a graduate of Elon College where he made the Small College All American football team under Coach Clyde "Peahead" Walker. He coached all three sports—baseball, football, and basketball—here from 1938 until the spring of 1942. He left here to coach in Rocky Mount and later in Henderson and New Bern before he went to Florida in 1956.

Finding lost pieces of Tarboro history.

CORRECTION—I am to blame for an error which appeared in Greg's story on local election results.

In reply to his question, I told him Henry Cherry was Tarboro's first black mayor and that he was elected in 1883.

It was only an hour or so later that I realized I was wrong, but it was too late to change Greg's story before it was published.

It was in May of 1881 that Frank Dancy, a black blacksmith, was elected mayor of Tarborough. In those days the town voters chose six commissioners, and from their members, the commissioners chose a mayor.

That year—and it was a full five years after the end of Reconstruction Tarborough elected four Republicans (Radicals), Henry Cherry, black; Frank Dancy, black; A.P. Williamson, white; and Alexander McCabe, white.

The Democrats, both white, were Judge George Howard and C.J. Austin.

At least five ballots were held along party lines, with the Republicans divided, until Frank Dancy was elected with both Howard and Dancy voting for him.

While Dr. Moses Ray is not the first black to serve as mayor of our town, he most certainly is the first to be elected by popular vote. And as far as I know he is the first black man to seek the office, and it should be noted that this man was elected without opposition.

Frankly, I am fed up with labels regarding race, religion and previous condition of servitude.

In fact, had I been editor of this family journal after this month's municipal election, I would have been tempted to headline my story: "Moses Ray First Dentist To Be Elected Tarboro Mayor".

As the old song goes, "A Good Man Is Hard To Find."

STORM—It is generally agreed that last weekend's ice storm was much more damaging than Hurricane Hazel, that has become the milepost from which the severity of all storms hereabouts are measured.

The storm also marked a first for this family journal.

As far as I can determine Sunday marked the first scheduled publication day that the paper didn't make it since that July day in 1863 when the Yankees came to town and got careless with matches.

What about Hurricane Hazel?

On that Friday afternoon at the height of the storm is appeared the power wouldn't be restored until the following day and all of the back shop crowd went home. About 5:30, Billy Evans, Herman Creech and I decided we would put out a paper.

One of use remembered that Mrs. Mary Whitley, our bookkeeper, had an old hand-operated mimeograph machine. We contacted her, and Mary agreed to help.

Billy and I worked our way around to the fire and police stations and took notes around downtown. Back at the office, I typed the stories, May cut stencils and we went to her house on E. Church Street to put out a newspaper.

It was getting dark, so while Mary's husband, Bill, held a kerosene lantern and her mother fed paper into the mimeograph machine, Mary cranked away. Billy caught the papers and together we collated and stapled the three or four pages together.

We printed several hundred copies and then the three of us—Billy, Herman and I—set out delivering our paper. We climbed over fallen trees along Main, St. Andrew and St. Patrick until the supply of *Daily Southerners* and the carriers were exhausted.

Sure, in retrospect it was a trivial thing, but it was a matter of pride. Pride in keeping alive a tradition and a love for doing what is expected of you and the special feeling you get within yourself for doing more.

By today's standards, I suppose that's trivial too.

Miss Sally Staton's final trick on her home town.

TREAT—The now accepted Halloween practice of Trick or Treat didn't make the local scene until sometime in the 1950s, and it took residents hereabouts several years to get use to the annual autumn blackmail.

When the foolishness began, Miss Sally Staton was a maiden lady in her 80s who lived on the southeast corner of St. Patrick and Wilson streets across from the low school. Some folks said Miss Sally was overeducated and peculiar. Throughout the community it was generally agreed she was as tight as the bark on a tree. She was super frugal.

When the first Trick or Treat Halloween arrived, Miss Sally was ready. She purchased a dime bag of candy corn from the Colonial Store. Each time that Halloween night when she answered a knock, she would clutch three four of the small bits of candy in her fist, reach down into the caller's bag, drop the pittance of sweets and drum her fingers on the paper bag to make it sound like a rain of goodies.

That Halloween routine lasted several years until, I suppose, Miss Sally decided she was spending too much on foolishness.

The next Halloween she answered the door carrying a box of brown sugar and a teaspoon. The would-be tricksters walked slowly down her front walk still not believing what had been doled into their bag or treats.

Sally Baker Staton, daughter of Dr. L.L. and Kate Baker Staton, died on August 26, 1962, at the age of 87, of burns suffered when she inadvertently turned on the scalding hot water while in her bath tub and was unable to get out.

When her handwritten will was read we learned that through her miserliness and despite our snickers and snide remarks, Miss Sally had thoroughly tricked us all. Most important, however, the little old lady had provided a magnificent treat worth thousands upon thousands of dollars for local girls, many of whom are to this day yet unborn, in the form of scholarships.

When all the legal dust was finally settled the annual process of awarding scholarships to Vassar College, Miss Sally's alma mater, began. Since then 18 girls have been recipients, and because of wise investing by the scholarship fund trustee, the annual awards have been increased in value.

I like to think that every Halloween when Tarborough abounds in ghosties, ghoulies and beasties and things that go bump in the night, Miss Sally Staton sits in her old high-backed Panama chair high atop the pecan tree on the old low school grounds, adjusts her rimless spectacles on the tip of her nose, peers across Wilson Street, and every a little spook raps on the door of her house, she laughs and laughs and laughs......

(Ramblin told and retold the story of how the old soldier atop the Confederate monument was shot in the behind in 1906. Did he really find out who did it?)

SHOOTING—Back in the 1950s and again in the early 1980s I wrote the story as told me by Dr. Spencer Bass about the Confederate Memorial Day ceremony during which some member of the Edgecombe Guards, during a salute, shot the soldier atop the Confederate monument in the Town Common squarely in the behind.

This week I found an account of the incident in *The Southerner* for May 17, 1906:

"Thursday when the Edgecombe Guards were firing a salute at the Confederate monument, one of the men slipped in a ball cartridge and aimed at the figure of the soldier, which surmounts this monument, and struck it.

"It was a disgraceful act. We trust that Capt. (Paul) Jones and every member of the company who has the slightest regard for the reputation of the Guards will spare no effort to ascertain who fired the shot.

(The newspaper then offered a $5 reward to bring the culprit to justice but the mystery was never solved. Half a century later, Ramblin remembers this:)

No one was ever charged with the dastardly deed, but in Paul Nobles' Fairview Grocery on a winter night, over a cold beer by a hot stove, Mr. John Taylor and Mr. Johnny Carpenter told me the name of the shooter. However, they first made me swear I wouldn't publish the name until both of them were dead.

On the first Memorial Day after Mr. Carpenter's death I began writing the story, but when I reached the climax I suddenly realized I had forgotten the name of the Guard member who "debehinded" the statue. *(And it remains a mystery to this day.)*

RIVER—In this century when you wanted to know the level of the Tar River here you called either E.V. Zoeller, E. Harvie

Ward, M.A. Moore, Jr. or the boys at the waste water treatment plant. Over the years one succeeded the other as the official river reader. But no more.

Early this week or late last week the National Weather Service people—with no advanced notice—removed the electronic river level reader.

1990

(Opening his fifth decade as a newspaperman, Ramblin' was still boosting Tarboro.)

DECADE—A couple of folks have asked me what I considered to be the town's top story for the past decade.

Without hesitation and not caring about possible contradiction, I replied, Downtown.

Since the day when those entrepreneurs V.E. and R.M. Fountain opened the Fairview Shopping Center I have always capitalized Downtown when referring in this column to Main Street from the Common to the river. I considered and still consider it to be a special place.

Drive through the downtown area of almost any Eastern Carolina town, with the exception of Tarboro and Washington and you cannot help but be depressed by the plywood masking vacant stores. A drive-through is more than enough to discourage rather than encourage a stop to shop.

I assume the same grants which Tarboro sought and received were available to other towns. But brick sidewalks and new storm drainage under Main Street don't attract shoppers.

HOUSE—The talk on the street is it now seems certain that what my generation calls the Mahler house at the southwest corner of Main and Baker has again been sold and will become a Bed and Breakfast facility.

How wonderful for Main!

The following week.

PORCH—Last week's column offering about the Morris-Powell-Mahler house on the southwest corner of Main and Baker brought fond memories to several readers.

Mostly they remembered the long front porch and what a wonderful place it was on sweet spring and hot summer nights. As soon as the supper dishes were washed and put away, the residents went out on the porch and settled down. It wasn't long before neighbors began drifting over, and nearly every passer-by was invited to come up and sit for a spell. It wasn't too long before all the big old rockers were filled and the swing on the south end was creaking softly.

As one local lady said this week, "The conversation was wonderful. You were afraid to leave for fear that you would miss something." Someone else remembered, "If there was a breeze anywhere in Tarboro it could be found on that porch, even in the hottest weather."

If by chance the porch began before 7 p.m., a radio was moved to one of the open front windows. For the next 15 minutes the only voices heard came from the Atwater-Kent, and those were of Amos and Andy, and the Kingfish and Lightening and Lawyer Calhoun, and Miss Blue, and Madam Queen. Only that program and perhaps, Lowell Thomas with the news could silence the conversation on the Mahler porch.

When the talking resumed, the neighbors down the street could always tell when Bill Mahler had favored the rockers with one of his countless stories. Laughter could be heard in all directions.

At least four generations of girls were courted on that porch—the Morrises, the Powells, Blake and Mahlers. The old swing bears silent witness.

It was late one Saturday morning that I learned the Mahler girls were having an inside yard sale preparatory to selling the house. It was bitterly cold when I went inside the house and found Cynthia and Elizabeth and their spouses and younguns huddled around a gas heater.

Cynthia said, "We're about sold out? What do you want?"

I told her I was interested in the old swing and although I didn't have a porch to hang it from, I wanted to make sure it stayed in Tarboro.

Cynthia smiled and told me, "We've decided the swing goes with the house. It isn't for sale."

I couldn't have been happier.

HISTORY—February is Black History Month, and a couple of years ago I reprinted here some items from this family journal about members of the black community in years past. So far as sparking any interest or comment, the offering was almost a dud. However, at the library one day last month a young black man asked if I would share some more of my findings which should be of interest to those interested in the community's black history.

I have written before about William Morgan, 87, who died in 1837, and his obituary noted he was a black man, a Revolutionary soldier and a pensioner who was much respected by his neighbors.

Just ask and a flood of local history came forth.

TRIVIA—At coffee one morning this week I was asked, "It's been a long time since you've written a column on Tarboro trivia. What are you gonna write another?"

Another seat-warmer at the table said, "If you really read his weekly stuff you'd know it's all trivial."

With friends like that, who needs enemas?

So here is another dose of Tarboro trivia:

One of the hottest temperatures ever recorded here was 106 degrees on Aug. 31, 1932.

The first meeting of the local United Daughters of the Confederacy chapter as held at the home of Mrs. W. H. Johnston (present site of the post office, I think), in October of 1902.

In 1885 Dr. Arnold was using the Thomas Blount house for a school.

Near Wiggins Crossroads are beds of clay which are smooth and almost free of grit. The clay is much sought after for eating. (Dr. J.P. Keech, 1932).

In 1853 it required four hours for a stagecoach to travel from Tarboro to Rocky Mount.

The first bale of cotton shipped over the Wilmington and Weldon Railroad branch between Tarboro and Rocky Mount was sent by Dr. W.S. Baker to N.A. Martin Brother and Co. in Petersburg, Va. It sold for 15 cents a pound on September 8, 1860.

The Wahree Knitting Mill, which was on Sunset Avenue was named for the Wah-Ree Cotillion Club. The name is believed to have been coined by Frank Powell, owner and editor of *The Southerner.* Its meaning is unknown, but the first mention in the paper was in October of 1883.

Baker Staton bought the Cotton Valley Farm in 1844, and made it an agricultural showplace.

In 1902 electric lights were installed in Calvary Episcopal Church.

In 1887 the Masonic Lodge was located in the southwest corner of St. James and St. Andrews, across the street from the Methodist Church.

In the early 1900s, James B. Lloyd called his home (the present Elks Lodge) Oakland. John A. Wedded and George Howard Jr. (the Barracks) called their homes Oakhurst.

On February 10, 1910 the paper announced H.H. Philips, the son of the late Judge Fred Philips, would open a law office in the Elks Temple in New Bern.

In March of 1909 The Victor Mattress Company opened in the old Central Tobacco Warehouse on the west end of Water Street. One of its first products was a felt mattress called the "Restmore."

There was a heavy frost on May 31, 1845.

On March 6, 1910 James B. Lloyd agreed to sell Henry Johnston 100 acres of what is today East Tarboro for $9,500.

C.C. Lacier, father of Miss Miriam Lacier, died in 1883. He was 51.

In August of 1887 it rained 11.35 inches in 17 hours.

On March 2, 1920, at the call of Miss Ora Lee Brown, there met in the rooms of the National Bank with her the following: T.B. Jacocks, Mrs. Adah Bass, Mrs. W.D. Leggett, J.P. Keech, George Howard, H.P. Foxhall, R.G. Shackell, R.A. Lapsley, Paul Jones and Miss Meta Liles, and the Edgecombe Public Library was organized.

SORRY—I wish to apologize to the readers of this space for recent Friday absences.

The breadwinner and I went to Ocracoke to celebrate our 40th wedding anniversary.

For those of you who wonder about such things, what transpired was exactly as it was 40 years ago, except this time I was the one who went in the bathroom and cried.

(The Cypress Grill in Jamesville was one of Ramblin's very favorite eating places in all the world but the restaurant, hardly more than a river-bank shack, was open only during the herring run up the Roanoke River and usually closed before May 1. There is something poignant about the following item.)

CONFLICT—I found myself in something of a quandary of major proportions Wednesday when I was invited by a distinguished group of local gentlemen to join them for a noon repast at the Cypress Grill on the mighty Roanoke River at Jamesville.

Alas, because of a previous engagement, I could accept neither.

I couldn't help but be reminded of General William Gaston Lewis, who farmed and ran a hardware store here in the years after the War of the Late Unpleasantness. He said that if anything in this world did worry him it was to be invited to two barbecues on the same day in different directions.

The best I can do is hope for rainchecks.

(There would be no raincheck. He began writing his column Tuesday afternoon on May 22 but something interrupted and he lay down to take a nap. The following is what they found in his typewriter.)

NAME—We spent several delightful days last week at Cokertown-on-the-Crystal Coast. One of the first things that caught my attention was a sign which warned turtle crossing, or some such. I'm not sure, but along the stretch of road for a goodly distance there were those turtle signs.

That is really caring.

Right here in Tarboro we have an entrance sign which proclaims Tarboro to be a Bird Sanctuary. Since that time, the powers that be in Tarboro have installed signs urging motorists to be . . .

(The unfinished sentence was the last ever written by Mabrey Bass. Southerner editor Ginger Bishop's front page story Wednesday afternoon of May 23, tells what happened.)

"Baker Mabrey Bass Jr., editor emeritus of *The Daily Southerner* and author of the weekly column, 'Ramblin',' died in his sleep Tuesday afternoon after penning those lines for this week's column.

"Bass, who for 35 years was editor of this newspaper, never finished the column. His funeral service will be conducted Thursday at 3 p.m. at Calvary Episcopal Church. He will be buried in Greenwood Cemetery.

"Bass, born Jan. 9, 1925, became editor in June, 1950, after graduating from the University of North Carolina with a degree in journalism. He served in that position until 1985 when he was named editor emeritus, devoting most of his time to historical pursuits and his column.

"'Mabrey had a long association dealing with people in Tarboro and Edgecombe County,' said Julius R. Creech, owner and publisher of *The Daily Southerner*. 'He was a valued employee as well as a personal friend. It is a tremendous loss to us even now. We regret it very much.'

"The son of the late Baker M. and Jennie Louise McLauchlin Bass, he graduated from Tarboro High School where he played tackle for the school's football team.

"'He was a very good tackle,' said teammate Pete Clark. 'He was big and very aggressive.'

'After graduation from high school, he attended N.C. State University until beginning service in the U.S. Marine Corps. He saw considerable action in the Pacific during World War II.

"'When Mabrey came back from the Marines, he looked like the all-American boy,' said Herbert Taylor, who has been the attorney for the county commissioners, Town of Tarboro and city and county school board throughout Bass' career.

"I have a great deal of respect and affection for him,' Taylor said. When he printed, he printed like he saw it. He never hesitated to express his opinion in a very timely manner.'

"His concern for the people of Tarboro and Edgecombe County were reflected in those editorials and writings, said George Dudley who worked with Bass as an assistant before being named editor upon Bass' retirement.

"Mabrey was an excellent writer,' Dudley said. 'He had a good command of the language and the ability to write both informatively and enjoyably.

"As far as what was going on in Tarboro and Edgecombe County, Mabrey was aware of it. That was a huge asset for anyone in the news business. He clearly loved Tarboro and Edgecombe County.'

"Billy Evans, who worked with Bass as sports editor, Linotype operator, photographer and fishing buddy, agreed.

"That's what he loved,' Evans said. 'The history of Tarboro and Edgecombe County and the people.'

"Bass was noted for his historical research, writings and knowledge.

"He was a source of information,' Dudley said. 'Everybody went to Mabrey for information. If he didn't know the answer, he could tell you who did.'

"Additionally, Bass had a sense of humor both in his writings and personal contacts that many remember.

"He loved jokes,' Evans said. 'Every morning, we'd get a cup of coffee and crowd around his Cuba hole to hear the new joke of the day. People would wander in during the morning to hear his jokes.'

"Above all, Bass was a journalist.

"Mabrey did what was necessary to get the job done,' Evans said. "We put out *The Daily Southerner* on a mimeograph machine when Hurricane Hazel hit in 1955 and then hand-delivered it to every house the next morning. It was mimeographed, but we got a paper out.'

"Lately, Bass had turned his interest to the protection of the Tar River and was an avid supporter of the Tar River Foundation, a non-profit group which promotes environmental responsibility and protection of the waterway and its tributaries.

"In lieu of flowers, his family has requested that donations be made to the Tar River Foundation, 908 St. Andrew St., Tarboro.

"Bass is survived by his wife, Mrs. Patricia Bass, and two children, Mrs. Betsy Broom of Zebulon and B.M. Bass III of Tarboro. Also surviving are his brother, William M. Bass of Dallas, Texas, and two grandchildren.

"The family will receive friends today from 7 to 9 p.m. at Carlisle Funeral Home."

ARTICLES BY DR. SPENCER BASS

(Dr. Spencer P. Bass was one of the best known physicians in Eastern North Carolina. The uncle of Daily Southerner *Editor Mabrey Bass Jr., he was mentioned often in "Ramblin' 'Round" and wrote several articles of his own for* The Southerner *and for Rocky Mount's* Evening Telegram. *In 1966, Penny Bridgers, a Tarboro native, wrote the following column about Dr. Bass for* Edgecombe County Chronicle *and we use it as an introduction for those who are not familiar with one of Tarboro's best known citizens.)*

Dr. Spencer Bass is a native Tarborean who made his debut into this world on October 23, 1883. It is said that those born during this time of year often become followers of the medical profession. It was not just fate, but a keen interest in science as well as people that led Dr. Bass to his calling. As a doctor of medicine he distinguished himself not only in Tarboro but throughout this entire area. Spencer Bass is known to the citizens of Edgecombe for much more than his medical ministrations. He is to Edgecombe County what the Renaissance man was to Italy centuries ago.

His education began here in Tarboro under the eye of that "noted educator" Frank Wilkinson. When the proper time arrived, young Bass went off as an enthusiastic freshman to the University at Chapel Hill. He vividly remembers the ordeals of "hazing" up there. It was due to an unfortunate incident during his sophomore year, in connection with the hazing, but in which he was not involved, that his career at Chapel Hill came to an untimely end. Undaunted, however, he went, on the advice of his father, with bags not even unpacked, straight to Charlottesville.

While at the University of Virginia, he distinguished himself in all phases of college life. He was captain of the track team and earned his letter in football. He was a member of the Honour Society of the University and president of his class. He graduated in medicine at Virginia and received his hospital training there.

He came home to North Carolina, and set himself up as a general practioner in Tarboro. There was no hospital here in Tarboro at the time, but Dr. Bass trained himself to perform an increasing amount of hospital-type work in his office. He recalls, with a smile, that obstetrics was his biggest "line". Recently the Kiwanis Club, of which he is a long-time member, awarded him a certificate naming him "Father of the Years" because he helped so many members into the world. He chuckles when he sees many of his graying "babies" walking down the street.

When the medical demands of the town began to increase, Dr. Bass responded in kind. In 1928, he built a small hospital which operated in conjunction with Parkview Hospital in Rocky Mount. Although it was a "shoestring" effort. Tarboro's hospital was distinguished by recognition from the American Hospital Association.

Like all doctors, Dr. Bass gradually took up a special field of medicine. He became the first doctor in Tarboro to practice modern pediatric medicine. In later years he became Chairman of the Pediatrics section of the North Carolina Medical Association. He has also served as president of the Medical Societies of Nash-Edgecombe, the 4th District, and the Seaboard Society of North Carolina and Virginia.

In line with Dr. Bass's diverse interests, however, the Department of Internal Revenue classifies him as "a farmer who does some doctoring". Dr. Bass has a great interest in growing things. He finds it to be most fulfilling from all points of view.

At his table, the good doctor is a connoisseur of everything from young corn to a good glass of beer. He recalls fondly the times in New York City when one could walk into "Luchow's" for a cool stein at ten cents and get a whole table full of luncheon delicacies to boot.

Mrs. Spencer Bass, the former Ethel Denver Pike of Leesburg, Virginia, maintained the harmony of the Bass household until her death in 1960. Dr. Bass met her while at Carolina at a house party at the home of his roommate. It was love at first sight. Today their two children, Eleanor Bass Howard and

Dr. Spencer Bass, Jr. "take care" of their father (although I suspect that it might still be the other way around).

Dr. Bass still keeps morning office hours and maintains his interest in farming. He avidly pursues his other hobby, people, and continues to be one of Edgecombe's foremost authorities on tales of its people and places.

(This is the first of Dr. Bass's stories from "In Olde Edgecombe". He began the series during the 1960's but the dates of publications are not important. We only ask that you enjoy what Dr. Bass offered.)

This is the first in a monthly series of articles concerning people, places, houses and happenings in old Edgecombe which will be presented by members of the Edgecombe Historical Society.

Today's offering is about the Parker-Cheshire house, now the home of Mr. and Mrs. Don Gilliam, Jr.

In 1808, Theophilus Parker, a merchant of Tarboro bought from John Andrews for the sum of 100 pounds, lots 20, 21, 31 and 32 in the Town of Tarboro. This was the square bounded by Church, St. Patrick, St. John and St. David streets.

In 1810 he built on this property the house in which he and his wife, then their daughter and her husband, and finally a granddaughter of the building lived, in turn. It was sold out of the family to the late Judge Don Gilliam and is now the home of Mr. and Mrs. Don Gilliam, Jr.

The grandson of the builder, the Rt. Rev. Joseph Blount Cheshire, the fifth bishop of North Carolina, was born and brought up in this house. He described it thusly:

"It is a plain framed house with four rooms downstairs and four in the second story . . . . It was a fine house in those days, the first in that part of the country to have an entrance hall and the staircase going up from this hall. Up to that time it was customary to have the staircase go up from the parlor of 'best room', where the company was entertained. The family in this part of the 'old South' usually made the Mother's chamber their sitting room. Consequently, when young men called on the ladies, and the ladies did not have on their company attire, a servant would often have to be sent through the room where the company was waiting, to go upstairs for the ladies' best dresses;

and these would be thrown from the back window, so that the young ladies might be able to attire themselves properly before going in to see their beaux!"

The bishop (in his manuscript, "Life of My Father", has this to say this about his grandfather, the builder of the house:

"Theophilus Parker began business as a merchant in Tarborough in the early nineteenth century, his place of business being on Main or St. George's St., as it was then called. In the War of 1812, I think he had some position in the Commissary Department. He was part owner of the privateer, 'Snap Dragon', Captain Otway Burns, which sailed out of New Bern. I once had the deed for his share but I have lost it. He was a successful man, and owned the large plantation, since known as 'Panola", lying east of town. He succeeded Mr. Edmund D. MacNair as president of the Tarborough branch of the State Bank, which he continued as president until his death. He was universally regarded as a man of the highest integrity, benevolence and sagacity."

A deed recorded May, 1815, shows that Theophilus Parker bought from Joseph Branch and his wife, Susan, 163 acres of land for the sum of $2,720, "adjoining the Town of Tarboro on the upper line, the line of Henry Dolandson, John A. Irwin and Henry Cotten."

This was the Panola plantation; it lay, according to the bishop's account, "just across the street running along the east side of town (St. David Street) half a block from his residence. The 'Quarters,' therefore, were near at hand, the whole being closely associated as if he lived on a plantation in the country. Many of the buildings ordinarily confined to the plantation were on his town lot.

There were barns, stables, a carriage house, houses for curing meat and smoking bacon, a spinning house, etc. My grandmother and her daughters must have led a busy life. In those days the mistress of the house, besides the affairs of her immediate family, had to keep an oversight of the work of the women in spinning, weaving and making clothes.

There was some kind of an elementary spinning-machine, called a 'spinning-jenny' set up in the spinning house. Flax was cultivated on the plantation, as well as cotton, and I remember seeing in the spinning house and in other places, hackles, a flax wheel, and implements for dressing and spinning flax; and also old homemade linen sheets of flax raised, dressed, spun and woven on the plantation. I do not know whether this was common at the time, or only an experiment of my grandfather's, but I think it must have been not unusual.

"All kinds of handicrafts were practiced on the old-fashioned plantations. Each plantation was largely self-supporting, with its home-made clothing, shoes, carts, wagons, harness, etc. I do not remember my grandfather's plantation. It was sold after his death, just about the time I was born. I am only mentioning from memory of the remnants and reminders of its old industries."

Thus the plantation house again became a town residence. One by one by one lots were sold from the original square, until today less than a fourth of the early Parker purchase of the four town lots, numbers 20, 21, 31 and 32 remain. The house has been added to in the Twentieth Century, but it keeps its early-Nineteenth Century charm.

The Old Veterans

It was about 30 years after the Civil War that I began to notice the veterans in the community. There were many of them and some were minus an arm or leg.

They had numerous local reunions and parades and barbecues and were much cherished by everyone.

North Carolina furnished 125,000 troops and had 40,000 casualties. She furnished one-seventh of the troops with one-ninth of the population of the Confederacy.

She was first at Bethel (Va.), farthest at Gettysburg and last at Appomattox.

Edgecombe furnished her full quota of men. I lost five kinsmen killed and several wounded.

One of the wounded was my Uncle Cal. Captain Ed Foxhall said that they were at Marie's Heights at the Battle of Fredricksburg. He told Calvin to get down behind the stonewall. Calvin said he wanted to watch the yankees coming.

Great waves of Burnside's men in blue were approaching. A shell cracked overhead and Cal lost part of his left hand. He was sent to the rear with another walking wounded. He held his wounded hand behind him, but he still had his gun. The general rode up to him with drawn sword and ordered, "Get back into line you damn coward." Cal tried to shoot the general, "No man can call me a coward," he said. In parting he asked the general to take his place in the front line.

General W.R. Cox was a tall, straight gentleman, immaculately dressed. His home was Penelo Plantation on the way to Rocky Mount. He was wounded five times and it was his brigade that saved the day for Lee at Spotsylvania Courthouse. At the Battle of Winchester where Sheridan made his famous ride, the Confederates drove the Federals from the field and captured the camp and supplies.

The poor, hungry, ragged, barefoot men became disorganized amid such plenty. Sheridan rode out from Winchester, rallied his men and drove the Confederates in confusion down the valley. The Cox brigade was one of the few which held together. At Chancellorsville, it was Cox's men who, thinking they were shooting at Federals, shot Stonewall Jackson and his staff. Cox was in the last charge at Appomattox.

Mr. S.S. Nash was too young to enlist in his own town, so he went to another. He was in the front of the line at Fredricksburg running for the trenches. He stumbled and fell just as a volley crashed over him. Soon after he was captured and spent several years in a Northern prison.

In the first part of the war, prisoners were exchanged, but when Grant took command he stopped this because it helped the South. Bruce Catton wrote that the South did not have enough food, clothing and shelter to care for the large number of prisoners it held. The North, though a land of plenty, retaliated, and there was little difference in the treatment of prisoners. The North hanged the officer in command of Andersonville Prison.

Mr. Elisha Felton was known as Mr. 36. He was a scout in front of the lines at Fredricksburg. He stepped around a big boulder and there were 36 Yankees with arms stacked, eating. He could not retreat, so he yelled, "Come on, boys, here they are!" He got between them and their guns. There were no boys to come to his aid, but he marched the 36 to the Confederate prison.

Many of the veterans adopted or acquired titles. There were many "colonels," "majors" and "captains." I attended a meeting of veterans in the old opera house. The adjutant called the roll of colonel this or major that. The old boys answered, "Here" in the fiercest voice they could muster. Finally, he came to Private Dennis Johnson.

A soft voice in the back of the hall answered, "Here, and I am the last living private in the Confederate Army."

Private Johnson was in Pickett's charge at Gettysburg, among the few who went over the stone wall among the Federal batteries, the high water mark of the Confederacy. He played dead and crawled away during the night.

Most of the troops in the charge were from N.C., but Virginia got credit for the gallant charge. I knew La Salle Corbel Pickett, the child-bride of the general.

In the early 1900s, the Blue and the Gray held several joint reunions. The first was in Washington. I was waiting in the lobby of the Raleigh Hotel. It was very hot and in those days there were no drinking fountains and with the heavy demand for water it was almost impossible to keep the cooler filled.

A tall gentleman strode in. He was buttoned up in a resplendent gray uniform with gold braid, a red sash, a star on the collar and a hat with large black plumes. I knew he was roasting. He walked to the cooler, took a paper cup and got only a few drops. He shook the cooler and the ice rattled. He tried again and then with one mighty blow he sent the cooler clattering across the tile floor.

He walked out muttering, "A damned Yankee cooler."

Sketches

I drove with my grandfather over the old wooden bridge across the Tar. Above the bridge a large raft of logs was being floated downstream, guided by two men with long poles.

Below the bridge was another raft of logs tied to the shore on the Princeville side and logs were being pulled up a chute to the screaming saws in a large two-story building. There had been a mill there a long time for it was mentioned in Civil War writings.

Lumber was stacked beside a railway almost to the present 258 bypass. In later years, I saw this mill and its great piles of boards burn.

To the left of the bridge on the Princeville side was a platform. It was level with the bridge and extended to the water. On it was a small house, the ticket office of the Tarboro terminal of Frank Hitch's railroad. A small locomotive hitched to a train of bright red cars was on a track parallel to the river.

The Hitch narrow gauge road was primarily a log road, but it did carry passengers. It ran from Tarboro to Coakley, to Goose Nest (now Oak City), and on to Hamilton on the Roanoke River.

I think that most of his logs were shipped by water from Hamilton to Norfolk. The road operated until the timber accessible to it was exhausted. Hunters who have hunted in Gatlin's Pocosin, the big woods now owned by Tom Pearsal, know well the remnants of the old log road.

Before removing his rails and trains to parts unknown, Hitch offered it to the businessmen of Tarboro. They were not interested.

In Norfolk, Hitch invested much of his fortune derived from Edgecombe and Martin County logs in real estate at inflated values prior to the Jamestown Exposition and lost it in the depression which followed.

Years later, Frank Hitch came back to Tarboro, the scene of his financial triumphs and in a small way, again bought and sold timber.

He lived in the old hotel at the corner of Main and St. James. His health was bad and he could not climb to his second floor room so he built a hoist, operated by a winch, turned by a faithful attendant. His second visit to Tarboro did not last long. I guess he sent for me because my father had helped him with some injured by his railroad. His end came in the old hotel with his son of the same name by his bedside.

~

Hotel Farrar, Hotel Tarboro - it brings many memories. It was built by O.C. Farrar and in its day, was the finest hotel east of Raleigh. It had many ups and downs with downs predominating. While operated by Carlos Fritch, it was advertised as the worst hotel in North Carolina. While Tom Farrar was manager, he was asked by a stranger, "Who runs that hotel in Tarboro?" Tom answered, "No one. It's automatic."

Baron Von Probst was a graduate of Heidleberg and had traveled the world over. He lived on a houseboat at Manteo where he found the hunting and fishing on the N.C. coast to his liking. When war was declared with Germany in 1917, his remittance money could not reach him and he had to go to work.

Tom Farrar gave him a job as night clerk. I knew the old gentleman as a hunting companion.

Toward the end of the war, President Wilson promulgated his 14 points to make the world safe for democracy. The papers were full of the prospects for the wonderful world which would follow, peace and the League of Nations and the world safe for democracy.

The baron was sipping gin in the sunshine in front of the hotel reading the morning paper. I greeted him with, "What do you know this morning?" He answered, "Doctor, I know the world will still be safe for HYPOCRISY."

The Cleveland Celebration

In the days before the turn of this century Tarboreans enjoyed their politics, but there was never such a celebration as the one which came when Grover Cleveland was elected president.

Main Street from the river bridge up was decorated with bunting. The entire county population came to Tarboro. Every precinct sent a covered wagon with its number painted on the side. Many carried slogans.

The Edgecombe Guards were there in full force. Confederate veterans, most of them on horseback, were at the head of the procession and were led by Mr. Bush Williams, a tall old man with a white beard, who was with Henry Lawson Wyatt when Wyatt was killed at the Battle of Big Bethel. Williams proudly carried the Stars and Bars.

The big parade formed on the Princeville side of the river ridge and marched up Main to the railroad in north Tarboro. It was so long that as the last of the marchers were crossing the bridge to go up Main they met the head of the marchers waiting to go back across and disband.

One side of the Town Common was transformed into a huge barbecue pit, more than 100 yards long, and pigs roasted there throughout the day. When properly done and seasoned they fed the hungry hundreds who thronged to town for the celebration.

When night came there was a torchlight parade almost as long as the one during the day. Some of the marchers carried blazing pine knots, while others carried flares consisting of a can of kerosene and wick mounted on the end of a stick.

At each intersection in town was placed a barrel of rosin which was doused with kerosene and set ablaze. When the wooden sides burned away, the blazing rosin spread out over the dirt street, burning the toes of more than one of the marchers.

The wagons were in the parade as before, but this time they were loaded with casualties. There was much alcoholic shouting and singing and an occasional pair of legs could be seen sticking out from under the canvas sides or hanging off the tailgates.

Tarboreans enjoyed their politics in the old days!

Inventions

It is generally taught that man's greatest invention was how to make fire. It certainly made man more comfortable and heat is the chief factor in the progress of man.

The next most important invention was the wheel and its many uses.

But one of my professors insisted that man's greatest invention was soap. He taught hygiene.

How the splitting of the atom will rank, I don't know, but heat accomplished that.

The safety bicycle with pneumatic tires came into general use in the 90s. This was the first time man (and woman) was able to propel himself with relative ease.

The bicycle was welcomed to Tarboro with enthusiasm.

The streets were unpaved, rutted and there was a town ordinance, which never has been repealed, against riding bicycles on the sidewalks which were very little better than the streets. But people walked in those days.

The town built a dirt track in the Common which encircled the area from St. Andrew Street to Panola and along side Panola back to St. Andrew. A cycle club was formed which formulated rules of the road. In the evening Tarboro, both male and female, young and old, rode round and round.

There were races in which cyclists from other towns competed. One great attraction was a tournament in which rings were suspended over the track and the contestants, going at full speed, were to capture the rings with a lance.

The women riders were much bothered by the long skirts of the period catching between the chain and the sprocket. Two girls from Bath were visiting in town and brought their bicycles and a new style. Their skirts were just below the knee and their legs were encased in boots to the hemlines. There was no exposure and Tarboro's hemline ascended and with a few pauses has gone up until we now have the revealing mini-skirt.

This brings to mind a few lines from the Anglican Digest:

I think that I shall never see
A thing as ugly as a knee
Above whose gnarled and knotted crest
The mini hemline comes to rest
Or one that's even worse than that,
When padded with repulsive fat.
A knee that may in summer wear
Nothing at all but be quite bare
Behind whose flex there oft remains
A net of blue and broken veins
Some knees continue to perplex
Now they can form the letter "X"
While in another set one sees
A pair of true parentheses.
Some nuts write verses such as these
But greater nuts display their knees.

I think the Digest had indigestion and had never seen some Tarboro knees.

But we must take the bad with the good.

Gleanings

Seventy-two-year-old Henry pounded his chest with his fists and said, "Examine me. A little old lady says she will marry me and I want to know what shape I'm in."

I assured him that he was very fit for his age and gave him the required medical certificate for matrimony.

Several months later, Henry returned. He looked dejected and was very uncomfortable with a respiratory infection. After prescribing appropriate medication, I advised him to go to bed and let his wife wait on him.

"I ain't got no wife," he said.

I asked, "Why, you planned to be married when I last saw you."

He answered, "Doctor, I live hard. All my children are married and gone. I was sitting by the fire one mighty cold night trying to warm a yarn shawl. I have always had cold feet. My first wife had a way of warming that shawl and wrapping it around my feet. I was wondering how I was going to get in bed and wrap that shawl around my feet before it got cool. I have a little dog. He is mighty friendly. He rubbed against my leg and I put my hand on him. He was warm. I said to myself, what's warm to my hand is bound to be warm to my feet. I put that dog under the covers, put my feet on him and slept warm all night.

"I decided not to get married."

~

I asked a husband to get me a spoon so that I could hold his wife's tongue down to examine her throat. My supply of wooden tongue depressors was exhausted.

He returned with a big iron pot spoon and said, "If this don't do, I will get the shovel."

~

I was busy with a patient. I heard a door slam, stumbling noises and then a loud voice saying, "I got a broken leg. I come to the doctor to fix it. I know he can do it. I had a daughter who couldn't see nothing. He taken the eyes out and scraped them, put them back and now, she can see as good as anybody."

I knew it was my old friend, Preston.

We doctors are appreciative of praise, even if undeserved. We often are held responsible for the inevitable.

Preston's praise was in appreciation of a very simple operation, the removal of a superficial growth from the cornea.

Preston was a big man whose very presence commanded attention. In Reconstruction Days, he was a power in politics and his efforts sent his brother to the legislature. He said his father was an African king who came to this country and slavery because he loved molasses. The captain of the ship said if he would come aboard he would give him all the molasses he wanted and when he finally had enough, the ship was so far from land that he could not swim back.

X-ray showed a fracture near the ankle, so I applied a cast. Preston waited all day for his son for whom he had just bought a car to come and take him home. It was dark and his son had not returned.

I told him I would take him home. He jumped up from the bed and would have tried to walk had I not stopped him.

He said, "Ain't you done fixed it?" I explained he would have to wait before he could walk and presented him a pair of crutches. He hobbled to the car, but he had forgotten his bag containing his preacher-son's baptizing suit. A nurse brought it.

We drove toward his home and as we emerged from a big woods, he said, "I see my light! I see my light!" We drove into the yard and stopped. In a loud voice, he called, "Come out here and help me."

His large family poured out. The small voice of his little wife called, "What's the matter?"

Preston answered, "I've got a broken leg. Fix that bed in the company room. I want to get in it. I have waited on you all and now you are going to wait on me." A son helped him from the car and into the company bed.

He said he was hungry.

Soon, a little girl came in with a large platter. On it was a fried pig's ear, pig feet, collards, sweet potatoes, black-eye peas, a generous portion of cornbread, and a cup brim-full of molasses.

Tarboro's Epidemic

The Crusaders brought home from the wars the story of the "Old Man of the Mountains," who with his band of assassins maddened themselves with hashish, an opiate of hemp leaves, and spread terror throughout the Mohammedan world. Sixty years ago Canobis was in the official, though little - used list of drugs.

The Indian hemp was the most potent and the most active preparation made from the flowering heads.

Hemp was once extensively used for the fiber to make rope. It was then not a problem, but a World War I veteran told me that he had seen the boys smoke hemp rope for kicks.

Now it has come to us with a Mexican name—marijuana—and Tarboro and Edgecombe gained notoriety when a large field of the once useful, now evil, weed was found in our good soil.

When our soldiers went into the island of Mindanao, the home of the Moro, after we "liberated" the Philippines from Spain, the official sidearm was the 38 - caliber Colt revolver. The Moros would madden themselves with hashish and go "Juramentado," which meant they had sworn to kill a Christian.

An officer on a street of Elio saw one of the madmen coming. He emptied his revolver into him, but the Juramentado chopped down the officer with his bolo. The 38 was discarded and replaced by the 45.

Pershing's order that all Juramentados were to be buried with a pig did more to control the situation than did the 45.

The little town of Tarboro made national news in 1822.

Nine years before, the Congress passed an act to encourage the use of smallpox vaccine. They appointed Dr. James Smith of Baltimore coordinator of the program and provided that the free vaccine could be sent by mail without charge. Dr. Smith sent to Dr. James Ward of Tarboro by mistake crusts from smallpox sores rather than vaccine. Dr. Ward inoculated his patients and caused an epidemic in which ten died. There was a tremendous uproar and two N.C. congressmen had Congress repeal the vaccine act. They insisted the "act was a nuisance of the most dangerous kind which slaughtered with indifference the citizens of N.C."

Smallpox for years without number had been a scourge of the civilized world. It was universal. One medieval king cried, "Bring me a mistress without pock marks."

Smallpox was introduced into Mexico by the Spaniards and killed millions of Indians. John Lawson in his travels in N.C. told of Indians covered with horrible sores drowning themselves. Smallpox and other diseases of the White man destroyed more Indians than his whiskey and bullets.

Lady Mary Montegue (1689-1762) came back to England from Turkey with the idea that inoculation with the matter from a mild case of smallpox would protect one from a malignant form. It often did, but it often proved to be a bad form of the disease.

In the country there were rumors that those who milked cows with smallpox and got sores on their hands from the cows did not have smallpox. Edward Jenner, who had been a student under the great Hunter, was practicing in a small village. An apprentice under Jenner heard a milkmaid say she could not catch smallpox because she had had cowpox.

Jenner was interested and in 1796 he inoculated young James Phipps from the sores on the hands of Sara Nelms. About six months later he inoculated Phipps with virulent smallpox. Phipps was immune. Thus was born the first vaccine against disease, but many years passed before smallpox vaccine was universally accepted. The vaccine was often contaminated and did at times cause trouble, but now the purified vaccine has made smallpox a rare disease in civilized countries.

I was health officer of Edgecombe in the early days of this century. A mild form of smallpox had gained considerable headway in the Runnymede Mill area before it was recognized. Runnymede was not then within the corporate limits of the town. The law required that I quarantine the disease. I offered free vaccine to all, but even in 1910, there was considerable opposition to vaccination.

Some Tarboro citizens, encouraged by some of the older doctors, did not like the way the young doctor was handling the situation. They wanted a stricker quarantine and they called a meeting of the Edgecombe Board of Health and hired an attorney, too.

Dr. W.S. Rankin had just been installed as the first full time state health officer. I called on him for help.

The attorney and his employers stated their case.

Dr. Rankin replied that he had reviewed the situation and approved of what I was doing and that vaccination was the only way to control smallpox. He added that, when the next Legislature met he would ask that the quarantine law be repealed and rely entirely on vaccination.

The attorney said, "Do you mean that I should be vaccinated? I am just out of the hospital where I was operated on for a ruptured appendix."

Dr. Rankin replied that the attorney needed vaccination more than anyone he had seen in Tarboro.

Dr. Rankin went on to head the Duke Foundation and whenever we met, we laughed about the Tarboro epidemic.

All About Alcohol

Virginia has legalized liquor by the drink as have several other states. Man will have his alcohol and many methods of regulations have been tried. Those states which have liquor by the drink claim that alcohol is slightly less a factor in auto accidents than when sold by the bottle.

I doubt if the old saloons will ever return, but all saloons were not bad. The saloon was good or bad, depending upon its clientele.

David Pender, the founder of what is now the Colonial Stores' chain, was a native of Tarboro and clerked for D. Litchenstine's general store, now occupied by Marrow-Pitt Hardware. He told me that one of his first duties when the store opened for the day was to ready the saloon which was in the rear of the store. He placed bottles of various liquors, water, sugar and glasses on the bar.

He mentioned specifically such gentlemen as Col. Dowd, Captain Foxhall and Mr. Buck Barlow as patrons who with little or no aid would mix their drinks and on leaving the store would pay for what they had consumed.

The proprietors in Tarboro just prior to prohibition were Mack Dixon, Glasgow Evans, Dick Parker, Dick Denton and Boston Lewis. They were orderly and the only thing wrong was that they sold intoxicating drinks. I heard of a German who, before my day, instructed his bartenders when drawing beer to, "Make the bubbles come. That's where the profit is."

The best whiskey sold for $1.25 a full quart. North Carolina "went dry" before the nation as a whole. I attended a meeting of doctors where we were addressed by Dr. Charles O'Hagan Laughinghouse of Greenville. His subject was alcohol and he gave statistics, painting a picture of what a wonderful world it would be without the evils of alcohol. He asked us to use our influence to aid the passage of the act of prohibiting the manufacture and sale of alcohol in North Carolina. When he finished his exhaustive and informative speech there was much applause. He leisurely folded his papers, put his glasses in his pocket and waited until there was quiet.

"Well, boys," he said, "we all know that alcohol is the greatest curse of the human race, but among friends it is the most delectable thing we have. Let's take a drink."

After the state went dry one could still get liquor by the jug from Norfolk, and the express office was a popular waiting place. I have seen groups of 20 or more waiting for the train to come.

When the Volstead Act was passed, the great drought began. It soon evolved into the alcohol deluge.

In 1923, I was in St. Louis, which never did obey the law. I went into a bar and ordered a beer. I paid for it and poured it out. I voted dry. I would drink dry.

Soon there were stills in the woods, on the ditch banks, in the barns and in the kitchens. Whiskey was selling for a dollar a gallon. The stores displayed kegs of various sizes, jars, copper sheets and tubes and there was brisk trade in sugar, corn meal and rye.

One Edgecombe officer being paid $25 for each still captured would damage the still slightly, take a sheet metal worker who would repair it, sell it, and notify the officer to whom he sold it.

I attended a party in Williamston where drinks were served by the chief of police and the sheriff of Martin County.

One of the most popular brands of moonshine whiskey in Edgecombe was made by old Lee. It had aroma.

I followed a flushed covey of birds into a wood, and there was Lee's distillery. There were several big vats and more than

200 barrels, all filled with mash. The still was pouring out the fiery stuff.

I assured Lee that I was not an informer, and as Lee's distillery was on my favorite hunting ground, I saw him often.

Returning from a hunt late one afternoon, I witnessed a raid on Lee's home. The officers searched his house and under it, his chicken coop, and his stable. They were about to abandon the search when an officer stepped into Lee's pig pen. The pen was built over a pit in which there were barrels of whiskey.

I watched Lee's cache of whiskey being destroyed and thought of its popularity and flavor, and the old saying, "everything with pig in it is so good."

Unreasonable Woman

Mr. Bertram E. Brown was rector of Calvary Episcopal Church for many years. He was universally loved and respected and was truly a man of God. A monument in his memory was placed on the Common in the form of a sun dial on a white marble base. The base is there, but a thief took the dial.

I was talking with him while watching the sheriff pour moonshine whiskey down the drain. I asked, "Why don't you church people see that prohibition doesn't prohibit and brings on many other evils?". He replied that the American people are prone to go too far and then the pendulum swings the other way. Wait.

I hope it is true today.

Mrs. Blank came into my office, dressed in a well-worn calico dress and a sun bonnet. She was weeping. She asked me to take her to the home of her sister who lived several miles in the country. She had left her husband because he had beat her. I asked if she had her children with her. She said, "No" and cried more. I could not take her to her sister's so I called Mr. Brown to help.

About a week passed and Mrs. Blank appeared again, dressed as before. She wished to wait in my office until Mr. Brown could take her home. She had to see her children, but she would not live with John Blank unless he promised not to beat her.

A few days later I met Mr. Brown at a filling station. While he talked he twirled his watch chain around his finger. The chain had a Phi Beta Kappa key and a small gold crucifix attached. He looked up at the distant clouds.

And this is his story:

"I took Mrs. Blank back to her husband. I drove up to the door. I did not know exactly how to proceed, so I left Mrs. Blank in the car while I went in and talked to her husband. He was at dinner and asked me to join him but I declined. I said, "I have brought your wife back. She says she will live with you if you promise not to beat her."

Blank: "I ain't promising nothing."

Brown: "If you tell me about the troubles between you and your wife, perhaps I can find some solution."

Blank: "I don't know."

Brown: "Isn't she a good wife?"

Blank: "Yes, she's a fine smart woman."

Brown: "Is she a good cook?"

Blank: "None better."

Brown: "Does she keep house and help you with the garden and your crops?"

Blank: "She is a smart woman."

Brown: "Is she a good mother?"

Blank: "Yes, sir."

Brown: "What have you done about the children since your wife has been away?"

Blank: "I went to the county home and got an old woman to help. She is in that room with the baby now. But she ain't got no sense. Seems like I got to have a woman here to look after the house and children."

Brown: "From what you have told me, I do not see why you have any reason to beat your wife. Just what is wrong between you two?"

Blank: "I tell you, Mr. Brown, she is the most onreasonablest woman in the world. She is just so onreasonable that I just got to spank her."

Brown: "So she is just unreasonable and you say you must have a woman here to help you with the house and children. Is that woman now with the baby reasonable?"

Blank: "She ain't got no sense."

Brown: "Now, Mr. Blank, God made woman to be loved and cherished and protected and God did not make woman with reason in them. You say you have to have a woman to help you. So you must live with an unreasonable person. Why not let that unreasonable person be your wife?"

Blank: "I ain't never thought of it just that way. I promise not to beat her. Let her come on in."

Old Frank and His School

Mr. Frank Wilkinson taught many generations of Edgecombe boys. He was an old man when I went to him in the 90s. Stout, not very tall, and bald, he was known far and wide as Old Frank.

He was just, but a strict disciplinarian. There was always a stout switch handy, but his favorite weapon was part of an old yardstick made of some dark wood and not flimsy as are those of today. He kept this stick in his old homemade desk. All of his school furniture was made by some local carpenter and the seats were uncomfortable.

His first school was about where the town electric light plant now is. It was burned. The school which housed me was a two-room affair with a breezeway between. One room paralleled St. Patrick and the other Wilson Street. He always opened his yearly session by telling how he and George Wimberly went to Chapel Hill by stagecoach and stopped at Duke's farm for a year's supply of tobacco.

The battleship, Maine, was blown up in Havana harbor and all the newspapers were yelling for war to save the poor Cubans from the tyrannical Spain. Vocal patriotism was very vocal.

Washington's Birthday came soon after the sinking and we boys asked for a holiday.

Old Frank refused.

There were juvenile delinquents then as now and we, delinquents, planned to disrupt the school.

Thad Hussey went to Royster's Fertilizer Factory and got some fish scrap which he placed in the sand underneath the hot stoves. It was bitter cold and soon the odor in the room was a far cry from a lady's perfume.

Several of us had powered red pepper which, as we passed, we tossed on the hot stoves, being careful that Old Frank or his assistant did not see us. The effect was like modern tear gas. While one room was being aired, we went to the other, back and forth, until the fish scrap was discovered and the supply of pepper exhausted.

Old Frank got out his favorite weapon and lined us up against the wall. He asked each of us if we had put the pepper on the stove and the answer was always, "No." He came to me. I forgot that I had pepper on my hands and rubbed my eyes and then I stood before him with eyes red and tears streaming down my cheeks. In a sarcastic voice, he asked, "And now, Mr. Bass, did you by chance put pepper on the stove?"

I looked at the stick in his hand and in a quivering voice, answered, "Yes."

Old Frank was so astonished that he paused, took a chew of tobacco, scratched his head, and questioned the next boy. All denied it. It was not any innate honesty which made me confess, but the sight of that stick and hope for less punishment.

He ordered us to our seats. There was no recess that day and no lunch time. About 4 o'clock, he said, "Bass, get your books and come up here."

I had found an old geography and stuffed the pages under my clothes in areas where parents and teachers are wont to apply their chastising.

He kept me standing before him and that desk containing the stick for a long time. Finally, he said, "You see that door? Get out of here and come back tomorrow knowing your lessons. All you liars stay in until dark."

Here is a word to delinquents—Neither Thad Hussey nor I have ever been in jail.

Little remains of Old Frank in Tarboro today.

There is the reading, writing and arithmetic which he drummed into a few, now old men, an abandoned home last occupied by Miss Sally Staton, and a bell which called so many boys to work, now rings joyfully when Tarboro High School makes a touchdown.

Old-Time Politics

Just before the Civil War, Mr. William S. Battle built the house which is now the home of Dr. Curtis Norfleet on Albemarle Avenue. West Battle Avenue, with a wide space on each side of his driveway, was his front yard. Glenburnie was part of his home which included land far beyond the present site of North Tarboro School. He owned many thousands of acres and many slaves. He was one of the most influential men of his day in Edgecombe and Nash. He owned the Rocky Mount Cotton Mills.

When I went to Chapel Hill in 1900 I had a class in North Carolina history which was taught by Dr. Kemp P. Battle, the retired former president of the university. The lecture room was in Old East. The seats were highly polished by use and Dr. Battle sat behind a table such as you would find in many kitchens of that period.

In the midst of one of his lectures, which were very informal, he began to laugh and he told this story:

"I have a relative, William S. Battle, in Edgecombe County, who decided to run for the legislature. His opponent was an uneducated man named Hardy Flowers. A political rally was held in number nine township. There was a crude platform for the candidates to speak from, and the farmers in the neighborhood were gathered around.

"Mr. Battle drove up and the crowd cheered. He was escorted to the platform, was introduced and began his speech. He finished and the crowd cheered.

"Hardy Flowers stood, spit out his quid, and said, 'Well, boys, we have just heard the finest speech ever made in this here county, for Mr. Battle is a fine man - the finest man in this county. But Mr. Battle don't live like we'uns does. He lives in a fine house and lives fine, and he don't know how we'uns live or what we'uns need.

"Now look at that carriage Mr. Battle rides in with them fine horses and one colored man to drive him and another to help him in and out.

"I come here on that mule tied to that sapling over there, just like we'uns all come.

"Look at that hat Mr. Battle wears. That is a beaver hat. It come from Europe, cause there ain't no hat fitten for Mr. Battle's head in this county. My hat is a old coonskin cap. I treed the coon, skinned him, and my wife made the cap.

"That coat Mr. Battle got on is a broadcloth coat that come from Parie.

"My coat - my wife spun the yarn, made the cloth and the coat, just like we'uns all wear.

"Them boots Mr. Battle has on come from Europe, too. My boots - my old brindle cow broke her leg. I skinned her, tanned the hide, and old man Brown by Otter's Creek made the boots.

"I tell you, Mr. Battle is a good man, a fine man, but he don't live like we'uns and he is just too danged fine to represent us.

"Now I have saved this about Mr. Battle for the last: When Mr. Battle gets ready to go to bed at night, he don't go out under the firmament, look up at the stars and wets on the ground. He uses a China mug."

Mr. William S. Battle was defeated.

About Mr. and Mrs. Bond

The neat letterhead read:

> Mrs. M. E. Bond
> Dress Maker
> Dealer in Bonnets and Dress Trimmings
> F. L. Bond.
> Manufacturer and Dealer in All Kinds of Furniture and Mattresses.

A book on cabinetmakers of the South recently published by Chapel Hill Press rates Bond as a skilled artisan. Many of his pieces of walnut and mahogany in the style of Chippendale and Hepplewhite are in the houses of Tarboro. He autographed them with stencil. Much of his furniture fell into unappreciative hands in the period when it was replaced by glaring, golden oak.

Why do we have such periods of abstract art, abstract architecture and Hippies? Who but America would destroy Sanford White's N.Y. Pennsylvania Station masterpiece and build over it a box-like structure?

The Bonds lived and worked in a pleasant house at Main and Water streets, now the site of an Esso filling station.

John Cummings of Tarboro inherited from his father a walnut desk which had been bought at auction. He, by accident, found a secret drawer and in it was a small, worn notebook-the journal of Frank Lewis Bond.

The first entry was on April 14, 1854.

The journal contained clippings from the papers of the day, formula relating to his trade and remedies for most human and animal ills. He must have had a desire to be a physician.

On nearly every page there was a remedy. He had a cure for alcoholism, snake bite and mad dog bite. He was a century ahead of Ladybird Johnson, for he repeatedly advocated the planting of multiflora rose and peonies on the right of way of the railroad.

The railroad from Rocky Mount did not extend beyond Tarboro and our town was the railhead for the Confederates in action around Plymouth, Washington and Kinston. Troops and their munitions came to Tarboro and marched over the bridge across the Tar.

While Bond worked, he watched and recorded in his journal many things which happened in town and who passed over the bridge.

He wrote:

May 20, 1862 - 417 Yankee prisoners from the Salisbury Prison Camp were brought to Tarboro and were taken down the river on flatboats and by steamer to Washington to be exchanged. 297 were floated down later.

July 16, 1862 - The Yellow Fever commenced at Wilmington. It was brought there by the steamer Kate from Nassau.

November 11th, 1862 - The following regiments passed over the bridge - 17th, 26th, 59th, 44th, 42nd, 56th, and 47th N.C. troops, and two South Carolina regiments of Holcomb's Legion. The Confederate impressing officer came to town. He took the horses belonging to Robert Austin, Wm. Battle, Wm. Dozier and Mrs. Dancy.

July 20, 1863 - The Yankee General Potter entered Tarboro. He had burned the cotton mill at Rocky Mount and looted. He and his cavalry crossed the bridge and were driven back by Major Kerney. He fired the bridge to prevent the Confederate advance. The citizens extinguished the fire. Among the citizens were Dr. Joe Baker, Philip Garnett, and Isaac Palamountain.

April 1, 1864 - 2,410 Yankee prisoners captured at Plymouth arrived in Tarboro. They were from Pa., Conn. and Mass. regiments.

Among these prisoners were two who wrote of their captivity. They survived Andersonville.

One of them wrote that on the march they passed the farm of a Mrs. Pippen (my great-grandmother). She had her slaves place tubs and barrels filled with water beside the road from which the prisoners could drink.

The other prisoner wrote of camping across the river, passing over the bridge and marching up Main Street, lined with magnificent elms, on his way to the cars and Andersonville. His conclusion was the Tarboro was a pretty little town.

When I was a small boy I heard the repeated boom of a cannon down by the riverside. They were trying to "jar the water" to make F. L. Bond's body rise. He had jumped off the bridge to his death.

I remember Mrs. Bond as a patient about 1909.

Bond willed to the Masons of Tarboro the tavern in which Washington slept when he visited the "little village of Tarboro" upon which now stands the Masonic building at Main and Pitt streets.

The River and Tarboro's Name

No one knows why the river is named the Tar. Is it an Indian name or is it because of the tar, pitch and turpentine which the early settlers floated down to what is now Washington?

The river was the most practical way for the products of our forests and fields to get to market. At first there were rafts and barges and then there were the steamboats.

Our Community House was built by Thomas Blount. He was a member of a family which had a fleet of ocean-going ships which loaded our cotton, tobacco and naval stores at Washington and sold them abroad. Several fortunes were made transporting goods on the Tar.

There was another way to market livestock. A group of farmers would gather their hogs and cows, mark them by notches and holes in their ears, fill their wagons with corn, and drive the animals to Petersburg. It must have been an arduous journey. Joshua Lawrence, the famous Baptist preacher and farmer, wrote over his doorway, "God be my helper, I will never drive another hog to Petersburg."

Tarboro could have received its name either from the river or from a large turpentine distillery at the foot of Albemarle Avenue. The distillery burned and the river was a river of fire as the volatile product of the pines floated down.

A few years ago the railroad was driving piles for a new pier under its bridge. The piles refused to be driven. A driver went down to inspect what was thought to be a rock. He found a bed of rosin which had to be blasted before the piles could be driven.

Was the rosin a waste product or the result of the fire?

Several early fortunes were made transporting goods on the Tar.

When the Yankees came to Tarboro, they burned three steamboats and one which was being built. The last steamboats to navigate the Tar was the Shiloh and the Tarboro, owned by the Shiloh Oil Company. Billy Bryan and I were stowaways on the Shiloh's maiden voyage from Tarboro to Shiloh and back.

Tarboro is where it is because of the river which is fordable at average water level at Trade Street. Later there was a ferry which was owned by Joseph Howell, upon whose farm the original Tarboro was built. The legislature gave Howell the right to build a bridge and fixed the toll rate, so many pence for a man and a horse, a cow, etc.

The little river is very capricious. When I was a boy I heard my elders speak of the disastrous flood of 1889. Like in Noah's time of "40 days and 40 nights, the rain, she kept a drapping." The crops were ruined and there was near famine in Edgecombe.

I remember many floods when Princeville had to be evacuated. The flood to beat all floods was in 1919. The water was much higher then than in 1889. The river was more than a mile wide. I watched cows caught in the flood trying to climb upon the railroad bridge. The water touched the cross ties.

There is a cypress tree on the downstream side of the highway bridge in which are driven iron rods, now covered with poison ivy, indicating the height of various floods.

An indication of the vagaries of the river: The editor of *The Southerner* walked across it in 1968 and did not get his knees wet.

I have seen the river freeze several times. The hardest freeze was in 1893 when there was skating on it and a horse was driven across at Trade Street. It froze in 1900 and again in 1919.

The records may prove me wrong, but it seems that there were more and deeper snows and harder freezes in the old days than recently. I remember the dead birds by the roadside in 1893 and in 1919.

When the snows came, the horses with bells were hitched to sleighs.

I remember going to the old County Home in a sleigh with my father. The doctors of Tarboro would rotate in the care of the poor at the home, and the pay went into a fund to build a hospital. The money so earned helped to build the first community hospital.

The home consisted of a number of snug little cabins, an infirmary, and a comfortable house for the superintendent.

I waited in the sleigh while my father made his rounds. He walked in the snow with the superintendent and standing by the sleigh, he said, "Jim, when I was here last I told you to clean up this place and it is worse now than then."

Jim replied, "Turner, you are the feardest man of a louse I ever see'd."

With a resigned chuckle, my father drove through the snow back to Tarboro.

(The following articles appeared in the Evening Telegram or elsewhere with the titles "As I Remember It" or with individual headlines.)

Potter's Raid

Union General Edward Elmer Potter was born in New York in 1823. After studying law, he went to California with the gold rush. How successful he was in the gold rush is not recorded, but he returned to New York and engaged in farming.

At the outbreak of the War Between the States, he was commissioned captain, and later made lieutenant colonel of a regiment of Negroes which he had raised. At the time of his raid, he was a brigadier general.

In July of 1863 he commanded an expedition composed of New York calvary and a company of Negro troops whose objective was to burn the railway bridge at Rocky Mount, over which supplies went to Lee's army, and to destroy as much public and private property as was expedient. He left New Bern on July 19 and without opposition reached Greenville, "a pretty little town," which he sacked, and burned the bridge over the Tar.

Mrs. Peyton Atkinson, in a letter to Gov. Vance asking that he take steps to prevent another such raid, described how "wretches" broke open safes, broke down doors to ladies bedrooms at night and stole jewelry and watches.

Potter left part of his command at Sparta and detached about 300 men under Major Jacobs to go to Rocky Mount, while his main force came to Tarboro. A few shots were fired at him as he entered the town.

Major Jacobs, on his way to Rocky Mount, met Confederate Bennett Jenkins of Edgecombe, who was home on leave. Jenkins fled, but his horse failed to jump a ditch and he was captured.

There was no telegraph between Tarboro and Rocky Mount, and the surprise was complete. Here is what Jacobs said he did in Rocky Mount:

"The advance captured a train of cars, although it was in motion. Upon it were five officers; vis., one captain, two second lieutenants, two first lieutenants, and ten privates. This train, together with the depot, was burned. Railroad, telegraph offices, the county bridge and the railroad bridge were burned. A cotton mill six stories high, made of stone, employing 150 white girls, one flouring mill four stories high, 1,000 barrels of flour and immense quantities of hardtack, cotton and cloth filled the storerooms at the factory; a machine shop filled with munitions; several separate storehouses; three trains of government wagons (total 37) loaded with all manners of supplies, all burned. Destruction was large and complete. At 11 a.m. I marched leisurely back toward Tarborough, burning large quantities of cotton and five wagons on the way. Cotton destroyed exceeded 800 bales."

There is a story that Jacobs would have burned the house at the mill (now used as the office) and then occupied by the mill manager, but that the manager was from the North and was a Mason. There is no record of Potter's troops burning residences.

In Tarboro, General Potter burned the jail and other public stores, "and then thc wretches ate a sumptuous meal at Mrs. Gregory's hotel."

Confederate Major Kennedy brought from near Hamilton by what is now Rt. 43, 84 cavalry and one cannon to within about three miles of Tarboro "at a convenient crook in the road with trees on both sides." Here he set up an ambush.

He sent a squad of six men to Tarboro to entice the Federals into the trap. One of this squad was Mr. Ed Lewis, grandfather of Miss Mary Hester Lewis, who is secretary of the Tarboro school system.

Mrs. Lewis told me of the battle of Daniels School House, which was near "the crook in the road."

The squad rode up to the Tarboro bridge on the side opposite town. The Yankees were watering their horses at the foot of Trade Street. The Confederates fired on them.

General Potter reacted quickly and sent two troops of New York cavalry under Major Clarkson in pursuit of the Confederates. The Yankees were led into the ambush and received a volley at close range and were much disorganized. The few mounted Confederates with their officers charged into the confused Yankees and there were hand-to-hand encounters. The Yankees retreated. General Potter sent a larger force under Major Cole to help Clarkson. The Yankees dismounted and prepared to attack, but grossly over-estimated the number of Confederates who had a cannon which outranged the Yankee mountain howitzer. They again retreated and set fire to the bridge over the Tar.

The wounded were placed in Daniels School House. When I was a boy on my grandfather's farm, I peeped through the bullet holes in the school.

There is a legend that a wounded Yankee officer, instead of retreating to Tarboro, rode down a path to the house of Captain Daniels, about a mile away, where he collapsed. He was taken in and nursed until he was able to be moved.

General Potter left Tarboro in a hurry and the citizens extinguished the fire on the bridge. The leader of the fire fighters was Gov. Clark.

Major Kennedy's force was not large enough to attack Potter's main force, but after leaving Sparta, he was under constant attack from the rear. A Confederate force under General

Martin, a Mexican War veteran with one arm, tried to intercept Potter, but he escaped. A Yankee sympathizer led him during the night by a path in the woods around the Confederates.

General Martin did not follow as he was ordered to bring his troops to Virginia to protect Petersburg from General "Spoon" Butler, but the cavalry continued to annoy Potter until he crossed the Neuse River on pontoons.

Potter's raid was, from the northern viewpoint, a great success. He destroyed thousands of both public and private property and escaped with his prisoners, horses, mules and other booty.

He lost 64 men.

Flim Flams

I do not know how many flim flams Tarboro residents have perpetrated upon each other, but I remember two quite expensive ones which were the result of attractive strangers coming to town. Tarboro has always been addicted to embracing the strangers within our gates, often to the exclusion of some native of much greater worth.

About 1895, six men came to town. They were well-dressed, all had well-trimmed beards and they quickly made friends at the Sand Packers Club which was the loafing place in the back room of MacNair's Drug Store. The store was open until 11 p.m. and every evening there was a gathering of Tarboro's elite.

These men were selling bins. In those days of bad roads and when so many of the everyday necessities of life were made at home, people bought things in bulk a barrel of flour or a bag of meal.

The bins were made of sheet iron and painted in gay colors. The flour could be dumped into the bin and the top fastened. At the bottom was a shaker which could sift flour into a pan as needed. On the side of the line of little drawers each marked for a different spice.

The strangers hired horses and buggies from the livery stable and had a extension fixed behind the buggies so that they could carry about three bins. Each morning they went into the country and came back in the evening minus the bins.

Wagons would come from the railroad station piled high with bins. This went on for several months until the county was presumably saturated with bins.

They had demonstrated there was a great market for bins and since they had the rights to sell in all the counties of North Carolina they said they would be glad, for a consideration, to sell the rights in some of the counties in the state to their friends who had been so nice to them during their stay in Tarboro.

Local businessmen invested heavily in the rights to sell the bins and the bearded men departed with much handshaking and good will, but leaving some debts to the livery stable and others.

The Tarboro magnates made up teams and sent them into the various counties. They had bought a supply of bins from the manufacturer. But the bins did not sell and upon investigation, they found that very few of the bins had been sold in Edgecombe.

The bearded strangers had only one carload of bins which they had carried from Tarboro to Hobgood and had them shipped by rail back to Tarboro. So the bins had simply gone round and round. The strangers were traced to a place in Illinois, but they could not be identified for they had shaved their beards.

In another instance a man came to town and rented a vacant store under the Hotel Farrar. He was selling peg-toothed harrows - a farm implement. He brought in several loads of sand and spread it on the floor. He had men pull his harrows through the sand to show how they worked. The harrows did a good job.

He had manufactured harrows down in Georgia and made all the money he wanted and he wished to sell his factory and retire.

He helped Tarboro businessmen form a corporation which bought his equipment and built a house to hold it by the East Carolina railroad tracks. The building is still standing today.

The Tarboro corporation began to manufacture harrows, but the harrows had a defect. The teeth of the harrows were fixed in the working position. There was no way to adjust the pegs so that the harrow could be dragged from field to field without tearing up paths and bridges over ditches.

The harrows did not sell and the corporation floundered.

So much for Tarboro business acumen.

About Joe Bunn

Eighteen-year-old Joseph Powell Bunn joined the Edgecombe Guards in June of 1917.

They were in camp in Goldsboro where they had come from the Mexican border guarding against bandit raids. The Guards were part of the 119th Regiment in the 30th Division.

Joe gained rapid promotion to first sergeant in the regimental machine gun company. The guns were of British manufacture and mounted on little carts drawn by horses or mules up near the firing line and then man-handed into action.

The regiment left for France in April of 1918. The 30th Division and the 27th were attached to the British Army and went into action near Ypres on ground that had beenfought over by British, Canadian, Australian, Indian and South African troops for three years. The mighty Hindenburg Line was in front of and above them. Shelling was constant. The boys could often tell where the big low velocity shells would fall, but not the smaller high-speed shells.

Life in the trenches was hard. Rats, lice and stench. German shells would often disinter some poor British who had been buried where they fell.

Rations were poor by American standards. The Stars and Stripes which told of the rations issued the troops under Pershing, made Australian frozen goats and rabbit unpalatable.

The Edgecombe boys were so desperate that they paid $100 each for several hogs and had an Edgecombe barbecue.

Joe saw a yellow cloud of chlorine gas blowing toward the American line. The wind changed and blew it back on the Germans.

He witnessed the last cavalry charge. The British thought they could breach the German line and lead the infantry through with a cavalry charge, but they never reached the Germans. Machine guns piled up the poor horses and men and that charge ended the soldier on a horse.

At last the great day came. Behind the American lines were massed cannon, hub to hub. The little ones in front and the big ones behind. The greatest barrage of the war fell on the Germans and then Joe went over the top with his buddies. Many boys fell, but the Hindenburg Line was taken and the German retreat began.

Joe went back over the field. He saw an American with his head shot off. There was an empty pistol in his hand and five dead Germans in front of him. Joe thought it was the body of a friend and reported him dead, but it was not his friend who was captured and survived the war.

After the Armistice, the boys tried to improve their rations and Joe hunted partridge in the no-man's-land which was grown high with weeds. He did not have a shotgun, so he used a grenade. Poor birds!

The boys had saved $1,600 of ration money and planned to spend it in one grand night in New York, but Uncle Sam sent them home a few at the time and kept the money.

Joe was honored at home during the war. Miss Mattie Shackleford and others planted a tree and named it "Sergeant Joe Bunn Oak." The beautiful scarlet oak stands at the corner of Main and West Wilson streets.

Joe was not hit by a German bullet, but he has been unable to dodge various American and foreign germ viruses.

His trips to many hospitals have left him a monument to surgery.

Between these illnesses he runs a tobacco warehouse which is a wonderful occupation. You work three months and hunt and fish the other nine.

There are many less turkeys because of Joe, but Joe is not a killer.

He has birds and squirrels eating from his hand. One old squirrel in his yard bites his finger when Joe's offering is not to his liking, which proves that man is not the only animal that bites the hand that feeds him.

A boyhood friend tells of taking Joe with him to dinner. His friend's mother noticed that Joe's blouse was full and that it moved. Joe had his bantam chicken in his shirt because the Gypsies were in town!

Joe is a good neighbor, even if he did take my empty whiskey bottles which I put on his lawn after a party and place them on the preacher's lawn across the street. And one morning at daybreak his car backfired and alarmed the neighborhood. The preacher called, "What is wrong?" Joe said, "Nothing. Dr. Bass is shooting squirrels."

Joe is just home from a two-week bout with pneumonia.

You can't keep a good man down!

Back From the Past

The British Broadcasting Co. wrote to a TV station in Texas that the program of the Texas station had been received in England. The Texas station had been off the air for about two years, but their program had been going round and round where no one knows and came back to earth. The happenings and words of an individual come back from the past.

During the summer of 1903, the University of Virginia at which I was a student, sent me around N.C. to recruit some athletes. To go to Edenton, one went by rail to Tunis and then by boat down the Chowan River.

I was sitting in front of the pilot house in the late afternoon, enjoying a brisk breeze and the beautiful river when I was summoned to dinner in the small cabin. I had just been seated when something like an electric shock hit me on my knee and the shock was repeated rapidly, again and again. I jumped up with a yell and shed my trousers and stood there in my BVDs. Some wasps had flown in my trousers and stung me.

Several ladies at an adjoining table screamed and ran from the room.

The purser brought the medicine chest and applied some ammonia to the stings, and I put on my trousers.

The ladies returned with some shy glances at the funny man.

About 20 years later, I was returning from Norfolk. The train stopped at Tunis, leaving the cars on the bridge over the river. All was quiet. Two men were sitting in the seat in front of me. One said to the other, "I saw the dang funniest thing on one of those boats down there," and told about the fellow who had the wasp in his pants.

I touched him on his shoulder and said, "I heard your story. Did you really see it or was it hearsay?". He said he saw it and I said, "I am the guy who shed his trousers.

The dignity of the medical man is as old as the witchdoctor. This dignity is manifested in various degrees. Some medical men wear it as if they are God's gift to medicine, but all the great men of the profession that I have known are modest. The great Dr. Sir William Osler advised equanimity.

My friend, Dr. William DeB. McNider, a much-beloved professor at Chapel Hill in the School of Medicine, was a model of equanimity. In the summer of 1903 I had come from Fayetteville to Raleigh on the early morning train and I had registered at the Yarboro and was waiting for breakfast. I was standing in front of the building when Bill McNider, driving a horse, saw me and stopped. I had known Bill at UNC. He had recently graduated in medicine and was then assisting Dr. Hubert Royster, who was dean of the UNC two-year medical school in Raleigh. I followed Bill as he made the rounds, and he introduced me as Dr. Bass, though I was only a second-year student. I did not correct him.

He came to a ward with about six patients who had been operated on for ruptured appendices. I stood with my back to the wall watching Bill dress a suppurating odoriferous abdominal wound. I felt my feet slipping from under me, and when I regained consciousness, I was on a bed and a nurse was holding some aromatic spirits of ammonia to my nose.

I left Rex Hospital completely devoid of equanimity, and never told of that episode.

About 1920, I entered a patient's room and was introduced to the nurse on duty, who said, "Doctor, I have met you before. Do you remember coming to Rex Hospital with Dr. McNider and fainting? I picked you up and put you on a bed."

I do not know with how much dignity I entered that room, but I was deflated.

The woman was then Mrs. Stella K. Barbee. Jessie Helms of WRAL last week devoted his whole broadcast to a review of the life of and praise of this remarkable woman who had done so much for the welfare of her hometown, Raleigh.

Mrs. Barbee had just died.

We believe that everything that breathes
In earth and sea and sky
Has a speech and language of its own
Even as you and I.

The world is full of sounds that the human ear cannot detect for our own range of hearing is quite limited. The throat of the wood thrush continues to move long after his beautiful song does not register in our ears. Dogs hear sounds which we humans do not.

It was the first day of hunting season and we stopped the car on a farm path at the head of a ditch. I went with the dogs away from the ditch. My companion, while assembling his gun, walked up the ditch and had gone only a few yards when up flew a big covey. Unafraid, they flew only a short distance and settled down - all but one old cock who saw us with the guns and dogs just out of range. He realized that his family of young and inexperienced was not following him. He began to "talk" and slowly flew back and over his family, telling them to get up and follow him to the woods and safety, which they did.

A rather voluminous book, "Bob White Quail and His Habits", by Stoddard is full of Bob White calls.

⁂

The crow is one of the most intelligent of birds, and can be taught to talk a bit of our language.

A farmer had surrounded a small peanut field with a wire fence for his hogs. It was raining gently and the curtains of my buggy were up and I was well-hidden. The hogs were busy rooting the peanuts and on the back of each of the hogs was a crow. As the hog would root up a peanut, the crow would jump off, pick up the nut before the hog could and return to the hog's back to eat the meat. Every fence post had a crow perched on it waiting his turn for a hog back.

⁂

There is a bird in the West called the white-neck raven. He is smaller than our crow and where the crow is a rather clumsy flyer, this raven is most expert. He is called white-neck because the feathers near the skin in his neck are white, but the whole bird is black and rather iridescent.

I was on a prairie in New Mexico and saw some of these birds. They were so much like a crow that I wished for a closer view. I hid in a small evergreen oak and called the distress call of our eastern crow. It did not make any impression. I changed the pitch and the birds began to answer and fly toward me. I was well-hidden and they came near. Their cry of alarm was answered far and wide. They came from the mountains in the distance. Soon there were hundreds calling and trying to locate the one in trouble. I called until I was hoarse. I stepped from my hiding place and instantly there was silence or perhaps my ears could not register their conversation about me. They began to disperse and the sky full of birds put on an exhibition of flying. They would fly up, up, until they were almost mere dots in the sky and down they would dive almost to earth and display all kinds of acrobatic flying.

It was about 2 a.m. on an April night. The moon was shining brightly. I was on a white sandy road. There was on one side mostly wasteland, and cultivated fields on the other. I drove around a curve and the lights of my car no longer lighted a white road. Ahead, as far as I could see, the road was dark. The change was startling and as I drew nearer, the road cleared. There were hundreds and hundreds of rabbits in the road. When I returned about an hour later, the rabbits were gone.

Ernest Seaton Thompson, in his "Wild Animals I Have Known," tells of seeing a rabbit dance in Yellowstone Park. I had seen a rabbit dance in Edgecombe.

I wonder how the rabbits sent out invitations to that dance?

Makeshift Medicine

I hope my motive in describing the treatment of the little boy with the broken leg will not be misunderstood.

I wish to show the difficulties of practice in a rural community, even 50 years ago, and how in emergency we had to improvise. In those days of poor roads, relatively few automobiles, and fewer hospitals, most of the treatment of the sick or injured was done in the home and often with surprisingly satisfactory results.

It was in 1919 during the greatest flood of Tar River that I received a request from Doctor X of Conetoe to come and give an anesthetic for him. He often called me to give anesthetic on obstetric cases, so I put some ether and an inhaler in a bag and started.

Water was across the road in Princeville and rising rapidly.

I stopped in front of the office of Dr. X, who with a cheery greeting put his bag, which usually contained obstetric equipment, in my car and said, "Let's go."

The ditches were overflowing and the farm paths were deep in mud. We had gone about two miles when we got stuck and after much palaver, the Model T was pulled out by a mule.

In the frustration and excitement of being pulled out, Dr. X produced a bottle and began to fortify his spirit. I had already noticed that he had been drinking.

We finally reached the patient's home; a two-room cabin on the banks of Ballyhack Canal, which was overflowing. By that time Dr. X was almost asleep and remained in the car.

I went into the house and there I found a little boy with a broken thigh bone (the femur), at about the middle third of the thigh.

The boy was lying on a lumpy mattress of corn shucks, and all the surroundings were crude and poor. I looked through the equipment in our several bags and found a roll of adhesive plaster and some absorbent cotton. There was no place to take the boy and time was limited because of the flood, so I went to work.

First, there had to be a smooth, firm bed. We spread a quilt on the floor and gently placed the child upon it and then removed the shuck mattress. There was a wide ironing board leaning against the wall, which I padded with a quilt and nailed it on securely. The nails were pulled from the wall with pliers and a broken hammer. I nailed some of the bed slats together, and fixed them across the bed to hold the ironing board. I went to the chicken coop and took some slabs off its roof and with my always-sharp pocket knife, whittled four splints. These I padded with absorbent cotton and wrapped securely with bandages torn from a dingy sheet.

It is necessary in such a fracture to have some way to put traction on the lower fragment to keep the muscles from pulling the lower fragment past the upper.

There was part of an oak wardrobe which was far beyond any use for what it was built. I took enough of that to make what we call a Balkan frame by nailing a board at the foot of the bed to equal the height of the head of the bed. I left a space between the two top boards spanning the distance between the head and the foot because I did not have any pulleys. I used two empty sewing thread spools with a round nail through each as an axle. I unraveled a plow line for a cord and took some bricks from the fireplace for a counter-weight.

We placed the boy on the ironing board and applied the adhesive strips to make what is known as a Bucks extension to pull on the lower portion of the leg.

I gave the boy ether until he was asleep and with the father dropping ether under my direction, I put the broken bone together as best I could, applied the splints and bandaged them securely with the strips of the sheet. I suspended the leg and adjusted the weight. All this took time and the river was rising.

I awakened Dr. X and took him to his home.

I was among the last cars to drive through flooded Princeville into Tarboro.

The days following were almost like the time of Noah when "40 days and 40 nights the rain she kept a drapping." The river was more than a mile wide, the greatest recorded flood in the history of the Tar.

I forgot about the boy. I thought Dr. X would attend him and I could not reach him.

Five weeks from the day I worked on him, the boy and his father WALKED into my office. I did not recognize them until the father said, "I just cut him down yesterday," and that Dr. X had not been to see him. I marveled that the fracture had healed enough to permit the boy to walk. There was no shortening. Both legs were the same length. He limped a little. X-ray showed that I had by chance put the jagged end of one fragment into the marrow of the other.

I saw a man in consultation with another doctor at the patient's home in Pitt County. He had meningitis and was unconscious and in extremes. I did a spinal puncture for diagnosis and the spinal fluid, instead of dripping slowly from the hollow needle, was under such pressure that if spurted more than a yard.

There was not anything we could do, for it was before the days of antibiotics or serum. Bacterial culture of the spinal fluid showed he had pneumococcic meningitis, then considered 100 percent fatal.

I heard the doctor who had called me tell the family that we had done all we could and their only hope was to "do some hard praying."

About a month passed and the meningitis patient came to me. He said that he had been told that I had been to see him. He complained of double vision. One of the muscles which moved the eye was paralyzed and he saw two objects where there was only one.

He is still living.

God moves in mysterious ways
His wonders to perform
He plants His footsteps in the sea.
And rides upon the storm.

Carolina Capers

In 1900, five Edgecombe boys entered the freshman class at Chapel Hill. They were Albert Cox, Marshall Staton, Vines Cobb, W.W. (Cap) Eagles, and Spencer Bass.

Cox, Staton and I roomed in the Carr Building, which had just been completed and was the first dormitory built after the Civil War. The total enrollment in the university was less than 500.

Hazing was the order of the night and every freshman, if he lived on the campus was blacked more than once with either printer's ink or lampblack.

Cox and Staton roomed together, but Staton, to avoid being blacked, slept at the inn which was on the right of the campus, facing Franklin Street. My roommate and I were not congenial and I moved in with Cox.

One night Cox said that there was a rumor that a blacking party would visit the building that night and that he was tired of being blacked. So was I. We swore a solemn oath we would not be blacked again.

We locked the door, nailed bed slats across it and pulled a bureau against it. We put a baseball bat on each side of the bed and went to sleep.

In the small hours, we were awakened by the command, "Freshmen, open up".

I said, "They are here. You stand on the right and I will take the left, and I will crack the first head that comes in".

Cox said, "You reckon we are doing right?"

I replied, "I don't want to be blacked. I have had enough."

Cox said, "Some of our friends may be in that party".

There was more banging on the door and commands to open up.

Cox said, "I think we ought to let them in. If we were to hurt one of those boys, it would ruin our careers."

Cox was most persuasive. We foreswore our oath and removed the barricade.

The "Friend" who wielded the brush started at my face and finally said, "Freshman, hold up your foot".

The blackers had cut off the water in the building and we could not turn it on. There were no baths in the other buildings, so we went outdoors and with other painted boys, turned on a hydrant. We soaped and scrubbed and half-clean and half-frozen, went back to bed.

I doubt if the blacking effected our careers, but Cox had a brilliant one. He was a colonel of a fighting N.C. regiment in World War One. He was a successful lawyer in the nation's capital and major general of National Guard troops in World War II.

Staton practiced law in Tarboro.

Cap Eagles of Crisp was a merchant, farmer and legislator.

Vines Cobb, an esteemed citizen, farmed the land of his ancestors at Cobbs Crossroad.

Attendance at chapel was compulsory. The Warren Court had not outlawed prayer in the schools. Unless one had an early morning class, chapel was not always agreeable.

Each student was assigned a numbered seat and when the eight o'clock bell in the South Building stopped ringing, the doors to Gerard Hall were closed and the vacant seats recorded.

Chapel consisted of a short prayer service by one of the Chapel Hill preachers. The most frequent to preside was Billy

Jones, a short, fat man with a long white beard. He had been chaplain at Gen. R.E. Lee's headquarters and wrote a book about Christ in the camps.

One day at chapel President Venerable announced that the next morning he wished a full attendance as some very important visitors would speak to us.

When Cox and I became sophomores we did unto the freshmen as had been done unto us. In the small hours of the night we took up our paint and by candlelight, painted over the numbers on the back of the chairs in Gerard Hall, we painted and put a daub of paint in each seat. On the wall behind the rostrum in large letters, "I DID IT. I CAN NOT TELL A LIE".

We went to chapel and watched "Old Ven" and his VIPs come up from downtown. There was full attendance outside the building, but inside only an irate president.

Juvenile delinquency had not been invented.

This was just a prank.

Thoughts

Everyday I meet men and women whom I remember as their first acquaintance. Some are older than their years and unhappy, others full of life and joy.

I often wonder what they think.

I received a book with a card as bookmark, upon which were written the lovely thoughts of a lady whom I helped into the world. She is Mrs. Helen Roche, the daughter of Mr. and Mrs. J.B. Arnold, and lives in Bethesda, Maryland:

The simple things are best, they say
So I pick out from every day
Some little wondrous work of art
And try to store it in my heart.

* *

The acorn that I found in the garden
The bug house under a stone
The silvery trail of a slimy ole snail
The spider that spins all alone.

* *

The bird on its nest in the rosebush
The weed growing out of the wall
The tulip that blooms from a bulblet
The apple blossoms that fall
The cool of the moon in the nighttime
The warmth of the sun in the day
The colors that meet in a rainbow
The stars in the Milky Way
The rustle of leaves in the treetop
The glistening dew on the grass
The spatter of rain on the sidewalk
The sound of the winds as they pass
The smell of perked coffee at breakfast
The wonder of yeast rising rolls
The spice in a dish of plum pudding
The shimmer of Jello in molds
Oh! I could go on forever
Naming things that we often think small
Yet if we only pause and consider
They're the most important of all.

* *

I took a little walk into a garden fairyland
Sniffed a pretty yellow rose
Held it in my hand
A little bit of earth and sky
What beauty to behold
A treasure from God's artistry
Its petals brushed with gold.

-Helen-

Foundry and Fair

Behind the filling station by Thorne's Drug Store on North Main is a substantial brick building and over its wide entrance in faded letter is written Edgecombe Foundry.

As a small boy I saw there men pouring molten iron into molds. Many beautiful and useful things came out of this old foundry.

The iron fence at the Henry Bridgers home by the Hilma Golf Course was made there. This fence was first installed at the old courthouse and was sold when the building was repaired and enlarged after a fire in 1912.

On the Pitt Street side of what is now Adler's was an iron stairway leading to the door on the second floor. This stairway was beautifully molded and a racing horse adorned each riser. A similar stairway was erected on the Courthouse side of Marrow Pitt's Store.

The famous Edgecombe cotton planter was made there and sold all over the South.

Boot jacks in the form of a huge beetle were made there and helped many a man get his feet free of his boots.

Also cast there was a large frog doorstop, so lifelike that a little boy kicked it to make it jump.

In early 1900 a group of citizens bought the area presently known as Fairview and established the Edgecombe County Fair.

Time was short before the opening of the first fair in the fall, and while workmen were working in the grandstand and other buildings, stores were closed in the afternoons and with hoes and axes, we worked on the race track.

The fair prospered.

The first airplane ever seen in Tarboro was the chief attraction one year.

I do not know why the fair that I remember was about 1890. The present Runnymede Mill and village occupy the fair area.

There was a special train which shuttled from the cotton yard at Water Street and Albemarle and took us to the fair. There I saw my first squeedunk and balloon! I can see the horses hitched to sulkies with high wheels racing around the track. The Edgecombe Guards in dress-uniforms were drilling to martial music.

That fair also failed.

I remember on a fox hunt we ran the fox aground underneath the abandoned and rotting Floral Hall.

My last memory of the old fairground was when Billy Bryan and I were riding a horse bareback hunting bird eggs for Billy's collection. We did not have a box or other receptacle in which to keep the eggs, so we put them in our mouths. On the way back to town, the horse stumbled and threw us.

The eggs were bad!

This fairground was given by Miss Minerva Pittman to the doctors of the county to build a hospital in memory of her father, Dr. Newsome Pittman, the grandfather of Dr. Newsome Battle of Rocky Mount. It was later either sold or exchanged for a house on St. Andrew Street which was remodeled and named Pittman Sanitarium. This evolved into the Edgecombe General Hospital.

Cotton was once KING in Edgecombe.

Some farmers bought hay and grain from the West to feed their mules so all their land could be devoted to cotton.

It came to town three or four bales to a wagon and Main Street was often lined with these wagons. The buyers would slash open the bales and pull out samples and they were often accused of "shaking hands in the middle of the bale."

From the street the bales went to the cotton yard, a big platform at Water Street and Albemarle. There it was weighed by official weighers and sent to its destination by train.

The trucks, the government programs, the bonded warehouses, synthetic fibers and the weevil changed the handling of cotton."

In 1923, Edgecombe raised 48,000 bales. In 1968 it raised 3,504 bales and in 1967 only 1138 bales.

Cotton has been divested of all royalty and is now a plebeian stepchild.

A Jury of Peers

Our much - mutilated Constitution provides that every citizen has a right to be tried by a jury of his peers. Of course, this means his legal equals, for many a man is tried by juries not his equal intellectually, socially, economically or morally.

One can seldom explain the vagaries of a jury, but I guess the system comes nearer to dispensing justice than any other. Sometimes one is tried by a jury which exceeds in quality more than the legal requirement.

The neighbors heard the lady scream for help and rushed to her aid. Her clothes were torn and she was bruised and scratched. Her assailant escaped through a window. He was recognized, arrested and charged with assault on a female.

I was present at the trial as a medical witness. The defendant pleaded not guilty, but his defense was fictitious.

The jury was out several hours and brought in a verdict of not guilty. The court was astounded and the judge reprimanded the jury.

A few days after the trial, one of the jurors consulted me and after prescribing for him I asked why the jury brought in a verdict so contrary to t he evidence.

He said, "Well, we took a vote and it was eleven to one for conviction. I was standing alone looking out a window when Jim came to me and said, 'John, you voted to convict that man.' I said yes he is as guilty as hell and then Jim said, 'I know he is, but you don't understand. We men who run after women have got to stand together.' We took another vote and it was ten to two for conviction. We kept on talking, and voting and we found that there were twelve men on that jury who ran after women."

Even the Warren Court could not deny that this man was tried by a jury of his equals.

In 1967 there were 983 children born in Edgecombe. Two hundred and sixty-one of them were illegitimate. Ten were white and 251 were non-white. A few years ago I read in a national publication that Edgecombe County led the nation in illegitimate births in proportion to its population.

Edgecombe cannot boast about its morals unless it is proud of its ultra-liberal state, but it can boast about its land.

Mr. Zeno Moore of Whitakers was our first county agricultural agent and a very fine gentleman.

I had a call to Whitakers in midsummer and the crops were beautiful. I met Mr. Moore on the street and asked him if the land above Leggett, between Swift Creek and Fishing Creek, was the best land in the county.

He replied, "Doctor, I will answer you in this way: I attended a meeting of agricultural agents in Des Moines. We were addressed by the chief of the Bureau of Soils of the U.S. Department of Agriculture. After his talk, he asked if there were any questions. An agent asked, 'What is the best land in America?'

"The bureau chief said, 'You are going to be surprised at my answer. We used to think that the deep soil of the Mississippi

Valley was the best, but we know now that it can be depleted, and can only be restored by the slow and expensive use of animal manure. The kindest soil in America is the Norfolk sand loam as typified by the soils of Edgecombe County, North Carolina, and Marlboro County, South Carolina. It is easily depleted, it is easily restored. It lends itself to the economical use of commercial fertilizer. It is a kind soil and will give a return commensurate with what you do for it.'"

I have quoted this many times and wondered why we do not do more with this kind soil.

About Folks

My friend Joe had a stroke. He was paralyzed on one side and he could not talk or write. His girl friend was most attentive. She visited him daily and added to his comfort.

She consulted me about a vital problem.

She said, "Joe wants me to marry him and I wish to know if you think I should."

I told her that while some improvement could be expected, he would always be an invalid and unable to work and that she should consider such a step most carefully.

She said, "I know all that, but I am afraid that Joe will over persuade me."

He did!

⁂

There was a loud knock at my back door at daybreak.

Faithful Jim was there. I asked him why he had come so early. He said he was in trouble and had to have $3.85 at once.

He was treasurer for the church and last night he had walked home with one of the ladies of the choir and, "Doctor, ladies is the luringest things in the world."

With these two examples before me and considering Joe's wonderful powers of persuasion, I think the "female of the species is more deadly than the male."

⁂

During the days when whiskey was rationed, little books of tickets were issued. An old fellow bragged that he had tickets in three counties and one of his neighbors accused him of damming a ditch with his empty bottles.

This alcoholic consulted me and after a lengthy examination, I asked the obvious question:

"Are you drinking too much?"

There was a long pause and then he said:

"Now, Dr. Bass, you have done stopped practicing medicine and gone to meddling."

The story was published in Reader's Digest, but it happened to me several years before publication. It is my story.

Some people are more cooperative.

It was snowing hard one dark night. I answered a call several miles in the country. There was a lantern on the porch to guide me.

An old gentleman was sitting by the fire smoking a pipe with a long stem and with it he pointed to a door.

"She is in there," he said. "She has a broken arm. Excuse me for telling you what ails her, but I have found that when I send for a doctor and don't tell him what is wrong with me, he is a damn long time finding out."

How true!

(The concluding article is an account of efforts to treat Dr. Bass's grandfather who was wounded during the Civil War. So far as the editors can determine, it was never published.)

As a small boy I sat before the fire on winter evenings with my grandfather, James Spencer Pippen, and listened to him tell about The War. This is the story of his wound.

Grandfather was a Sergeant Major in a Confederate Cavalry regiment. When General Lee evacuated Petersburg, Grandfather's unit, with their mounts, was placed behind high breast works near Old Banford Church to hold the Yankees while the infantry retreated. When the order to mount and ride was given the cavalry made a dash up a steep hill with the Yankee artillery shelling them. From that day on in the Confederate rear guard Grandfather was in daily conflict.

Near Farmville, Virginia, there was a big field with a small hill in its center. A group of Yankees was seen on this hill and the Confederates charged them from the woods to the west. When they reached the hill the Yankees had retreated to their side of the field and the Confederates did not follow. There was firing all about. In the confusion of reforming at the hill Grandfather received a blow on the upper third of his right thigh. He at first through he had been kicked by a horse, but soon his boot was filled with blood and he knew he had been hit. He sat on his horse for some distance, but became so weak that he asked to be helped from the saddle.

They placed him in the corner of a rail fence beside the road, and, as the Yankees were pressing, his comrades went on. Grandfather lay in the fence corner for most of the day.

A Confederate surgeon stopped and examined him and said that he could not help. The fifty caliber minnie bullet had passed through a canteen and blanket rolls and struck the femur or thigh bone and been deflected upward into his bladder.

Late in the afternoon some ambulances passed and he was placed in one of them. Every jolt of the rough road was agonizing. Progress was slow as the road was full of Confederate supply wagons and stragglers. In the small hours of the night he heard voices the distance calling his name. They came nearer and nearer until they reached his wagon and he answered. Two men from his company had come back to look for him.

The name of one of the men I have forgotten. The other was Sam Jenkins, a neighbor in his native Edgecombe. Tom Pearsall, of Rocky Mount, and Sam Jenkins, of Tarboro, are his descendants.

These friends did all they could for Grandfather. They brewed a tea from the pitch of alder which grew beside the road and Grandfather believed that this hot drink saved his life. They took him to Farmville, Virginia, and placed him in a temporary hospital. Within in a few days Farmville was occupied by the Yankees and the hospital filled with their wounded.

Grandfather said that there was a great difference in the food and care given the Confederate wounded and their victors. The cot next to him was occupied by a Yankee captain who had been shot through the chest. They became friends and the Captain shared his rations with Grandfather. One day the captain said, "Johnny, you look hungry. Let me give you something good which I have under my cot." The Captain sat up in bed. Blood poured from his mouth and he fell back dead.

A physician from Farmville, whose name I have forgotten. became interested in Grandfather and took him to his home. This extra care without doubt saved his life. The war rolled on to nearby Appomattox and the paroled soldiers of Lee's Army made their miserable journey home. Sam Jenkins, upon reaching Edgecombe, told my Grandmother, Susan Mabrey Pippen, where to find Grandfather. With little delay she set out for Farmville, a distance of about 150 miles.

She was accompanied by her uncle, Drew Bryan, a paroled Confederate Officer. He drove Grandmother in a carriage. They were followed by a wagon with springs containing a mattress and provisions, and driven by Mathy, a newly liberated slave. Progress was slow. It was springtime and rabbits plentiful. Whenever one ran across the road Mathy would jump down from the wagon, make a cross mark in the dirt and spit on it, so that the would find "Marse Spence" alive.

Such activity was unusual in Mathy, who was famed for her indolence. It was said that when sitting before a blazing pine knot fire with his trousers rolled above his knees, rather than move he would call to his brother, "Starling, Starling, pour some water on the fire, my shins is scorching."

Somewhere in Virginia they met Federal Cavalry. Regardless of explanations or protest, their horses were taken from them and wagon and carriage left stranded on the road. Lt. Bryan left Grandmother guarded by Mathy and walked up the road. In some way, he found Grant's headquarters and got an interview with the General. I have always felt kindly towards Grant for he restored their horses and gave them an escort into Farmville and part of their journey south.

After jolts and disagreeable experiences in obtaining lodging in wayside farm houses, they reached home.

Grandfather's recovery was slow. The local doctors advised that nothing could be done. In the year of the Philadelphia Centennial Exposition, he was taken to the great Dr. Agnew, professor of surgery at University of Pennsylvania, who also advised against operation.

(Family members today report that Grandfather Pippen was unable to urinate standing up and had to lie down to achieve normal bladder relief. Dr. Bass did not report that in this original account of the wounding.

There is little wonder Pippen constantly looked for someone to remove the minnie ball from his bladder.)

Nineteen years after his wounding, Dr. Lycurgus Lafayette Staton, having graduated in medicine, came home to Tarboro to practice his profession. On Grandfather's farm was a negro boy who had a stone in his bladder. Dr. Staton removed the stone. One day, Grandfather said to the doctor: "If you removed the stone from that boy's bladder, why can't you remove the bullet from mine?"

The time was set and doctors from far and wide came to observe and to assist. Grandfather was placed on the dining room table. Dr. Westry Jones, of Tarboro, who had been a Confederate Army surgeon, gave chloroform using a cup with a wad of cotton in it as an inhaler. There were no sterile instruments or dressings, as the work of Pasteur and Lister was unknown.

Dr. Staton, using the perineal approach, got the bullet. Grandfather was placed in bed. Before leaving. Dr. Don Williams, of Tarboro, said to Dr. Staton: "Here is a Pare Syringe and some morphia which you can give under the skin. You made need it. I'll leave it on the mantle." During the night the watchers by Grandfather's bed heard a sound as of dropping water. Grandfather had bled through the mattress and the blood was dropping on the floor.

A messenger was sent for Dr. Staton on a running horse. The doctor was soon at his patient's bedside. He said: "Bring me a chicken—bring me a chicken!" A hen was quickly jerked from her roost and brought in. The Doctor severed her head and collected the blood in a cup. With the Pare Syringe he attempted to inject the blood into his patient. Of course, this was impossible. The clotting blood jammed the little syringe. In the light of present knowledge, this was most fortunate, but the doctor had the right idea. Undismayed, he cleaned the syringe and, grasping a bottle of brandy, he injected brandy into his patient. All these punctures subsequently abscessed. But Grandfather recovered. The blood transfusion was unsuccessful, but the patient did enjoy chicken broth on the following day.

Grandfather always carried the flattened old bullet in his vest pocket and was much distressed when he lost it a few months before he died in 1896.

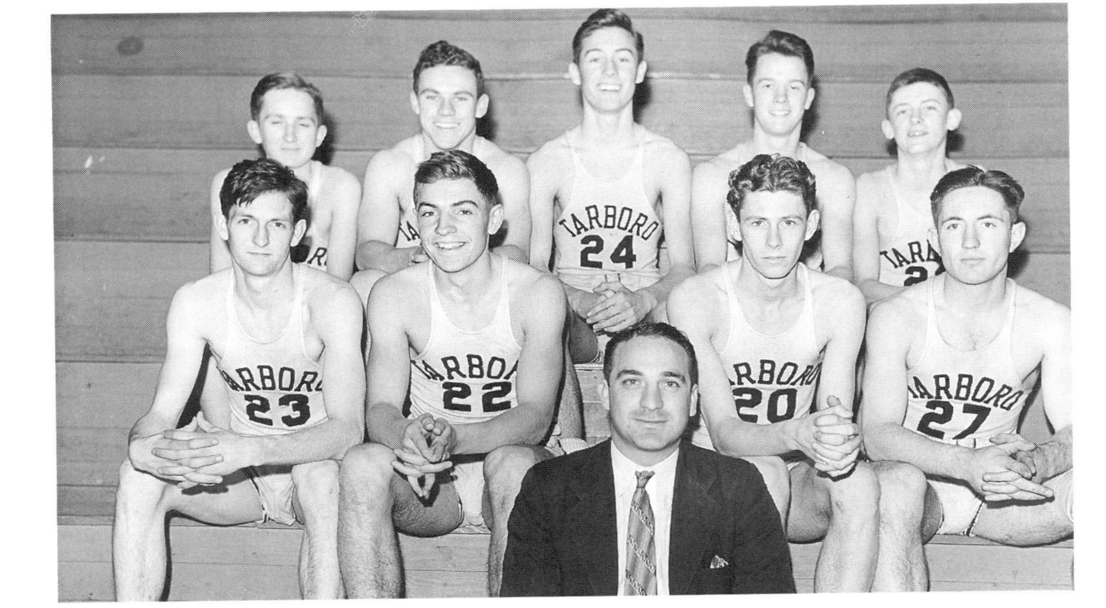

(Search as we might, the editors of this collection of columns could not find a photograph of Mabrey Bass in his natural environs around Tarboro. But we did find many pictures of his friends, neighbors and team mates.)

TARBORO HIGH BASKETBALL TEAM IN THE LATE 1930'S: Center foreground: Coach Joe Caruso. Bottom row, left to right: Bill Mewbern, Bill Hatton, Richard Thayer and Thurman Strickland. Top row, left to right: Dink Edmondson, Harry Palmer, Watt Smoot, Don Nicholson and Bud Shook.

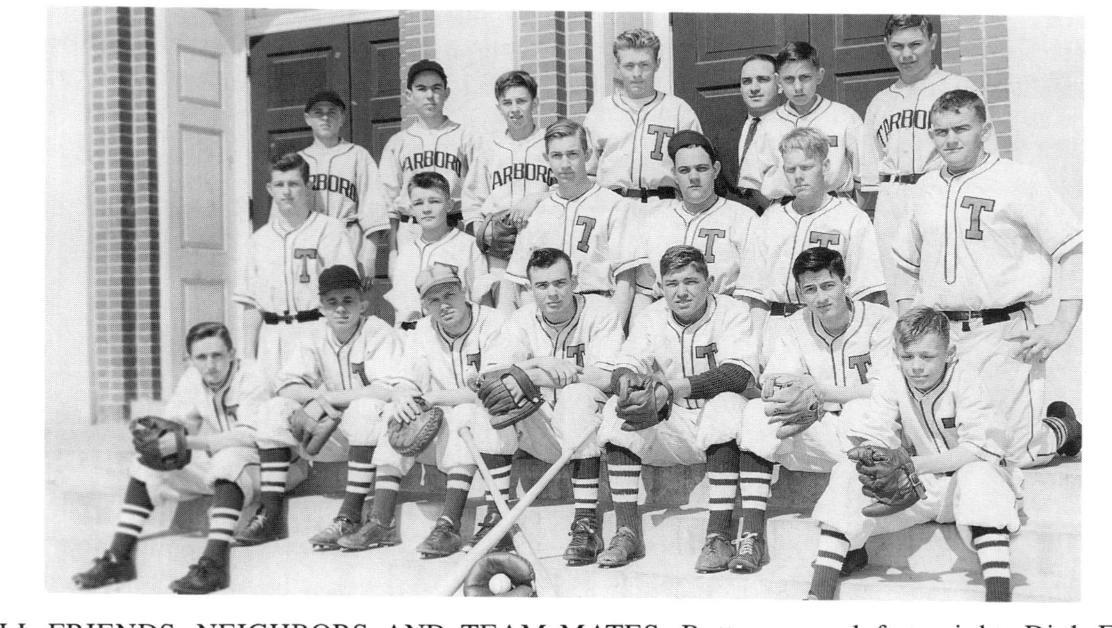

BASEBALL FRIENDS, NEIGHBORS AND TEAM MATES: Bottom row, left to right: Dink Emondson, Boo Boo Gilliam, unknown, Monk Guill, Martin Sasser, Charles Whitley, and Bo Carpenter. Middle row, left to right: Ottie Graham. Forrest (Slug) Sledge, Bill Stell, Mance Bogey, Paul Nobles, Bill Webb. Top row, left to right: Harvie Ward, Dirkum Strickland, Pete Clark, Russell Carter, Coach Joe Caruso, Jack Hagans and James Ballar. (The editors made every effort to identify the player seated between Boo Boo Gilliam and Monk Guill but failed.

FOOTBALL FRIENDS, NEIGHBORS AND TEAM MATES; Bottom row, seated, left to right: Charles Fountain, Harry Palmer, Earl Purvis, Thurman Strickland, Bill Hatton, Bill Webb. Second row, kneeling: Dink Edmondson, Russell Carter, Frank Ballard, Ottie Graham, Don Nicholson, Richard Thayer, Monk Guill, Son Creech. Third row, left to right, standing: Henry Slaughenhaumpt, Bud Shook, Johnny Hudson, Noah Baker Jr., Watt Smoot, Ted Williamson, Bill Mewbern, David Gatling. Top row: O. L. Pittman, Bob Peters, Seward Parks, Bunny Shugar, Julian Gatling, Corky Webb and Mac Proctor.

HOME FRONT NEWS HONIES: Sent to our fighting men overseas in the famous Home Front News to remind them what they were fighting for, left to right: Randall Hudson (known to all as Ruby). Sue Gaines, Kate Irwin Johnson, Evelyn Shugar, Dale Creech, Jean Darrow, Ruth Ballard, unknown, Mary Marshall Farrar.

THAT OLD GANG OF MINE: A representative picture of Tarboro's youth about the time World War II erupted in Europe. This picture was taken at a Howard Memorial Presbyterian Church function and identification of all the youngsters in the picture was virtually impossible, leaving that game for the readers. But every person pictured here grew up with Mabrey Bass. He frequently dated Sonora Lindsey, fifth from the right in the second row.

The All American Marine.

NO EXPLANATION NEEDED: Mabrey Bass, United States Marine Corps. (Family collection)

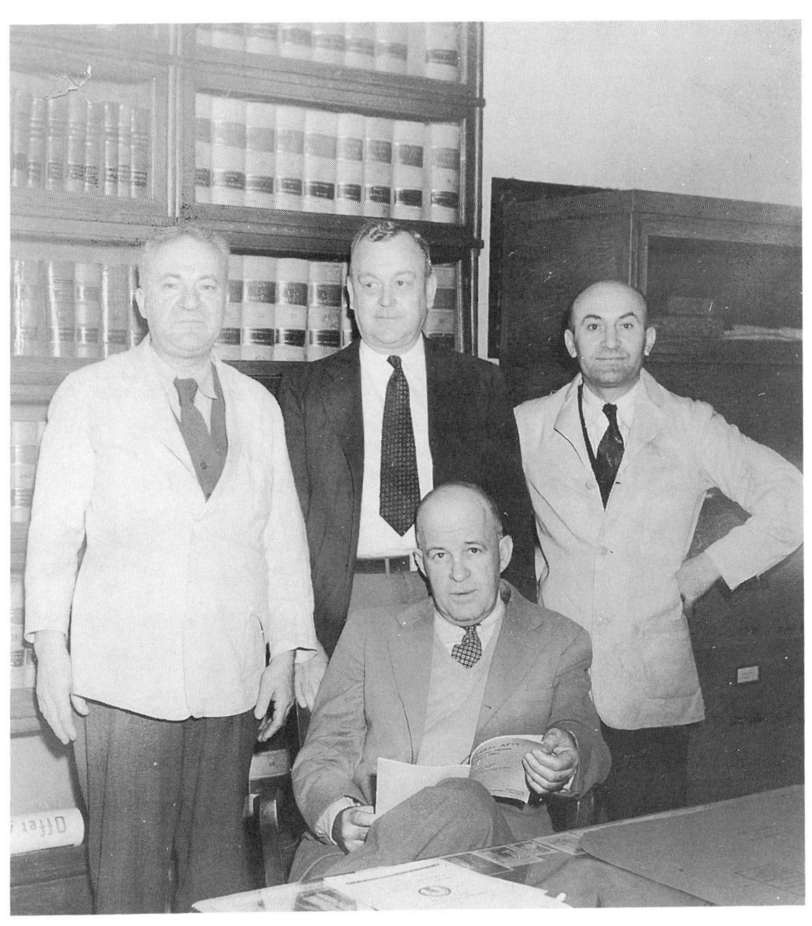

DIXIE CAFE PROPRIETORS: Standing with Mayor Rawls Howard between them, Gus Pistolis, left and Cris Pistolis, right, ran the always-popular Dixie Cafe on Main Street. The man seated is United States District Judge Don Gilliam and the scene suggests Gus and Cris had just earned their citizenship papers to become American citizens. Mabrey frequently mentioned the Dixie Cafe in his columns.

PRINCEVILLE FLOOD: A common sight at Mewbern's Mill just across the river bridge in Princeville before the dike was constructed—a motor boat at the front door of the store. This photograph was apparently taken about 1940. The people trying to do business in spite of the flood could not be identified.

HART MILL HONOREES: Hart Mill was one of Tarboro's largest employers during Mabrey Bass's early years and is still in operation today. This photograph, apparently taken in the early 1950's shows some of the employees there. The purpose of the picture has been lost in time.

THE FUZZ—AND OTHER TOWN OFFICIALS: Teenagers in Tarboro during the 1940's were as full of mischief as they are today. Mabrey Bass knew and respected the habits of the policemen how to avoid them. He grew up to report the activities of the other city officials. Left to right, first row: Reddin Pittman, City Court Judge and local historian, J. P. Keech, Mark Ruffin and Frank O'Neil. Second row: Dan Freuler, Mabrey Bass's uncle A. B. (Pug) Bass, a city commissioner. Third row: H. B. Keehln, R. M. Cosby, J. R. Spruill and Police Chief Robert Worsley. Top row: Wiley Bullock, Mayor Rawls Howard, Romaine Howard, City Clerk George Earnhart, Lewis Heilbroner and J. L. Sherrod. Missing is Commissioner M. S. Brown, who took the photograph.

DOWNTOWN TARBORO: A classic scene of the heart of town in the late 1930's. It is 11:30 on a summer morning, there is a parade and the streets are jammed with spectators. Notice the Coca-Cola sign hanging on the corner drug store. Like most others, the Edgecombe Drug store offered curb service. Pull up out front, toot the horn and a youngster like Mabrey Bass would bring you a Coke for a nickel.

HELPING THE WAR EFFORT: Students from Central School did their part in pushing War Bonds. These students are not identified but the three standing young boys on the right appear to be David Summerlin, Jack Brinson and Bill Clark III.

WAR TIME PARADE: It is possible this parade involved black fire companies that often staged fire fighting exercises in Tarboro. The Colonial Theater is "Cooled by Washed Air" and the wooden structure on the left is the old Tarboro House, which took in roomers. The movie, "Seven Days Ashore" starring Wally Brown and Alan Carney, did not win any Oscars.

BIG BOY SCOUT RALLY; Tarboro was host to a Camporee for area black Boy Scouts of America in about 1938. This picture shows the old Marrow-Pitt Hardware store and the trees that shaded the front of the County Couthouse. The old town clock is in the back ground and the turnout for the parade was obviously very good.

THE ENTIRE STAFF OF THE HOME FRONT NEWS, which featured local news about Tarboro and mailed to all Tarboro men serving in the armed forces are, left to right: George Earnhart, Alice Evans, Dail Holderness and Bill Babcock.

BASEBALL LEGEND CONNIE MACK VISITS TARBORO: The legendary baseball Hall of Famer, C
Mack, center, visited Tarboro in the late 1930's at an exhibition major league baseball game. Tarbor
Eagle Scout, Frank Ballard, is sitting to Mack's right.

GOOD IDEA THAT RARELY GOT OFF THE GROUND: An idea that just did not work: Town officials, including Mrs. Mary Godfrey of the Tarboro Chamber of Commerce in the center, at the dedication of the Tarboro Airport located a few miles out of town on the Oak City Highway in the mid 1940's. Second from the right in his aviator's helmet and flight jacket in chief pilot George Hatch. The project failed and ·abrey Bass crusaded to close down the operation.

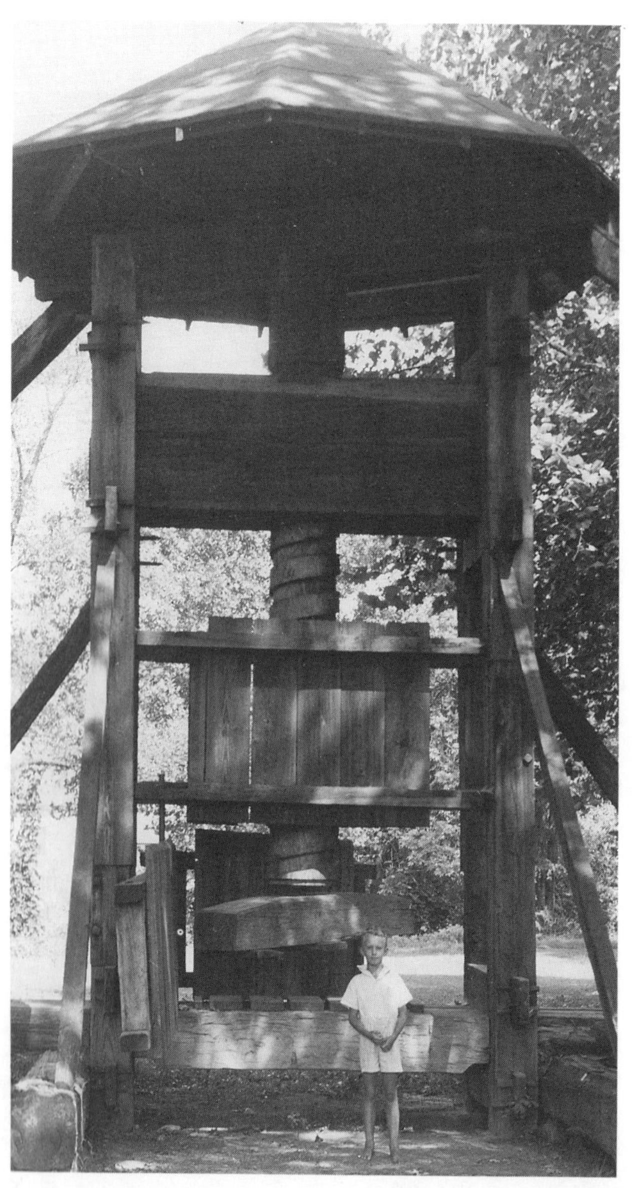

THE OLD COTTON PRESS: This photograph was taken shortly ftter the press was initially erected on the Wilson Street side of Town Common. The young boy here is not identified.

POST WARPARADE: This parade took place in the early 1950s. The Midway grocery car is a Jeep station wagon. Notice the 2-digit telephone number.

Spencer P. Bass, author of twenty-two articles of historic st included in this volume. (Family collection)